Alternate Assessment
for Students with
Significant Cognitive
Disabilities

Alternate Assessment
for Students with Significant Cognitive Disabilities

An Educator's Guide

by

Harold L. Kleinert, Ed.D.

and

Jacqui Farmer Kearns, Ed.D.

Human Development Institute
University of Kentucky

with invited contributors

·P·A·U·L·H·
BROOKES
PUBLISHING CO.®

Baltimore • London • Sydney

Paul H. Brookes Publishing Co.
Post Office Box 10624
Baltimore, Maryland 21285-0624
USA

www.brookespublishing.com

Typeset by Spearhead Global, Inc., Bear, Delaware.
Manufactured in the United States of America by
Sheridan Books, Inc., Chelsea, Michigan.

Painting sidebars on front and back cover by Alma Quenemoen; used by permission of Harold L. Kleinert.

Library of Congress Cataloging-in-Publication Data

Kleinert, Harold L.
  Alternate assessment for students with significant cognitive disabilities: an educator's guide/by Harold L. Kleinert and Jacqui Farmer Kearns; with invited contributors.
      p.   cm.
Includes bibliographical references and index.
   ISBN-13: 978-1-59857-076-2
   ISBN-10: 1-59857-076-5
   1. Children with disabilities—Rating of.   2. Educational tests and measurements.   I. Kearns, Jacqui Farmer. II. Title.
   LC4019.K543 2010
   371.9'043—dc22

2010027671

British Library Cataloguing in Publication data are available from the British Library.

2014   2013   2012   2011   2010

10   9   8   7   6   5   4   3   2   1

Contents

v

About the Authors

Harold L. Kleinert, Ed.D., Executive Director, University Center for Excellence, Human Development Institute, 126 Mineral Industries Building, University of Kentucky, Lexington, Kentucky 40506

Dr. Harold Kleinert has directed a broad range of federally funded research and demonstration projects, especially in the area of education of children and youth with severe disabilities, including research focused on alternate assessment, peer tutoring, community-referenced instruction, and service learning for students with developmental disabilities. He has led projects designed to teach physicians, as well as medical, dental, nursing, and physician assistant students, how to provide high-quality care to patients with developmental disabilities. He was the lead author of the text *Alternate Assessment: Measuring Outcomes and Supports for Students with Disabilities* (Paul H. Brookes Publishing Co., 2001), which he coauthored with Dr. Jacqui Farmer Kearns.

Jacqui Farmer Kearns, Ed.D., Principal Investigator, National Alternate Assessment Center, Human Development Institute, University of Kentucky, 1 Quality Street, Lexington, Kentucky 40502

Dr. Jacqui Farmer Kearns is nationally recognized for her work on alternate assessment based on alternate achievement standards, and together with Dr. Harold Kleinert, developed the nation's first alternate assessment for students with significant cognitive disabilities. She coauthored *Alternate Assessment: Measuring Outcomes and Supports for Students with Disabilities* (Paul H. Brookes Publishing Co., 2001), with Dr. Kleinert. Dr. Kearns has 9 years of classroom experience in teaching students with significant cognitive disabilities and has provided extensive training on inclusive education. She completed two additional federally funded research projects, Including Students Who Are Deaf-Blind in Large Scale Assessment and Universal Design for Assessment: Applications of Technology, related to assessment systems. Dr. Kearns serves as Acting Director for Inclusive Large Scale Standards and Assessments, a University of Kentucky–based assessment design group.

About the Contributors

Lynn Ahlgrim-Delzell, Ph.D., Assistant Professor of Research, Department of Educational Leadership, University of North Carolina at Charlotte, 9201 University City Boulevard, Charlotte, North Carolina 28223

Dr. Lynn Ahlgrim-Delzell has researched issues related to gaining access to the general curriculum for students with severe cognitive disabilities for 15 years, focusing on alternate assessment, literacy, and mathematics. She has authored or coauthored numerous articles in peer-refereed journals, presentations at national conferences, and book chapters. Her work has been published in the following journals: *Exceptional Children, Research and Practice in Severe Disabilities, Journal of Special Education, Journal of Disability Policy Studies, Remedial and Special Education,* and *Reading Psychology.* She is coauthor of the *Early Literacy Skills Builder* (Attainment Company, 2007), a reading curriculum specifically designed for this population.

Diane M. Browder, Ph.D., Lake and Edward P. Snyder Distinguished Professor of Special Education, Department of Special Education and Child Development, 9201 University City Boulevard, University of North Carolina at Charlotte, Charlotte, North Carolina, 28223

Dr. Diane Browder has completed more than 2 decades of research and writing on assessment and instruction for students with severe disabilities. Recently, she has focused on alternate assessment and linking both assessment and instruction to the general curriculum. She is Principal Investigator for two Institute for Educational Sciences–funded research projects—one on early literacy and the other on math and science for students with significant cognitive disabilities. Dr. Browder is also a partner in the National Center on Alternate Assessment and currently serves on the technical work groups for the National Center on Education Outcomes and the National Study on Alternate Assessment. She was a recent member of the U.S. Department of Education No Child Left Behind National Technical Advisory Council. Dr. Browder received the 2009 Distinguished Researcher Award from the American Educational Research Association Special Education Special Interest Group and was the 2009 First Citizens Bank Scholar at the University of North Carolina at Charlotte.

Michael Burdge, M.A., Alternate Assessment Consultant, Keystone Alternate Assessment Design, 3688 Salisbury Drive, Lexington, Kentucky 40510

Mr. Michael Burdge has consulted with several states, territories, and countries on developing, implementing, and maintaining their alternate assessment systems as a result of his work with the Inclusive Large Scale Standards and Assessment group at the University of Kentucky and the National Alternate Assessment Center. His focus on improving the inclusive education of students with significant cognitive disabilities is grounded in his

27 years of teaching and his research and direct professional development involvement with thousands of special and general educators.

Jean Clayton, M.Ed., Alternate Assessment Consultant, Keystone Alternate Assessment Design, 3688 Salisbury Drive, Lexington, Kentucky 40510

Ms. Jean Clayton has 23 years of teaching and extensive experience in inclusive environments. Since 2002, she has been consulting with several states, U.S. territories, and the Pacific Freely Associated States on alternate assessment and instruction. Along with her focus on alternate assessment, she has worked on projects addressing peer tutoring, access to the general curriculum, and assistive technology.

Belva C. Collins, Ed.D., Professor, Department of Special Education and Rehabilitation Counseling, 229 Taylor Education Building, University of Kentucky, Lexington, Kentucky 40506

Dr. Belva Collins's current research interests fall in three areas: 1) systematic instruction of functional core content, 2) distance education delivery in special education personnel preparation, and 3) inclusion of students with special needs in their faith communities. Dr. Collins is the author of *Moderate and Severe Disabilities: A Foundational Approach* (Pearson, 2007) on moderate and severe disabilities and has been Principal Investigator on a series of personnel preparation projects to prepare rural special education personnel and to prepare leaders in special education distance education delivery.

Ginevra Courtade, Ph.D., Assistant Professor, Department of Teaching and Learning, College of Education and Human Development, University of Louisville, Louisville, Kentucky 40292

Dr. Ginevra Courtade has conducted research on alternate assessments, literacy, and science instruction for students with moderate to severe intellectual disabilities. Her current research is focused on access to the general curriculum and inclusive instruction for students with moderate and severe disabilities. Dr. Courtade has numerous publications, including journal articles and book chapters, and she coauthored the following curricula and texts: *Early Literacy Skills Builder* (Attainment Company, 2007), *Teaching to Standards: Science* (Attainment Company, 2008), and *Aligning IEPs to Academic Standards for Students with Moderate to Severe Disabilities* (Attainment Company, 2005).

Anne Denham, Ed.S., ATP, Alternate Assessment Consultant, Inclusive Large Scale Standards and Assessment, Human Development Institute, University of Kentucky, 1 Quality Street, Lexington, Kentucky 40502

Ms. Anne Denham has an extensive background in assistive technology combined with years of teaching students with significant cognitive disabilities in an inclusive environment. Her background provides a strong, practical base for her work on developing alternate assessment systems and access to the general curriculum with the Pacific Island entities and several U.S. territories and states. Her focus on universal design for learning with the National Alternate Assessment Center and CAST has furthered her experience and passion for accessible instruction for all students.

Karen M. Guettler, B.F.A., Technical Assistance Specialist, Inclusive Large Scale Standards and Assessment, Human Development Institute, University of Kentucky, 1 Quality Street, Lexington, Kentucky 40502

Ms. Karen Guettler has worked in the development of statewide alternate assessments and facilitates stakeholder meetings to review and revise alternate assessments. She has managed alternate assessment scoring centers and presented at a low incidence institute. She also serves as a representative on her county's Special Education Advisory Council.

Karen D. Hager, Ph.D., Assistant Professor, Department of Special Education and Rehabilitation Counseling, 229 Taylor Education Building, University of Kentucky, Lexington, Kentucky 40506

Dr. Karen Hager conducts research in the areas of effective supervision of student teachers, use of self-monitoring by student teachers to improve instructional practices, and use of technology in supervision. Prior to completing her doctoral program, she taught students with moderate and severe disabilities in public schools in Colorado, Utah, and Minnesota.

Karin K. Hess, Ed.D., Senior Associate, Center for Assessment, Post Office Box 351, Dover, New Hampshire 03821

Since 2002, Dr. Karin Hess has brought to the National Center for Assessment more than 30 years of deep experience in curriculum, instruction, and assessment as a classroom teacher and school administrator. She has assisted more than a dozen states in major development of grade-level expectations, revisions to state content standards, and creation of detailed assessment specifications aligned to content standards that are both educationally and technically sound. Dr. Hess's most recent research and writing focus has been on development and alignment of educationally sound and accessible alternate assessments (alternate assessment based on alternate achievement standards and alternate assessment based on modified achievement standards) and the use of content-based learning progressions with formative and interim assessment practices that support improved achievement. Dr. Hess has worked as a program specialist with the New Jersey Department of Education, as program evaluator for the Vermont Mathematics Project, as a content specialist for development of the Vermont Science assessment, and as the developer/editor of *Science Exemplars.*

Bree A. Jimenez, Ph.D., Research Associate for Project MASTERY, Department of Special Education and Child Development, University of North Carolina at Charlotte, Charlotte, North Carolina 28223

Ms. Bree Jimenez was a grant liaison with the Charlotte-Mecklenburg School system and the University of North Carolina at Charlotte, for the Reading, Writing, Math, and Science for Students with Significant Cognitive Disabilities grant. She helps design and conduct research in the area of general curriculum access. She has spent extensive time writing extended content standards for state departments of education, as well as training educators and administrators on alternate assessments. She recently received her doctorate in special education. Her doctoral dissertation focused on the area of general curriculum access for secondary level students with significant disabilities.

Jane O'Regan Kleinert, Ph.D., CCC-SLP, Assistant Professor, Division of Communication Sciences and Disorders, College of Health Sciences, University of Kentucky, Lexington, Kentucky 40506

Dr. Jane Kleinert has more than 30 years of experience as a speech-language pathologist specializing in services to children and adolescents with the most severe disabilities. Her areas of research and grant activity are in the area of communication services to students with intellectual disabilities and complex communication needs and the relationship between communication and self-determination for students with significant cognitive disabilities.

Lou-Ann E. Land, M.Ed., Technical Assistance Specialist, Inclusive Large Scale Standards and Assessment, Human Development Institute, University of Kentucky, 1 Quality Street, Lexington, Kentucky 40502

Ms. Lou-Ann Land is currently responsible for the development, planning, and execution of state and other agency alternate assessment programs, as well preparing and conducting teacher training on the development of instruction and assessment linked to grade-level standards. Ms. Land relies on her 19 years of experience teaching students with significant cognitive disabilities in her work. She has presented nationally on topics about assessment, instruction, and inclusion and has coauthored a book chapter on teaching and assessing students with significant cognitive disabilities on functional math within grade-level content.

Pamela J. Mims, Ph.D., Research Scientist with the National Alternate Assessment Center, College of Education/Special Education and Child Development, 9201 University City Boulevard, University of North Carolina at Charlotte, Charlotte, North Carolina 28223

Dr. Pamela Mims teaches an undergraduate course on systematic instruction for students with significant cognitive disabilities. Her areas of interest and research include access to the general curriculum for students with severe disabilities, systematic instruction, alternate assessment, dual sensory impairments, and students with significant multiple disabilities.

Jacqueline M. Norman, M.Ed., Disability Program Administrator II, Inclusive Large Scale Standards and Assessment, Human Development Institute, University of Kentucky, 1 Quality Street, Lexington, Kentucky 40502

Ms. Jacqueline Norman has assisted several states in the development and implementation of their alternate assessment programs for students with the most significant cognitive disabilities. In addition, she has been involved in state and federal grant programs focused on improving instruction and/or alternate assessment, specifically the Inclusive Education Initiative and the Colorado Enhanced Assessment Grant. As an advocate for inclusion, she spent more than 10 years in the classroom as both a general education teacher (foreign languages) and a special education teacher.

David K. Pugalee, Ph.D., Director, Center for Mathematics, Science, & Technology Education, 317 College of Education Building, University of North Carolina at Charlotte, Charlotte, North Carolina 28223

Dr. David Pugalee earned his doctorate degree in mathematics education from the University of North Carolina at Chapel Hill. He taught at the elementary, middle, and secondary levels before moving into higher education. His list of publications includes research articles in *Educational Studies in Mathematics* and *School Science and Mathematics* and several books and book chapters published by the National Council of Teachers of Mathematics. Dr. Pugalee's research interest is the relationship between language and mathematics teaching and learning.

Rachel Quenemoen, M.S., Senior Research Fellow, National Center on Educational Outcomes, 207 Pattee Hall, 150 Pillsbury Drive SE, University of Minnesota, Minneapolis, Minnesota 55455

Ms. Rachel Quenemoen is the technical assistance team leader for the National Center on Educational Outcomes. Ms. Quenemoen has worked for 30 years as an educational sociologist focused on research to practice efforts, providing training and professional development to educators at the district, state, and national levels. She has been a multi-district cooperative administrator in both general and special education. For the last 15 years, she has worked at the state and national levels on educational change processes and reform efforts related to standards-based reform and students with disabilities, building consensus and capacity among practitioners, researchers, and policy makers. She is the proud parent of an adult daughter with Down syndrome.

Robert J. Rickelman, Ph.D., Professor of Literacy Education, Reading and Elementary Education Department, 367B College Of Education Building, University of North Carolina Charlotte, Charlotte, North Carolina 28223

Dr. Robert Rickelman has worked as a literacy specialist in schools in Ohio and Pennsylvania. His teaching and research interests include reading and writing across content areas and the uses of technology in the teaching of literacy. He is the former president of the College Reading Association and coeditor of *Reading Research and Instruction*. He has authored or coauthored over 60 publications in the area of literacy education. He has served as a consultant to the National Alternate Assessment Center and provided his expertise on alternate and modified alternate assessments to several states, including Georgia, Hawaii, Kentucky, and New York.

Leah Riggs, M.S., Teacher of Exceptional Children, Elizabethtown High School, Panther Lane, Elizabethtown, Kentucky 42701

Ms. Leah Riggs is currently in her fourth year teaching high school students with moderate and severe disabilities. She completed her alternate certification and master's degree in special education in moderate and severe disabilities at the University of Kentucky. She has worked closely with both the Kentucky and Missouri departments of education to validate and align alternate assessment standards with the general education curriculum. Her lesson plans for teaching general education core content standards in science to students with moderate and severe disabilities were accepted by the Kentucky Department of Education's lesson planning project for teaching all students. She also served on the Kentucky Department of Education's Low Incidence Initiative Task Force as a teacher representative for students with significant cognitive disabilities.

Deborah A. Taub, Ph.D., Senior Associate, edCount, LLC, 5335 Wisconsin Avenue, NW, Suite 440, Washington, DC 20015

Dr. Deborah Taub currently serves as the project director for Gallaudet curriculum development for edCount, LLC, a small, woman-owned business dedicated to building capacity in the fields of education policy, standards, assessment, and evaluation. Prior to joining edCount, Dr. Taub served for 3 years as a technical assistance specialist with Inclusive Large Scale Standards and Assessment at the University of Kentucky. Dr. Taub's responsibilities included the development, implementation, and evaluation of high-quality alternate assessments for students with significant cognitive disabilities, development of standards-based curricula and instruction, and alignment evaluation. Dr. Taub has also worked as a school reform specialist and education researcher. She has written articles and presented internationally on working with students who have autism.

Elizabeth Towles-Reeves, Ph.D., Senior Associate, Alternate Assessment and Disabilities Specialist, edCount, LLC, 318 Redding Road, Georgetown, Kentucky 40324

Dr. Elizabeth Towles-Reeves currently serves as deputy project director for Evaluating the Validity of English Language Proficiency Assessments (EVEA) project, providing oversight and coordination of project management meetings, leadership for development of project instruments, and management of grant and contracts. In addition, she works directly with the District of Columbia, Puerto Rico, and Hawaii to conduct validity evaluations of their alternate assessment systems. Since 2001, she has authored and coauthored more than a dozen research reports, the majority of which have appeared in peer-reviewed academic journals. She has authored several book chapters and presented regularly at national and regional conferences since 2003. In 2007, she was awarded TASH's Alice H. Hayden Emerging Researcher Award.

Martha Thurlow, Ph.D., Director, National Center on Educational Outcomes, 207 Pattee Hall, 150 Pillsbury Drive SE, University of Minnesota, Minneapolis, Minnesota 55455

Dr. Martha Thurlow has emphasized during her work since the 1990s the need to obtain valid, reliable, and comparable measures of student performance, while ensuring that the assessments are truly measuring the knowledge and skills of students with special needs rather than their disabilities. Her studies have covered a range of topics, including participation, decision making, accommodations, universal design, computer-based testing, graduation exams, and alternate assessments. Dr. Thurlow has provided technical assistance to states on topics that promote better assessment of students with disabilities and English language learners with disabilities, including setting policies on accommodations, reporting assessment results, and monitoring the provision of accommodations during assessments and instruction.

Shawnee Y. Wakeman, Ph.D., Clinical Assistant Professor, Department of Special Education and Child Development, 9201 University City Boulevard, University of North Carolina at Charlotte, Charlotte, North Carolina 28223

Dr. Shawnee Wakeman has served as a special education teacher, an assistant principal, and a research associate for the National Alternate Assessment Center. Her research interests include the relationship of the principal to the education of students with disabilities, access to the general curriculum and how it is enacted for students with significant cognitive disabilities, alignment of the educational system and the policy implications of those alignment issues, and alternate assessment. Dr. Wakeman is currently involved in several federally funded projects and publications related to alternate assessment and curriculum alignment.

Donna Wickham, Ph.D., Director of Program, Keystone Alternate Assessment Design, LLC, 3688 Salisbury Drive, Lexington, Kentucky 40510

Dr. Donna Wickham has been a teacher of adolescents with severe disabilities and deaf-blindness, a technical assistance coordinator of Deaf-Blind and Positive Behavior Supports National OSEP Centers, and a university faculty member in two special education departments in the area of severe disabilities. She was a past director of Inclusive Large Scale Standards and Assessment and is currently employed by an alternate assessment design company working with states to improve their accountability systems and classroom instruction for students with significant cognitive disabilities.

James M. Zeller, B.S.Ed., Retired Teacher, Lexington, Kentucky

Mr. James Zeller, a native of North Dakota, received degrees in the areas of history and art education and taught for a number of years in North Dakota and Kentucky. While teaching in North Dakota, he taught art at the high school, middle school, and elementary school levels, as well as middle school social studies. After moving to Kentucky, he resumed teaching art to elementary school students. His teaching competencies include illustration, painting, ceramics, sculpture, printmaking, American history, world history, and European history.

Mariel L. Zeller, M.S.Ed., Technical Assistance Specialist, Inclusive Large Scale Standards and Assessment, Human Development Institute, University of Kentucky, 1 Quality Street, Lexington, Kentucky 40502

Ms. Mariel Zeller has served as a regional special education coordinator with the North Dakota Department of Public Instruction and the North Dakota State Deaf-Blind coordinator. She has assisted several states in standards and curriculum alignment, alternate assessment development, administration, scoring, and professional development. She has worked with state Technical Advisory Committees and written technical manuals for alternate assessments. She has presented at conferences conducted by TASH, the Council of Chief State School Officers, and statewide education agencies.

Foreword

Looking back, alternate assessment based on alternate achievement standards was the next logical step in the progression toward full inclusion for students with disabilities. If you were an inclusion believer, you had to favor greater curriculum access, universal participation in assessments, and visibility in the accountability system. However, students with significant cognitive disabilities could not have participated in the assessment system the way it was configured. Retooling meant that many preconceptions—about standards-based curriculum, flexibility of assessments, and comparability of results using multiple measurement formats—had to shift. In short, new instructional methods, accommodations, and alternate assessments were needed to allow *all* students to participate equitably, validly, and visibly in the system.

The authors have neatly captured this rich and recent history and have provided perspectives that can assist state policy makers, local educators, higher education faculty, and students preparing to enter the education profession. Rapid advances and innovations in thought and practice have occurred in the area of inclusive assessment since the 1990s, when only a handful of states were attempting alternate assessments with their students. Several contributors to this book were on hand in those days to share the experiences of the early adopters (notably Kentucky), with other states just embarking in the wake of the Individuals with Disabilities Education Act Amendments (IDEA) of 1997 (PL 105-17). These newer states invented alternate assessments that measured what educators valued and that related to state cultures, and as a result, a wide range of models and approaches was born, unique to each state.

In Massachusetts, close attention was paid to grade-level content standards and the level of instructional complexity to allow all students to attain those standards. For each learning standard, a continuum of outcomes called "entry points" was developed and vetted by content experts who also helped frame the "essence," or Big Ideas, of each standard. Although educators certainly experienced growing pains, they involved stakeholders in guiding the system, and teachers rose to the challenge. Teachers relayed their surprise and delight as their students learned important new skills that had not been anticipated. Following intensive professional development, teachers themselves learned critical new skills—such as curriculum alignment and data collection. It is apparent from experience that virtually every student with a significant cognitive disability in Massachusetts can receive instruction in the academic curriculum at appropriately challenging levels, and more than four in five students with significant cognitive disabilities can demonstrate steady progress in learning increasingly difficult academic skills and content. As expectations mounted for both teachers and students, efficiencies were created along the way, as portfolio evidence documented skill attainment and signaled the need for more complex instruction.

Massachusetts was a success story, but in some states, the road was more difficult, as contributors to this book can also attest. States stumbled over low expectations and teachers' objections to the extra work involved in alternate assessments and the implication that they had not been teaching their students effectively in the past. States also were caught in the larger web of education reform in which all students were expected to learn academics at higher levels and, in many cases, meet new graduation standards that may have precluded students with significant cognitive disabilities from receiving diplomas. What began largely as a political, philosophical, and procedural conversation in the 1990s subsequently lit up the worlds of research, higher education, and government, resulting in new theoretical models, validity arguments, exploration of effective practices, and sponsorship of such entities as the National Alternate Assessment Center.

Along the way, states were required to document the validity of their assessments and demonstrate to federal peer reviewers, among others, that these assessments met the purpose for which they were intended. A "second wave" followed in which many states reexamined and subsequently overhauled their alternate assessments to provide greater fidelity to grade-level content, balance system flexibility with internal consistency, and allow schools and individualized education program teams to make decisions that benefited students.

Moving forward, states are likely to continue to face challenges to the validity of methods and results for students with significant and wide-ranging disabilities, as well as opposition to universal participation in assessments, especially for students with the *most* significant cognitive disabilities. Discussions are likely to continue on the relative merits of individualization versus standardization in alternate assessments and on the primary purpose of alternate assessments in general. Should they simply measure the status quo or provide information to improve instruction? Questions will persist as to which methods and approaches work best to promote access to grade-level content for such a diverse population and which method (or combination of methods) offers the greatest opportunity for students to show what they know. Perhaps most significant, resisters will continue to question whether these students are able to learn academic content in the first place and challenge the wisdom and importance of including these students in academic instruction.

I am thrilled that Harold and Jacqui have revised and reissued their original work, in light of the many recent advances in theory and practice and our own shared and individual research and experience. They remind us why this work is important, even in the face of continuing challenges, and their ideas, and those of their coauthors, advance the domain of education for *all* students.

Daniel J. Wiener
Administrator of Inclusive Assessment
Massachusetts Department of Elementary and Secondary Education

REFERENCE

Individuals with Disabilities Education Act (IDEA) Amendments of 1997, PL 105-17, 20 U.S.C. §§ 1400 *et seq.*

Preface

This is a book about alternate assessment based on alternate achievement standards (AA-AAS), and, most important, the implications for these assessments on what students with significant cognitive disabilities are taught and expected to learn. This is a text designed primarily for special and general education teachers and for related service personnel (e.g., speech-language pathologists, school psychologists) who work with students with significant cognitive disabilities. Although we provide chapters useful for policy makers and researchers, including a broad overview of the place of alternate assessment under the accountability rubric of the No Child Left Behind (NCLB) Act of 2001 (PL 107-110; Chapter 1), a discussion of key validity and technical issues related to alternate assessments (Chapter 2), and a synthesis of the research on alternate assessments (Chapter 12), we have tried to write these and all of the chapters from a practitioner perspective.

This classroom perspective is emphasized throughout the text, which is divided into three major sections. The first section presents an overview of key principles and fundamental dimensions that must be addressed in the development and implementation of AA-AAS. Chapter 1, coauthored by Harold L. Kleinert, Rachel Quenemoen, and Martha Thurlow, provides a general overview of AA-AAS, its historical development, and its place in a broader accountability system designed for all students, as required under NCLB. At the end of this first chapter, the authors also present what we believe are essential principles in creating and using alternate assessments based on alternate achievement standards.

Chapter 2, by Jacqui Farmer Kearns, provides an introduction to practitioners on the key terminology of alternate assessments, including content and performance standards. The author discusses the importance of validity in alternate assessments, and especially consequential validity—the "so what" question of how teachers and schools should use these scores. Dr. Kearns also discusses scoring considerations and teacher training within the context of high-quality alternate assessments. Chapter 3, by Jane O'Regan Kleinert, Jacqui Farmer Kearns, and Harold L. Kleinert, discusses first what the authors have learned about the communicative competence of students with significant cognitive disabilities and why the development of communicative competence lies at the heart of both access to the general curriculum and the broader educational outcomes essential for achieving independence. This chapter also provides strategies for teachers and speech-language pathologists in enabling students who do not yet have formal communication systems to develop symbolic language.

Chapter 4, by Shawnee Y. Wakeman, Diane M. Browder, Bree A. Jimenez, and Pamela J. Mims, presents the essential criteria for aligning instruction and assessment using academic content standards. These authors also discuss other critical issues in both instruction and assessment for students with significant cognitive disabilities, including how to differentiate instruction across grades or grade bands and how to make instruction and assessment accessible to all students.

Section II addresses teaching and assessing students with significant cognitive disabilities across each of the major academic content areas. In Chapter 5, Michael Burdge,

Jean Clayton, Anne Denham, and Karin K. Hess present a method they have used with hundreds of teachers to provide access to the general curriculum. Their "Four-Step Process" provides both a systematic approach to considering how to make grade-level content meaningful for students with significant cognitive disabilities and to develop student products that are directly applicable to AA-AAS. This chapter includes an extended example of the application of the Four-Step Process to a seventh-grade language arts general education unit for a student with significant multiple disabilities.

Chapters 6–9 present specific examples of subject-level instruction and assessment linked to grade-level content standards. For each of these academic subjects, the authors first present a rationale for why the study of that subject is important for students with significant cognitive disabilities. In Chapter 6, Lynn Ahlgrim-Delzell, Robert J. Rickelman, and Jean Clayton describe how grade-level reading content can be made accessible for students with significant cognitive disabilities with elementary, middle, and high school examples that include both instruction and assessment. In Chapter 7, Lou-Ann Land, David K. Pugalee, Anne Denham, and Harold L. Kleinert describe a similar process for accessing grade-level math standards (e.g., a class unit linear algebraic equations) for students with moderate, as well as severe, multiple disabilities.

In Chapter 8, Ginevra Courtade, Deborah A. Taub, and Michael Burdge describe how science instruction and assessment can be made accessible for students with significant cognitive disabilities. The authors provide two examples, a fourth-grade geology lesson and a high school biology lesson, to illustrate the process. Each example includes students of varying abilities and communication needs.

Reading, math, and science are, of course, NCLB-required subjects in states' AA-AAS. In Chapter 9, Karen M. Guettler, Jacqueline M. Norman, James M. Zeller, and Mariel L. Zeller describe the importance of social studies and arts instruction for students with significant cognitive disabilities and how elementary, middle, and high school units can be adapted to address the needs of students with significant cognitive disabilities across these subjects. Even though these subjects are not required for AA-AAS under NCLB, they are a part of the alternate assessments of some states, and the authors describe how students with significant cognitive disabilities can demonstrate grade-linked content on such assessments.

The final section expands the discussion of academic achievement, to consider how other important outcomes for students with significant cognitive disabilities can be addressed within the context of both instruction and assessment. In Chapter 10, Harold L. Kleinert, Belva C. Collins, Donna Wickham, Leah Riggs, and Karen D. Hager address the critical importance of embedding functional or life skill instruction within grade-level content, as well as how systematic instruction and the component skills of self-determination can enhance students' capacity for problem-solving, applying, and generalizing their knowledge.

In Chapter 11, Jacqui Farmer Kearns and Rachel Quenemoen address the relationship of the individualized education program (IEP) to the content of alternate assessments and how student teams can align IEPs with grade-level content standards. These authors further discuss the role of the family in the IEP process and the importance of ensuring that the student's family understands the purpose and content of their state's alternate assessment.

Finally, in Chapter 12, Harold L. Kleinert and Elizabeth Towles-Reeves describe what researchers have learned from alternate assessments, and most important, the implications of these "lessons learned" for practitioners. This chapter concludes with directions for future research, calls for the inclusion of families and students as active participants within that research, and notes the essential role of teachers as partners in expanding knowledge of what students with significant cognitive disabilities know and can do.

REFERENCE

No Child Left Behind Act of 2001, PL 107-110, 115 Stat. 1425, 20 U.S.C. §§ 6301 *et seq.*

Acknowledgments

As with any large undertaking, there are many people who have provided us invaluable assistance in the writing of this book. We first thank our co-contributors, who have written from their respective experiences as policy makers, teacher trainers, researchers, classroom teachers, and family members of students with significant cognitive disabilities and who have shared their considerable knowledge, expertise, and wisdom.

We thank Daniel Wiener of the Massachusetts Department of Elementary and Secondary Education for his gracious foreword and for sharing his state-level perspective on the importance of high expectations for all students and the impact of those expectations upon achievement for students with significant cognitive disabilities in his state.

We need to recognize the generous support of the United States Office of Special Education Programs for funding the National Alternate Assessment Center (Grant No. H3244040001), through which we and several of our coauthors have conducted a portion of the research reported in this text. Of course, the opinions we have expressed do not necessarily reflect the position or policy of the U.S. Department of Education, and no official endorsements should be inferred.

This book was made significantly better by the contributions of the editorial and production staff of Paul H. Brookes Publishing Co. We especially want to acknowledge our Editor, Ms. Rebecca Lazo, who initially brought to us the idea that it was time for a new text on alternate assessment directed to teachers and practitioners and who encouraged and guided us through the prospectus, development, writing, and editing phases. Ms. Lisa Koepenick, Project Manager, worked painstakingly, patiently, and tirelessly with us and our coauthors to improve wording, style, and format throughout the text. Her suggestions for improving the clarity and readability of each chapter were invaluable. Mr. Steve Plocher, Acquisitions Assistant, ensured the production quality of the book and diligently worked to keep us and our coauthors all on track with the myriad of details, permissions, and deadlines that are essential if a book is ever to be published in the first place. Thanks to each of you for your high standard of excellence!

Finally, we would like to thank our families for allowing us the time to write this book. Their support and love continue to make all the difference.

Alternate Assessment
for Students with
Significant Cognitive
Disabilities

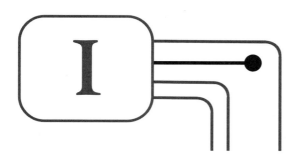

An Overview of Alternate Assessment

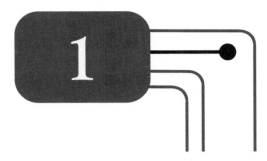

An Introduction to Alternate Assessments

Historical Foundations, Essential Parameters, and Guiding Principles

Harold L. Kleinert, Rachel Quenemoen, and Martha Thurlow

Students with significant cognitive disabilities—those students for whom regular educational assessments, even with accommodations and modifications, are not appropriate for their full participation in measures of school accountability—account for an estimated 1% or less of all students (Kearns, Towles-Reeves, Kleinert, Kleinert, & Thomas, in press; U.S. Department of Education, 2005). Students with significant cognitive disabilities *typically* include students with moderate and severe intellectual disabilities, as well as many students who are labeled as having autism, multiple disabilities, and deafblindness (Kearns & Towles-Reeves, 2007). However, children and youth with significant cognitive disabilities—the very students who are the subjects of this book—do not represent a categorical label under the Individuals with Disabilities Education Improvement Act (IDEA) of 2004 (PL 108-446) but rather are those students whose participation in school accountability is premised on their achievement on what are called *alternate achievement standards*.

So what are alternate achievement standards? Are they something wholly apart from the educational achievement standards expected of all other students? The U.S Department of Education (2003) has made it clear that alternate achievement standards can reflect reduced complexity within academic content, but they still must be aligned to the content standards for all students, and they must "reflect best professional judgment" about what students with significant cognitive disabilities can learn. The requirement for every state to create alternate achievement standards aligned to the content standards for all students has caused educators to rethink what is possible for students with significant cognitive disabilities.

Educators used to say that it was very good to include students with significant cognitive disabilities in general education classes. However, educators really did not expect those students to master key ideas in that general curriculum, nor did educators consider the possibility of holding schools accountable for students' learning within the general curriculum. Students with significant cognitive disabilities needed to be part of general education classes, educators reasoned, because they needed to develop the communication and social skills to develop friendships with their peers without disabilities, learn to be a part of the real world, and get along in that world. Perhaps in the process of this inclusion, students with significant cognitive disabilities might also learn a portion of the math or reading or science or social studies that was being taught, but that was not the primary reason they were there. Thoughts about this type of inclusion, however, have changed because all students, including students with significant cognitive disabilities, are to be assessed on performance standards that are linked to grade-level curriculum (U.S. Department of Education, 2004).

This book describes what this requirement means for teachers, students, and families, and how educators can teach and assess students in ways that reflect these new possibilities. This book is about holding onto what is best in what educators have learned from the past—that instruction and assessment for students with significant cognitive disabilities need to be presented systematically, that students and families are integral partners in determining instructional outcomes, and that what educators teach must promote independence in current and future environments, and ultimately improve life outcomes for students—while simultaneously expanding educators' horizons to include the essential elements of the curriculum for all students.

In this first chapter, we discuss the historical context for the inclusion of all students in large-scale educational assessments, especially alternate assessment based on alternate achievement standards (AA-AAS) for students with significant cognitive disabilities. We also introduce the major themes of this book.

PRESENT FRAMEWORK FOR ASSESSMENT AND ACCOUNTABILITY FOR STUDENTS WITH DISABILITIES

The present framework for assessing students with disabilities and including their assessment results within accountability systems includes an array of options that have emerged over time. Historically, students with disabilities had the options of participating in the regular assessment with or without accommodations. With IDEA 1997 (PL 105-17), however, the notion of alternate assessments emerged. Identification of different types of alternate assessments grew out of the No Child Left Behind (NCLB) Act of 2001 (PL 107-110), formerly known as the Elementary and Secondary Education Act, and its regulations. These were supported by the 2004 reauthorization of IDEA and its regulations.

The five assessment options for students with disabilities are 1) regular assessment, 2) regular assessment with accommodations, 3) alternate assessment based on grade-level achievement standards (AA-GLAS), 4) alternate assessment based on modified achievement standards (AA-MAS), and 5) AA-AAS. All options are to be based on the state's grade-level content standards. Each option is considered to be more or less appropriate for certain students, and each option is included in the federal NCLB accountability system in specific ways. These are depicted in Figure 1.1.

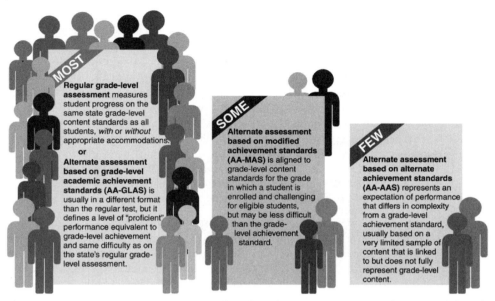

Figure 1.1. Assessment options. (From Cortiella, C. [2007]. *Learning opportunities for your child through alternate assessments: Alternate assessments based on modified academic achievement standards* [p. 7]. Minneapolis: University of Minnesota, National Center on Educational Outcomes; reprinted by permission.)

Regular Assessment with or without Accommodations

Most students with disabilities are expected to participate in the state or district assessment system via the regular assessment, the same assessment in which students without disabilities participate, either with or without accommodations. These assessments are to be based on grade-level content standards and to hold students to grade-level expectations for performance. Regular assessments typically include multiple-choice questions, and sometimes constructed response questions, which are presented via paper and pencil or computer formats. Accommodations are changes in the materials or procedures of the assessment that do not change what the assessment intends to measure (e.g., extra time on an untimed test, being read to when reading skills are not intended to be part of what is measured; Lazarus, Thurlow, Lail, & Christensen, 2009; Thurlow, 2007; Thurlow, Lazarus, & Christensen, 2008; Thurlow, Thompson, & Johnstone, 2007). NCLB and IDEA regulations have clarified that the scores of all students in the regular assessment with or without accommodations are included in the accountability system without restrictions. The scores of students who are assessed with accommodations that alter what the test intends to measure (e.g., extra time on a timed test, being read to on a reading test that measures decoding or fluency skills) are not included in the accountability system but do factor into the total number of students who should be assessed, thus effectively reducing participation rates.

Alternate Assessment Based on Grade-Level Achievement Standards

The AA-GLAS option allows states to use alternative methods or formats to those used for the regular assessment, such as portfolios or performance events. These assessments are based on grade-level content standards and hold students to grade-level expectations for performance. States are not required to provide this option, and few states have chosen to pursue it, with just two (Massachusetts and North Carolina) approved by the U.S. Department of Education as of January 2009 for use in the NCLB accountability system. Massachusetts described its AA-GLAS option in a report that indicated the number of students participating in the option was small but growing (Weiner, 2006). The number of students with disabilities needing this assessment option is generally expected to be relatively small, especially if accommodation policies are robust, but no limitations were placed on the percentage of students who could be counted as proficient for NCLB accountability.

Alternate Assessment Based on Modified Achievement Standards

The AA-MAS is the newest of the assessment options for students with disabilities. It was added by regulation to both NCLB and IDEA in 2007. These assessments are based on grade-level content standards and hold students to modified expectations for performance. The meaning of *modified achievement standards* is being refined as states explore or implement this option, but the AA-MAS regulation defined them as being "challenging for eligible students, but . . . less difficult than the grade-level academic achievement standards" (U.S. Department of Education, 2007, p. 17778). States are not required to offer the AA-MAS option, but the number choosing to do so, or to consider doing so, is growing. For example, as of July 2009, Texas had an AA-MAS approved by the U.S. Department of Education (U.S. Department of Education, 2009). Other states who have implemented the AA-MAS option include Kansas, Louisiana, California, North Carolina, North Dakota, and Oklahoma. The AA-MAS option was targeted by regulation to a specific group of students with individualized education programs (IEPs)—described as being a small group of students with disabilities who can make significant progress but may not reach grade-level achievement within the time period covered by their IEP (e.g., 1 academic year; U.S. Department of Education, 2007). An additional clarification in the regulation was that a student's participation in the AA-MAS should not preclude that student from meeting graduation requirements.

The U.S. Department of Education (2007) imposed limitations on the percentage of the total population that could be counted as proficient on an AA-MAS, although there was no limitation placed on the number of students with IEPs who could participate in this option. Generally, only up to 2% of the total population of students can be counted as proficient based on modified achievement standards; only when the percentage of students counted as proficient on the AA-AAS is less than 1% can the 2% be increased for the AA-MAS, but never so that the total percentage of students rated proficient across *both* of these alternate assessments exceeds 3%.

Lazarus, Rogers, Cormier, and Thurlow (2008) described the participation criteria of nine states that submitted their AA-MAS to the U.S. Department of Education for approval to be used in their accountability systems. The criteria most often focused on include 1) consideration of previous performance on multiple measures, 2) learning grade-level content, 3) not progressing at a rate expected to reach grade-level proficiency within the school year covered by the IEP, 4) not demonstrating knowledge on the regular assessment even with the provision of accommodations, and 5) not based on disability category label. All states included the requirement that the student have an IEP; some included the idea that a student's participation in this assessment could not preclude the student from meeting graduation requirements. A study of the states' AA-MAS designs (Albus, Lazarus, Thurlow, & Cormier, 2009) revealed that most states were approaching the construction of the AA-MAS by using formats associated with regular assessments but with modifications such as removing a distracter, using shorter reading passages, requiring the student to read fewer passages, or simplifying the language of the items.

Alternate Assessment Based on Alternate Achievement Standards

The AA-AAS, first introduced with the 1997 reauthorization of IDEA (PL 105-17) and required for implementation by July 2000, is an assessment for students with significant cognitive disabilities that is based on grade-level content standards and holds students to different expectations for performance. These assessments, which are the topic of this book, are now implemented in all states, although they have evolved over time to where they are now. Much has been learned about the students for whom this assessment is intended, as well as about the assessments themselves, and perhaps about assessment in general.

HISTORY AND RATIONALE FOR ALTERNATE ASSESSMENT BASED ON ALTERNATE ACHIEVEMENT STANDARDS

The history of AA-AAS begins with the earliest efforts of standards-based reform in two pioneering states, Maryland and Kentucky, in the early 1990s. In the wake of national reports in the 1980s such as *A Nation at Risk* (National Commission on Excellence in Education, 1983), educators, parents, and policy makers across the country were defining what all students should and could learn. In Maryland and Kentucky, these efforts were part of new state requirements designed to promote public school accountability through a state system of assessments of student achievement. State stakeholders realized that the term *all* truly had to mean *all* students to ensure that all students benefited from these accountability systems. The potential negative consequences of some students falling outside of the accountability system were being documented by researchers as early as the 1990s (e.g., National Center on Educational Outcomes [NCEO], n.d.). These consequences included increased rates of referral to special education, exclusion from the curriculum, and no information on the educational results of students with disabilities to inform educational improvement. The reports generated from research conducted beginning in the 1990s led to one major conclusion: All students must be included in school accountability, including students who cannot participate in the general assessments, even with accommodations, adaptations, or other supports, because of the potential negative consequences of exclusion (Kleinert, Haigh, Kearns, & Kennedy, 2000; Ysseldyke et al., 1996).

Some students had never been included in large-scale assessments of academic achievement, particularly those students with severe disabilities. The last 3 decades of the 20th century ushered in the philosophy of normalization for all people with disabilities (Wolfensberger, 1972)—the idea that people with severe disabilities needed the opportunity to participate in the same valued activities and rhythms of life as everyone else. Partially as an outgrowth of normalization, the inclusion of students with severe disabilities in general education classrooms emerged as a new and powerful tool for opportunities for socialization in the 1980s and 1990s. These movements, along with increasing options for assistive technology, helped support broad shifts in thinking about who was included in the definition of *all* students who would play a part in defining and measuring school accountability.

These broader shifts in thinking coincided with the inclusive accountability efforts in Maryland and Kentucky to influence federal policies in the 1990s. The Improving America's Schools Act of 1994 (PL 103-382) and IDEA 1997 both emphasized the need to include all students in assessments used for accountability purposes as part of a monumental movement to standards-based reform that has continued for more than 2 decades. IDEA 1997 specifically required for the first time that all state and district assessments must have an alternate assessment to allow full inclusion of students who could not participate in the general assessment, even with accommodations. IDEA 1997 additionally reinforced the accountability provisions by focusing the reauthorization on access to and progress in the general curriculum as the foundation of special education services. As one legal advocate observed,

> An IEP that sets lower goals and does not focus on these standards is usually illegal. Nor is it generally legal to assign a student with disabilities to a low-track regular program that does not teach to these standards. These rights are protected by the federal IDEA and Section 504 of the Rehabilitation Act of 1973. (Weckstein, 1999, p. 314)

From that point on, all students with disabilities were part of the standards-based reform movement, and like all other students, were to participate in a standards-based assessment for purposes of system accountability.

The predominant curriculum being taught to students with severe disabilities at the time of IDEA 1997 was not the general curriculum; it was primarily a functional life-skills curriculum, and the field of severe disabilities did not respond quickly to the emphasis on access to and progress in the general curriculum. That shift in curricular focus to include the content of the general curriculum became one of the major challenges—and opportunities—of these new alternate assessment requirements.

NCEO surveys of state directors of special education over the decade following the 1997 IDEA amendments documented the rapid development of these new assessments and the rapid shift in curricular thinking that followed that development (Thompson, Johnstone, Thurlow, & Altman, 2005; Thompson & Thurlow, 1999, 2000, 2001, 2003). In response to the 1999 NCEO survey, 20 states indicated that they were developing some type of alternate assessment. Still, only Kentucky and Maryland reported that they had the alternate assessment in place. By 2003, nearly all states had at least one alternate assessment in place, although what content was assessed—functional, academic, or some type of blend—varied greatly. Table 1.1 shows the shifting nature of the assessed content on alternate assessments over the time span.

For example, in 1999, 16 states assessed functional content with no link to the state content standards, and 1 additional state assessed a blend of state content standards and functional skills. In this same year, 19 states assessed content extended from the state content standards, and 24 states indicated that their alternate assessments were still in development. However, the focus on assessing only functional content in alternate assessments changed very rapidly. In 2000, only 9 states still reported assessing only functional skills, whereas 28 states reported measuring only extended state content standards. By 2005, no states reported assessing *only* functional content, and only 1 state reported assessing any functional skills, apart from the general curriculum, at all. Furthermore, in 2005, 10 states indicated that their respective alternate assessments were based on grade-level state

Table 1.1. Content addressed by state alternate assessments: Changes over time

Year	Functional skills, no link to content standards	Functional skills, linked to content standards	Content standards plus functional skills	Expanded or extended content standards	Grade-level content standards	IEP team determines content for assessment	Other or uncertain response	State revising content
1999	16	—	1	19	—	—	24	—
2000	9	3	7	28	—	—	3	—
2001	4	15	9	19	—	—	3	—
2003	2	—	4	36	—	3	3	2
2005	—	—	1	21	10	1	7	10

From Quenemoen, R. (2008). *A brief history of alternate assessments based on alternate achievement standards* (Synthesis Report 68, p. 8). Minneapolis: University of Minnesota, National Center on Educational Outcomes; adapted by permission.
Key: IEP, individualized education program.

content standards. That shift corresponded with the clarification in the NCLB Act of 2001 that assessments used for accountability under Title I had to include all students and cover the academic content for the grade in which each student was enrolled. This requirement was further defined in practice nationally through the peer review process under Title I as a condition for states to continue receiving federal funding.

As states began implementing these standards-based assessments, instruction also began to shift. Pioneering states that emphasized academic instruction and alternate assessments based on the state content standards began finding evidence of surprising student achievement. As the field started seeing student work that suggested students with severe disabilities could learn much more than anyone had previously expected when they were taught an academic curriculum, there began to be simultaneous shifts in the field of severe disabilities, including demonstrations of student learning directly linked to grade level content in such subjects as reading and math (Browder, Ahlgrim-Delzell, Courtade, Gibbs, & Flowers, 2008; Jimenez, Browder, & Courtade, 2008). These shifts have not been without considerable controversy, and even fear, among teachers and parents of these students. Examples of these curricular shifts, and how they can be applied for students with even profound and multiple disabilities, are presented throughout this text, especially in Chapters 5–9.

The shifts in the field of severe disabilities were more than matched by shifts in understanding of technical adequacy of large-scale assessments of students with severe disabilities. As the states developed and implemented alternate assessments, measurement advisors were puzzled about how to ensure that results of these assessments were of sufficient quality to be included in accountability systems. It quickly became clear that existing measurement paradigms, using traditional statistical methods of documenting technical qualities, were not working well. These challenges stimulated discussion across measurement, curriculum, and special education partners (Quenemoen, Thurlow, & Ryan, 2004). It quickly became apparent that the technical challenges of alternate assessment were not going to be solved with the expertise and tools of one educational discipline alone. These challenges required collaboration that would yield educationally sound but technically defensible strategies. Chapter 2 describes what educators have learned from this important collaborative effort.

Although this book is about alternate assessments for students with significant cognitive disabilities, that is AA-AAS, we believe it also important for the reader to understand the full framework under which students with disabilities can participate in standards-based assessments under NCLB and IDEA 2004.

PARAMETERS OF ALTERNATE ASSESSMENT BASED ON ALTERNATE ACHIEVEMENT STANDARDS: THE WHAT, WHO, AND HOW

What Is Assessed

Both NCLB and IDEA 2004 have specified that AA-AAS for students with significant cognitive disabilities must be based on the state's academic standards for all students. As defined in NCLB, the state may identify or set alternate achievement standards for students with significant cognitive disabilities provided that these alternate standards 1) are aligned with the state's academic content standards, 2) promote access to the general curriculum, and 3) reflect professional judgment of the highest achievement standards possible (U.S. Department of Education, 2003). IDEA 2004 mandates that states "shall provide for alternate assessments that—are aligned with the State's challenging academic content standards and challenging student academic achievement standards" (§ 612[a][16][C][ii][I]).

Alternate achievement standards are "an expectation of performance that differs in complexity from a grade-level achievement standard" (U.S. Department of Education, 2005, p. 20). Alternate achievement standards must 1) be aligned with the state's academic content standards, 2) describe at least three levels of achievement (i.e., basic, proficient, advanced), 3) include descriptions of competencies associated with each level of achievement, and 4) include assessment or cut scores that differentiate between achievement levels (U.S. Department of Education, 2005). Although alternate achievement standards for students with significant cognitive disabilities may differ in complexity from grade-level achievement standards, or be reduced in breadth or coverage, they must still be linked to grade-level content. In its *Standards and Assessment Peer Review Guidance* for states, the U.S. Department of Education (2004) has explicitly delineated this linkage:

> For alternate assessments in grades 3 through 8 based on alternate achievement standards, the assessment materials should show a clear link to the content standards for the grade in which the student is enrolled although the grade-level content may be reduced in complexity or modified to reflect pre-requisite skills. (p. 15)

Who Is Assessed

AA-AAS options are designed for the small percentage of students with significant cognitive disabilities for whom the regular assessment, even with appropriate accommodations, would be an inappropriate measure of student progress within the general education curriculum (IDEA 2004, § 614[d][1])[A][VI])[bb]). For those students who cannot participate in regular assessments, even with accommodations, states (or districts, in the case of local assessments) must develop alternate assessments. "In general, the Department [of Education] estimates that about 9 percent of students with disabilities (approximately one percent of the total student population) have significant cognitive disabilities that qualify them to participate in an assessment based on alternate achievement standards" (U.S. Department of Education, 2005, p. 23). Researchers have noted that students taking this assessment typically have been labeled as having special education labels such as autism, intellectual disability, and/or multiple disabilities. However, not *all* students with these labels will need an alternate assessment, and students with other special education labels (e.g., orthopedic disability, deafblindness) may also qualify for an AA-AAS. In short, the term *significant cognitive disability* does not in itself denote a specific IDEA disability category or categories, but rather a set of educational considerations based upon individual student needs.

However, even if educators do attempt to describe the population of students in each state AA-AAS by their reported disability categories, this would *not* be especially helpful for at least two reasons. First, although researchers have found sizable variations across states in the percentage of students in each IDEA disability category reported as participating in the state AA-AAS (Kearns et al., in press), this variation may really reflect the considerable variation in how states assign students to IDEA categories in the first place. For example, for all states in the United States, the percentage of all students identified as having intellectual disabilities varies by a factor of eightfold—from a low of 0.35% of all students (New Hampshire) to a high of 2.75% of all students (West Virginia; U.S. Department of Education, 2007). Thus, differences in the percentages of students in each

IDEA category participating in the AA-AAS across states may not primarily reflect which students get identified for the alternate assessment, but rather how students were originally assigned to disability categories in their respective states. Second, IDEA disability categories are only broad eligibility labels, and are not predictive of individual learner needs. These are important reasons why educators need a more objective, descriptive measure across states to define characteristics of students participating in the AA-AAS option.

In attempting to define students with significant cognitive disabilities eligible for AA-AAS, states have used criteria such as "the student requires intensive individualized instruction or extensively modified instruction to acquire, maintain, or generalize skills," and/or "the student requires direct instruction in multiple settings to successfully generalize skills to natural settings, including home, school, and community," or the "student requires extended standards" (Kearns et al., in press). Such criteria certainly do not rule out instruction and assessment on grade-level academic content for students with significant cognitive disabilities—rather, these criteria would suggest that academic content for students with significant cognitive disabilities should be taught with "intensive individualized" instruction and that the academic content should be personalized or made meaningful for each student so that the student can learn to apply that content to new situations, especially those associated with real-life or authentic tasks.

In 2009, researchers developed and validated a simple tool—the Learner Characteristics Inventory (LCI; Kearns et al., in press; Towles-Reeves, Kearns, Kleinert, & Kleinert, 2009)—to describe the population of students taking the AA-AAS. The LCI is a quick, teacher-scored checklist that rates the student on the following variables: receptive and expressive communication, hearing, vision, motor skills, engagement, health/attendance, and reading and mathematics skills (see Chapter 3 for a more detailed description of the LCI). In a study of seven states' AA-AAS (including states from all parts of the country, as well as both urban and rural states), Kearns et al. found that students were perhaps best differentiated by levels of receptive and expressive language use. The majority of learners in each state's respective alternate assessment communicated *symbolically* (using oral speech, signs, or other symbol systems across a range of communicative situations) and could follow one- to two-step directions independently. The next largest percentage of learners included those who used *emergent symbolic* communication (e.g., beginning to use pictures or signs to communicate) and who needed additional cues for assistance to follow directions. The final set of students were those who communicated *presymbolically* (communicating expressively via facial expressions or muscle tone) and needed physical prompts to respond to verbal directions. These three groups, clearly evidenced in similar proportions across all seven states, represent significant developmental differences that, in turn, have an impact on the acquisition/demonstration of skills in reading and mathematics. The results of this research are described in greater detail in Chapter 3; however, suffice it to say for now that who is assessed using AA-AAS is a very heterogeneous population of students that makes up approximately 1% of all students, for whom perhaps the best descriptor of functioning level may well be the extent to which the students are able to use *symbolic communication*, both to convey their needs and to understand directions.

How Students Are Assessed

A key issue for states and local districts in the development of alternate assessments is, of course, what those assessments will look like—how they will be structured and what the sources of data will be. Ysseldyke and Olsen (1999) originally described a broad range of possible options for alternate assessments, including performance event tests (e.g., structured problems that require a student to solve a problem or perform a task), adaptive behavior skills or performance checklists (a listing of standardized or criterion-referenced critical skills that a student has mastered), interviews with significant others knowledgeable about the student's performance, analyses of progress on current IEP objectives, portfolios (collections of student work that reveal what students can do), or some combination of these measures. As alternate assessments for students with significant cognitive disabilities have become increasingly aligned with academic standards for all students (and less focused on functional skill content and the specific content of the student's IEP; Browder et al., 2004), the following three approaches to alternate assessment have become the most widely used (Roeber, 2002):

1. A *portfolio*, or body of evidence, approach: Portfolios are systematic collections of student work that are scored against predetermined criteria for accountability purposes.

2. A *checklist* approach: This approach requires that teachers identify whether students are able to perform certain predetermined skills, tasks, or activities. Evidence for performance can come from direct observation, interviews, and/or examples of student work samples. With this approach, a student's accountability score is based on the number or complexity of skills that he or she is able to perform successfully.

3. A *performance assessment* or *performance event* approach: This is a direct measure of a skill under controlled assessment conditions (e.g., the student responding to questions about interpretations of bar graphs taken from grade-level math content in a one-to-one assessment task). Performance events may or may not be timed and are often referred to as "on-demand" tasks, in that students are expected to demonstrate performance under what would be called more typical testing conditions.

As noted by Towles-Reeves, Kleinert, and Muhomba (2009), several states are using more than one of these approaches (e.g., requiring student portfolios to reflect a broad range of content in math and reading performance, but perhaps using performance event tasks for assessment in science or other academic subjects).

These three approaches, however, can vary widely in how they are applied across states. For example, some states may require highly structured portfolios in which both the kinds of entries and targeted skills are specified, whereas other states might identify the grade-level content standards that must be evidenced in the portfolio but allow teachers to select the targeted skill most appropriate for the developmental or communication level of the student to illustrate that standard. Thus the format of the assessment may not be as critical in describing state approaches to alternate assessment as the degree of flexibility versus standardization within the assessment, as well as the specific points at which greater flexibility is given (e.g., teacher selects the skill and activity in which the skill is to be measured versus an assessment in which the exact skill, the activity for that skill, and the testing conditions are precisely given by the assessment itself). Gong and Marion (2006) discussed the importance of describing this dimension of standardization versus flexibility, which is essential in understanding how states conceptualize their AA-AAS to accurately capture the learning of such a heterogeneous population of learners.

ESSENTIAL PARTICIPANTS IN AA-AAS: THE ROLES OF SPECIAL AND GENERAL EDUCATION TEACHERS, RELATED SERVICE PERSONNEL, PARENTS, STUDENTS, AND ADMINISTRATORS

When alternate assessments were first introduced, they were seen largely as the province of special educators (Kleinert, Kearns, & Kennedy, 1997), who attempted to apply what they knew about inclusion in general education classrooms to the content measured in alternate assessments by their respective states. As alternate assessments began to focus much more clearly on academic standards for all students, and most recently on grade-level content standards, general educators have become essential partners in defining the link to grade-level content standards, providing instruction that enables students with significant cognitive disabilities to make that link, and aligning the assessment items in the AA-AAS to grade-level content standards (see Browder et al., 2007). Without question, general education teachers are increasingly becoming critical players in their respective states' alternate assessments.

Yet there are other essential partners as well. For example, the role of related service personnel, including speech-language pathologists, is highlighted by Kearns et al. (in press) and Towles-Reeves et al. (2009), in that students in the alternate assessment form three discreet groups in terms of expressive and receptive communication (symbolic, emerging symbolic, and presymbolic) and that even at the secondary level, approximately 10% of students in the AA-AAS are still functioning at a presymbolic level. Because academic content is by definition symbolic content, it becomes tremendously challenging to provide meaningful instruction on grade-level content standards to students at a presymbolic level of communication, and it becomes essential that general and special education teachers, in collaboration with speech-language pathologists, work to establish a formal, symbolic communication for these students while enabling access to grade-level academic content as a part of establishing that symbolic communication. The importance of other related service personnel (e.g., physical therapists, occupational therapists) in both instruction and assessment also is illustrated by the finding across three geographically distinct states that approximately 18%–24% of students with significant cognitive disabilities in their states' respective alternate assessments required adaptations as a result of motor or physical disabilities (Towles-Reeves et al., 2009). Without needed adaptations and supports, students with significant cognitive disabilities will not be able to meaningfully access the general curriculum or be able to demonstrate what they really know on their state's alternate assessment.

Principals, as the instructional leaders for their schools, play a key role in large-scale assessments for students with significant cognitive disabilities. In a survey across two states of principals who had students in their respective alternate assessments ($N = 389$), Towles-Reeves, Kleinert, and Anderman (2008) found that responding principals perceived themselves as instructional leaders for all of the students in their respective schools, including students with significant cognitive disabilities. (In fact, they rated their role as instructional leaders for all of their students as the most important part of their jobs.) Principals' perceptions of the AA-AAS in these two states were generally positive. The majority of responding principals perceived that their state's alternate assessment increased 1) instruction on grade-level content, 2) general education and special education teacher expectations of students with the most significant cognitive disabilities, 3) sharing of instructional responsibilities for these students with other school personnel, and 4) special education teachers' understanding of academic content standards (Towles-Reeves et al., 2008). Yet without high expectations for students with significant cognitive disabilities and an adequate understanding of the purpose of AA-AAS for these students, principals will not be able to fulfill their role as instructional leaders for all students.

Parents also play an essential role in shaping expectations for children's education, though their role in alternate assessments has received little attention thus far. In one study that did investigate parent perceptions (Roach, 2006), results suggested that parents believed the assessment was useful and that it was important for their child to learn academic content in reading, writing, and math. Results also suggested that they generally agreed that all students should have the opportunity to participate in statewide assessments. Parents in this study expressed their strongest agreement in the confidence in the results of their *own* child's performance (a mean of 4.25 on a 5-point Likert scale). Yet parent perceptions were less positive as students got older and as the percentage of functional to academic objectives on their child's IEP increased. Parents are critical partners, and it is essential that they have confidence in their state's alternate assessments to reflect important learning for their children.

A final essential participant is the student. Kampfer, Horvath, Kleinert, and Kearns (2001) found that in the context of one state's alternate assessment, the extent to which students were involved in constructing their *own* portfolio assessments was significantly and positively related to their actual scores but that the amount of teacher time spent on actually completing the assessment was significantly less related to student scores. Similarly, Karvonen, Flowers, Browder, Wakeman, and Algozzine (2006) found that teachers who provided extensive amounts of direct instruction on targeted skills, took frequent data on student performance, and enabled students to participate in monitoring their own learning (e.g., self-monitoring, self-evaluation strategies) had students who scored well on their state's alternate assessment. Clearly, students need to have a voice in determining what they should learn and how they should learn it, and they should be able to participate in evaluating that learning. This also means that students receive direct feedback on their performance on their state's alternate assessment in order to improve their learning.

IMPORTANT PRINCIPLES OF
ALTERNATE ASSESSMENTS: WHAT WE BELIEVE

Each of us operates not only from what we have learned from experience and from the research base of our field, but from our beliefs or our "essential principles" as well. The authors of this chapter believe that the requirements of IDEA and NCLB for the inclusion of all students in large-scale educational assessments, including the AA-AAS for students with significant cognitive disabilities, present not only very real challenges, but a singular opportunity to improve educational programs for the students with whom we work.

The list that follows includes our principles of what constitutes effective alternate assessment strategies—principles that we believe will result in improved programs and outcomes for students with significant disabilities. We have developed and expanded this list from an earlier set of principles (Kleinert & Thurlow, 2001) that we developed for our original text on alternate assessment, *Alternate Assessment: Measuring Outcomes and Supports for Students with Disabilities* (Kleinert & Kearns, 2001), and we have based our revised list on the lessons we have since learned.

1. Alternate assessment must be integrally tied to effective instruction, including direct student engagement; high rates of student responses; and structured, systematic teaching opportunities specifically designed to elicit those responses.

2. Alternate assessment must allow the student to apply what he or she has learned; skills are not evidenced in isolation but are parts of complex performances that integrate skills across developmental and academic areas.

3. Alternate assessment is not meant to be a one-time test or single snapshot of student performance; rather, it is based on continuous assessment of student performance.

4. Alternate assessments are a team responsibility—it is not just the role of the special educator to implement these assessments, but general educators, related service personnel, school administrators, parents, and students themselves have essential roles in the process.

5. The ultimate purpose of alternate assessments for students with significant disabilities is to improve instruction and results for these students. Teachers must learn to use alternate assessment not only to document what the student has learned but also to actually *enhance* and *extend* that learning. It is for this reason that we have written this book, and it is for this reason that it is addressed primarily to teachers and other direct practitioners.

REFERENCES

Albus, D., Lazarus, S.S., Thurlow, M.L., & Cormier, D. (2009). *Characteristics of states' alternate assessments based on modified academic achievement standards in 2008.* Minneapolis: University of Minnesota, National Center on Educational Outcomes.

Browder, D., Ahlgrim-Delzell, L., Courtade, G., Gibbs, S., & Flowers, C. (2008). Evaluation of the effectiveness of an early literacy program for students with significant developmental disabilities. *Exceptional Children, 75,* 33–54.

Browder, D., Flowers, C., Ahlgrim-Delzell, L., Karvonen, M., Spooner, F., & Algozzine, R. (2004). The alignment of alternate assessment content with academic and functional curricula. *Journal of Special Education, 37*(4), 211–223.

Browder, D., Wakeman, S., Flowers, C., Rickelman, R., Pugalee, D., & Karvonen, M. (2007). Creating access to the general curriculum with links to grade-level content for students with significant cognitive disabilities: An explication of the concept. *Journal of Special Education, 41*(1), 2–16.

Cortiella, C. (2007). *Learning opportunities for your child through alternate assessments: Alternate assessments based on modified academic achievement standards.* Minneapolis: University of Minnesota, National Center on Educational Outcomes.

Gong, B., & Marion, S. (2006). *Dealing with flexibility in assessments for students with significant cognitive disabilities.* Dover, NH: National Center for the Improvement of Educational Assessment. Retrieved August 20, 2009, from http://www.nciea.org/publications/AERA_BGSM06.pdf

Improving America's Schools Act of 1994, PL 103-382, 20 U.S.C. §§ 630 *et seq.*

Individuals with Disabilities Education Act Amendments (IDEA) of 1997, PL 105-17, 20 U.S.C. §§ 1400 *et seq.*

Individuals with Disabilities Education Improvement Act (IDEA) of 2004, PL 108-446, 20 U.S.C. §§ 1400 *et seq.*

Jimenez, B., Browder, D., & Courtade, G. (2008). Teaching an algebraic equation to high school students with moderate developmental disabilities. *Education and Training in Developmental Disabilities, 43*(2), 266–274.

Kampfer, S., Horvath, L., Kleinert, H., & Kearns, J. (2001). Teachers' perceptions of one state's alternate assessment portfolio program: Implications for practice and preparation. *Exceptional Children, 67*(3), 361–374.

Karvonen, M., Flowers, C., Browder, D., Wakeman, S., & Algozzine, B. (2006). Case study of the influence on alternate assessment outcomes for students with disabilities. *Education and Training in Developmental Disabilities, 41*(2), 95–110.

Kearns, J., & Towles-Reeves, E. (2007). *Who are the students who take alternate achievement standards assessments.* Retrieved February 21, 2010, from http://www.naacpartners.org/products.aspx

Kearns, J., Towles-Reeves, E., Kleinert, H., Kleinert, J., & Thomas, M. (in press). Characteristics of and implications for students participating in alternate assessments based on alternate academic achievement standards. *Journal of Special Education.*

Kleinert, H., Haigh, J., Kearns, J., & Kennedy, S. (2000). Alternate assessments: Lessons learned and roads to be taken. *Exceptional Children, 67*(1), 51–66.

Kleinert, H.L., & Kearns, J.F. (2001). *Alternate assessment: Measuring outcomes and supports for students with disabilities.* Baltimore: Paul H. Brookes Publishing Co.

Kleinert, H., Kearns, J., & Kennedy, S. (1997). Accountability for all students: Kentucky's alternate portfolio system for students with moderate and severe cognitive disabilities. *Journal of The Association for Persons with Severe Handicaps, 22*(2), 88–101.

Kleinert, H.L., & Thurlow, M.L. (2001). An introduction to alternate assessment. In H. Kleinert & J. Kearns, *Alternate assessment: Measuring outcomes and supports for students with disabilities* (pp. 1–15). Baltimore: Paul H. Brookes Publishing Co.

Lazarus, S.S., Rogers, C., Cormier, D., & Thurlow, M.L. (2008). *States' participation guidelines for alternate assessments based on modified academic achievement standards (AA-MAS) in 2008* (Synthesis Report 71). Minneapolis: University of Minnesota, National Center on Educational Outcomes.

Lazarus, S.S., Thurlow, M.L., Lail, K.E., & Christensen, L. (2009). A longitudinal analysis of state accommodations policies: Twelve years of change 1993-2005. *Journal of Special Education, 43*(2), 67–80.

National Center on Educational Outcomes. (n.d.). Archived publications. Retrieved February 22, 2010, from http://www.cehd.umn.edu/nceo/OnlinePubs/PublicationsArchives.html

National Commission on Excellence in Education. (1983). *A nation at risk: The imperative for educational reform.* Washington, DC: Author.

No Child Left Behind Act of 2001, PL 107-110, 115 Stat. 1425, 20 U.S.C. §§ 6301 *et seq.*

Quenemoen, R. (2008). *A brief history of alternate assessments based on alternate achievement standards* (Synthesis Report 68). Minneapolis: University of Minnesota, National Center on Educational Outcomes.

Quenemoen, R., Thurlow, M., & Ryan, J. (2004). *I say potato, you say potahto: An AERA Conference discussion paper and side-by-side glossary.* Minneapolis: University of Minnesota, National Center on Educational Outcomes.

Roach, A. (2006). Influences on parent perceptions of an alternate assessment for students with severe cognitive disabilities. *Research and Practice for Persons with Severe Handicaps, 31,* 267–274.

Roeber, E. (2002). *Setting standards on alternate assessments* (Synthesis Report 42). Minneapolis: University of Minnesota, National Center on Educational Outcomes. Retrieved November 28, 2005, from http://education.umn.edu/NCEO/OnlinePubs/Synthesis42.html

Thompson, S.J., Johnstone, C.J., Thurlow, M.L., & Altman, J.R. (2005). *2005 state special education outcomes: Steps forward in a decade of change.* Minneapolis: University of Minnesota, National Center on Educational Outcomes.

Thompson, S., & Thurlow, M. (1999). *1999 state special education outcomes: A report on state activities at the end of the century.* Minneapolis: University of Minnesota, National Center on Educational Outcomes.

Thompson, S.J., & Thurlow, M.L. (2000). *State alternate assessments: Status as IDEA alternate assessment requirements take effect* (Synthesis Report No. 35). Minneapolis: University of Minnesota, National Center on Educational Outcomes.

Thompson, S., & Thurlow, M. (2001). *2001 state special education outcomes: A report on state activities at the beginning of a new decade*. Minneapolis: University of Minnesota, National Center on Educational Outcomes.

Thompson, S., & Thurlow, M. (2003). *2003 state special education outcomes: Marching on*. Minneapolis: University of Minnesota, National Center on Educational Outcomes.

Thurlow, M.L. (2007). State policies and accommodations: Issues and implications. In C.C. Laitusis & L.L. Cook (Eds.), *Large-scale assessment and accommodations: What works?* (pp. 13–22). Arlington, VA: Council for Exceptional Children.

Thurlow, M.L., Lazarus, S.S., & Christensen, L.L. (2008). Role of assessment accommodations in accountability. *Perspectives, 34*(4), 17–20.

Thurlow, M., Thompson, S., & Johnstone, C. (2007). Policy, legal, and implementation issues surrounding assessment accommodations for students with disabilities. In L. Florian (Ed.), *The Sage handbook of special education* (pp. 331–346). Thousand Oaks, CA: Sage.

Towles-Reeves, E., Kearns, J., Kleinert, H., & Kleinert, J. (2009). Knowing what students know: Defining the student population taking alternate assessments based on alternate achievement standards. *Journal of Special Education, 42*, 241–254.

Towles-Reeves, E., Kleinert, H., & Anderman, L. (2008). Alternate assessments based on alternate achievements standards: Principals' perceptions. *Research and Practice in Severe Disabilities, 33*, 122–133.

Towles-Reeves, E., Kleinert, H., & Muhomba, M. (2009). Alternate assessment: Have we learned anything new? *Exceptional Children, 75*, 233–252.

U.S. Department of Education. (2003, December 9). Improving the academic achievement of the disadvantaged. *Federal Register, 66*(236), 68698–68708.

U.S. Department of Education. (2004). *Standards and assessment peer review guidance*. Washington, DC: Author, Office of Elementary and Secondary Education.

U.S. Department of Education. (2005). *Alternate achievement standards for students with the most significant cognitive disabilities: Non-regulatory guidance*. Washington, DC: Author, Office of Elementary and Secondary Education.

U.S. Department of Education. (2007). *Modified academic achievement standards: Non-regulatory guidance*. Washington, DC: Author. Retrieved July 30, 2007, from http://www.ed.gov/policy/speced/guid/modachieve-summary.html

U.S. Department of Education. (2009, June 23). *Letter from Joseph C. Conaty, Delegated Authority for the Assistant Secretary for Elementary and Secondary Education, to Robert Scott, Commissioner of the Texas Education Agency*. Retrieved July 24, 2009, from http://ritter.tea.state.tx.us/student.assessment/special_education/usde_ltr_alt_assessment.pdf

Weckstein, P. (1999). School reform and enforceable rights to quality education. In J. Heubert (Ed.), *Law and school reform: Six strategies for promoting educational equity* (pp. 306–389). New Haven, CT: Yale University Press.

Weiner, D. (2006). *Alternate assessments measured against grade-level achievement standards: The Massachusetts "competency portfolio"* (Synthesis Report 59). Minneapolis: University of Minnesota, National Center on Educational Outcomes.

Wolfensberger, W. (1972). *The principle of normalization in human services*. Toronto: National Institute of Mental Retardation.

Ysseldyke, J., & Olsen, K. (1999). Putting alternate assessments into practice: What to measure and possible sources of data. *Exceptional Children, 65*, 175–186.

Ysseldyke, J., Thurlow, M., Erickson, R., Gabrys, R., Haigh, J., Trimble, S., et al. (1996). *A comparison of state assessment systems in Maryland and Kentucky with a focus on the participation of students with disabilities* (Maryland-Kentucky Report 1). Minneapolis: University of Minnesota, National Center on Educational Outcomes.

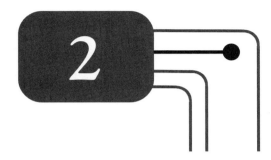

Principles and Practices for Achievement Assessments in School Accountability Systems

Jacqui Farmer Kearns

Andrea, a new special education teacher, has just received the scores for her 10 students from the alternate assessment based on alternate achievement standards (AA-AAS) reading, math, and science assessments administered during the previous year. The principal, Mrs. Jones, wants to have a discussion with her later this week about what they can do to improve their school results for this group of children. Next week, she has a meeting with a parent of one of the students on her caseload to answer some questions about the individual student's results that she received in the mail.

Similarly, Mrs. Jones is "under the gun" because her school did not meet the adequate yearly progress goals under the No Child Left Behind (NCLB) Act of 2001 (PL 107-110) for the subgroup of students with disabilities, some of whom are on Andrea's caseload, but many of whom take the general assessment or general assessment with accommodations. Mrs. Jones will have to discuss strategies for improving results with the expert assigned to her school, the superintendent of the district, and the parents on her site-based council.

This vignette illustrates the types of scenarios facing teachers, administrators, and families as they seek to understand the requirements of their state assessment and accountability system as well as NCLB. The good news in this vignette is that the principal wants to know what her school should do to improve results for students with significant cognitive disabilities. Her positive reaction suggests that the accountability system is having the intended effect of focusing on improved instruction for all students. However, with each additional layer of professional staff members, including administrators at the district and even state levels, a different set of questions and concerns emerge about what steps they should take.

This chapter explicates the principles and practices of assessment for school accountability purposes, as these principles relate to an AA-AAS. In addition, we hope to begin to build a basic vocabulary of commonly used assessment terminology that is often misinterpreted or has different meanings across the disciplines of special education, measurement, and curriculum experts. We open the chapter with a discussion of the fundamentals of validity (i.e., purpose and use of the assessments) of both assessment and accountability systems. Next, we describe key components of an assessment design including observation tools, content standards, scoring the assessments, and setting the standards for achievement. Finally, we provide Andrea and her principal with some key questions to consider as they prepare for the conversations they will have with a wide array of constituents to improve instruction.

VALIDITY OF AN ALTERNATE ASSESSMENT BASED ON ALTERNATE ACHIEVEMENT STANDARDS IN SCHOOL ACCOUNTABILITY SYSTEMS

The ultimate validity criterion for any assessment is the extent to which it accomplishes the purpose for which it was intended. Validity of an assessment is determined by a body of research that demonstrates a relationship between the test and the behavior it is intended to measure. For example, a reading test is valid if it measures reading as it claims and if it measures reading for the *intended* use of the reading score (e.g., large-scale accountability). If the score is to be used in an accountability system, then it must be *valid* for use in accountability systems. Indeed, the American Educational Research Association (AERA), the American Psychological Association (APA), and the National Council on Measurement in Education (NCME) point to purpose and use as fundamental validity criteria in their *Standards for Educational and Psychological Testing* (1999).

For NCLB purposes, the assessment must measure reading for the purpose of school accountability. This distinction between the purpose of using an assessment to judge school accountability and the purpose of using an assessment for diagnosing a reading problem, for example, is important to understand. Assessments that are valid for the purpose of accountability may not be valid for diagnosing a reading problem for a specific child. Furthermore, assessments should only be used for the intended purposes.

Likewise, the validity of an accountability system is based on the extent to which the accountability system accomplishes the purpose for which it was intended (Hill et al., 2005). For our discussion, the purpose of accountability systems is to qualify student achievement into evidence of school quality (Betebenner, 2009). The distinction between assessment and accountability is essential for determining the validity of each. The purpose of the assessment is to acquire, summarize, and report information. The purpose of accountability is to assign *consequences* to the results of the assessment (Hill et al., 2005).

Our discussion of validity is limited to the explication of validity for summative achievement assessments in reading, math, and science for purposes of accountability or making valid judgments about the quality of a school. Summative achievement assessments are administered annually, whereas formative assessments are administered more often within the school year (Betebenner, 2009). At the time of this writing, only summative assessments are included in state accountability systems under NCLB.

Although valid assessments are necessary for valid accountability systems, valid assessments represent only one part of the "validity argument." Documenting the validity of an accountability system that relies on those assessments requires that a body of research verify the relationship between student achievement as defined by the assessments and school quality. In addition, accountability systems may also include other measures or indicators of school quality (e.g., attendance, promotion/retention, drop-out rate). The NCLB legislation uses achievement assessments in reading, math, and science as accountability measures in the determination of adequate yearly progress, a federally mandated accountability measure. The accountability system under NCLB ensures that federal funding to states is used appropriately to improve student assessment results in reading, mathematics, and science. In addition, some states have accountability requirements that exceed the NCLB assessment and reporting requirements. For example, some states require social studies or arts and humanities assessments, which are not required for NCLB, or the state may require a norm-referenced test at a particular grade level (e.g., all students have to take the ACT exam in the 11th grade). In these cases, the Individuals with Disabilities Education Improvement Act (IDEA) of 2004 (PL 108-446) requires that students with disabilities be assessed as well and their results reported to the extent to which all students are assessed and their results reported. To that end, students with disabilities not only are assessed in the same content areas as other students are assessed but they also must have assessments that mirror other state assessment requirements. For those students who participate in an AA-AAS, IDEA requires that states develop alternate assessments in those additional content areas for those students who cannot take the regular assessment, even with accommodations.

HISTORICAL PERSPECTIVES

Using an AA-AAS is a relatively recent development in the area of achievement assessments. The first AA-AAS emerged in state accountability systems in the early 1990s (Kleinert & Kearns, 2001; Kleinert, Kearns, & Kennedy, 1997). The purpose of these early alternate assessments was to ensure that students with significant cognitive disabilities were represented in state accountability systems. In at least one state, teachers received cash rewards if the school met its achievement goals, and school councils had the authority to determine how professional development and other discretionary dollars could be spent at the building level. Ensuring that all students were represented in the accountability system was a policy decision intended to protect access to resources for students with disabilities and their teachers, as well as to minimize the unintended negative consequences of accountability. For example, an accountability system that does not include all students increases the possibility that those students and their teachers will be marginalized and resources directed to those who are more likely to meet the established criteria for achievement. In addition, if students with disabilities are not included in accountability systems focused on academic achievement, then the lack of opportunities to develop academic skills results in a self-perpetuating system of low expectations. Even in the early 1990s, although alternate assessments relied heavily on indices of program quality, including some indicators that were not direct measures of academic achievement (e.g., extent of participation in general education classes, generalization of skills across settings), these early assessments often did tie, at least in part, to achievement in academic content (Kleinert & Kearns, 2001). Since then, we have come to understand that although initial gains may have been realized, heavy reliance on program quality indicators (and not direct measures of student achievement) resulted in continued low expectations for academic achievement for students with disabilities (Quenemoen, Thompson, & Thurlow, 2003). The requirement for links to grade-level academic content, although controversial, has the potential to raise our expectations for the achievement of academic content for these students (Cortiella, 2006).

TECHNICAL QUALITY OF AN ALTERNATE ASSESSMENT BASED ON ALTERNATE ACHIEVEMENT STANDARDS

The NCLB requirements for academic content linkage and technical quality of an AA-AAS have resulted in careful consideration of the technical properties of these assessments, while simultaneously balancing the need for flexibility in order to accommodate a very heterogeneous population. To better understand the factors affecting alternate assessments, the National Alternate Assessment Center (NAAC) proposed applying the theoretical framework developed by Pellegrino, Chudowsky, and Glaser (2001) in the National Research Council's *Knowing What Students Know*. Their framework illustrated the relationship of three important assessment features—cognition, observation, and interpretation—which interact with each other to delineate fundamental aspects of technical quality. The cognition vertex refers to characteristics of the student population and how students demonstrate competence in the academic domains of reading, math, and science. The observation vertex refers to the instrument (i.e., test) used to gather information. The interpretation vertex describes reporting results, determining error sources, setting achievement standards, and analyzing responses for bias and other interpretation issues. Each of the three vertices of the assessment triangle (Figure 2.1) is reflexive in that each vertex informs the other two.

In addition to these three important components of assessments (discussed in more detail in the following sections), the fourth component—the validity evaluation *itself*—remains the central component. The validity of the assessment rests with the extent to which the information is useful for the intended purpose. In other words, the assessment data must be useful to schools as they work to improve results for students in learning the academic content.

Cognition Vertex: Content Standards and Student Population

This vertex of the assessment triangle refers to the population of students who will or are taking a particular assessment and the extent to which there is a "theory of learning," or a research base describing how the population demonstrates competence in academic domains (Pellegrino et al., 2001). Chapter 3 describes the student population that participates in an AA-AAS as highly varied in expressive and receptive language development, motor skills, and engagement (Kearns, Towles-Reeves, Kleinert, Kleinert, & Thomas, in press; Towles-Reeves, Kearns, Kleinert, & Kleinert, 2009). Furthermore, the population also exhibits highly varied access to academic content within and across grades (Browder, Flowers, & Wakeman, 2008; Kearns et al.). The heterogeneity of the student population

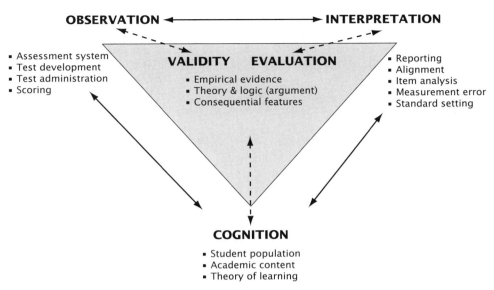

Figure 2.1. The assessment triangle (From Marion, S., & Pellegrino, J. [2006]. A validity framework for evaluating the technical quality of alternate assessments. *Educational Measurement: Issues and Practices, 25*[4], 52; reprinted by permission.)

and the lack of a coherent theory of academic learning for this population present multiple issues for balancing the observation and interpretation vertices of the assessment triangle—that is, in how the target behaviors are observed and what inferences can be made about those behaviors in reference to what students have learned.

Content Standards

Central to the discussion of academic content is the basic understanding of what is meant by *grade-level academic content standards*. Under NCLB, grade-level academic content standards refer to the content standards (e.g., reading, math, science) that are emphasized and assessed at each grade. It is important to note that the term *grade-level* in this case does not assume performance on grade-level. It simply means that students with significant cognitive disabilities will gain access to the same curriculum activities and materials that are used by students without disabilities of a similar age/grade and that the assessment items link or approximate as closely as possible grade-level content standards. Most important, assessment items must reflect reasonably high expectations for learning among the assessment population.

Content standards represent the foundation on which curricula (i.e., instructional activities) are built. Although the term *grade-level* may presume a level of performance for students without disabilities, in the case of an AA-AAS, performance is judged against a separate set of achievement standards that include different definitions of what it means to be proficient within a content domain. Although teaching academic content (e.g., reading, math) is documented in research literature (Browder et al., 2007), little is known about how students with significant intellectual disabilities progress through that curriculum. In particular, we have not fully determined which skills and concepts are essential building blocks for future learning or which are immediately useful in real life. Chapters 6–9 in this book are specifically dedicated to the descriptions of approximating and gaining access to the general curriculum, as well as understanding the content standards and how these can be applied to students with significant cognitive disabilities.

Student Population

Federal guidelines recommend alternate assessments be used for students with "significant cognitive disabilities" or "significant cognitive impairments" (U.S. Department of Education, 2003). These population designations, however, are not well defined. In a review of participation criteria from state administration manuals, Musson, Thomas, Towles-Reeves, and Kearns (in press) found the majority of states use similar terminology, but they do not include measures of IQ or disability categories as the primary indicators of alternate assessment eligibility; rather, states often reference the intensity of instruction required by the student as the key determinant. Similarly, in a national study of alternate assessments, Cameto, Knokey, Nagle, Sanford, and Blackorby (2009) found that 92% of the states surveyed used terminology such as "severe cognitive disability" to describe the need for extensive modifications to instruction or curriculum, but these states did not include the student's disability category as a criterion for participation in the AA-AAS.

In order to find more detailed knowledge about the assessment population, the NAAC conducted a seven-state study of the learner characteristics of students participating in an AA-AAS. Kearns et al. (in press) found that in states where the rate of participation in an AA-AAS was significantly less than 2% of the total population, similar learner characteristics emerged. The student sample size across the seven states exceeded 12,000 students. Teacher observation data for each student included 11 descriptive indicators, in addition to traditional student demographic data (e.g., age, gender, ethnicity). Three important student characteristics, as well as teacher perception of the student's skill in reading and mathematics, emerged as the primary descriptive categories for students in the AA-AAS: 1) disability category, 2) expressive and receptive language development, and 3) reading and mathematics skills.

Disability Category

Findings revealed that all disability categories were represented in students participating in these states' AA-AAS programs, although the majority of the population came primarily from three categories: intellectual impairment/mental retardation (58%), multiple disabilities (13%), and autism (17%; Kearns et al., in press). It is important to note that the population did not represent any disability category *in its entirety*. As such, there were students with intellectual disabilities, multiple disabilities, and autism who did not participate in their state's AA-AAS.

Expressive and Receptive Language Development

The population of students participating in an AA-AAS is highly varied in expressive and receptive language. The majority of the population (70%) in the Kearns et al. (in press) study communicated symbolically using oral speech or symbol-based augmentative communication. An additional 15%–20% of the students were "emerging" in their level of symbolic language; these students used pictures, gestures, and signs to express intents and exhibited consistent receptive responses, but they needed cues to follow directions. Another 8%–12% communicated expressively at a presymbolic level and alerted to sensory information, whereas only 2% of the population had inconsistent receptive responses. This latter group of students also had more complex disabilities involving hearing, vision, motor, and health concerns. About 50% of the students identified as presymbolic and emerging symbolic learners also used augmentative and alternative communication systems. Finally, the percentage of presymbolic and emerging symbolic learners remained essentially the same from elementary to high school. This finding was troubling; as students participate in language-rich environments with appropriate communication supports, their level of symbolic language should increase. Indeed, symbolic language is an essential component of reading (Koppenhaver, Pierce, & Yoder, 1995).

Reading and Mathematics Skills

From a series of five descriptors, teachers in the Kearns et al. (in press) study selected the best description of the student's academic skills in both reading and mathematics. Consistent with the levels of symbolic language, approximately 70% of the population read basic sight words or read with basic understanding of text. In mathematics, most students counted with correspondence or used a calculator to solve basic math problems. Smaller percentages were found for both lower and higher skill levels in reading and math. Approximately 13% had no awareness of text or of number systems, and an additional 10%–15% exhibited only a basic awareness of text and numbers. On the higher skill level, approximately 2% read with critical understanding. Although this was not a longitudinal study, it is noteworthy that the percentages in the academic indicators did not change significantly across the grade span from elementary to high school. Some small changes in these percentages were observed at the high school level, however, these changes are more likely attributable to slight population shifts caused by the complexity of high school content and graduation policy than from actual instructional gains for students in the AA-AAS.

Assessment Population and Domain Content: Relationship to Validity

The assessment population in an AA-AAS is highly diverse, particularly in the areas of language or communication development and skill levels in academic content. Symbolic language in particular is essential for the development of skills in academic content. Access to academic content that is grade specific is best described as inconsistent for this population within and across grades, with relatively little apparent change across grade span. In addition, little is known about how students with significant cognitive disabilities progress in content across grades, what content is essential for development of future skills, and how to move beyond basic recall of facts and words to application of knowledge and skills. The application of knowledge and skills ensures that the skills learned will be useful as the student advances through school to successful transition to adulthood. How students achieve competence in academic curricular domains is an important criterion for validity that as yet is not fully met in the development of states' AA-AAS programs. This is because few children with significant cognitive disabilities have had continuous access to the general curriculum with the supports and services to maximize their opportunities for learning. The lack of understanding about how children with significant cognitive disabilities *should* progress has implications for assessment design, the extent to which testing inferences are useful, and the extent to which the results can be used successfully to improve instruction.

Implications of the Cognition Vertex for School Staff

Andrea and her principal Mrs. Jones will want to ensure that the appropriate students are participating in the alternate assessments according to the participation criteria. In addition, they will want to ensure that all of the students participating in the alternate assessment have communication systems that allow them to respond to the assessment items. They plan to work closely with their related services and assistive technology team to determine appropriate communication supports. (See Chapter 3 for a further description of the steps in this process.)

Next, Andrea and her team will want to review the content standards in their alternate assessment and align the curriculum, learning activities, and instruction with those content standards. Generally speaking, teachers who provide services to students with significant cognitive disabilities have student case loads that span multiple grades. Andrea and Mrs. Jones will utilize collaborative planning with general education teachers at each grade for specific content activities in reading, math, and science. To facilitate planning across grades, they decide to use a simple form to collect curriculum activity information for 2-week periods. Once completed, the content catalog allows Andrea to collect content activities and prepare adaptations and supports to maximize student participation. Figure 2.2 illustrates a content catalog for academic content.

Andrea's district uses a curriculum pacing guide that is aligned to the standards. This allows the assistive technology staff to develop and maintain a catalog of content supports in a variety of forms, including objects and pictures, as well as electronic resources. Finally, Andrea implements systematic instructional procedures utilizing data-driven instructional decisions (Wolery, Bailey, & Sugai, 1988). This information allows her to make instructional changes to maximize student performance.

Grade: 3	Teacher: Smith		Week of: October 15
Reading/writing	**Math**	**Science**	**Social studies**
Read *The Enormous Potato* (Davis, 1997) to identify the author's problem and the solution. Write a personal narrative about a personal problem.	Math rules: using number line Number + 1	Electricity investigation What makes the light come on?	Map skills

Figure 2.2.　Page from a content catalog.

Observation Vertex: Assessment Design and Administration

Based on the population and the theory of how students with significant cognitive disabilities develop academic domain competence, the observation vertex of the assessment triangle considers what content standards will be assessed, how the assessment will be administered to the student, and how the student's responses will be scored. The challenge for an AA-AAS is that unlike students in the general assessment who respond independently to what are typically multiple-choice or open-response items, students with significant cognitive disabilities must rely on the teacher's direct observation of the student engaging in the behavior. At this time, nearly all alternate achievement standards assessments are individually administered, generally by school-level personnel, and in most cases by the student's teacher (Gong & Marion, 2006). The teacher's level of involvement in an accountability environment represents an inherent validity problem that must be accounted for in the assessment design.

Assessment Design

An ongoing conversation in the area of alternate achievement standards assessments continues to be which assessment format (i.e., performance tasks, portfolios, checklists, or rating scales) is "best." In 2005, results of the National Center on Educational Outcomes State Survey (Thompson, Johnstone, Thurlow, & Altman, 2005) suggested that 25 states (50%) reported using a body of evidence or portfolio format; 7 states (14%) reported using a rating scale or checklist approach; 8 states (16%) reported their alternate assessments were under revision; an additional 7 states (14%) reported a format in the "Other" category; and 2 states (4%) identified that they were using an individualized education program (IEP) analysis, which is no longer approved under NCLB. Furthermore, of the 25 states that reported using a portfolio, 7 of those states described structured performance tasks as integral components of the portfolio. In addition, of the seven states reporting the use of a rating scale or checklist, three of those states described their system as "performance on a standardized set of events, tasks, or skills" (p. 11). In other words, states, although nominally indicating that they were using one assessment type (e.g., portfolio), often integrated components of another assessment type (e.g., performance tasks within a portfolio model). In a later study, Cameto et al. (2009) found the largest nominal category of assessment design reported by states was again the portfolio format, followed by performance tasks, and rating scales.

Since the 2005 NCEO survey, eight states volunteered to participate with a team of measurement, special education, and content experts in reviewing the technical documentation of alternate achievement standards assessments. Examining the technical documentation of these assessments allowed the team to examine not only the structural format but also the extent to which the assessment was being used as intended and the extent to which the purposes of the assessments were being achieved, as well as the positive and negative implications of the results. Although the data collected on purpose, use, and consequences were at best minimal for these relatively new assessments, this critical look confirmed the findings of the NCEO survey that the nominal or assessment format category is not very useful for understanding or describing alternate achievement standards assessments. Indeed, states found that the best way to describe an alternate assessment format was to describe the interaction between the student and teacher (Gong & Marion, 2006). For example, does the teacher develop the assessment task/item or does the teacher read a script? Does the student give an independent response, or can the correct response be prompted? What flexibility is given to assist the student to make an independent response? Who scores the student's response? Does the teacher rate the student's response or does a third party consider the evidence independent of the teacher? All of these questions are critical in understanding or interpreting the results of alternate assessments, and all of them are independent of the type or format of the alternate assessment.

It is also important to note here that the format or type of the assessment is also not necessarily an indicator of the quality of the assessment. All of the nominal categories of assessment used with students with significant cognitive disabilities (e.g., portfolio, performance task, rating scale, multiple choice), have relative strengths and weaknesses from a technical quality point of view. Technically sound assessments account for the weaknesses they present and clearly explicate the interpretations or inferences that can and cannot be made from the assessment results (AERA, APA, & NCME, 1999). As a result, many hybrid AA-AAS systems are beginning to emerge that include features from the three major formats. Although technical quality of an AA-AAS continues to improve, poorly designed alternate assessments are simply poor assessments, regardless of the name given to the assessment format.

Assessment Design Examples

The assessment item in Figure 2.3 is labeled as a performance task. In this design, the teacher reads a script and provides picture answer choices. The student must independently choose the correct picture choice. The teacher codes the student's answer choice on the answer sheet.

Although this assessment is labeled a performance task, the characteristics are more similar to an individually administered multiple-choice format with picture answer choices. These formats can sample a wider array of content standards than portfolios but typically sample fewer items than rating scales. Documenting procedural fidelity and reliability in the administration of the items is difficult to monitor for the purposes of large-scale accountability because such documentation requires direct observation of both teacher and student performance.

Similarly, rating scales and checklists may require that a body of evidence or portfolio be maintained for each student. Figure 2.4 provides an example of a rating scale item.

Teacher script and directions	Answer selection pictures
"We are going to explore some cultures to better understand our history. Here are shelters or homes that people lived in a long time ago or may still use." *Show each item to the student and describe (e.g., "This shelter is made from leaves, bark, branches and mud..."). Allow the student to explore the materials before moving on to the questions.* "Show me the shelter or home used by the Woodland Indians."	

Figure 2.3. Example of an alternate assessment item.

Rating Scale Scoring
- Standard: Students use appropriate strategies before, during, and after reading to construct meaning
- Sample item
  - Indicate what is known based on details.
  - Predict what might happen in text.
  - Determine if prediction is correct.
- Scoring
  - 0 = Does not demonstrate
  - 1 = Demonstrates with support
  - 2 = Correct and independent
- Evidence:

Figure 2.4. Rating scale sample item.

It asks the rater to indicate the best description of the student's performance on each item from an array of choices. Rating scales generally have larger numbers of items than the other format types, which allows for a broader sample of standards to be included in the design. Rating scales also are dependent on the rater's understanding of the items and the rater's accurate recall of the student's performance. Given the relatively recent exposure of students with significant cognitive disabilities and their teachers to the teaching of academic content (and hence, their unfamiliarity with this content), many rating scale systems require the maintenance of student work samples or cited evidence so that the results can periodically be verified.

Finally, portfolio assessments often require the teacher to establish the assessment task or item as individually determined for each student, based on prescribed content standards at each grade level. Teachers specify the behavior that is closest to the age/grade content standard for each student and the conditions under which the student will respond. The performance criterion for each item/task is often specified in the scoring rubric. These target behaviors are generally assessed within the context of ongoing instruction through data collection procedures. Portfolio assessments often include student work and/or instructional data for the target behaviors. In these cases, annotation of the work sample with dates and results may also be specified in the administration manual. The examples in Figure 2.5 are types of portfolio evidence.

Portfolio formats must account for a high degree of flexibility in the collection of the samples, the alignment of the student work with the content standards, and the relatively small number of standards that can be sampled effectively (Gong & Marion, 2006). These examples represent the primary types of an AA-AAS. Hybrid examples—which include multiple formats coordinated to account for the measurement weaknesses in each of the individual examples—continue to emerge. The introduction of formative assessment systems, in which assessments are administered multiple times throughout the year with results provided in real time, may provide better formative feedback to guide instruction than any of the formats administered on an annual accountability basis. Formative assessments coupled with assessments that can be administered annually, if well designed, could revolutionize an AA-AAS by controlling for the weaknesses in each individual format and accomplishing both instructional improvement and accountability purposes. It is for this reason that the chapters in this book on reading (Chapter 6), math (Chapter 7), science (Chapter 8), and social studies and the arts (Chapter 9) provide examples of formative, classroom assessments that can be used as important data sources for large-scale alternate assessments.

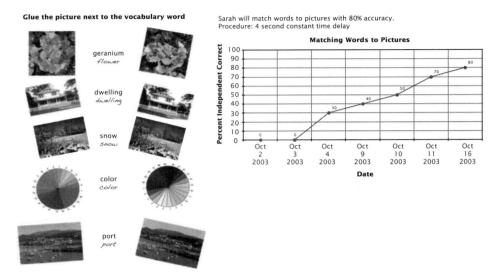

Figure 2.5. Portfolio work samples.

Administering an Alternate Assessment Based on Alternate Achievement Standards

There are several critical elements within the administration of an AA-AAS. These include the teacher's role, the importance of the state's administration manual and ongoing teacher training and support, the allowance for prompting in eliciting student performance, and providing accommodations and individualized supports to students.

The Teacher's Role

As we have discussed, most AA-AAS programs in use are generally described using nominal terminology or names (e.g., performance task, multiple choice/picture array, portfolio, rating scale or checklist). Each nominal category—to the extent that the assessment actually conforms to that nominal category—has strengths and weaknesses with respect for validity (Gong & Marion, 2006). However, all alternate assessments share a common problem or threat to validity when used to judge school performance in accountability systems; that threat is the heavy involvement of the teacher in administering and/or scoring student assessment results (Marion & Pellegrino, 2006). To control for this threat, states may require student work folders be maintained at the school level in addition to the assessment information, audit student work periodically, require another knowledgeable individual to administer the assessment, and/or use external reviewers to score the assessments.

Administration Manuals and Teacher Support

Because assessment formats vary, it is important to rely on the assessment administration manual provided by each state. These manuals are generally updated annually and found on state assessment web sites. In addition to providing an administration manual, many states also provide teacher training through regional face-to-face training sessions, train-the-trainer networks, or electronic training formats. Electronic training formats are growing in popularity because of the need for consistency in the training message, continuous availability of the training materials, and the ability to assess the user to ensure quality and minimize sources of error. These trainings include a range of topics, but generally the following topics are discussed: assessment population; participation criteria; IEP team role and responsibilities; observation/assessment format (e.g., how to present the assessment items, rate the students' performance and/or select student work as evidence of their performance); assessment timelines; and packaging and submitting student results, as would be the case for rating scales or performance tasks, or in the case of portfolios, submission of assessment materials for scoring, including how to label the materials and pack the submission box.

The observation of the student is the critical element to the validity of the assessment design whether observed directly, recalled, or inferred from evidence. As such, it is very important to read and follow the instructions in the administration manual. Administration errors increase the probability that a student's score could be invalidated. If the assessment administration manual calls for reading a script and presenting items in a prescribed order, it is critical to comply with a high degree of fidelity to the script. If the assessment includes a list of skills in which the teacher recalls the student's performance as correct and independent, correct but prompted, or incorrect, for example, it is important to respond to each item as indicated and not be tempted to skip to the easy items or even the difficult ones.

Prompts, Scaffolds, and Task Directions

The terms *prompts, scaffolds,* and even *task directions* are used differently in individual states' AA-AAS programs, and often the definitions for these terms for assessment purposes are different from their common uses for instructional purposes. A word about the term *prompting* is important here. In the special education instructional literature, the term *prompting* refers to "leading the student to the correct response" (Wolery et al., 1988, p. 254). Prompting is used often during instruction to reduce errors and increase the efficiency of instruction (Browder, 2001; Westling & Fox, 2004; Wolery et al., 1988). Indeed, in the special education literature, it is recommended that if a prompting strategy or hierarchy is being used during instruction, it is important to conduct noninstructional probes during the assessment condition in which the prompt is *not* delivered in order to determine the student's level of accuracy and independence (Wolery et al., 1988). Alternate assessment administration manuals vary greatly in this area, in that some states allow prompted responses, provided these prompts are identified as such. Some states do not allow prompted responses at all. In some cases, such as in performance tasks, the allowed prompt is prescribed within the script. It is important to follow the directions exactly as they are provided in the administration manual, so as not to compromise the validity of the assessment or the inferences that can be made about the student's performance. However, providing a prompt that leads the student to a correct response during assessment can be problematic in most assessment designs. As an example, assessment protocols in which a hierarchical prompting system is implemented result in repeated item presentation which in turn results in increased assessment time. The students most affected by the increased time are often the students who demonstrate the least reliable responses from the outset. The assessment design should account for this additional time requirement and the resulting implications for interpreting results.

Student Accommodations and Supports

Depending on the assessment format, the administration manual may also describe appropriate accommodations and supports for students. The use of accommodations or supports in this context allows a measure of flexibility that also minimizes bias in the assessment. These allowable accommodations provide students the opportunity to gain access to the item and make a response. Accommodations are most often used or considered in the context of states' regular assessments. In these cases, accommodations must be determined by the student's IEP team and used consistently during instruction as well as assessment (Christensen, Thurlow, & Wang, 2009). Accommodations used in an AA-AAS would follow similar procedures or be specified in the state's administration guide. AA-AAS manuals may also use the term *supports*, which are intended to achieve the same function as accommodations—that is, increasing the probability that more students will be able to provide an independent response. States vary in the use of and interpretation of supports within their respective AA-AAS programs. Some states include student supports in the scoring criteria, whereas in other states, the supports are built into the assessment design (i.e., picture arrays provided as part of a multiple-choice item). Because providing inappropriate supports may invalidate a student's score, it is essential to follow the administration guide exactly.

Scoring the Alternate Assessment Based on Alternate Achievement Standards

Scoring student assessments is another important component of the AA-AAS. Increasingly, states in which the AA-AAS is a portfolio are using independent, professionally trained scorers. These scorers are specifically trained using previously scored student assessments and a predetermined scoring rubric. The rubric assigns points (generally 1–4) for each variable that describes a quality performance. For example, the scoring rubric in Table 2.1 considers independence and accuracy, as well as the complexity or difficulty of the skill/item presented to the student. Rubrics are most often used in portfolio assessments in which the evidence represents multiple performance variables that are being measured (e.g., independence, accuracy, complexity, supports).

Rubric scores can be derived in a *compensatory* manner, in which each cell in the rubric holds independent value and a high score in one dimension, such as performance or supports, can offset a lower score in another dimension. Within a compensatory model, scores are thus essentially averaged. Scores may also be derived in a *conjunctive* manner, in which score requirements in certain dimensions may prevent offset scoring. For example, in order to reach proficiency in a conjunctive model, a student may have to score enough points to attain proficiency in *every* dimension. A student who scores sufficient points in the performance and supports dimensions to attain proficiency but not enough points to attain proficiency in the complexity dimension would fall short of overall proficiency in a state using a conjunctive model of scoring.

Table 2.1. Sample scoring rubric for a state portfolio alternate assessment

	1	2	3	4
Accuracy/ independence	Student's independent performance is at or below baseline levels and below 50% correct responses.	Student's independent performance minimally exceeds baseline at 50%–74% correct responses.	Student's independent performance exceeds baseline at 75%–89% correct responses.	Student's independent performance exceeds baseline at 90%–100% correct responses.
Complexity	Student demonstrates basic recall of information.	Student makes inferences or explains information.	Student demonstrates application and analysis of information.	Student evaluates and/or critiques information.

Preparing for Administration of the Assessment

———● *Andrea is preparing for the administration of the alternate assessment. She has read the administration manual and has prepared an administration checklist to assist her in planning. She has assembled the necessary materials and practiced reading the script and presenting the items. She has prepared the accommodations for some students, as the administration manual directs. Mrs. Jones has provided release time for Andrea to attend training opportunities provided by the local district. Andrea has thus taken all of the important steps to prepare herself and her students for the second part of the assessment triangle—the actual observation of student performance according to the specified dimensions of her state's alternate assessment.*

Interpretation Vertex: Interpretation or Inference from Assessment Results

The third vertex of the assessment triangle refers to the interpretation or inferences that can be made from the assessment results. Topics of discussion important to this vertex include setting achievement standards, reporting and using the data to improve results, ensuring the items align with the content standard, determining sources of error, analyzing item response results by population characteristics. In this section, we discuss the three most important topics for classroom teachers: 1) setting achievement standards, 2) reporting and interpreting the assessment results, and 3) using the data to improve results for students and schools.

Setting Achievement Standards

As described earlier in this chapter, achievement standards refer to the descriptions of achievement that are represented by the distribution of scores. Table 2.2 illustrates descriptions of achievement levels for Grade 5 reading.

Performance or achievement standards generally take the form of descriptive definitions with labels such as *basic, proficient,* or *advanced.* Achievement standards are described in the form of performance level descriptors developed *prior* to administering the assessment, but the range of scores associated with those definitions are determined following

Table 2.2. Performance descriptor example: Grade 5 reading

Below Basic	Basic	Proficient	Advanced
Student aware of text, follows directionality, makes letter distinctions, or tells a story from the pictures that is not linked to the text. May read or identify environmental print.	Student uses pictures to tell a story. Reads basic sight words, simple sentences, directions with pictures, bullets, and/or lists in print. Uses one to two strategies to decode words.	Student reads fluently with minimal errors and basic understanding from paragraphs/short passages from narrative/informational text. Follows written directions with minimal errors.	Student reads fluently with critical understanding from narrative or informational texts. Comprehends text from a variety of genres. Draws author inferences and makes connections between texts, and between texts and real-life situations.

the administration of assessment and are based on the range and distribution of scores compared with the descriptions of the achievement levels. Once the assessment has been scored and the range and distribution of scores has been determined, the descriptions of performance are then matched with a distribution of scores to determine the cut-off points for each performance level (i.e., "cut" scores) in a highly structured process called *standard setting*. It is recommended that a committee of knowledgeable stakeholders or a standard-setting team be convened to determine the numerical values associated with the definitions of basic, proficient, or advanced scores (Cizek, 2001; Perie, 2007). This committee considers a range of relevant evidence within a highly structured process to determine where within the score distribution the performance definitions align. Most states utilize a standard-setting team, although achievement standards may also be set without stakeholder involvement. As an example, if the range of possible scores on an assessment is 0–60, then proficiency is likely to fall within the top range of 45–55 of the possible score points. However, the standard-setting committee may consider the range of possible score points that match the performance descriptors, student work or examples that represent the score points, or the distribution of scores once the recommended cut scores are applied.

Requirements under NCLB for an AA-AAS call for achievement standards to represent the "highest achievement level appropriate" (U.S. Department of Education, 2005, p. 22), meaning that the achievement standards for students participating in the AA-AAS should be no less challenging for students with intellectual/cognitive disabilities than the standards set for all other students. Simply put, this means that if in the general assessment only about 25% of the students are reaching proficient and advanced levels, then approximately the same percentage of students who are assessed in the AA-AAS would meet similar levels of proficiency. Given the lack of well-defined academic learning progressions for students with significant cognitive disabilities, and the lack of consistent instruction in academic content especially for older students, high percentages of proficient and advanced scores could lead to the unintended consequence of complacency, thereby reinforcing low expectations in academic achievement. Conversely, consistently low scores can lead to teacher frustration, which also reinforces low expectations of students. The delicate balance of defining and maintaining reasonable definitions of achievement and the corresponding distribution of scores in order to avoid the consequences on either end of the continuum will continue to challenge the validity of the assessments and the accountability programs for students with disabilities. The key to this challenge lies in describing what students should know and do across the grade span and supporting the descriptions with evidence.

Reporting and Using the Data to Improve Results

The purpose for measuring student achievement is to use the data to illustrate improvements in instructional practices. We describe the issues in reporting and interpreting the results to improve instruction for students with significant cognitive disabilities.

The Individuals with Disabilities Education Act Amendments (IDEA) of 1997 (PL 105-17) required states to report the results of assessments for students with disabilities with the same frequency as they reported results for the general student population. In addition, NCLB requires states to meet specific timelines for reporting so that students who attend schools that have persistently low performances may choose a different school. To further complicate this challenge, children with significant cognitive disabilities often attend classes in districtwide programs or special schools. States are unique in how they report individual student scores and how those scores are included in the accountability system. Figure 2.6, for example, presents a sample report for an individual student's alternate assessment scores.

In this individual student report, the scores indicate that the student is performing at the basic level in all content areas. The student's raw score points are 20 for each of the tested subjects from a total possible raw score of 60 for each subject. The student's scores indicate a relative strength in performance accuracy and independence; however, the student's performance is at a low level of complexity, or basic recall. (See Chapter 10 for a further discussion of depth of knowledge or complexity.) Likewise, the student does not use supports that would increase his or her access to apply the skills in reading, math, and science in everyday situations. A score report for a group of students would look slightly different in that it would indicate the raw scores and performance levels for *each* student assessed at that particular school level.

Interpreting Results

In order to determine a specific student's assessment results, it is important to again review the performance level descriptors. To that end, the numerical results must be translated into the description of performance at that level. To use the example in the previous

Subject area	Performance level	Raw score	Scores by rubric dimension		
			Performance	Complexity	Supports
Reading	Basic	20/60	10	5	5
Mathematics	Basic	20/60	10	5	5
Science	Basic	20/60	10	5	5
Social studies	Basic	20/60			

Figure 2.6. State alternate assessment score report for an individual student.

section, the student's raw score was 20 out of 60 points, and performance is described as basic. The performance level of basic is, in turn, translated into the following description:

> Student uses pictures to tell a story. Reads basic site words, simple sentences, directions with pictures, bullets, and/or lists in print. Uses one to two strategies to decode words.

The performance description translates the numerical number into a description of what the student knows and can do based on the assessment results. Similarly, a student performance at a different numerical value would result in a different description of performance.

Although the score for one student has some useful information, the purpose of these assessments is to consider the scores for all of the students who were assessed. Some important questions to consider when reviewing scores at the local school level include

- How did our students perform on the AA-AAS?

- What was the distribution of scores across grades?

- What were the relative student performances in reading, math, and science?

- What appears to be working well?

- Where could we improve?

- Were our students able to respond to all of the items?

- Does every student have a system for communicating content?

- What else can we do to make the content more accessible to our students?

- How does student performance align with our curriculum and instruction?

- Did we have assessment administration errors?

- What training, technical assistance, or supports do we need to minimize administration errors and maximize student participation?

These questions focus on the intent and purpose for which assessments are used in accountability systems—which is the ultimate criterion for validity.

Revisiting Validity

It is important to understand that NCLB achievement assessments, including an AA-AAS, are administered for the purposes of school accountability. Furthermore, the purpose and use of an assessment is central to the validity of the instrument. Inferences, decisions, and actions must be considered within the constraints of the purpose and use of the instrument. As such, achievement assessments administered as a requirement of NCLB are intended to measure student achievement in reading, math, and science and to hold schools, districts, and states accountable for improving achievement results in those content areas. Within the overall intent of NCLB, all of this is done in an effort to 1) inform professional development at school, district, and state levels; 2) inform the alignment of assessment, curriculum, and instruction; 3) inform and improve instructional practices; and 4) report results for individual students. If a test is likely to be used inappropriately, then specific warnings against those purposes should be specified, as noted in Standard 1.3 in the *Standards for Educational and Psychological Testing* (AREA, APA, & NCME, 1999).

Finally, the appropriate interpretive materials must be included in the score report. Not all assessments used for large-scale achievement and accountability purposes are appropriate for *individual student decision making*. In fact, few are valid solely for the purpose of making high-stakes (e.g., placement, retention/promotion, graduation) decisions at the individual student level. Indeed, as IDEA requires, IEP teams *must* use multiple sources of data in making program decisions for an individual student.

BACK TO THE BEGINNING

Andrea met with her principal Mrs. Jones to consider the scores from the previous year. Together, they looked at the percentage of students scoring in each category (below basic, basic, proficient, and advanced). They found that the majority of students' scores fell in the below basic and basic categories. Upon review of the performance descriptors in those categories, they realized that there was not sufficient alignment between what the students were taught and the content standards on which they were assessed. They also noticed one or more documentation errors (teacher administration errors) that were coded by the scorers. Finally, at least one student was unable to respond to the assessment items because of the lack of consistent communication. Together Andrea and Mrs. Jones formulated the following action plan:

1. *Review the administration manual to correct documentation errors.*

2. *Use a matrix to align the curriculum standards at each grade with the classroom activities for each student. (See Figure 2.7 for an example of a standards/activity matrix. Also, see Chapter 4 for a further discussion of curriculum alignment strategies.)*

3. *Work with related services to identify appropriate strategies for supporting the development of a communication system for the student who failed to respond to assessment items. (See Chapter 3 for further information about completing this essential part of the action plan.)*

Next Andrea and Mrs. Jones met with parents to describe the assessment results. In that meeting, Andrea and Mrs. Jones reiterated the purpose and use of the accountability assessment. They recommended interpreting the results at the individual student level with caution, as the results were not intended to be used for individual student planning. However, they did work with the parents to identify strategies for building the students' communication skills as an integral first step to developing competence in academic content. They encouraged the parents to develop a story time or reading routine at home, as well as family game night to incorporate opportunities to practice essential literacy and numeracy practice within age-appropriate routines and leisure activities.

Finally, Andrea and the principal integrated their action plan into the school action plan, which included regular and ongoing collaboration with the general education faculty.

The promise of including all students in accountability systems is that teachers will get the supports they need to make the changes necessary to improve results for all students.

General class activities content standards	Sentence dictation	Piecing cut-up sentence	Writing sentence	Self-selected reading with a peer	Teacher read aloud	Computer reading program
Students will know that some words have multiple meanings and identify the correct meaning as the word is used.						
Students will identify the purpose of capitalization, punctuation, bold-face type, italics, or indentations to make meaning of the text.						
Students will describe characters, plot, setting, or problem/solution of a passage.						
Students will identify the correct sequence.						
Students will identify main ideas or details that support them.						

Figure 2.7.   Aligning content with activities: A planning matrix.

REFERENCES

American Educational Research Association, American Psychological Association, & National Council on Measurement in Education. (1999). *Standards for educational and psychological testing.* Washington, DC: American Educational Research Association.

Betebenner, D.W. (2009). *Growth, standards and accountability.* Dover, NH: The Center for Assessment. Retrieved July 30, 2009, from http://www.nciea.org/publications/growthand Standard_DB09.pdf

Browder, D. (2001). *Curriculum and assessment for students with moderate and severe disabilities.* New York: Guilford Press.

Browder, D.M., Flowers, C., & Wakeman, S.Y. (2008). Facilitating participation in assessments and the general curriculum: Level of symbolic communication classification for students with significant cognitive disabilities. *Assessment in Education: Principles, Policy, and Practice, 15*(2), 137–151.

Browder, D.M., Wakeman, S.Y., Flowers, C., Rickelman, R.J., Pugalee, D., & Karvonen, M. (2007). Creating access to the general curriculum with links to grade level content for students with significant cognitive disabilities: An explication of the concept. *Journal of Special Education, 41*(1), 2–16.

Cameto, R., Knokey, A., Nagle, K., Sanford, C., & Blackorby, J. (2009). *National alternate assessment study*. Retrieved October 9, 2009, from http://ies.ed.gov/ncser/pdf/20093014.pdf

Christensen, L.L., Thurlow, M.L., & Wang, T. (2009). *Improving accommodations outcomes: Monitoring instructional and assessment accommodations for students with disabilities*. Minneapolis: University of Minnesota, National Center on Educational Outcomes.

Cizek, G. (2001). *Setting performance standards: Concepts, methods, and perspectives*. Mahwah, NJ: Lawrence Erlbaum Associates.

Cortiella, C. (2006). *NCLB and IDEA: What parents of students with disabilities need to know and do*. Minneapolis: University of Minnesota, National Center on Educational Outcomes.

Davis, A. (1997). *The enormous potato*. Toronto: Kids Can Press, Limited.

Gage, S.T., & Falvey, M.A. (1995). Assessment strategies to develop appropriate curricular and educational programs. In M.A. Falvey (Ed.), *Inclusive and heterogeneous schooling: Assessment, curriculum, and instruction* (pp. 59–110). Baltimore: Paul H. Brookes Publishing Co.

Gong, B., & Marion, S. (2006). *Dealing with flexibility in assessments for students with significant cognitive disabilities*. Dover, NH: National Center for the Improvement of Educational Assessment. Retrieved October, 15, 2009, from http://www.naacpartners.org/products/whitePapers/18010.pdf

Hill, R., Gong, B., Marion, S., DePasquale, C., Dunn, J., & Simpson, M. (2005). *Using value tables to explicitly value student growth*. Dover, NH: The Center for Assessment. Retrieved October 15, 2009, from http://www.nciea.org/publications/MARCES_RH07.pdf

Individuals with Disabilities Education Act Amendments (IDEA) of 1997, PL 105–17, 20 U.S.C. §§ 1400 *et seq.*

Individuals with Disabilities Education Improvement Act (IDEA) of 2004, PL 108-446, 20 U.S.C. §§ 1400 *et seq.*

Kearns, J., Towles-Reeves, E., Kleinert, H., Kleinert, J., & Thomas, M. (in press). Alternate achievement standards assessments: Understanding the student population. *Journal of Special Education*.

Kleinert, H.L., & Kearns, J.F. (2001). *Alternate assessment: Measuring outcomes and supports for students with disabilities*. Baltimore: Paul H. Brookes Publishing Co.

Kleinert, H., Kearns, J., & Kennedy, S. (1997). Accountability for all students: Kentucky's alternate portfolio system for students with moderate and severe cognitive disabilities. *Journal of The Association for Persons with Severe Handicaps, 22*(2), 88–101.

Koppenhaver, D., Pierce, P.L., & Yoder, D.E. (1995). AAC, FC, and ABC's: Issues and relationships. *American Journal of Speech Language Pathology, 4*, 5–14.

Marion, S., & Pellegrino, J. (2006). A validity framework for evaluating the technical quality of alternate assessments. *Educational Measurement: Issues and Practices, 25*(4), 47–57.

Musson, J.E., Thomas, M.K., Towles-Reeves, E., & Kearns, J.F. (in press). An analysis of state alternate assessment participation guidelines. *Journal of Special Education*.

No Child Left Behind Act of 2001, PL 107–110, 115 Stat. 1425, 20 U.S.C. §§ 6301 *et seq.*

Pellegrino, J., Chudowsky, N., & Glaser, R. (2001). *Knowing what students know: The science and design of educational assessment*. Washington, DC: National Research Council, National Academies Press.

Perie, M. (2007). *Setting alternate achievement standards*. Lexington: University of Kentucky, National Alternate Assessment Center. Retrieved October 9, 2009, from http://www.naacpartners.org/products/whitePapers/18020.pdf

Quenemoen, R., Thompson, S., & Thurlow, M. (2003). *Measuring academic achievement of students with significant cognitive disabilities: Building understanding of alternate assessment scoring criteria* (Synthesis Report 50). Minneapolis: University of Minnesota, National Center on Educational Outcomes. Retrieved October 9, 2009, from http://education.umn.edu/NCEO/OnlinePubs/Synthesis50.html

Thompson, S.J., Johnstone, C.J., Thurlow, M.L., & Altman, J.R. (2005). *2005 State special education outcomes: Steps forward in a decade of change*. Minneapolis: University of Minnesota, National Center on Educational Outcomes.

Towles-Reeves, E., Kearns, J., Kleinert, H., & Kleinert, J. (2009). An analysis of the learning characteristics of students taking alternate assessments based on alternate achievement standards. *Journal of Special Education, 42*, 241–254.

U.S. Department of Education. (2003, December 9). Improving the academic achievement of the disadvantaged. *Federal Register, 66*(236), 68698–68708.

U.S. Department of Education. (2005). *Alternate achievement standards for students with the most significant cognitive disabilities: Non-regulatory guidance.* Washington, DC: Author, Office of Elementary and Secondary Education.

Westling, D., & Fox, L. (2004). *Teaching students with severe disabilities* (3rd ed.). Upper Saddle River, NJ: Merrill/Prentice Hall.

Wolery, M., Bailey, D., & Sugai, G. (1988). *Effective teaching: Principles and procedures of applied behavior analysis.* Boston: Allyn & Bacon.

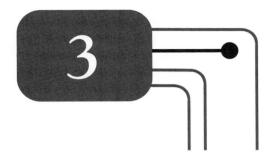

Students in
the AA-AAS and
the Importance of
Communicative Competence

Jane O'Regan Kleinert, Jacqui Farmer Kearns, and Harold L. Kleinert

Until recently (Towles-Reeves, Kearns, Kleinert, & Kleinert, 2009), we could only describe the population of students participating in alternate assessment based on alternate achievement standards (AA-AAS) as 1% of students with the "most significant cognitive disabilities" (U.S. Department of Education, 2005). Because the terminology *most significant cognitive disabilities* is not defined in the literature or in federal statutes and does not necessarily align with disability categories used to determine eligibility for services, describing this population in order to design an appropriate assessment has been somewhat problematic. Indeed, findings from a National Alternate Assessment Center study in seven states revealed that participating students represented all disability categories (Kearns, Towles-Reeves, Kleinert, Kleinert, & Thomas, in press). Although the percentages of students participating in the AA-AAS in some Individuals with Disabilities Education Act (IDEA) of 1990 (PL 101-476) categories were quite low across these states (Towles-Reeves et al., 2009), this assessment population appears to be mostly represented in three specific IDEA eligibility categories: mental retardation, multiple disabilities, and autism. It is also important to note that only a percentage of each of these three categories was represented in state AA-AAS programs; no IDEA category had 100% representation in alternate achievement standards assessments.

In addition to disability categories, Kearns et al. (in press) and Towles-Reeves et al. (2009) described the population of learners participating in state AA-AAS programs through the use of a Learner Characteristics Inventory (LCI). Characteristics in the inventory included level of expressive and receptive language; level of responsiveness or social engagement; sensory characteristics such as hearing and vision; motor characteristics; use of augmentative and alternative communication; speaking a language other than English at home; and broad, single measures for reading and mathematics. Towles-Reeves et al. found that expressive and receptive communication were significant predictors of participation in an AA-AAS. Interestingly, the largest percent of students (63%–74%) participating in an AA-AAS included students who communicated expressively using symbolic language (generally oral speech) to express a variety of intents and who responded to directions or requests independently. An additional 17%–26% represented emerging symbolic language users. These were students who may have used a few signs, pictures, or gestures to communicate a variety of intents and who may have required additional cues in order to follow requests or directions. Finally, 8%–11% of students were communicating at a presymbolic level, meaning that they used facial expressions and/or body movements to communicate basic intentions; what these students understood receptively was often uncertain (Towles-Reeves et al.).

Not surprisingly Towles-Reeves et al. (2009) found that low levels of expressive and receptive language were highly correlated with lower skill indicators on reading and math items. More troubling, however, was a finding noted by Kearns et al. (in press) of only minimal change in the percentage of students communicating at a presymbolic stage across the grade spans from elementary to high school. Although the Kearns et al. seven-state study was not a longitudinal study of the same students over time, one would expect to find significantly lower percentages of students in high school at a presymbolic level than students in the earlier grades. Indeed, the percentage of students communicating at a presymbolic level remained relatively the same across the grade spans in all but one of the seven states in the Kearns et al. study.

The LCI used in these studies relied on teacher reports to gather the data. Although the agreement among raters observing the same student was quite high, presymbolic learners may have been overrepresented because of a lack of understanding among teachers of what constitutes *intentional* communication (e.g., facial expressions, body movements, vocalizations) from students with significant cognitive disabilities who do not have oral speech (Kearns et al., in press).

Consistent expressive and receptive communication, beyond a simple greeting, is absolutely essential if educators hope to shape expressive intentions and receptive responses into a level of symbolic language necessary for social conversations about books, movies, television, sports, or any number of recreation leisure endeavors, as well as informational conversations about work or daily living activities, including issues of health and safety. Indeed, Rankin, Harwood, and Mirenda (1994) suggested that competent use of language for multiple purposes, audiences, and contexts facilitates the metalinguistic skills required for reading comprehension. Furthermore, language learners must use symbols repeatedly, interactively, and generatively during meaningful and ongoing activities in language-rich environments (Cafiero, 1998, 2005; Goossens, Crain, & Elder, 1992; Mirenda, 2003; Romski & Sevcik, 2005; Yoder, 2001).

Given the broad range of communication competence found within students taking the AA-AAS, as well as the percentage of students that teachers report have no formal means of communication, this chapter focuses on teaching academic content and building communication competence *simultaneously*. We discuss the role of related service professionals in facilitating access to the general curriculum and provide examples of how students at the presymbolic, emerging symbolic, and symbolic levels of expressive and receptive communication can be engaged in learning grade-level content. We also illustrate the importance of a truly transdisciplinary approach for integrating speech-language, physical, and occupational therapy services in supporting access to the general curriculum and enabling students to demonstrate what they know through their state's AA-AAS.

The role of communication, and facilitating students' communication development, is at the heart of true access to grade-level content and to student performance on alternate assessments linked to grade-level content standards. All academic content is by definition symbolic; if students are never taught to express or to understand progressively higher forms of communication, curricular access will simply not be meaningful or relevant to them, and their participation on any assessment linked to grade-level content will be problematic at best.

ALL BEHAVIOR COMMUNICATES

The first primary understanding in facilitating the development of communicative competence is that all behavior communicates (McDonald, 1982), and educators can facilitate communication in individuals with complex communication needs regardless of age or disability (Beck, Stoner, & Dennis, 2009; Rowland & Schweigert, 1990). From birth, all individuals make assumptions regarding the communicative intent of behavior. For example, initially adults interpret an infant's early output as meaningful and respond in kind. Individuals *do not* have to use true language, or real words (symbolic communication), to communicate. Young children evidence several easily recognizable forms of communication development on their way to use of true language or symbolic communication.

The idea that all behavior communicates is the single most important lesson in this chapter if we are to enable children and youth with significant cognitive disabilities to move through the various levels toward symbolic language use, promote overall language development, mitigate the potential for abuse and neglect, and ensure positive education outcomes.

IDENTIFYING COMMUNICATIVE COMPETENCE: LEVELS OF COMMUNICATION DEVELOPMENT

There are essentially three levels of communication development: presymbolic communication (perlocution stage), emerging symbolic communication (illocutionary stage), and symbolic communication (locutionary stage; Bates, 1979; Bates, Thal, Whitesell, Fenson, & Oakes, 1989). We begin by examining the stages of early communication development. We describe this early development not because students with the most severe disabilities are like very young children (they are not and should never be treated as such!). Rather, it is essential to understand how children typically move toward more sophisticated forms of communication (and the specific sequence of communicative levels through which they move) if we hope to facilitate those more complex forms of communication for our students with significant cognitive disabilities who currently are at a presymbolic level.

Presymbolic Communication (Perlocution Stage)

When infants cry, parents interpret those cries to communicate a need (e.g., feeding, changing). When an infant smiles or laughs, parents interpret or give meaning to those behaviors and in the process of interpreting and *repeatedly responding to the infant's output as meaningful* model communication and reinforce the infant's earliest attempts at communication. Parents (and others) are essentially teaching the infant that if the infant gives those signals, it means that he or she wants or needs something, and the parents will respond—*that is communication.* Gradually, infants learn to expect that their caregivers will respond to their output. By using exaggerated speech or gestures when responding to an infant (e.g., picking up the infant and saying, "Oh, you want to get up! Okay, we can get up.") the infant learns that there are more standardized ways to communicate needs and wants. The infant then begins to imitate the more recognizable output *and* attach meaning to that output. For example, the infant now cries ("I'm hungry!"), reaches ("Pick me up!"), or smiles and vocalizes ("I like that; do it again") to express *specific intents.* Parents' recognition of the infant's output and their interpretation and consistent response to the infant's output *as if it is meaningful* teaches the infant to be an intentional communicator long before he or she uses symbolic (true representational/abstract words or symbols) speech/language.

For older children with significant disabilities who may not be using oral speech or whose oral speech is inefficient, others often fail to interpret their body movements (which might seem to be erratic), their cries, changes in muscle tone or position, or facial expressions as communicative. Therefore, communication partners fail to respond in a manner that facilitates the development of communicative competence. For example, Felicia, an 8-year-old with severe disabilities with whom we worked, was identified as a presymbolic communicator by her teachers and other professionals; that is, she did not use words or signs and did not even seem to be using any clear gestures. During an observation, when Felicia was facing away from several of the individuals in the room and could not see them, she increased loud vocalizations, turned her head, and increased spasticity in her arms. When we turned her around to face the people in the room, she stopped these behaviors and began to display a new set of behaviors (e.g., smiling, head turning, eye gazing, relaxed arms). Clearly, Felicia's first set of behaviors was an *expression of the intent* of protesting her position facing away from the other people in the room. When we interpreted her output as meaningful, and responded to it in kind, Felicia was able to successfully communicate her intent (e.g., "Hey, I want to see these folks and interact with them. I don't like sitting alone!"). If we had not interpreted and responded to Felicia's output, she may have become so upset that she could not participate in the activities that were offered to her. Indeed, she might have been labeled "uncooperative" or "noninteractive." Such a result would have been the opposite of her *real intention,* which was to *interact* with all the people in the room.

Emerging Symbolic Communication (Illocutionary Stage)

Students communicating at an emerging level of symbolic communication use more clear behavioral output such as gestures and use repeated, specific activities or vocalizations, but not words. Children at this stage may have more intact motor skills than the little girl described in the previous section, but their output may still be ignored or misinterpreted. These children might even exhibit behaviors that are more difficult to control, or less socially acceptable, but are nonetheless still communicative. For example, when Daniel, another child with disabilities with whom we worked, would get frustrated, he would bite or hit the individual closest to him. Using an analysis of behavior (Mirenda, 1999), we determined that Daniel used these behaviors to communicate boredom or frustration. Of course, everyone communicates frustration and boredom; however, we needed to teach Daniel appropriate ways to communicate his frustration and boredom. When Daniel began to show signs of frustration, the teacher, in a proactive strategy, would say, "Oh, you are getting upset; you need to tell me that," and then she helped Daniel to hit his single switch communication device with the message, I'M UPSET; HELP ME PLEASE. This provided Daniel with an acceptable way of expressing his frustration and reinforced his expressive communication development.

Symbolic Communication (Locutionary Stage)

The highest level of communication development is the use of true (symbolic) language. True language is the use of symbolic or representational communication involving a set of symbols and rules for the use of those symbols that are accepted by a given population of people. These symbols can take many forms including spoken words, printed words, manual signs, or braille, for example. Most of the students in state AA-AAS programs appear to communicate at the symbolic level; as Towles-Reeves et al. (2009) reported, 63%–74% of students participating in the AA-AAS used symbolic language. Of course, there is great variation in the complexity of symbolic language and its users. An 18-month-old child may use symbolic language in a very rudimentary form, whereas a college student would use very complex symbolic language to write a research paper.

The goal of communication intervention is to move students as close and as quickly as possible to the use of symbolic language and, having achieved that, to increasingly complex forms of language.

IDENTIFYING COMMUNICATIVE COMPETENCE: STUDENTS WITH SIGNIFICANT COGNITIVE DISABILITIES

To become more effective at teaching students with significant cognitive disabilities to communicate at higher and more recognizable levels, educators and other communication partners must learn to recognize *when students are communicating and how they communicate*. To do this, it is essential to have a common set of terms to describe and identify various forms of communication. It is very important to note that communication is not only about expressing intent (expressive communication). Communication has two parts that are equally important: *expressive communication* (output) and *receptive communication* (understanding others). Sometimes, students are referred to as "noncommunicative," simply because they do not speak and they have not been given a means of augmentative or alternative communication to express themselves. These students are often described as having complex communication needs. Although these students may not be able to speak, *they may often understand language* and are learning; they simply are not able to express what they understand. Our definition of *communication* then, must take into account both expressive and receptive communication.

It is also important to differentiate between the terms *language* and *communication*. These terms are *not* interchangeable. Communication encompasses all types of interactions among people, regardless of the level of complexity of those interactions. As we have noted previously, language specifically refers to a set of abstract symbols governed by a set of rules that are used by a given community or culture to communicate. Language refers to various means of communication (e.g., speech, signs) that are clearly symbolic or abstract and that follow certain rules in order to be used correctly; however, one does not have to use formal or symbolic language to communicate. In fact, many students with significant disabilities do not use formal language but definitely do communicate. Too often, we hear descriptions of a student who does not use formal language or speech as one who does not communicate. It is essential not to make this mistake. *All students communicate in some way.*

Defining the Term *Communication*

When we ask teachers and speech-language pathologists (SLPs) to define communication, we often get responses such as

"Sending and receiving messages"

"Using some way to tell others what I want, need, like, don't like, and so forth"

"Using words, gestures, and so forth to get people to do what I want them to do"

Of course, all of these definitions are partly correct. Each one describes one or more of the elements that contribute to successful communication. However, we need to establish a simple definition of communication that includes *all* of its important elements and can easily be applied to *all* individuals, including those with significant disabilities who have complex communication needs. For clarity and simplicity, we express the definition that follows as a simple equation, which includes all of the elements needed to successfully transmit thoughts and intents to others and to understand the thoughts and intents of others:

Communication = an intent or function + a form or mode + listener comprehension

The elements included in this definition have been offered in one way or another by numerous researchers and authorities in communication over a period of many years (Light & Binger, 1998; McDonald, 1982; McLean & Snyder-McLean, 1978; Mirenda, 1999; Paul, 2001; Rowland, 2005; Stremel-Campbell, 1985).

Intent/Function

Simply put, successful communication occurs when an individual has an *intent* or a thought, idea, need, and so forth that he or she wishes to express. This is the *function* of communication, or the reason for communicating in the first place. One might wish to convey many intents. Intents include such functions as greeting, asking, refusing, demanding, telling a story, getting attention, and so forth. Some people think of the *intent* as the *topic* or *content* of the communication.

Form/Mode

Next, individuals encode the intent or function of their communication into a *form* or *mode* to express what they want to convey. Forms or modes can be almost any observable output, such as gestures, facial expressions, movements, muscle tone changes, words, signs, print, braille, and so forth. Some of these initial forms are more difficult to understand and, as we have noted, may be referred to as *presymbolic* communication, whereby the individual uses some nonstandard and often nonregularized means to communicate, such as a facial expression, change in muscle tone, or cry to convey a message. The individual at the presymbolic communication level does not yet have the ability to express him- or herself by use of symbols or representations that are abstract, such as words or signs.

Forms for individuals at the emerging symbolic communication level include more regularized, recognizable output, such as clear gestures, head nods or shakes, looking or pointing to a specific item, or beginning to use a few real objects or very simple pictures to express an intent. Although an individual at this level is not considered a symbolic communicator because he or she is not using formal language, individuals at the emerging symbolic level are much more easily understood than individuals at the presymbolic level because they use more regularized ways to express intents.

The highest level of communication is then the use of formal language or true *symbolic* communication (e.g., speech, signs, braille).

Listener Comprehension

Finally, communicators hope their listeners understand or comprehend what they are trying to convey. If all of these steps fall into place, there is successful communication. Unfortunately, sometimes a listener does not understand the mode or form an individual has chosen to express his or her intent, or the listener misinterprets what the individual is trying to convey (i.e., the intent). When this occurs, there can be a breakdown in communication, or worse yet, the listener may not even realize that the individual is trying to communicate something. Such communication problems happen frequently with students with significant disabilities and complex communication needs.

Students who are not using a symbolic form of communication are often mislabeled as "presymbolic" without even considering that they may *understand receptively* much more than they are able to express. For example, unfortunately, some individuals understand symbolic language (receptively) but have not yet been given the appropriate means (e.g., an augmentative and alternative communication [AAC] device) to express their symbolic knowledge. If an individual understands true or symbolic language, then *that student is at a symbolic level and is able to learn symbolic material at school.* Of course, some students may well be at a presymbolic level *both* receptively and expressively; however, it is of utmost importance to determine if a student is able to understand symbolic language but not able to express that understanding because he or she lacks a viable communication system.

It is important for educators and others who work with students with complex communication needs to be aware of all the elements that comprise communication—both to accurately describe a student's receptive and expressive communication abilities and to facilitate development of higher levels of communication usage. It is our job as educators and SLPs to correctly determine how students are communicating, interpret their output as communicative, respond to them consistently, and facilitate their use of higher levels of communication.

Identifying Communication Competence

The following steps are intended as suggestions for determining the level at which students with significant cognitive disabilities and complex communication needs communicate:

1. Observe the student and record the types of behavior that might be communicative acts, both *expressive* output and *receptive* understanding. For a student who is difficult to interpret, teachers, families, paraeducators, and/or SLPs can list the various behaviors

that the student usually displays (e.g., crying, vocalizations, changes in muscle tone, biting, hitting, looking, reaching, clapping).

2. Observe the antecedents and responses to the student's behavior. For example, when the student reaches or screams, is there an attractive object or a favorite person nearby (antecedent) that elicits this output? Is the student perhaps requesting attention or the attractive object? Do others respond or ignore the student when he or she reaches or screams toward the person or object (response)? As a second example, consider what is happening (antecedent) when the student bites his or her hand. *Nothing* is really happening, it might appear. Could that mean that the student is bored or tired and no one is paying attention to him or her, or that the student has no part in an activity in which the other students are engaged (response)? These types of questions help to identify the intent/function and form/mode of the student's communicative output. If communication partners acknowledge and interpret this output as meaningful and respond appropriately, the student likely will increase and modify his or her communicative behavior. If the student's output is ignored, he or she may well increase undesirable output (biting) or stop trying to communicate altogether and withdraw. Providing students with a usable communication system often markedly reduces undesirable behaviors (Franco et al., 2009).

Completing a communication log, such as the log presented in Figure 3.1, provides an organized way to observe student behavior and evaluate the level of the student's communicative output. This log can be used to determine when and how the student is communicating with others. Figure 3.1 provides an example of a completed Student Communication Observation Recording Log for three students: Sherry, Donnetta, and Jamal. (A blank log is included in the appendix at the end of the book.) The first two student examples, Sherry and Donnetta, are typical of a number of students with severe disabilities and will thus be used for most of the examples in this chapter.

A word of caution, however, is in order here. Students who have *severe expressive communication* disorders are often assumed to have severe cognitive disabilities. However, this *may* indicate that educators have not assessed the student's *receptive communication abilities* and may have grossly underestimated the student's overall abilities. The authors have often met children in self-contained classes who displayed severe motor disabilities that impeded expressive communication but who nevertheless had age-appropriate or only mildly impaired receptive language abilities. When these students were provided appropriate, often complex, electronic AAC systems, they were able to complete age-appropriate academic curricula. Look closely at student 3, Jamal, in Figure 3.1, for an excellent example of such a student.

Another caution is in order: Be sure that each student for whom you are responsible has had a complete assessment of his or her receptive communication/language skills. *Adapted materials* may be needed to complete such an assessment so that the student can display his or her true abilities. In addition to the SLP, occupational therapy, physical therapy, and vision or hearing specialists may be needed to complete an accurate assessment of the student's abilities. If the student has strong receptive skills but does not have an adequate AAC system, *such a system must be developed and put in place immediately so that the student can gain access to age-appropriate academic curriculum.*

3. Ask the family to complete the same type of observation activities at home, or ask them to describe to you how the student communicates at home and in other

Student Communication Observation Recording Log

Date _02/02/2009_

Student's output and/or behaviors that may signal receptive or expressive communication (Mode/Form)	What's happening around or with the student? (Antecedent)	What could the student have meant to communicate? (Intent/Function)	Did the student receive any type of a response from others? (Consequence/Response)
Student 1:			
Sherry is sitting in her wheelchair and begins to bang on her tray.	Other students are working with the teacher on a math lesson.	"Hey, I'm bored. I want some attention and to be involved in some way."	Teacher glances at Sherry to be sure she is OK, but no other response is given. Sherry eventually goes to sleep in her chair.
Student 2:			
Donnetta is working on her science project with typically developing peers. She wants	The students are building a DNA model in science class. While Donnetta does	"Excuse me, may I have the glue please. I can't reach it. I know that I	The student was nice to Donnetta and smiled when she tapped, but the student did

Figure 3.1. Student Communication Observation Recording Log. (*Key:* AAC, augmentative and alternative communication.)

(continued)

Figure 3.1. *(continued)*

Student Communication
Observation Recording Log

Date 02/02/2009 _____

Student's output and/or behaviors that may signal receptive or expressive communication (Mode/Form)	What's happening around or with the student? (Antecedent)	What could the student have meant to communicate? (Intent/Function)	Did the student receive any type of a response from others? (Consequence/Response)
Student 2: (continued)			
the glue. She reaches, says /m/ as an attempt to say "mine," taps one of her peers and points to her part of the project. Finally she gives up and watches the other two students work.	not understand exactly what the project is about, she does know that she is to glue parts on the project as directed and imitate the other students in doing so. All the students are gluing parts on the model. Each student was a glue stick, but someone borrowed Donnetta's and accidentally put it down out of her reach. The student whom Donnetta taps smiles and says "hi," but does not realize that Donnetta is asking for the glue.	am supposed to glue this part on, but I don't have any glue because someone borrowed mine and put it out of my reach."	not see that Donnetta had been pointing to the glue or that another student borrowed Donnetta's glue. Because Donnetta does not have an AAC device that uses voice output, and she does not have clear speech or sign, she is not successful in her request for the glue.

Student 3:

Jamal is at lunch and refuses to eat a certain food. He closes his mouth and looks away. He gives a thumbs-down sign to indicate he does not want to eat the food offered. He shakes his head "no." He becomes frustrated when the paraeducator tells him repeatedly to "try this."	Jamal is being offered a food that he knows is too hard for him to chew. The paraeducator is insisting that he take a bite and at least try the food.	Jamal has good receptive skills and knows what he can and cannot eat well. He understands what the paraeducator wants him to do, but he knows the food is not one that he can easily eat. He does not have an AAC device, however, so he is having difficulty relaying this information.	School personnel are underestimating Jamal and do not realize that he has good receptive skills and can make sound judgments about what is and is not safe for him to eat. This is extremely frustrating for this student who has strong receptive language but very limited expressive communication skills at this time.
Jamal laughs and smiles, waves his arm in a "high-five" gesture, nods his head in agreement, and vocalizes. He clearly understands what his peers are discussing.	Two male peer tutors are talking about their favorite college football team that played the day before and won.	"Hey, I saw that game. UK is my favorite team of all!"	While the peer tutors smile at Jamal, they do not include him in their conversation. After all, he is in the classroom for students with severe disabilities, so he surely does not understand football, does he? In reality, Jamal has good receptive

(continued)

51

Figure 3.1. *(continued)*

Student Communication Observation Recording Log

Date _02/02/2009_

Student's output and/or behaviors that may signal receptive or expressive communication (Mode/Form)	What's happening around or with the student? (Antecedent)	What could the student have meant to communicate? (Intent/Function)	Did the student receive any type of a response from others? (Consequence/Response)
			language skills (he is clearly at a symbolic level receptively) and he understands and enjoys conversations about his favorite team. Jamal's communicative competence has been underestimated as a result of his severe motor disabilities. He should be in classes and settings that match his receptive and cognitive abilities AND have a complex, symbolic communication system that is designed to meet his motor problems.

environments outside of school. This increases the richness of information about the student's communication ability and style, as frequently, families have a much greater awareness of the student's true abilities. Here, again, there may be indications that the student is at a symbolic level of receptive communication, even if he or she is not using symbolic expressive communication (think of Jamal).

4. Develop a list of the types of intents the student expresses and the mode or form he or she uses to express these intents, and teach ALL team members to observe and respond appropriately to the student's communicative output. Once you have had an opportunity to carefully observe and respond to a student's communications, make an inventory of the various communication skills and levels. The appendix at the end of the book provides a sample Student Communication Competency Inventory worksheet to use to develop such an inventory. You can transfer and summarize what you have learned about each student from the Student Communication Observation Recording Log to the Student Communication Competency Inventory in order to 1) begin to determine each student's communicative intents and how these intents are expressed and 2) begin to decide how to respond to that student in order to increase the frequency and quality of his or her communications.

The inventory should be shared with all individuals who come in contact with the student. Include the information regarding the student's communication behaviors at home as well. Students may be more interactive at home because the family often is better able to understand the student's communicative output. It is important to know as much about the student's skills as possible in order to elicit the same level of ability at school as is used at home.

Figure 3.2 provides a completed inventory for Sherry as an example of how this process is completed. Sherry is 19 years old; has multiple disabilities, including vision impairment/cortical blindness; uses a wheelchair; is nonverbal; and has significant cognitive disability. Note that the team has decided to implement a few preliminary suggestions regarding responding to Sherry's communicative output, though there are many questions left to be answered. The main question is to determine a more clearly understood system for Sherry to express herself.

FACILITATING COMMUNICATION COMPETENCE: A FOUR-STEP PROCESS

Communication training for students with significant disabilities and complex communication needs requires a team approach. The teacher works with the SLP, the specialist trained in communication development and AAC, to determine the student's level of receptive and expressive communication, describe the types of intents and forms the student currently uses, and determine the intervention strategies that will move the student toward symbolic communication and language use. In addition, if the student has motor, muscle tone, or sensory impairments, the team will include the physical and/or occupational therapist. If the student has hearing or vision disorders, specialists in those areas will also be needed. The following steps will help guide a team approach to facilitating communication competence.

Student Communication Competency Inventory

Student: Sherry   **Age:** 19   **School:** Midtown High School

Content/ Intent/Function	Mode/ Form of output	Suggested responses to the student
(List the intents the student exhibits below.)	(List the mode or form the student uses to express his or her intents listed in the previous column.)	(Record the manner in which everyone should respond to the student and indicate which **AAC** should be used, if appropriate. Also list any **adaptive equipment needed** for the student to participate in ongoing activities.)
Asking for attention/ calling	Sherry bangs on table when she is trying to gain attention or to call	Acknowledge her; go talk to her; engage her in ongoing activities; ensure she is not uncomfortable; engage a peer. Provide a single switch and teach Sherry to use this to call attention to herself.
Refusing	Sherry turns head away when she does not want to participate, is upset, or does not like a food, etc.	Acknowledge that she does not like the food, activity, and so forth. Consider an alternative to the ongoing activity; ensure she is not uncomfortable. Provide AAC to express refusal.

Figure 3.2. Student Communication Competency Inventory for Sherry. (*Key:* AAC, augmentative and alternative communication.)

Figure 3.2. *(continued)*

Content/ Intent/Function	Mode/ Form of output	Suggested responses to the student
Boredom	When Sherry is bored, she bites self or goes to sleep.	Ensure she is included in all classroom activities; ensure she has available adapted items of interest to her; ensure she is not uncomfortable; BE SURE HER DAY INCLUDES MANY OPPORTUNITIES TO COMMUNICATE WITH AND RESPOND TO OTHERS. Provide adaptive equipment so that Sherry can participate in on-going activity or for an alternate activity.
Wants more of an activity or food (requests)	When Sherry likes or wants to continue an activity or wants more of something, she smiles and vocalizes.	Respond to her request appropriately. Acknowledge her communication. Provide a single switch for requesting.

Step 1: Review the Student's Current Inventory of Communicative Intents and the Modes or Forms the Student Uses to Express These Intents

While reviewing this information, think about the following questions:

1. Is the student communicating expressively at a presymbolic, emerging symbolic, or symbolic level? This question can be answered using the Student Communication Inventory described in the previous section.

    Once the student's communication level is determined, it is important to decide how to respond to his or her communicative output and how to make that output more understandable. This information can then be used to develop an action plan designed to increase the frequency and quality of the student's communicative output. Specifically, Questions 2–6 that follow need to be addressed.

2. Can others readily understand the student's communications, and what barriers are making the student difficult to understand?

3. Does the student initiate interactions with others?

4. Does the student respond to others?

5. Does the student have sufficient opportunities to communicate?

6. Does the student require an AAC system or assistive technology to help him or her communicate more clearly?

Step 2: Observe the Student and Talk with the Full Classroom Team and the Family in Order to Answer Questions 2–6 Listed in the Previous Section

If the student is difficult to understand or it is difficult to *interpret* his or her communication output, determine why this is happening. Consider the student's strengths and challenges within the key physical and cognitive abilities that support communication output. These areas include hearing, vision, motor skills (including, e.g., muscle tone and movement patterns), ability to vocalize, comprehension, cognitive levels, and so forth. Difficulties in these areas may be impeding the student's ability to clearly express him- or herself either verbally or nonverbally. Note whether the student initiates and responds to others and the best way for him or her to do so. Investigate how often the student *actually has an opportunity to communicate and with whom*. Figure 3.3 provides an example of a simple way to inventory a student's skills in the noted areas and to analyze how these problems might interfere with the student's ability to clearly express him- or herself. (A blank form is included in the appendix at the end of the book.)

Step 3: Work with the Entire Team to Review All of the Information Already Gathered to Determine the Student's Current Communication Skills and to Determine How to Support Increased Communication

During this step, complete the following:

1. Summarize the student's current communication skills.

2. Determine the barriers to producing understandable output or more complex output.

3. Determine the student's strongest abilities that will support increased communication.

4. Determine what needs to be done to increase the student's opportunities to communicate more often.

5. Determine, along with the classroom team and especially the SLP, the type and content of an AAC system that will assist the student toward development of more symbolic communication usage.

How does one complete this daunting task? Do so simply by working together as a team to review the information gathered on the Student Communication Observation Recording Log (Figure 3.1), the Student Communication Competency Inventory (Figure 3.2), and the Potential Barriers and Supports to Clear Communication inventory (Figure 3.3).

Potential Barriers and Supports to Clear Communication

Student: *Sherry* **Age:** *19* **School:** *Midtown High School*

Sensory/ Receptive systems (Describe each type)	Strengths (Facilitating abilities)	Weaknesses (Inhibitory/ Distracting)	How is communication affected?
Auditory	Sherry alerts to sound and voice.		Sherry responds to others and will be able to hear voice output from an AAC device.
Vision	Sherry seems to track people in the environment sometimes.	Sherry has cortical blindness.	This will limit the type of AAC used.
Touch/Tactile	Sherry enjoys touch and searches for items if they are close to her.		Sherry will be able to feel a switch attached to an AAC device.
Cognition/ Receptive abilities	Sherry responds to sounds and voices of her favorite people and some peers, she loves country music, and she smiles when she smells her favorite foods.	It is difficult to know what Sherry understands, as her severe motor and vision problems impede her ability to make clear responses.	
Motor characteristics		Sherry cannot sit independently, has difficulty	Motor difficulties will limit the type, position, and

Figure 3.3. Potential Barriers and Supports to Clear Communication inventory for Sherry. (*Key*: AAC, augmentative and alternative communication.)

(continued)

Figure 3.3. *(continued)*

Potential Barriers and Supports to Clear Communication

Sensory/ Receptive systems (Describe each type)	Strengths (Facilitating abilities)	Weaknesses (Inhibitory/ Distracting)	How is communication affected?
		with head control, and has limited use of her arms/hands.	access to an AAC device.
Muscle tone		Sherry's muscle tone is increased and limits movements.	Motor impairments have limited Sherry's ability to vocalize.
Abnormal movement patterns and reflexes		Physical therapist reports that Sherry has reflexes that inhibit her ability to reach and move.	Physical therapy consultation will be vital to developing an AAC system for Sherry.
Environmental opportunities to communicate	Sherry responds with a smile when others talk to her, and she bangs on her tray when she wants attention, but this is often ignored.	Currently, Sherry stays in her self-contained class for the full day. She has limited opportunities to interact with students from other classes. She has limited opportunities for choice due to a set schedule in class.	Sherry needs to have more choices in her day, more interactions with peers from other classes, and an AAC system to help her communicate with and initiate to others.

Sherry: A Presymbolic Learner

Sherry is 19 years old and attends school in a self-contained classroom for students with the most significant disabilities. Using the information regarding Sherry's current communication characteristics from her Student Communication Competency Inventory (Figure 3.2) and the information from her completed Potential Barriers and Supports to Clear Communication inventory (Figure 3.3), we can determine Sherry's current communication status and then develop strategies to facilitate her movement toward symbolic communication. As we noted previously, here are each of the questions that need to be considered:

1. **Is the student communicating expressively at a presymbolic, emerging symbolic, or symbolic level?** *Sherry's Student Communication Competency Inventory indicates that she uses primarily modes such as banging, smiles, nonregularized vocalizations and cries, turning her head away, and sometimes biting herself to express a variety of intents such as requests for attention, enjoyment, refusal, and boredom. In addition, although she alerts to others, she has not been observed to meaningfully respond to directions. It would appear at this point that she is functioning at a presymbolic level of communication, both receptively and expressively.*

2. **Can others readily understand the student's communications, and what barriers are making the student difficult to understand?** *Sherry's Student Communication Competency Inventory indicates that people in her environment are not responding to her or interpreting her output as communicative. Sherry's completed Potential Barriers and Supports to Clear Communication form provides information as to why this may be happening: Her multiple physical impairments (motor difficulties, lack of vocal output, cortical blindness) are barriers to her ability to produce clearly understandable verbal or nonverbal output. Listeners are not viewing her output as communicative.*

3. **Does the student initiate interactions with others?** *Both inventories indicate that Sherry is trying to initiate exchanges but listeners are not viewing her output as communicative.*

4. **Does the student respond to others?** *Both inventories also indicate that Sherry is trying to respond to others as best as she can. Unfortunately, the people in her school environment are not recognizing her attempts. Her Student Communication Competency Inventory indicates that when she is ignored, she stops trying to communicate and either goes to sleep or begins to bite herself.*

5. **Does the student have sufficient opportunities to communicate?** *Sherry's Potential Barriers and Supports to Clear Communication form describes an environment with limited opportunities for Sherry to communicate. Her day is so scheduled that few choices of activities are offered, she has little opportunity to interact with her typically developing peers, and her attempts to gain attention are often ignored.*

6. **Does the student require an AAC system or assistive technology to help him or her communicate more clearly?** *It is very clear that Sherry does indeed require an AAC system. First, due to her many physical challenges, her communicative output is limited and difficult to understand. Second, the listeners in her environment are not recognizing her output as communicative. If an AAC system is introduced, which is designed to be accessible and useful to Sherry, and which is*

recognizable to her listeners, her communication output will be greatly enhanced. A word of caution is needed here, however: All too often teachers or therapists offer students an AAC device that happens to be readily available or one with which they are familiar but which is not suitable for a particular student. We have seen many, often expensive, AAC devices stored in a closet in the classroom because they had been purchased simply because someone had heard of the device but it had not been selected specifically to meet the needs of an individual student. Remember too, that AAC systems can range from the use of manual signs, hand-made picture boards, and single switches that activate one or two messages, for example, all the way to complex electronic or computer-based instruments. AAC systems need to be selected based on the needs of each particular student, and the system must be individualized for that student.

Step 4: Develop a Communication System

Developing an appropriate communication system is a process that requires a team that includes the SLP, teacher, family, and possibly a motor specialist such as an occupational or physical therapist if the student has motor impairments, as well as other specialists depending on the student's sensory (hearing/vision) abilities. In order to develop a viable communication system for a student with complex communication needs and significant disabilities, it is important to look primarily at what the student *can* do, not at what he or she cannot do. Educators must put a communication system in place for students as soon as possible—it is not appropriate to wait for the development of prerequisite skills before allowing a student to communicate. For example, some believe that a student must display a certain level of cognitive skills before he or she can communicate or believe that a student must have eye contact before beginning communication programming. We know that since all behaviors communicate and that if we respond to students regularly, regardless of the form through which they communicate, we do not have to wait for the development of "prerequisite" skills. In fact, waiting for such development simply delays the development of true, meaningful communication. Remember: All students communicate, and educators must be careful listeners and observers to determine *how* students are communicating and then assist them in becoming understandable to others as soon as possible.

To do this, answer two simple questions: 1) What skills does the student already have/use, and 2) What does the student need? To indicate how to meet the student's communication needs it may be helpful to develop a simple Decision Chart. Figures 3.4, 3.5, and 3.6 present completed Decision Charts for Sherry, Donnetta, and Jamal, respectively. (A blank chart is included in the appendix at the end of the book.)

————● Sherry: A Presymbolic Learner

Sherry is a 19-year-old student who has severe and multiple disabilities. She uses a wheelchair, has limited use of her arms and hands, poor head control, and very little response to people or sensory input. She also has a diagnosis of cortical blindness. She cries, bites herself, and sleeps much of the school day. She currently functions both receptively and expressively at a presymbolic level. The team first reviews what Sherry can do (Figure 3.4, columns 1 and 2). Then, the team thinks about the most important ways to make her communications more understandable and more typical. Team members consider what challenges and skills she has in order to decide what type of communication system or assistive devices will help her move to more understandable output.

Decision Chart for Developing a Communication Program

Student	What the student already has/does		Challenges/ Abilities	What the student needs	What actions can satisfy the communication needs of this student?
Sherry	Intents: Discomfort Refusal Pleasure Gaining attention Boredom Wanting more of something	Modes: Cries Turns away Smiles and laughs Screams and bangs table Screams, bangs table, bites self, goes to sleep Bangs table and smiles	Sherry has vision, motor disabilities; does not appear to understand any spoken language Sherry can use hand/arm to hit table; uses voice to laugh, cry, scream; smiles to touch and voice	Sherry needs a way to indicate intents without screaming, biting, going to sleep.	1. Determine a list of preferences. 2. Offer a preferred activity and then stop activity. 3. Have a single message switch that has a relatively large surface, and be sure to cover it with a texture that Sherry likes to touch. The switch should activate easily when touched or hit. Place it in close proximity of her hand. Assist her to hit switch. Then reinitiate activity. 4. Have switch available to her at all times and place it where she usually hits the table, especially when she is bored. If she hits the switch (when she goes to hit the table), respond as if she is calling for attention.

(continued)

Figure 3.4.　Decision Chart for Developing a Communication Program for Sherry.

Figure 3.4. *(continued)*

Decision Chart for Developing a Communication Program

Student	What the student already has/does	Challenges/ Abilities	What the student needs	What actions can satisfy the communication needs of this student?
				5. The message on the switch should be somewhat generic (e.g., "more" for requests for continuation of a favorite activity or item), but should be changed to a more appropriate message for other situations. For example, the switch might say HEY, LOOK or COME HERE PLEASE when Sherry will use it to call for attention when she is bored. *Other Steps to Begin:* 6. Respond to cries and screams as if she is requesting attention. 7. Honor head turn as a refusal. 8. Offer more opportunities for choices of preferred items, and assist her to reach toward the item she wants. 9. Provide more opportunities for interactions with peers and adults. Respond to her initiations.

Decision Chart for Developing a Communication Program

Student	What the student already has/does		Challenges/ Abilities	What the student needs	What actions can satisfy the communication needs of this student?
Donnetta	Intents: Requests	Modes: Donnetta points, looks, vocalizes, and/or reaches to request.	Donnette has limited mobility with walking and in walking; can use hands for gross activities, but not fine movements; uses a walker.	A way to request and initiate that others understand so that she can more fully participate in classroom activities	1. Provide a simple voice output communication system or a picture book or board that has several picture choices. Be sure she can wear the book or device when she goes from class to class.
	Gaining attention	Donnetta taps others to gain their attention.	Donnetta has no clear oral speech; has mild vision problems but has glasses. Donnetta follows simple directions with demonstration or pictures; imitates others; participates in activities; tries to initiate to others.		2. Be sure to have a page or level of the instrument or book for each classroom activity and a page for social interactions, initiations, responses, and simple questions. Be sure to put print under each picture so that Donnetta is receiving reading/literacy input as well.
	Frustration	Donnetta just gives up and watches when she is frustrated.	Donnetta learns sequences of activities by following directions with pictures.		3. Ask her friends for common phrases that all the kids use with each other.

Figure 3.5. Decision Chart for Developing a Communication Program for Donnetta.

Decision Chart for Developing a Communication Program

Student	What the student already has/does		Challenges/ Abilities	What the student needs	What actions can satisfy the communication needs of this student
Jamal	**Intents:**	**Modes:**	Jamal has severe cerebral palsy, does not walk or speak, and has only gross arm movements on the left side. He can separate out one finger on his right hand to gain access to a keyboard with large keys. His vision and hearing are fine. He reads some words and types on a computer but is hesitant because his spelling is limited. He was not received much work in reading and spelling, as his abilities have been underestimated in the past. He is sometimes uncooperative in class and gets angry because no one understands his communications.	A complex, electronic communication system in order to initiate to others, participate in age-appropriate academics, make friends, share his feelings and thoughts, and participate in decisions about his future	1. Contact a specialist in AAC instruments and assessment.
	Answers: Yes	Head nod			2. Look for an AAC device that has text to speech and links to pages from a home page.
	Answers: No	Head shake			3. Develop pages for high interest topics with pictures and print initially until reading improves; include social interaction pages and emotion pages, as Jamal has experienced anger and frustration from his communication difficulties.
	Shows agreement	Gross approximation at a "high five"			
	Shows disagreement	Approximation of a "thumbs down" gesture			
	Shows pleasure	Smiles, laughs			4. Be sure that the instrument is either software that can be put onto a laptop computer or is a dedicated device that can gain access to a printer, and so forth, so that class assignments can be completed using the device.
	Initiates to others	Smiles at peers and tries to be part of conversations, vocalizes a loud "Ah"			
	Frustration and anger	Looks away, refuses to participate, frowns			5. Begin age-appropriate academics.
	Responds readily and understands complex directions	If physically able			

Figure 3.6. Decision Chart for Developing a Communication Program for Jamal.

Finally the team proposes a set of steps to move Sherry toward more understandable communication output (i.e., a very simple AAC device that makes use of her current abilities).

To teach Sherry to use a single output switch, the team employs some very basic communication elicitation strategies. Educators sometimes hear these strategies referred to as "sabotage strategies" or strategies utilized in "milieu" teaching (Hancock & Kaiser, 2006). Whatever they are termed, these strategies have proven successful with students having severe cognitive disabilities. Some of these strategies include the following:

1. **Determine the student's main preferences and have these available but out of reach.** When the student reaches, cries, gestures, and/or fusses, the adult responds to the student's output as if it is meaningful. The student needs to learn that he or she can get the listener's attention or request by his or her output, yet unless the listener consistently responds to the student's output, he or she will not learn.

2. **Block access.** Again, a favorite activity or item is present, but the student cannot gain access to the item. This time when the student attempts to gain access to the desired item or activity, the teacher/SLP provides a new way for the student to request. This can be done in many ways. One strategy is to have the item almost within reach. When the student reaches toward the item, place a single message switch in front of the item and have the student touch the switch, which activates the message (e.g., I WANT THE _____).

3. **Repeat and practice.** Repeat access blocking over and over to establish the new behavior and help the student learn that activating the switch elicits the required response from the listener (e.g., OH, I SEE. I GET THE _____ WHEN I HIT THE SWITCH!).

4. **Provide choices.** Watch to see which choice the student looks or reaches toward. Again, give the student a new way to ask for the item. This could include using a switch again, or placing a picture in front of the real item and having the student touch the picture before he or she is given the item.

So, how might some of these strategies be used with our student, Sherry? The team first determines her preferred activities and/or items, and then looks for a way for her to request those. They know that she can hit the table consistently, so they decide to use a single message switch that is activated by hitting or touching it. The switch has a relatively large area so that Sherry does not have to be precise in where she hits it. In addition, the switch is covered with a texture that Sherry likes to feel (as we know her vision is poor due to cortical blindness). Then, the teacher uses simple sabotage and training techniques (Neetz, Haring, & Tomlenson, 1984; Reichle, Beukelman, & Light, 2002; Stremel-Campbell, 1985) to teach Sherry to hit the switch to get more of a preferred activity or item.

The team actually used this type of a simple program to teach Sherry to ask for more of her favorite activity—going fast in her wheelchair during gym class. First the team determined that she loves to go fast in her wheelchair. Next team members placed a switch on her lap tray near to the point where she usually hits her tray. Then they started going fast, stopped, and waited to see what Sherry would do. She fussed and hit at her tray. The team made sure that the switch was close to her hand. Someone on the team said, "Oh Sherry, you want to go more. You have to tell us." Then members helped her hit the switch that said I WANT TO GO SOME MORE. The team repeated this strategy when going to gym class from her classroom. The sequence was repeated about 6–8 times on the way to the gym. By the time Sherry reached the gym, she would look up when the chair stopped, smile, and reach toward the switch when verbally prompted. Because the team used a highly preferred activity, chose an action Sherry could already complete (hitting), coupled that with a new way to communicate (hitting the switch rather than the tray), helped her find the switch by covering it in a tactile material due to her vision loss, and repeated this meaningful activity over and over, Sherry learned the new skill in 1 day.

The team addresses Sherry's other communication intents by teaching everyone who comes into contact with her to respond to her communicative output as meaningful in order to increase her initiations. Finally, the team realizes that Sherry has not been offered choices or given enough opportunities to interact with others and will increase such opportunities in her day. These choices must include opportunities to interact with typically developing peers whenever possible in the context of the general curriculum.

To summarize, educators can teach students to communicate in a new way by completing the following steps:

1. Review the student's level of communication output, receptive abilities, intents expressed, and mode of communication.

2. Review challenges and abilities that can be utilized for communicative output.

3. Determine the student's greatest communicative needs at the time.

4. Match the student's physical and cognitive abilities with a system that will satisfy his or her needs, match his or her abilities (how he or she will gain access to the system), and lead toward more understandable and more symbolic communication. Begin with the easiest system for the student and then use it in different environments.

5. Address all of the student's communicative intents in some way. A student with complex communication needs may use more than one communication system to communicate.

Because Sherry is going to start with a single-message voice output device (switch) to request and to gain attention, the team still needs to address her refusals, smiles for pleasure, and so forth. Although the team may decide to use the single-message switch to encourage Sherry to gain attention or ask for "more," the team may decide to respond to her other intents in other ways. Because Sherry has a clearly understandable output to express pleasure (e.g., smile, laugh), these behaviors will be the form that Sherry uses to express those intents. Because Sherry has a clear refusal behavior (e.g., fusses, turns away), these behaviors will be accepted to express those intents. The team decides to respond to Sherry consistently, honor her refusals if at all possible, and smile and laugh with her when she shows pleasure. If all those who come in contact with Sherry are taught to respond to her meaningfully, she will increase her communicative output and strengthen her receptive knowledge of what is happening in her world. The key for students such as Sherry is that all those in contact with her are taught to understand and respond to her various forms of communication.

Donnetta: An Emerging Symbolic Learner

The sequence just discussed to develop a communication system can also be used with Donnetta (Figure 3.5), the 9-year-old student who functions at an emerging symbolic level in expressive communication. Donnetta uses clear points and some vocalizations, and she understands pictures, and so forth. Receptively she can follow direction with visual cues and with picture supports and by imitating others. Although she has limited mobility, mild vision problems, and poor hand coordination, Donnetta interacts with others, understands pictures, imitates her peers, participates in classroom activities, and has many communicative intents (e.g., requesting, commenting, protesting) that she tries to express. Her greatest educational need at this time is a communication system that allows her to initiate and respond to peers and adults and fully participate in classroom activities.

The system the team develops for Donnetta matches her skills of picture knowledge, pointing, using multiple communication intents, interacting socially, and following simple directions. Although some might also consider the use of a few signs for Donnetta, the team noted that she had limited fine motor skills, which would impede her being able to produce a large number of signs.

Donnetta has much to say and is trying hard to do so. She needs a system that is readily available to her, can include a great number of options, and will easily be understood by others. The team chooses a picture book with pages for each class and for each school/home activity or a simple voice-output AAC device that is activated by touching buttons on the device. For example, the device may have picture slots for eight different messages. Moreover, if the device has levels, it would also be able to hold different messages at each level setting. Within those level settings, each level can hold eight different messages. The teacher can quickly change the level and slip in new pictures, and Donnetta is ready for her next class. The team is careful to include print under each picture to provide reading/literacy input. In addition, the messages are recorded by a student the same age as Donnetta and in language/vocabulary that the other kids use.

Jamal: A Symbolic Learner

The process is completed again for our third student, Jamal (Figure 3.6). Jamal is 16, and his communicative competence has been underestimated due to his severe motor impairments from cerebral palsy. He is nonverbal, cannot walk, and can produce only undifferentiated vocalizations. He has limited use of his left arm, but he can use the index finger of his right hand to gain access to a keyboard. He can read and spell some words, but he does not like to use the computer because he has not been given enough instruction in reading and spelling over the years. He understands at age level and has gotten very frustrated and angry when at school because he cannot display his true abilities. He uses many age-appropriate gestures and has a clear yes/no (head nod or shake) response.

The team realizes that Jamal needs an intensive assessment with specialists in AAC and assistive technology devices. The team knows that Jamal needs a device that has many options (e.g., text to speech, so that he can type a message that the device speaks, and topic- or academic content–specific picture pages with print for communication in a variety of settings, until his reading and spelling improve). Jamal could use either communication software on a laptop computer or a dedicated instrument that can be linked to a printer and computer in order to print and save his assignments. In addition, the team recognizes that Jamal needs to be able to express his feelings when frustrated and angry so that his cooperation at school can improve.

STRATEGIES TO FACILITATE COMMUNICATION: LINKING TO THE GENERAL CURRICULUM

Once students have communication system supports in place, educators must have strategies and techniques to encourage these students to *use* their communication systems. The most important strategy for fostering communication is to provide opportunities to communicate.

Academic Content

In thinking about how to merge academic content and communicative competence, we advocate teaching curriculum content early, often, and within an age-appropriate context as a means of facilitating communication regardless of whether or not the student exhibits the developmental prerequisite skills. Individuals start building a common frame of reference on topics about their world at a very early age and continue to build these shared understandings throughout their lives. So many times, goals on an individualized education program will include "social greetings," but communication development begins with and depends on shared meanings/conversations/exchanges after "hello." It extends to a shared sense of meaning about the world.

Rich, engaging curriculum activities can provide excellent opportunities for language development and provide something to talk about. In addition, the curriculum topics are socially relevant, as students with and without disabilities are sharing experiences in which communication is essential. Using peers in the development of language through the existing curriculum solves a number of logistical problems as well. The grade-specific curriculum provides more opportunities with increased frequency of interaction, more specific attention to communication development, chronologically age-appropriate topics, and less curriculum planning because the curriculum activities already exist, and peers without disabilities are already there as communication models (see Hunt, Staub, Alwell, & Goetz, 1994). Finally, frequent opportunities for social interaction around shared experiences lead to increased competence in social skills and the development of friendships (Schwartz, Staub, Peck, & Gallucci, 2006).

Curriculum, Communication, and Augmentative and Alternative Communication Systems

Let us take the example of Jamal who wanted to participate in conversations with his peers regarding his favorite football team. For students such as Jamal, determining an appropriate AAC system is essential to facilitating appropriate communication, but it provides access to much more. Using Jamal's communication system and his interest in sports, the team could effectively plan and teach math activities around player statistics and score spreads of his favorite team. However, without a communication system, neither content learning nor conversations with friends could occur. In the seven-state study discussed previously in this chapter, Towles-Reeves et al. (2009) found that only about 50% of students identified as communicating at a pre- or emerging-symbolic level had an AAC system in use. As we have noted, many students are unable to display their true abilities because they do not have an understandable communication system. However, once we provide a communication system, the students need *opportunities* to communicate, as well as *reasons* to communicate. By integrating the communication system into the academic curriculum we have a guaranteed set of topics and opportunities for communication. Conversely, by providing students with a clear communication system, they can display their true academic levels and abilities. Therefore, the AAC device must include curriculum-related items to ensure students truly have the opportunity to develop communicative *and* academic competence.

Curriculum Standards and Materials

Grade-specific curriculum standards and materials form the skeleton of the activities that occur in classroom instruction. For example, in reading and literacy, focusing on the same books that typically developing peers are reading is essential. It is important to identify grade-appropriate reading materials even if the student cannot read independently. Age-appropriate themes, settings, characters, and contexts provide rich topics for conversation. For example, Elliott, a high school student with a significant disability, is learning about the idiomatic expressions in Steinbeck's (1937) *Of Mice and Men*. Elliott interprets language quite literally, and because most teenagers use idiomatic expression extensively, it is important to teach him specifically multiple meaning of words. This will allow him to more fully participate in conversations and social interactions. Figure 3.7 illustrates examples of idiomatic expressions used in Steinbeck's *Of Mice and Men*. This figure depicts the ways in which common vocabulary can have two meanings. One is the every day meaning and the other might be an idiomatic use of the same word. By helping Elliot see the two meanings of the same word, he will be more able to understand age-appropriate literature.

As another example, one middle school student, Ryan, worked on reading the vocabulary words in Lois Lowry's *The Giver* (1993) by a sight word reading approach, and he showed comprehension of each key word by matching it to a picture. To help understand a major theme of the book (i.e., what it is like to live in a world without color), Ryan matched both color and grey scale pictures so that a peer could review with Ryan the idea that the main character in the book (Jonas) lived in a community that didn't have color. Ryan then learned that once Jonas started learning about color, Jonas realized all that he had missed. Ryan was asked which type of world *he* preferred. He matched the pictures to the vocabulary word each time other students worked on their vocabulary words. Ryan worked on a cumulative set of vocabulary words throughout the book, adding to the list as new ones were acquired.

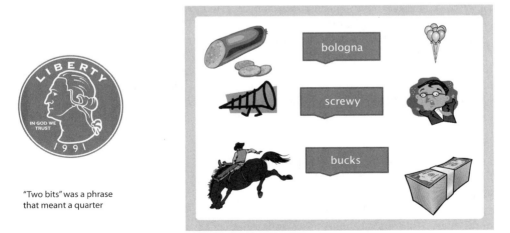

"Two bits" was a phrase that meant a quarter

Figure 3.7. Example of vocabulary building with idiomatic expressions.

Another student with a significant cognitive disability, Carlos, listened to the chapters read during class and then had the chapters summarized by a peer or teacher prior to working on his vocabulary words. He used an adapted keyboard with six picture keys that he pressed to type the picture and word into his *Writing with Symbols* computer software, which displayed the vocabulary word and picture while reading the word aloud to him. Rather than getting new vocabulary words each chapter, a few words to which Carlos could relate to were targeted for instruction within each chapter. During this unit, he spent time exploring the vocabulary with his keyboard and then was requested to type certain words.

Ecological Inventory

Determining what other students are reading and learning is essential for using the curriculum to develop communicative competence for students with disabilities. This job is easy if the student is included in a general education classroom; however, if the student is not included, then it becomes essential to conduct an ecological inventory with the teachers in your school or with the school librarian to determine the literature that other students are talking about. Developing this inventory is as simple as asking general education teachers what books they use in their literature lessons. If students are taught in a self-contained special education classroom, it may be helpful to have them participate in book clubs or literature circles with their typically developing peers. If these clubs do not exist, they can be formed. Keep the students' interests in mind, however; if a student is interested in horses, then books, movies, or information about horses will help connect that student to potential friends who share similar interests. This will further enhance vocabulary development and increase opportunities to practice conversations.

Transdisciplinary Approach

The choice of an AAC system should focus on the simplest and easiest to use for both the student and the recipient of the communication (Downing, 2004). The use of a transdisciplinary approach, including the participation of the SLP, special and general education teachers, physical and occupational therapists, and vision and hearing specialists, is critical to the selection of an appropriate system. A good example of the importance of this approach is that of a 9-year-old student named Felicia. Felicia had extremely high muscle tone, did not walk or use oral speech, and had a significant vision impairment. Her extremely high muscle tone and retention of early reflexes markedly inhibited her ability to voluntarily move her head or arm. When we first observed Felicia, despite her truly urgent attempts to communicate, her physical position within her wheelchair and the position of the materials on which she was to focus, forced her into an involuntary reflex whenever she attempted to make a voluntary response. The classroom staff urged her to turn her head and push the switch to activate a music tape. Unfortunately, Felicia was placed in such a position that when she made her sincere efforts to move, her muscle tone increased and an involuntary reflex pattern inhibited her ability to turn her head. Indeed, her very act of initiating movement actually prevented her from communicating an understandable response. A physical therapist, trained in pediatric treatment, immediately noticed this problem. The physical therapist recommended a more comfortable, normalized position for Felicia *and* an appropriate position for the class materials and the switch. The new positions allowed her to activate the switch and to display her response to the teacher's question (which she clearly understood). Felicia's inability to move was being interpreted as a lack of understanding of the direction to "hit the switch." Her true abilities would have remained hidden without the presence of a transdisciplinary team.

CONCLUSION

Students with significant cognitive disabilities—those students who participate in an AA-AAS—often evidence limited communication competence, with a significant percentage of these students rated by their teachers as being presymbolic learners (i.e., students who do not yet have formal communication systems; Kearns et al., in press; Towles-Reeves et al., 2009). Also, at least within cross-sectional, large-scale student data sets, students in upper grades do not evidence substantially higher levels of communicative competence (i.e., smaller percentages of presymbolic learners) than younger elementary age students (Kearns et al., in press). This is particularly distressing in light of the fact that the need and right to quality communication services for *all* students have been advocated and endorsed for decades by all of the primary educational and therapeutic professional associations (National Joint Committee for the Communication Needs of Persons with Severe Disabilities, 1992, 2005).

In addition, meaningful access to grade-level academic content and valid participation in alternate assessments require that students be able to understand academic content and be able to communicate what they know. Thus it is imperative that, within a transdisciplinary model, general and special education teachers, SLPs, assistive technology specialists, and other therapists work in partnership with students and their families to enable all students to achieve a formal means of communication, including using AAC systems. The context of the general education curriculum provides a rich environment to create topics of shared interest that promote further opportunities for communication, social interactions, and friendships.

Yet many teachers have students with significant cognitive disabilities for whom communication is a severe challenge; at times, teachers and therapists may mistakenly come to the conclusion that a student with severe disabilities really *cannot* communicate. Although this is *never* the case, both teachers and SLPs need practical strategies, based on normative development of communicative stages, in order to facilitate students' communication competence. Together, teachers and therapists need strategies to enable students who do not have formal communication systems to achieve this essential outcome of their education.

Although this has *not* been a chapter about alternate assessment per se, it is a foundational chapter critical to the education of students with significant cognitive disabilities. Without this foundation, it would appear very likely that any alternate assessment for these students would ultimately miss the mark. For if students have not been taught to communicate, it is not likely that participation in alternate assessments would have much effect on either their learning or their life.

REFERENCES

Bates, E. (1979). The emergence of symbols: Ontogeny and phylogeny. In W.A. Collins (Ed.), *Children's language and communication* (pp. 121–155). Mahwah, NJ: Lawrence Erlbaum Associates.

Bates, E., Thal, D., Whitesell, K., Fenson, L., & Oakes, L. (1989). Integrating language and gestures in infancy. *Developmental Psychology, 25,* 1004–1019.

Beck, A., Stoner, J., & Dennis, M. (2009). An investigation of aided language stimulation: Does it increase AAC use with adults with developmental disabilities and complex communication needs? *Augmentative and Alternative Communication, 25,* 42–54.

Cafiero, J. (1998). Communication power for individuals with autism. *Focus on Autism and Other Developmental Disabilities, 13,* 113–121.

Cafiero, J.M. (2005). *Meaningful exchanges for people with autism: An introduction to augmentative & alternative communication.* Bethesda, MD: Woodbine House.

Downing, J.E. (2004). Communication skills. In F.P. Orelove, D. Sobsey, & R.K. Silberman (Eds.), *Educating children with multiple disabilities: A collaborative approach* (4th ed., pp. 529–561). Baltimore: Paul H. Brookes Publishing Co.

Franco, J.H., Lang, R.L., O'Reilly, M.F., Chan, J.M., Sigafoos, J., & Rispoli, M. (2009). Functional analysis and treatment of inappropriate vocalizations using a speech-generating device for a child with autism. *Focus on Autism and Other Developmental Disabilities, 24,* 146–155.

Goossens, C., Crain, S., & Elder, P. (1992). *Engineering the preschool environment for interactive symbolic communication: 18 months to 5 years developmentally.* Birmingham, AL: Southeast Augmentative Communication Conference Publications.

Hancock, T.B., & Kaiser, A.P. (2006). Enhanced milieu teaching. In R.J. McCauley & M.E. Fey (Eds.), *Treatment of language disorders in children* (pp. 203–236). Baltimore: Paul H. Brookes Publishing Co.

Hunt, P., Staub, D., Alwell, M., & Goetz, L. (1994). Achievement of all students within the context of cooperative learning groups. *The Journal of The Association for Persons with Severe Handicaps, 19,* 290–301.

Individuals with Disabilities Education Act (IDEA) of 1990, PL 101-476, 20 U.S.C. §§ 1400 *et seq.*

Kearns, J., Towles-Reeves, E., Kleinert, H., Kleinert, J., & Thomas, M. (in press). Characteristics of and implications for students participating in alternate assessments based on alternate academic achievement standards. *Journal of Special Education.*

Light, J.C., & Binger, C. (1998). *Building communicative competence with individuals who use augmentative and alternative communication.* Baltimore: Paul H. Brookes Publishing Co.

Lowry, L. (1993). *The giver.* New York: Houghton Mifflin Co.

McDonald, J. (1982). Communication strategies for language intervention. In D. McClowry, A. Guilford, & S. Richardson (Eds.), *Infant communication.* New York: Grune & Stratton.

McLean, J., & Snyder-McLean, L. (1978). *A transactional approach to early language training.* Columbus, OH: Charles E. Merrill.

Mirenda, P. (1999). Augmentative and alternative communication techniques. In J.E. Downing (Ed.), *Teaching communication skills to students with severe disabilities* (pp. 119–138). Baltimore: Paul H. Brookes Publishing Co.

Mirenda, P. (2003). Toward functional augmentative and alternative communication for students with autism: Manual signs, graphic symbols, and voice output communication aids. *Language, Speech, and Hearing Services in the Schools, 34,* 203–216.

National Joint Committee for the Communication Needs of Persons with Severe Disabilities. (1992). *Guidelines for meeting the communication needs of persons with severe disabilities.* Retrieved March 12, 2010, from http://www.asha.org/docs/html/GL1992–00201.html

National Joint Committee for the Communication Needs of Persons with Severe Disabilities. (2005). *Communication services for persons with severe disabilities: Current Best Practices.* Retrieved March 12, 2010, from http://www.asha.org/uploadedFiles/NJC/ASHA2005NJCseminar.pdf

Neetz, J.A., Haring, T., & Tomlenson, C. (1984). *Instructional procedures for promoting communication behaviors in naturally occurring contexts: A self-training guide.* Santa Barbara: University of California.

Paul, R. (2001). *Language disorders from infancy through adolescence* (2nd ed.). St. Louis: Mosby.

Rankin, J., Harwood, K., & Mirenda, P. (1994). Influence of graphic symbol use on reading comprehension. *Augmentative and Alternative Communication, 10*, 269–281.

Reichle, J., Beukelman, D.R., & Light, J.C. (2002). *Exemplary practices for beginning communicators: Implications for AAC.* Baltimore: Paul H. Brookes Publishing Co.

Romski, M., & Sevcik, R. (2005). Augmentative communication and early intervention: Myths and realities. *Infants & Young Children: An Interdisciplinary Journal of Special Care Practices, 18,* 174–185.

Rowland, C. (2005). But what CAN they do? Assessment of communication skills in children with severe and multiple disabilities. *ASHA-DAAC Perspectives, 14,* 7–12.

Rowland, C., & Schweigert, P. (1990). *Tangible symbol systems: Symbolic communication for individuals with multisensory impairments.* Tucson, AZ: Communication Skill Builders.

Schwartz, I., Staub, D., Peck, C., & Gallucci, C. (2006). Peer relationships. In M.E. Snell & Fredda Brown (Eds.), *Instruction of students with severe disabilities* (6th ed., pp. 375–401). Upper Saddle River, NJ: Merrill Prentice Hall.

Steinbeck, J. (1937). *Of mice and men.* New York: Penguin Books.

Stremel-Campbell, K. (1985). *Prelanguage and emergent language: Communication intervention with young children.* Paper presented at the meeting of the Early Childhood Conference, Lexington, KY.

Towles-Reeves, E., Kearns, J., Kleinert, H., & Kleinert, J. (2009). An analysis of the learning characteristics of students taking alternate assessments based on alternate achievement standards. *Journal of Special Education, 42,* 241–254.

U.S. Department of Education. (2005). *Alternate achievement standards for students with the most significant cognitive disabilities: Non-regulatory guidance.* Washington, DC: Author, Office of Elementary and Secondary Education.

Yoder, D.E. (2001). Having my say. *Augmentative and Alternative Communication, 17*(1), 2–11.

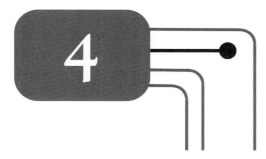

Aligning Curriculum with Grade-Specific Content Standards

Using Eight Criteria to Create Access

Shawnee Y. Wakeman, Diane M. Browder,
Bree A. Jimenez, and Pamela J. Mims

States typically define expectations for student learning as *content standards* (i.e., the academic content, or what the student is being taught) and *achievement standards* (i.e., the student's performance, or how the student would demonstrate what he or she knows). Alignment in education is an examination of the relationship or link among an assessment, the state standards, and classroom instruction. Although alignment is not a new concept in education, it is only since the requirements of states to meet Peer Review standards that educators have applied alignment to alternate assessment based on alternate achievement standards (AA-AAS). Aligning assessment and instruction to state content standards requires a shift in thinking about curriculum for students with significant cognitive disabilities who have traditionally had instruction in a functional curriculum (Browder, Spooner, Wakeman, Trela, & Baker, 2006). Although functional skills continue to be important, aligning assessment and instruction to state standards requires asking not only if skills are meaningful to the student but also if the content matches the intended target. Alignment also requires a three-way match from standard to instruction, from standard to assessment, and from instruction to assessment. Sometimes the match requires yet another consideration if states have translated or extended the state standards for students with significant cognitive disabilities. When extensions are used, consideration needs to be given as to whether they match the original target. Flowers,

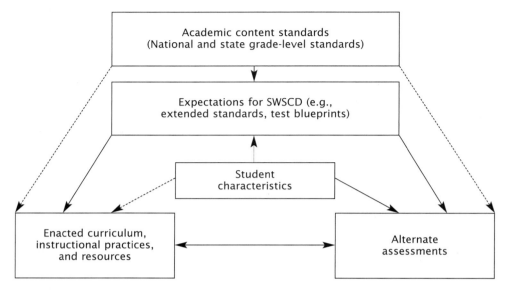

Figure 4.1. Educational components included in an alignment study. (*Key*: SWSCD, students with significant cognitive disabilities; From Flowers, C., Wakeman, S., Browder, D., & Karvonen, M. [2007]. *Links for academic learning: An alignment protocol for alternate assessments based on alternate achievement standards* [MANUAL, p. 17]. Charlotte: University of North Carolina at Charlotte; reprinted by permission.)

Wakeman, Browder, and Karvonen (2007) described the interaction among these educational components that need to match in a diagram on alignment (see Figure 4.1). Notice in this diagram that the characteristics of the student are considered when thinking about alignment. An assessment, for example, might be developed that perfectly matches state standards but is biased against many students with significant cognitive disabilities (e.g., requires verbal responding.) Although such an assessment might technically align, it would not be relevant.

Although states typically articulate both content and achievement standards, the desired match for an AA-AAS is in content since achievement is by definition alternate for these assessments. The U.S. Department of Education's *Alternate Achievement Standards for Students with the Most Significant Cognitive Disabilities* (2005) described a need for a clear link between the assessment and the grade-level content standards. Sometimes educators have difficulty understanding that grade-level content can be learned at different levels of achievement, and it can be argued that changing the achievement target changes the content. In contrast, other educators have described how content can be matched, even when achievement differs (Browder, Wakeman, et al., 2007).

This chapter is based on the premise that students with significant cognitive disabilities can learn content that is age and grade appropriate and that meaningful alternate achievement targets can be defined for this learning.

Most states base their general education content standards on those of national standards outlined by professional organizations (e.g., the National Council for Teachers of Mathematics, National Science Education Standards). In addition, many states provide guidance on the prioritized content for students with significant cognitive disabilities through extended or prioritized academic content standards or curriculum frameworks (e.g., Massachusetts Department of Education, n.d.; South Dakota Department of

Education, n.d.). States also develop performance or achievement standards by which they determine the degree to which a student is proficient in the domain assessed (e.g., Michigan Department of Education, n.d; Texas Department of Education, n.d.). To begin the process of aligning assessment and instruction, educators need to invest time in gaining deep understanding of their own state's standards and any extensions for students with significant cognitive disabilities.

Once the standards are well understood and planning for assessment and instruction begins, planning teams will face the challenge of how to determine what does or does not align. Assessment and instruction always reflect educators' curricular priorities. As Browder et al. (2004) illustrated in their research on the content of alternate assessments, these priorities may stem not only from the current thinking about curriculum but also past practice. For example, some educators may want all skills to be clearly linked to functional activities of community living. Others, trained in earlier eras when consideration was given to the mental age of students, may want to focus on early childhood skills. Others may want to target "real" academics such as reading and math, but they may not know how to extend standards for students with significant cognitive disabilities.

We propose using the eight criteria developed in the Links for Academic Learning (LAL) model (Flowers et al., 2007) to guide teams in planning assessment and instruction that align with state standards. Although LAL was originally developed to measure alignment of an AA-AAS system, these criteria can also serve as check points or guiding questions for planning classroom instruction (Browder, Spooner, et al., 2006). The purpose of this chapter is to help educators understand and use the eight criteria to develop instruction and assessment using academic content standards. We describe how to manage some of the challenges of aligning instruction with grade-level content standards, including how to 1) make learning functional or meaningful, 2) differentiate across grades or grade bands, and 3) design academic instruction including assessment that is accessible to all students. We also offer ideas for individualized education program (IEP) teams to help develop standards-based IEPs.

LINKS FOR ACADEMIC LEARNING CRITERIA

Browder et al. (2007) proposed a conceptual definition and criteria for linking instruction and assessment to grade-level academic content standards. This definition was used to shape the alignment criteria within the LAL model to include a two-part approach—one to specifically examine the demands from national policy (i.e., the Individuals with Disabilities Education Act Amendments [IDEA] of 1997 [PL 105-17], the Individuals with Disabilities Education Improvement Act [IDEA] of 2004 [PL 108-446], and the No Child Left Behind (NCLB) Act of 2001 [PL 107-110]), and one to address specific challenges for this population of teachers and students, such as a lack of training for teachers in the content areas and the nature of the students' disabilities. The definition includes eight criteria to be used for planning and evaluating alignment.

Criterion 1: The Content Is Academic

Given that past curricular priorities for students with significant cognitive disabilities de-emphasized academic learning, it is not surprising that assessment and instruction intended to align with state standards sometimes miss the academic focus entirely. For example, in trying to make a science lesson on weather patterns functional, the teacher ends up concentrating on how to open an umbrella. Sometimes special education teachers lack training in content domains, and general educators may not understand the concept of alternate achievement. One way to begin collaboration to plan assessment and instruction that align with state standards is to review the domains of the content and potential priorities. For example teams of special and general educators at the University of North Carolina at Charlotte developed some possible content priorities in math (Trela, Browder, Pugalee, Spooner, & Knight, 2008), science (Jimenez, Spooner, Browder, DiBiase, & Knight, 2008), and English/language arts (Wakeman et al., 2008). Furthermore, mathematics can be classified by the content area (e.g., geometry, algebra, numbers and operations, data analysis, measurement), the type of problem to solve (e.g., linear, spatial, quantitative), and the process that may be used (e.g., communication, reasoning and proof, representation, connections, problem solving). These areas of math surround the main priority suggested for students with severe disabilities, which is solving the problem and applying the solution to life, or "It's about the problem." In planning for students with significant cognitive disabilities, this forms the priority for math instruction. For example, although students may not be able to do all of the grade-level content in data analysis, they may be able to apply concepts to create bar graphs or compose a survey using assistive technology to solve questions, such as whether a fund-raiser met a goal or what students want in the school vending machines. (See Chapter 7 for a further explication of this main priority.) Similarly, in science it is important to keep inquiry at the center of planning, and in language arts it is important to focus on students gaining meaning from text.

Discussion of general priorities and the strands of content to be covered is an excellent starting point for an educational team planning for alignment, whether it be an IEP team or a school system or statewide planning meeting. Ongoing collaboration among general and special educators will also be essential to plan for aligned academic content across the school year. Such collaboration might focus on planning inclusive lessons or team teaching within general education or specialized instruction for the student with disabilities that parallels general curriculum content.

Criterion 2: The Content Is Referenced to the Student's Grade Level

Thinking about content at the student's grade level or band may be new for some educators. For instruction, one avenue to address the starting point is to either pair with a general education colleague, examine the pacing guides provided by the state or school system, or tap into alternate resources that provide general education lessons that are aligned to the standards appropriate for a student's grade level. Starting with the general education materials, activities, and lessons helps educators begin at the grade level and not below it. For example, students in a middle school classroom may be reading *Swiss Family Robinson* by Johann David Wyss (1990). By beginning with this same novel and creating adaptations for students with disabilities, instruction will be more aligned to the grade level than if the assumption is made that the students need a different book. All students in the class may be assigned to outline the chapters, make models of some of the lifestyle adaptations made by the family on the island, and compare the characters' quality of life before and after the shipwreck. Students with disabilities, however, might create outlines by selecting pretyped text with picture cues after hearing a chapter read aloud, help develop a model in a cooperative learning group, or create a chart of comparisons using objects used before and after the shipwreck.

Criterion 3: Fidelity with the
Grade-Level Content and Performance Standards

One of the most critical questions educators can ask about their instruction is how well it resembles the essence or core concepts and expectations within the content standard to which it is linked. This is the "matching" criterion in which educators ask how well a skill targeted for assessment and instruction reflects the content in the original standard. Rarely will the answer to an alignment be a simple "yes" or "no." Instead, the judgments about the links regarding content between the standard and instruction may identify a near link, a far link, or no link between the two areas. For example, the grade-level content standard may be *Analyze and identify types of clouds within weather conditions*. Instruction that focuses on identifying clouds could be considered to address one part of the standard (i.e., clouds) and therefore have a far link to the standard. A stronger link would address identifying types of clouds in different conditions. Following the same example, it is important to consider the performance expectations within the standards and instruction. Although it is critical that the content link is strong (i.e., either a near link or far link), the performance expectation may vary because the students participate in assessments based upon alternate achievement. In this example, the standard addresses the analysis and identification of types of clouds while the instruction focused on identification. This may be acceptable for a student based on his or her needs. It is important that instruction retains high expectations by finding the closest link possible to the original standard, even though these expectations will likely not be at the grade-level performance. The process of establishing the links for the content and performance expectations between standards and instruction can be challenging for students with significant cognitive disabilities due to a variety of reasons. Sometimes educators will need to consider complex standards that address several concepts within one standard and whether the expectation is for the student to master all concepts or some subcomponent. Sometimes the concept within a standard is not clear to teachers and more information will be needed before planning extensions. Educators will also need creativity to identify ways some students with complex challenges can engage with certain content. For example, how will a student who is legally blind and has physical challenges make observations during scientific inquiry?

Criterion 4: The Content Differs in
Range, Balance, and Depth of Knowledge

Instruction based on the content standards established by the state follow a pattern for range (how much of the content is addressed) and balance (to what extent each standard is covered). The standards reflect the intended range of what a student is to be taught during a school year and address the emphasis given to the concepts within the standards. For example, standards related to writing and composition may appear at the fourth-grade level but be minimized or nonexistent in the fifth-grade standards. Standards for algebra may represent a heavy emphasis for the focus in mathematics in the eighth- and ninth-grade standards but have less of an emphasis in the seventh-grade standards. The prioritization represented in the extended standards in a state may also help define the range of what is expected to be taught and the balance of what instruction should focus on.

Most teachers are familiar with taxonomies that represent depth of knowledge expectations. Bloom (Tileston, 2004) and Marzano (Marzano & Kendall, 2007) represent

Table 4.1. Adapted Bloom's Taxonomy Depth of Knowledge Scale that may be used for setting targets for student learning of grade-level content

Depth of knowledge	Examples for data analysis in mathematics
Attention (touch, look, vocalize, respond, attend)	Student hands materials to peer who creates object graph.
Caution: This level reflects engagement with instruction but not actual learning. This level may be a beginning point for some students' learning, but it is not a recommended outcome.	Student looks at bar graph as teacher creates it.
Memorize/recall (list, describe [facts], identify, state, define, label, recognize, record, match, recall, relate)	Student creates bar graph by using match to sample (pastes squares on colored area of bar graph). Communicates that it is total items sold.
Performance (perform, demonstrate, follow, count, locate, read)	Student fills in bar graph and circles number of total.
Comprehension (explain, conclude, group/categorize, restate, review, translate, describe [concepts], paraphrase, infer, summarize, illustrate)	Student fills in bar graph, circles number of total, describes which category has more/less, and communicates outcome.
Application (compute, organize, collect, apply, classify, construct, solve, use, order, develop, generate, interact with text, implement)	Student is given a problem (e.g., "Which movie was viewed by more people?"), collects data (e.g., polls class), generates graph, and communicates solution.
Analysis, Synthesis, Evaluation (pattern, analyze, compare, contrast, compose, predict, extend, plan, judge, evaluate, interpret, cause/effect, investigate, examine, distinguish, differentiate, generate) Recommendation: Be sure all students have the opportunity to demonstrate this greater depth of knowledge to avoid placing a ceiling on expectations.	Student is given a problem requiring inference (e.g., "Which type of movie are students likely to rent next?"), collects data, generates graphs, uses information to draw inference (e.g., more likely to rent a comedy based on past number of comedy rentals), and communicates prediction. Student may also confirm prediction by observing future patterns.

From Flowers, C., Wakeman, S., Browder, D., & Karvonen, M. (2007). *Links for academic learning: An alignment protocol for alternate assessments based on alternate achievement standards* (p. 56). Charlotte: University of North Carolina at Charlotte; adapted by permission.

two of the most familiar taxonomies. As instruction for this population of students includes alternate achievement, Flowers et al. (2007) adapted Bloom's taxonomy (see Table 4.1) to provide more options for alternate achievement targets. The adapted version includes attention as the lowest level, which would not be a target outcome because it reflects participation but not learning. In contrast, engaging students with materials may be an important starting point for some students. The adapted taxonomy also collapsed the higher levels for analysis, synthesis, and evaluation because these may be chosen less often. In contrast, it is important to target these higher levels for some learning so as not to place a ceiling on expectations. Students who never receive the opportunity to synthesize or evaluate material have no way to demonstrate that they can acquire these deeper levels of knowledge. It is especially important to ensure that students who use written symbols, representations of symbols such as sign language or braille, or picture symbols be given opportunities to use these skills (e.g., by selecting a symbol to show understanding) and not simply be asked to attend (e.g., staying awake during a story). See Chapter 10 for a further discussion of depth of knowledge and alternate assessments.

Criterion 5: Differentiation Across Grade Levels or Grade Bands

As content standards change to reflect the range of knowledge and skills and the balance within a grade level or band, instruction should also follow suit. It is expected that while a student who has not mastered some prerequisite skills continue to receive instructional support in learning those skills, the emphasis for instruction for that student should also reflect content within the grade level or band. One way this differentiation can occur is within the materials or context within which the instruction occurs. For example, whereas an elementary student may receive literacy instruction with a picture book, older students would need chapter books typical of the grade level. For these books to be accessible for students with disabilities, text summaries might be used along with vocabulary with picture symbol supports, definitions embedded within the text, a repeated story line to highlight the main ideas within chapters, and systematic reviews of prerequisite literacy skills such as orienting the book, identifying the author and title, and turning the pages of the text. Although some of these skills would appear in the expectations for an elementary student to engage in a read aloud, by applying them to age-appropriate novels, students acquire new skills as well (e.g., listening to text with fewer picture supports).

Another approach to differentiation is the broadening or deepening of concepts and content within content strands or domains. In mathematics, for instance, this could occur as students build on their previous knowledge. For example, one concept young children learn in geometry is the identification of shapes. To continue to focus on identifying shapes with older students does not differentiate by grade band and is not age or grade appropriate. Older students engage with shapes in more complex ways, such as understanding of the angles within shapes or solving problems related to the area and perimeter of shapes.

Criterion 6: The Expected Achievement of Students Is Grade-Referenced Academic Content

One question to address during instruction is, "How do I know what the student knows and can do?" The assessment of student performance should clearly reflect what the student can do and not something else. For example, when students receive full physical support for all of an assessment, it is difficult to know what they understood. Sometimes the solution is to use a different response mode or assistive technology so that opportunities for students to show what they know are not complicated by motor challenges. For example, a student may be able to eye gaze at an object, picture symbol, or written text or use a computer touch screen. Educators also need to be clear about the difference between instructional strategies and assessment strategies. In instruction, teachers often need to use systematic prompting to promote student responding. Sometimes physical guidance is part of this prompting system. Effective instruction also includes fading these prompts so that students can make independent responses (Collins, 2007). Typically when assessing student progress, the target for achievement is independent responding. Sometimes information may be collected on progress toward this outcome (e.g., partial credit for prompted responses), but again, physically guided responses may reflect teacher help more than student learning and probably should receive no credit on an assessment.

Educators also need to be clear on the difference between student achievement and program evaluation. Sometimes educators want to consider whether students are receiving a high-quality educational program. For this program evaluation, criteria to be considered may be whether students have inclusive opportunities, assistive technology, effective instruction, opportunities for self-determination, and so forth. Asking these questions is one way to help schools improve accountability for student progress. In contrast, a well-designed student assessment focuses on what the student does (e.g., how many independent responses the student makes) versus what the environment provides. Sometimes students may be asked to participate in their own assessment to promote self-determination goals. Acquisition of self-evaluation is an important goal for all students, but it is not a substitute for learning the content.

Criterion 7: Barriers to Performance

Students with significant cognitive disabilities may have difficulty demonstrating their achievement if the materials and activities require one way to engage with materials (e.g., paper and pencil). Because students within this population use a variety of formats to communicate, information needs to be presented in formats that allow all students to engage in the content and demonstrate their understanding. For example, students with visual impairments may require the use of braille or raised text in the presentation of information. Students with hearing impairments may need amplification devices along with a variety of visual supports. Students who are nonverbal may require technological supports, such as a Big Mac switch or a DynaVox. Accommodations used for general assessments (Salend, 2008) should also be considered for students taking alternate assessments (e.g., dictating answers to a scribe).

Because general assessments and instruction often focus heavily on the use of written text, another concern in removing performance barriers for students with significant cognitive disabilities is identifying alternative symbols for students who do not read. Browder, Ahlgrim-Delzell, Courtade-Little, and Snell (2006) described three levels of symbol use that can be used for planning access to general curriculum, including students who use 1) mostly nonsymbolic means to communicate, 2) symbols with concrete referents, and 3) abstract symbols. Some students (i.e., those who primarily use nonsymbolic communication) will be learning symbols concurrent with content. To show what they know, these students may need alternatives to paper and pencil tasks, such as indicating what comes next in a science experiment by setting out materials. Other students have begun to use symbols in concrete ways (e.g., pictures of food, picture of a ball to mean "play") and may similarly learn to use symbols to express basic academic concepts (e.g., picture of a dog to show what a story is about, use of an equals sign [=] to indicate "same" or a greater than sign [>] for "more," selection of object that is not "living" in science unit). Other students have a repertoire of abstract symbols including some reading, writing, and mathematics. These students may be able to express more abstract concepts using adaptations of text (e.g., circling the correct answer after reading a sentence, filling in a diagram on the layers of the Earth).

Browder, Flowers, and Wakeman (2008) found evidence that teachers can identify students' current level of symbol use. Identifying a student's current fluency with symbols should *not* be used to lower expectations for symbolic learning, however. For example, students who communicate nonsymbolically may learn the symbols for their actions if these are paired with words or pictures. Also, students should have the opportunity to show what they know using assistive technology. A student with physical challenges might rely on facial expressions in informal social settings but be able to communicate with abstract symbols when given access to appropriate technology. See Chapter 3 for a further discussion of the importance of communication and symbol use in making instruction and assessments accessible for all students.

Criterion 8: The Instructional Program Promotes Learning in the General Curriculum

Finally, teachers who consider the opportunities for students within their instructional program and the quality in which best instructional practices are evident may be better prepared to determine the degree of alignment between their instruction and the content standards. Reflection on what the enacted curriculum, or the taught curriculum, entails for students within the classroom allows for a greater understanding for what is and is not occurring for students. This information can lead teachers and IEP teams to discuss a rationale for why this pattern may be occurring and if that rationale makes sense for the student. In addition, a reflection on pedagogical (e.g., systematic instruction including data-based decisions and prompting approaches) and program practices (e.g., peer supports including inclusive practices and self-determination opportunities) provides teachers and IEP teams with greater information on which to base decisions about the educational needs and corresponding instructional plans for the student.

Summary

The eight criteria outlined from the LAL serve to identify considerations for practitioners regarding the alignment of instruction and assessment to content standards. These criteria are presented in Table 4.2 as a list of questions for educational planning teams. Criterion 8 serves as a springboard into additional considerations within instruction related to pedagogical strategies and planning to promote best practice for this population of students.

CURRICULUM ALIGNMENT INSTRUCTIONAL STRATEGIES

Once practitioners are familiar with the questions to ask of their instructional and assessment practices, it is important to put in place a plan to design and implement aligned instruction. Browder, Spooner, et al. (2006) and Clayton, Burdge, Denham, Kleinert, and Kearns (2006) have described steps to instruction that include reviewing standards, targeting outcomes, planning instructional adaptations, and incorporating the IEP. Teachers may ask several questions when developing this instruction such as

* How do I ensure my instruction retains the academic standard?

* Am I providing differentiated instruction across the grades for my students?

* Can all my students show what they have learned without the presence of confounding influences on their performance?

The following section describes several approaches teachers should consider when developing instruction that aligns with content standards.

Universal Design for Learning

The beginning point in aligning instruction for students with significant cognitive disabilities is collaboration to make instruction accessible and aligned for all students. Universal Design for Learning (UDL) is an approach for removing barriers and making learning accessible for all students (Center for Applied Special Technology [CAST], 2008).

Table 4.2. Links for Academic Learning criteria presented as questions for education teams to ask when considering alignment of assessment and instruction

Criterion	Question	Check
1	Have we targeted skills that are clearly academic?	General educator can identify the academic concept in the target skill.
2	Have we used the standards for this student's assigned grade in our planning?	Student's assigned grade is chronologically age appropriate (e.g., using middle school standards for a 13-year-old).
3	Do the target skills match the content of the original standards?	General educator identifies near link in extension to original.
4	Do the set of skills selected provide adequate range, balance, and depth of knowledge?	Multiple strands within the content are included in instructional efforts. Some skills require student to use deeper levels of knowledge (e.g., synthesis).
5	Is the content different from what is expected in earlier grades? Does it build knowledge needed to meet expectations in the next grade levels?	Although there may be some overlap, there clearly are also skills that are different for this grade level (e.g., new applications, deeper knowledge, new content) and that prepare the student for the grades ahead (e.g., by learning core concepts such as story maps or process of inquiry).
6	Are we expecting the student to demonstrate achievement of the standard?	Instruction will fade teacher assistance. Assessments allow student to show what he or she knows versus what the environment provides. (See Criteria 8 for what the environment provides.)
7	Have we minimized performance barriers?	Student will be able to use his or her current communication system, including level of fluency with symbols, to show learning. Accommodations for sensory and physical impairments are provided.
8	Have we provided high-quality instruction in the general curriculum?	The student will receive effective instruction on the target standards with appropriate supports (e.g., assistive technology) and with opportunities for inclusion and self-determination.

Source: Flowers, Wakeman, Browder, and Karvonen (2007).

UDL consists of three components: multiple means of representation, multiple means of engagement, and multiple means of expression (CAST, 2008). Table 4.3 provides an overview of each of the UDL components and barriers and how to avoid these barriers for students with significant cognitive disabilities who may be most at risk for these barriers. First, a planning team can consider the component of representation, or how best to present materials to the students. The barriers to representation may include text, audio, and images. To address these barriers, teachers may use larger text (e.g., for students with visual impairments), highlighted materials (e.g., for students that need that additional cue to focus in on materials), adapted books (e.g., for students that may not be able to participate in a nonadapted book due to complexity, length), and light boxes (e.g., for students with low vision).

Teams can also consider the engagement component, or how to keep students engaged in the materials or overall lesson. The barriers to engagement may include material that is too challenging or brand new or material that is presented repeatedly. Some ideas to address such barriers include reinforcement procedures (e.g., token economy system) or schedules of reinforcement (e.g., change from a fixed schedule of reinforce-

Table 4.3. Universal Design for Learning at a glance

Component	What does it mean?	Barriers	How do I provide equal access?
Representation	The presentation of information that will provide equal access for all learners. Modifications can be made to classroom materials that would make them more accessible to students with disabilities (e.g., modified books, larger print, light box, highlight text).	Printed text Audio Images/graphic	Handouts, pictures, modified books, Boardmaker, PicSyms, larger print, digital text Audio with captions, earphones Digital images with verbal description
Engagement	To increase the opportunity and motivation to provide equal access in engagement for all learners. Modifications can be made to provide strategies that involve students with disabilities more in the learning process.	Support and challenge Novelty and familiarity Developmental and cultural interest Flexible curricular materials	Flexible options and supportive scaffolding Repetition, familiarity, randomness Prompting, wait time, feedback Different concepts, broader representation of topics Opportunity to contribute to the curriculum by adding images, sounds, words, and texts
Expression	Alternatives of communication in order to provide equal access of expression for all learners. Modifications can be made for alternate methods of communication for students with limited or no speech (e.g., use of augmentative devices, computers).	Writing and spelling Speaking Drawing/illustrating	Computers, spell checkers Big Macs, Step-by-Step, pictures, augmentative and alternative communication Graphic programs

Source: Spooner, Baker, Harris, Ahlgrim-Delzell, and Browder (2007).

ment to a variable schedule of reinforcement), error correction procedures, prompting strategies (e.g., change from the use of constant time delay to the system of least prompts), and wait times between prompt levels (e.g., change from 3 seconds wait time to 5 seconds wait time).

The team should also consider expression, or the way for students to show what they know. The barriers to expression may include, but are not limited to, writing, speaking, or drawing. Students may be more successful with one form of expression versus another. Some of the changes that can be made may include picture support, object support, voice output devices, and so forth. Figure 4.2 provides an example format to help plan for each component of UDL during the development of a lesson. This figure also takes into

	Special education teacher	General education teacher	Paraprofessional(s)	Speech-language pathologist/ occupational therapist/other
Representation – adaptations in materials (e.g., adapt for sensory impairments)				
Engagement – how the student will participate in the activity				
Expression – how the student will demonstrate learning (e.g., use of assistive technology, alternative project)				

Figure 4.2. Universal Design for Learning planning worksheet.

consideration the person who is responsible for assisting with the changes in the lesson. For a further discussion of UDL as applied to students with significant cognitive disabilities, see Chapter 5.

Collaboration is an important part of planning instruction in English/language arts, math, and science. Special education educators tend to be experts in the delivery of instruction, including how to make instruction accessible for all learners. General educators typically are experts in the grade-level content. It is crucial that a partnership is created between special education and general educators to produce the best lesson for all students to not only ensure strong alignment of grade-specific content standards but also to address how all students will gain access to and respond to that content.

Work It Across

Although UDL helps planning teams determine how students will be engaged in instruction based on state standards, Work it Across is a way to extend standards to define expectations for student achievement. In this process, an educational planning team extends a state standard by first defining the grade-level expectation and then "working it across" examples for students at different symbolic levels (i.e., abstract, concrete, presymbolic). Browder, Spooner, et al. (2006) first outlined this process using the activities to address a standard for general education students and adapting them based on a student's symbolic communication level (described previously in the LAL Criterion 7). Browder, Wakeman, and Flowers (2009) have further detailed how to do this across grade levels. By using Work it Across, the teacher or planning team can define the goals for differentiated instruction.

Figure 4.3 provides a Work it Across example for a measurement standard: finding the perimeter of a geometric figure. The activity begins with the grade-level presentation

Mathematics Work It Across

Standard: Mathematics Standard 7.1: Generate strategies to determine the perimeters of geometric figures.
Essence of the standard: Find the perimeter of geometric figures.

Grade Level

7th Grade	On grade-level expectation (Not adapted)	Abstract symbolic	Concrete symbolic	Beginning symbol use
Student symbol use	Reads/writes at or near grade level	Reads sight words/picture cues. May count and recognize numbers	Recognizes pictures. May also use range of objects symbolically	Uses objects or gestures to communicate; relies on immediate context to use object symbolically (e.g. shows cup for drink)
Presentation of content: Adapted for symbol level	Geometric figures. Formula for perimeter	Line-drawn figures or raised figures. Visual Jig of steps for solving equations	Line-drawn figures with points at each angle, raised figures, or figures with Velcro edges. Visual Jig including pictures of steps for solving equations	Line-drawn figures with points at each angle, raised figures, or figures with Velcro edges. Visual Jig including pictures and/or objects of steps for solving equations

(continued)

Figure 4.3. Work it Across example for a math standard.

Figure 4.3. *(continued)*

Mathematics Work It Across

Standard: _Mathematics Standard 7.1: Generate strategies to determine the perimeters of geometric figures._

Essence of the standard: _Find the perimeter of geometric figures._

Grade Level			
Teaching activity	Provide figures. Ask students to generate strategies to solve equations. Work as groups. Have students evaluate strategies to determine effectiveness. Practice solving problems using formula and different figures.	Present visual of the steps for solving problem using written words and picture supports. Review steps for each problem. (teacher model and student guided practice). Provide figure with the length given OR figure without length given and students use rulers or other measurement instrument to find lengths. Model for students how to measure sides and record information. Model for students how to use formula and solve problems using different sizes of same figure. (Students can use a calculator or manipulatives if needed to solve problems.) Provide instruction on one type of figure at a time. Master first figure (e.g., square) before moving to next figure (e.g., rectangle).	Present visual of the steps for solving problem using picture supports. Review steps for each problem. (teacher model and student guided practice). Provide figure with the length given and string/yarn to measure sides. Model for students how to measure sides and cut string. Model for students how to compare outcome to given choices (provide two to three string options with corresponding written lengths with one matching correct length). Provide instruction on one type of figure at a time. Master first figure (e.g., square) before moving to next figure (e.g., rectangle).	Present visual of the steps for solving problem using picture or object supports. Review steps for each problem (teacher model and student guided practice). Provide figure with the length given and string/yarn to measure sides. Model for students how to measure sides and cut string. Model for students how to compare outcome to given choices (provide two string options with one matching correct length and one very dissimilar length). Provide instruction on one figure (e.g., square).
How student shows mastery	Uses formula to correctly solve perimeter problems.	Solves perimeter problems correctly for given figure by writing answer or selecting correct symbolic answer from given choices.	Matches string to correct perimeter string option.	Matches string to correct perimeter string option (using clear discriminating choice).

materials, activity, and expected student outcome that can be assessed. Based on the students' communication levels (i.e., abstract symbolic, concrete symbolic, presymbolic), the activities are adapted moving across the table to allow for student learning of the skill and an appropriate assessment of that learning. Although this instructional activity is written to address one standard, the example demonstrates how one activity can incorporate several different skills. The instructional activities based on student communication needs vary to help students build or reinforce the recognition of numeric symbols, use a jig to organize the information, use a calculator to enter the problem once generated, identify different geometric figures, and make comparisons of given choices. The concept of angles is implicitly introduced in this activity as well. As students are asked to determine the perimeter of a figure, the figure can be adapted to provide meaning for the students. For example, two- and three-dimensional figures could be used. Students could determine what size table cloth is needed for their dining room table, what size curtains are needed for their window, or how much fencing they will need to keep their dog in their backyard. By utilizing the Work It Across process, practitioners are more likely to provide instruction linked to a given standard that is differentiated to allow all students to participate in meaningful ways.

Systematic Instruction

Planning for a universally designed lesson and defining how to extend the standard are important forms of instructional support for students with severe disabilities to participate not only in general education content but also in inclusive contexts. Students with significant cognitive disabilities may also need systematic instruction to master general curriculum content. Systematic instruction is based on principles of applied behavior analysis and includes defining responses, using specific prompting strategies with fading, and shaping responding (Collins, 2007). Most research on academic learning for students with significant cognitive disabilities has used systematic instruction (Browder, Spooner, Ahlgrim-Delzell, Wakeman, & Harris, 2008; Browder, Wakeman, Spooner, Ahlgrim-Delzell, & Algozzine, 2006; Courtade, Spooner, & Browder, 2007). To apply systematic instruction to instruction that aligns with state content standards, educators would begin by defining an observable, measurable response or set of responses that link to demonstrating achievement of the content. For example, if the standard relates to solving linear equations, the target set of responses might be the steps required to use assistive technology in finding the solution. Or, if the standard relates to the plot of a story, the target response might be to sequence a set of pictures to retell the story. For students to learn these responses, the teacher may use some method of prompting.

Collins (2007) described a few methods of stimulus prompting (e.g., stimulus shaping, stimulus fading), in which cues are added to the materials, and response prompting, in which the teacher guides the student to make the response. Although there are several decades of research on applying these methods to daily living skills, there also are numerous examples of how systematic instruction can be used to teach academic content. In their review, Browder, Ahlgrim-Delzell, Spooner, Mims, and Baker (2009) found that time delay can be used to promote literacy learning. In time delay, the teacher provides an immediate prompt with the first trials of learning. For example, the teacher shows an array of four flash cards with vocabulary words and says, "Find 'constitution'" while pointing to the correct response. The student then imitates finding the correct answer and receives feedback (e.g., praise for correct response). Over trials the teacher delays pointing to the correct answer by a few seconds so that the student can anticipate the correct answer. Through this method, the student may learn to recognize the word with few or no errors. The student also receives instruction to learn the meaning of the word. For example, the student might pair the word with a picture or use it to complete a sentence. Most textbooks on severe disabilities have one or more chapters on systematic instruction (e.g., Collins; Snell & Brown, 2006; Westling & Fox, 2004).

Embedded Instruction

Systematic instruction takes an investment of teaching time, which is a challenge and major concern of teachers in the field of special education who are trying to find the time to "get it all in." Finding the balance among academic content, functional daily living skills, social and leisure skills, and vocational skills in educational planning is not easy. In addition, students with significant cognitive disabilities typically need additional practice, opportunities for generalization, and re-teaching to master a skill or behavior. In contrast, general education often progresses at a rapid pace with new content introduced daily. Finally, educators of students with significant cognitive disabilities often have the unique challenge of supporting learning in multiple content areas across multiple grade levels for students with diverse individualized needs. Special educators need strategies that work within this challenging new context.

One strategy that may maximize instructional time is to embed systematic instruction into other activities. This strategy allows the instructional trials to be presented during the natural course of the lesson rather than being presented at a separate time in massed trials (Jameson, McDonnell, Johnson, Reisen, & Polychronis, 2007). Experts have recommended embedding functional life skills in naturally occurring routines (Snell & Brown, 2006; Westling & Fox, 2004). For example, teaching students to communicate requests during mealtimes can be effective and efficient. Jameson et al. illustrated how systematic instruction (specifically time delay) of academic content can be embedded in general education lessons. One benefit to this method of instruction is that it allows for students with significant cognitive disabilities to remain in the general education lesson while getting the individualized priority skill instruction needed to show mastery of the content across multiple domains.

For example, Taylor is a seventh-grade student with a significant cognitive disability who attends an inclusive seventh-grade Earth science class. The students in this class are learning about the Earth's processes. A priority skill that may be identified for Taylor during this unit of instruction is to identify the picture symbol for the core and crust on a model of the Earth. During the course of the next week, other students in the class will learn several objectives surrounding the process of the layers of the Earth (grade-level achievement); however, Taylor will continue to work on mastery of the priority skill of identifying the core and crust (alternate achievement). Although Taylor will have the opportunity to participate in the full range of activities in the general education class, and may also show learning of this additional content, she will receive daily systematic instruction on identifying the core and crust. At some relevant point in the lesson, the teacher or a peer will give Taylor several opportunities to point to the core and crust using prompting with feedback as needed.

Although Taylor has priority skills related to specific content, she may also work on IEP objectives that promote learning across content areas. For example, she may apply her mathematical problem solving when the class focuses on mass and density. Or, she may use pictures to summarize the main idea after hearing a passage of science text read aloud. This context also allows for embedding social and daily living skills, such as communicating with a cooperative learning group or together cleaning a work area after an experiment. Taylor, however, should not be relegated only to the talking and cleaning tasks, but should also have full access to the science content learning. See Chapter 10 for a further example of the use of embedded instruction in teaching grade-linked science content to a high school student with significant cognitive disabilities.

Inquiry-Based Lessons

Inquiry is the process students can use to gain knowledge about the natural world by investigating, posing questions, and problem solving (National Research Council, 1996). Inquiry is especially important within science education as students learn to conduct experiments, make predictions, ask and answer questions, use appropriate tools and techniques to gather data, and develop understanding about the process and content of study (National Research Council, 2000). Sometimes educators make the mistake of teaching science as a "foreign language" with an overemphasis on the acquisition of science vocabulary. Students also need the more critical skills of problem solving and process development. Inquiry-based lessons can offer a greater balance in science education while allowing access for all students when universally designed. The National Research Council's *National Science Education Standards* (1996) has defined essential features of the inquiry process and the various ways in which all students may participate (see Table 8.1 in Chapter 8).

Although inquiry may be open ended, students with significant cognitive disabilities may need a guided inquiry approach to master processes such as posing questions. In fact, they probably will need systematic instruction to acquire these specific responses. Systematic prompting and feedback can be used to teach students specific responses, such as how to 1) engage with materials, 2) identify the materials to be used, 3) make a prediction about what will happen, and 4) identify appropriate tools to use to conduct an experiment. For example, Courtade, Browder, Spooner, and DiBiase (in press) trained teachers to follow a specific task analysis to engage middle school students with developmental disabilities in inquiry-based science lessons. A task analysis is a sequence of responses the learner performs to complete an activity. The use of inquiry-based instruction in science is further discussed in Chapter 8.

Although inquiry is a priority within science education, mathematics also lends itself to the use of critical thinking and problem solving. Math has many daily applications, such as buying an item at the grocery store, balancing a checkbook, measuring the dimensions of a room for a new piece of furniture, or determining how many stamps are needed to send holiday cards to family members. When students are simply taught computation (e.g., through use of a calculator), they may not apply these skills when these real-life activities arise. Instead, students can learn to ask questions, find answers, and develop greater content knowledge.

Figure 4.4 is an example of a task analysis that is used to teach a math lesson on medians. (A blank form is included in the appendix at the end of book.) To make the lesson meaningful, the teacher uses a story about a familiar theme (for these students, the Girls Club is familiar; Trela, Browder, Jimenez, & Courtade, 2007). In repetitions of the lesson, new stories are used to promote generalization of the math concept. To use an inquiry-based approach, the teacher applies use of a KWHL chart to ask four questions of the students: what do we Know? (K), what do we Want to know? (W), How do we find out? (H), and what did we Learn? (L). In a simple computation approach, students would use a technique to find the number in the middle. In this inquiry-based problem-solving

Mathematics Story-Based Lesson

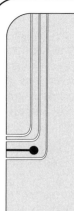

Math Strand: <u>Data analysis</u>
Skill (objective): <u>When provided with a set of numbers, the student will identify the median.</u>
Manipulatives: <u>Counting blocks</u>
Graphic organizer: <u>Bar graph</u>

What the teacher will do	Materials to present	What the student will do	Examples of student responses
Introduce the problem: "What does it mean to be in the middle?"	Anticipatory set: Use cubes to introduce median by discussing concept of middle.	Identify middle.	Put cube in middle, but switch when teacher touches middle cube.
Read a story problem about medians (e.g., Girls Club has girls who are many different ages. Sally is 9, Kara is 10, Cheri is 7, Jessica is 8, and Linda is 11. The girls talk about who is the oldest and who is the youngest. But one girl says, "I'm in the middle!" Whose age is in the middle? What is the median?) Repeat lesson with different stories with varied numbers and themes for generalization.	Median story	Follow the story by scanning the words and pointing to each number as it is read.	Text point using finger or assistive technology to highlight text.
Begin KWHL chart to guide inquiry. Ask, "What do we know?"	KWHL chart: Write numbers under "K" for "known" as student identifies; have cubes with numbers	Identify each known number (age) using cubes.	Move cubes; point to cubes.

92

Continue with KWHL chart. Ask, "What do we want to know?"	KWHL chart: Write problem statement under "W"	Identify problem statement (What is the median?).	Highlight text in story, say the statement, say "middle number".
Continue with KWHL chart. Ask, "How do we find out?" Let students experiment with cubes to see if they can identify how (as modeled at start of lesson).	KWHL chart: Write how under "H"	Identify median by putting numbers in order and finding one in the middle.	Move cubes, use augmentative and alternative communication device to tell peer which cube goes next.
Continue with KWHL chart. Ask, "What did we learn?" Have students identify number in middle.	KWHL chart: Write what was learned under "L"	Identify the median.	State the number, hold up the cube, point to number.
Check for understanding. Ask, "Which girl has the age in the middle?"	Some students might need girls' names/pictures on the cubes with their ages	Identify girl with median age.	State girl's name, point to her name in text, find her picture from several in an array.

Figure 4.4. Example of a story-based math lesson using an inquiry approach.

approach, students go through the KWHL process and try to discover for themselves how to find the answer using manipulatives.

Story-Based Lessons and Other Read Alouds

An additional strategy when planning curriculum alignment is the use of story-based lessons, also known as shared stories or read alouds. Providing a story as the basis for a lesson can be helpful to increase engagement, comprehension, and communication (Ezell & Justice, 2005; Justice, 2002). Story-based lessons are a strategy involving a shared book/ story/or text experience that includes the students and the teacher. Traditionally the material is read aloud, and throughout the story students are given opportunities to interact with the text (e.g., making predictions, asking questions, answering questions, identifying target vocabulary, anticipating repeated themes throughout, text pointing, turning pages).

Story-Based Lessons in English/Language Arts

Although read alouds have a long-standing history of use with young children, research has shown story-based lessons to be successful in increasing early literacy skills for older students with significant cognitive disabilities (Browder et al., 2007). When adapting this approach for older students, it is important to use literature that is age and grade appropriate. For example, Browder et al. used text summaries of middle school novels that were made into modified chapter books. While participating in reading these chapters aloud, students also worked on phonemic awareness, phonics, vocabulary development, and comprehension.

One important difference between a story-based lesson and simply reading text aloud is that the student is actively engaged in the reading of the story in a story-based lesson. To promote this engagement, researchers have used a systematic instruction procedure called *task analytic instruction* (Browder et al., 2007; Browder, Mims, Spooner, Ahlgrim-Delzell, & Lee, 2008). First, a task analysis is created of the sequence of responses the student will make while reading the book (e.g., identify title, turn pages, read a specific story line [maybe with augmentative and alternative communication (AAC)], point to key vocabulary). Next the teacher creates any adaptations needed for the books to be used. For example, Mims, Browder, Baker, Lee, and Spooner (2009) attached objects to the pages of the text for students with visual impairments to follow the story. The students then used these same objects to answer comprehension questions. When reading the story aloud, the teacher used systematic prompting and feedback to promote student responding (e.g., guided student to select correct object to answer comprehension question).

Figure 4.5 provides an example of a task analysis from Wakeman et al. (2008) that can be used to teach story-based lessons. This task analysis could be adapted in several ways. The task analysis could be adapted for use with expository text (e.g., a science lesson) by introducing science vocabulary. The repeated story line might be repetition of the major concept or "big idea" of the lesson. Additional state standards could be embedded in the lesson. For example, the student might be asked to find the current chapter's topic in the table of contents. This would promote a research skill. The student might create a story sequence summary using pictures and word captions (writing and comprehension). The task analysis could also be adapted for students with different disabilities. For example, students with physical challenges might use AAC or eye gaze to select a

Middle School Story-Based Lesson

Book or literature to be used: <u>Island of the Blue Dolphins by Scott O'Dell</u>

What the teacher will do	Materials to present	What the student will do	Examples of student responses
Get students' attention.	Anticipatory set: Allow student to interact with materials (e.g., sand to represent Island)	Interact with materials.	Eye gaze, touch, label
Review vocabulary and new symbols.	Flashcards with words/picture symbol/object of key vocabulary word(s) (e.g., Karana, girl, island, brother, Ramo, Father)	Say/repeat/point to word or symbol.	Touch, say, use voice output communication aid (VOCA)
Ask for prediction (e.g., "what do you think this chapter is going to be about?").	Picture walk through the book. Provide prediction options with words/pictures/objects. Present plausible, semi-plausible, and not plausible options.	Indicate response to prediction.	Verbally answer questions or look at, touch, or reach toward response board with options
Read the title (e.g., "The title of this chapter is called What will happen to Karana's Island? Can you find the title?").	Text point to title of book while labeling it as a "title."	Point to title.	Eye gaze word for word, point

State Standard to embed and where to embed (what step of the task-analysis): *Produce an artifact (e.g., short report) that can be a synthesis of what others said on a topic or issue, a formal presentation that may or may not include PowerPoint, a poster display, or webquest.* –Step 13.

(continued)

Figure 4.5. Sample middle school story-based lesson task analysis. (From Wakeman, S., Mraz, M., Rickelman, B., Browder, D., Mims, P., & Knight, V. [2008]. *A conceptual model for mathematics for students with significant cognitive disabilities* [Brochure]. Retrieved from http://education.uncc.edu/access/PDFlinks/Conceptual%20Model%20Brochures/ELA%20conceptual%20model%20brochure%202009.doc; reprinted by permission.)

Figure 4.5. *(continued)*

Middle School Story-Based Lesson

Book or literature to be used: <u>Island of the Blue Dolphins by Scott O'Dell</u>

What the teacher will do	Materials to present	What the student will do	Examples of student responses
Read the author (e.g., "The author of this story is named Scott O'Dell. Can you find the author?").	Text point to author of book while labeling it as "author."	Point to author.	Eye gaze word for word, point for word, point
Ask, "How do we get started?"	Present the book upside down and backward.	Open book to first page.	Reorient book and open, activate VOCA to request open
Read text and provide students chance to turn page.	Text point along with reading and pauses at end of page (e.g., "How do we keep the story going?").	Turn pages when appropriate.	Turn page, look at picture/symbol, or activate VOCA
Pause for repeated story line.	Read up to repeated story line or half of repeated story line (e.g., "What will happen to.....").	Anticipate repeated story line or finish repeated story line.	Say story line or activate switch

Pause for finding the vocabulary on page.	"Can you find one of our vocabulary words on the page?"	Point to picture/word/object that teacher says.	Look at, touch, say word
Give students an opportunity to point to chosen line on "text point page" in own book.	Wait for student to respond (e.g., "Can you help me read this line on the page?").	Text point to chosen line in book.	Point, eye gaze
Provide phonetic awareness opportunity (e.g., blending, segmenting a specific word).	Provide an opportunity for student to participate in phonetic awareness opportunity (e.g., "Can you tap out the syllables to the word island?").	Independently demonstrate blending, segmenting, or identifying a target sound.	Tap out, activate VOCA, speak
Ask comprehension question/review prediction (e.g., "What was this chapter about?").	Provide comprehension options with words/pictures/objects. Present plausible, semi-plausible, and not plausible options (can be same as prediction question).	Answer question.	Eye gaze, touch, speak, reach toward, activate VOCA, use augmentative and alternative communication

comprehension response. The student might use assistive technology to turn pages or read a repeated story line. Finally, additional state language arts standards might be embedded. For example, students may check off a list of story elements as they occur in the read aloud.

Story-Based Lessons in Math

Figure 4.4 provided a task analysis for a math lesson on median. One of the features of this lesson is the use of a story problem. Story-based lessons can also be used to address skills in math including data analysis, algebra, measurement, geometry, and numbers and operations. In the example in Figure 4.4, the focus of the task analysis is on the mathematics problem rather than on conventions of reading. In contrast, some teachers might have students generalize some of these skills (e.g., point to the title, predict what the story will be about).

One important strategy to consider when writing a math story is to use themes that are familiar to students' daily lives. The teacher may also use the names of the students in the class to add interest. To promote generalization of the math concept, additional stories are created with the same type of problem but different themes and math facts. The names of the characters should be changed, but it is important to keep the nature of the problem similar to that of the first story. A separate story should be developed for students to practice the skill. This story should include the same context but a different type of problem and facts. Again, the names of characters, facts, and nature of the problem should be changed. Finally, it is important to promote generalization of the skill to a new set of stories. It may be helpful for some students to support key words with picture symbols to help with further understanding (e.g., Writing with Symbols, Boardmaker), and when using unfamiliar vocabulary to the student, provide definitions within the text. In addition, a sequence of facts should be placed in the story (e.g., "The movie started at 3:00. The movie ended at 5:00"). Finally, the story should always end with a problem statement.

Story-Based Lessons in Science

Stories can also be used to help in science instruction. Figure 4.6 is an example of a "wonder" story that can be used to promote understanding of a certain topic in science. This particular example can be used along with a grade-aligned lesson on boiling and freezing points and may be used to introduce an experiment that takes students through the inquiry process. The story always ends with the question, "What would you like to learn?" This question is designed to pique the interest of students about a topic and is a helpful way to bridge into an inquiry lesson.

QUALITIES OF A WELL-DESIGNED STANDARDS-BASED INDIVIDUALIZED EDUCATION PROGRAM

IEP teams are charged to develop an IEP that addresses the needs of students including academic skills, daily life skills, behavioral skills, vocational skills, therapy goals, and others. Although the skills represented in an IEP are only part of the curriculum in which a student will be taught, the IEP provides the direction to teams related to considerations

Have you ever wondered?

Do you like to cook in the kitchen? Sometimes when we cook, we need

to freeze different food items. Sometimes when we cook, we need to

boil different food items. When we freeze things they get very cold.

When we boil things they get very hot. It is important to be safe in the

kitchen so we don't get hurt. What would you like to learn?

Figure 4.6. Science wonder story.

for instructional planning, including pivotal skills (i.e., those skills needed to create access), special supports and accommodations, and communication needs.

A well-designed IEP will have several qualities, as shown in Figure 4.7. At the core is the use of the grade-level content standards. These should be well reflected in the content and pivotal skills just described.

Objectives that Link to State Standards

A standards-based IEP will typically have three types of objectives: 1) priorities for content, 2) pivotal skills that promote learning across content areas, and 3) nonacademic priorities. This latter set, nonacademic priorities (e.g., social behaviors, life skills), may not align to state standards but can promote learning in the general curriculum.

Content Objectives

Some objectives in the IEP will relate to learning priorities within the grade-level content areas. To plan these priorities, the educational team needs to consider what will be the most important ideas of each instructional unit for the year. These IEP objectives will be those used for the focus of the embedded systematic instruction described previously. They may include skills such as reading 10 key vocabulary words related to a certain topic, identifying the author's point of view, or solving an algebraic equation. The alignment criteria presented previously in the chapter and shown in Table 4.2 are useful in selecting

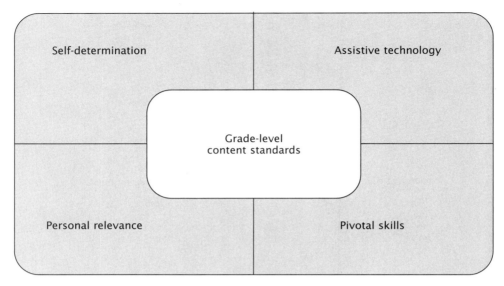

Figure 4.7. Components needed in designing a standards-based individualized education program.

these objectives. For example, the skills should be clearly academic, grade-level refer-enced, and match the content of some specific standards.

Objectives for Pivotal Skills

In addition to specific content objectives, it will be helpful to target some objectives that are pivotal to learning across content areas. Students need pivotal skills in communicat-ing understanding of text. For example, a student may have the objective of selecting a picture from a choice of four to answer the question, "What is the story about?" This skill would be applicable in all content areas and could be used for listening or reading com-prehension. Students also need to know how to pose questions. An example of an IEP objective might be that the student will ask a "why" question after having a lesson or story introduced (e.g., "Why is the story called 'The Day of the Dog'?" or "Why do I have dif-ferent color eyes than my sister?"). Students may also benefit in pivotal skills such as sequencing events (e.g., stories, science experiment), using a KWHL chart (e.g., for a story, math lesson, science experiment), and using Venn Diagrams to make comparisons.

Other Objectives

In contrast to objectives that solely link to state standards, the IEP will also have some long-standing values including promoting self-determination, the use of assistive technol-ogy, and personal relevance.

Self-Determination

Another quality of a well-designed standards-based IEP is that it will promote self-determination. The general curriculum activities can become the context for students to develop their self-determination skills. Students may learn choice making, decision making, problem solving, goal setting, self-management/evaluation, and self-awareness. Although these skills do not focus on content learning, they may be invaluable tools for students to use in learning the content. For example, Agran, Blanchard, and Wehmeyer (2000) taught teachers of students with severe disabilities to teach their students to set and reach transition-related goals. By providing students with specific questions to guide them toward planning and setting personal goals, active participation was achieved in setting lifelong goals. Students were asked what they wanted to learn, what they knew about it at the time, what needed to change for them to learn what they didn't know, and what they could do to make it happen. Although many of the students were not able to articulate direct responses for each question, the questions served as a focus point for planning. This questioning sequence enabled students to participate in the instructional process as well. Students were successful in achieving their goals. A well-developed IEP will have some objectives related to acquiring skills in self-determined learning. See Chapter 10 for a further discussion of the importance of self-determination in instruction and assessment for students with significant cognitive disabilities.

Assistive Technology

Another important tool for students to learn in the general curriculum is assistive technology. Students may also need IEP objectives on mastering the use of these devices. The use of assistive technology comes in the form of low-tech or high-tech devices. Clayton et al. (2006) suggested that IEP teams ask themselves questions in developing a standards-based IEP, such as "What does the student need to communicate?" Often students with significant disabilities need assistive devices to communicate their needs, wants, preferences, and knowledge. By planning for objectives within the IEP regarding the use of assistive technology, students may learn to respond using a variety of assistive technology supports across multiple content areas. In addition, assistive technology provides an appropriate method for students to use in assessment. Once students are able to make an accurate response (Downing, 2001), students are able to demonstrate what they know and are able to do on alternate assessments.

Personal Relevance

Finally, a well-designed IEP will have some objectives related to the student's individual needs that may or may not link to state academic content standards. A standards-based IEP can have objectives on daily living, social, vocational, and other skills that do not necessarily link directly to academic content standards. In contrast, sometimes these skills can be taught during the context of general education activities. For example, a student may practice washing his or her hands after a science experiment or greet peers in a math class. IEPs are also made personally relevant when they honor student preferences in selecting objectives.

For example, it may be a student's choice to learn about the ocean's current due to a love of boating and the student's geographical location of living on a large river. Students also can learn to write their own IEP objectives, which can intersect with writing instruction (Konrad & Test, 2007), and direct their own IEP meetings (Martin et al., 2006).

CONCLUSION

The purpose of this chapter was to provide educators with a foundation for reflecting on the alignment of their instructional and assessment practices and decisions with state standards, as well as to provide pedagogical strategies to promote that alignment. The criteria of the LAL model (Flowers et al., 2007) can help educational teams target instruction that is academic. Although this may be a given for other populations of students (e.g., students without disabilities or students who participate in an alternate assessment based on modified achievement standards), it is an important consideration for students with significant cognitive disabilities. In addition to this priority of teaching "real" academics, well-aligned instruction and assessment will lead students to acquire skills that clearly link to content standards for their grade level and prepare them for the next grade level. Through receiving high-quality instruction on the general curriculum, including fading teacher assistance, students should be able to demonstrate learning. The content learned will differ in scope and depth from that expected for the grade level but still clearly link to the content and have personal relevance.

This chapter has also described the use of instructional strategies to promote academic learning. Smith (1999) found that when teachers of students with significant cognitive disabilities operated using a deficit-oriented approach to instruction (e.g., accepting the student's nonparticipation, not calling on the student, having someone else complete the student's work), students became invisible and isolated within the classroom and, therefore, were undereducated. Effective instruction engages students in learning and gives them the opportunity to show the full extent of their learning. Meaningful instruction in academic standards may also broaden opportunities for students included in content and classrooms in ways they may never have been before. Through the use of UDL practices (e.g., addressing student communication systems in all instructional efforts) and explicit opportunities to embed unmastered prerequisite skills within other instructional efforts (e.g., using story-based lessons to address literacy skills and other content domains), teachers reduce the barriers for students to demonstrate their understanding.

REFERENCES

Agran, M., Blanchard, C., & Wehmeyer, M.L. (2000). Promoting transition goals and self-determination through student-directed learning: The Self-Determined Learning Model of Instruction. *Education and Training in Mental Retardation and Developmental Disabilities, 35,* 351–364.

Baker, J., & Harris, A. (2006). *UDL at a glance* (Reading, Writing, Math, and Science Grant H324M030003). Charlotte: University of North Carolina at Charlotte.

Browder, D., Ahlgrim-Delzell, L., Courtade-Little, G., & Snell, M. (2006). General curriculum access. In M. Snell & F. Brown (Eds.), *Instruction of students with severe disabilities* (6th ed., pp. 489–525). Upper Saddle River, NJ: Merrill Prentice Hall.

Browder, D., Alhgrim-Delzell, L., Spooner, F., Mims, P., & Baker, J. (2009). Using time delay to teach picture and word recognition to identify evidence-based practice for students with severe developmental disabilities. *Exceptional Children, 75,* 343–364.

Browder, D., Flowers, C., Ahlgrim-Delzell, L., Karvonen, M., Spooner, F., & Algozzine, R. (2004). The alignment of alternate assessment content with academic and functional curricula. *Journal of Special Education, 37,* 211–223.

Browder, D.M., Flowers, C., & Wakeman, S.Y. (2008). Facilitating participation in assessments and the general curriculum: Level of symbolic communication classification for students with significant cognitive disabilities. *Assessment in Education: Principles, Policy, & Practice, 15*, 137–151.

Browder, D.M., Mims, P.J., Spooner, F., Ahlgrim-Delzell, L., & Lee, A. (2008). Teaching elementary students with multiple disabilities to participate in shared stories. *Research and Practice for Persons with Severe Disabilities, 33*, 1–10.

Browder, D.M., Spooner, F., Ahlgrim-Delzell, L., Wakeman, S.Y., & Harris, A. (2008). A meta-analysis on teaching mathematics to students with significant cognitive disabilities. *Exceptional Children, 74*, 407–432.

Browder, D.M., Spooner, F., Wakeman, S., Trela, K., & Baker, J.N. (2006). Aligning instruction with academic content standards: Finding the link. *Research and Practice for Persons with Severe Disabilities, 31*(4), 309–321.

Browder, D.M., Trela, K.C., & Jimenez, B.A. (2007). Increasing participation of middle school students with significant cognitive disabilities. *Focus on Autism and Other Developmental Disabilities, 22*, 206–219.

Browder, D.M., Wakeman, S.Y., & Flowers, C. (2009). Alignment of alternate assessments with state standards. In W.D. Shafer & R.W. Lissitz (Eds.), *Alternate assessments based on alternate achievement standards: Policy, practice, and potential* (pp. 61–91). Baltimore: Paul H. Brookes Publishing Co.

Browder, D.M., Wakeman, S.Y., Flowers, C., Rickelman, R., Pugalee, D., & Karvonen, M. (2007). Creating access to the general curriculum with links to grade level content for students with significant cognitive disabilities: An explication of the concept. *Journal of Special Education, 41*, 2–16.

Browder, D.M., Wakeman, S.Y., Spooner, F., Ahlgrim-Delzell, L., & Algozzine, B. (2006). Research on reading instruction for individuals with significant cognitive disabilities. *Exceptional Children, 72*, 392–408.

Center for Applied Special Technology. (2008). *Universal design for learning guidelines* (Version 1.0). Wakefield, MA: Author.

Clayton, J., Burdge, M., Denham, A., Kleinert, H.L., & Kearns, J. (2006). A four-step process for accessing the general curriculum for students with significant cognitive disabilities. *TEACHING Exceptional Children, 38*(5), 20–27.

Collins, B. (2007). Identifying functional and age-appropriate skills: A curriculum for students with moderate and severe disabilities. *Moderate and severe disabilities: A foundational approach*. Upper Saddle River, NJ: Pearson/Merrill/Prentice Hall.

Courtade, G.R., Browder, D.M., Spooner, F., & DiBiase, W. (in press). Training teachers to use an inquiry-based task analysis to teach science to students with moderate and severe disabilities. *Education and Training in Developmental Disabilities*.

Courtade, G.R., Spooner, F., & Browder, D.M. (2007). A review of studies with students with significant cognitive disabilities that link to science standards. *Research and Practice in Severe Disabilities, 32*, 43–49.

Downing, J. (2001). Meeting the communication needs of students with severe and multiple disabilities in general education classrooms. *Exceptionality, 9*(3), 147–156.

Ezell, H.K., & Justice, L.M. (2005). *Shared storybook reading: Building young children's language and emergent literacy skills*. Baltimore: Paul H. Brookes Publishing Co.

Flowers, C., Wakeman, S., Browder, D., & Karvonen, M. (2007). *Links for academic learning: An alignment protocol for alternate assessments based on alternate achievement standards* [Manual]. Retrieved from http://education.uncc.edu/access/PDFlinks/AlignmentManualVersion8%203%20 FINAL%20110707.pdf

Individuals with Disabilities Education Act Amendments (IDEA) of 1997, PL 105-17, 20 U.S.C. §§ 1400 *et seq.*

Individuals with Disabilities Education Improvement Act (IDEA) of 2004, PL 108-446, 20 U.S.C. §§ 1400 *et seq.*

Jameson, J.M., McDonnell, J., Johnson, J.W., Reisen, T., & Polychronis, S. (2007). A comparison of one-to-one embedded instruction in the general education classroom and one-to-one massed practice instruction in the special education classroom. *Education and Treatment of Children, 30,* 23–44.

Jimenez, B. (2008). *Science story* (Project MASTERY: Math And Science Teaching that Promotes Clear Expectations and Real Learning across Years for Students with Significant Cognitive Disabilities, USDOE Grant R324A080014). Charlotte: University of North Carolina at Charlotte.

Jimenez, B. (2009). *Universal design for learning planning chart* (Project MASTERY: Math And Science Teaching that Promotes Clear Expectations and Real learning across Years for Students with Significant Cognitive Disabilities, USDOE Grant R324A080014). Charlotte: University of North Carolina at Charlotte.

Jimenez, B., Spooner, F., Browder, D., DiBiase, W., & Knight, V. (2008). *A conceptual model for science for students with significant cognitive disabilities* [Brochure]. Retrieved February 22, 2010, from http://education.uncc.edu/access/PDFlinks/Conceptual%20Model%20Brochures/Science%20conceptual%20model%20brochure%202009.doc

Justice, L.M. (2002). Word exposure conditions and preschoolers' novel word learning during shared storybook reading. *Reading Psychology, 23,* 87–106.

Konrad, M., & Test, D.W. (2007). Effects of GO 4 IT...NOW! strategy instruction on paragraph writing and goal articulation of middle school students with disabilities. *Remedial and Special Education, 28,* 277–291.

Martin, J.E., Van Dycke, J.L., Christensen, W.R., Greene, B.A., Gardner, J.E., & Lovett, D.L. (2006). Increasing student participation in their transition IEP meetings: Establishing the self-directed IEP as an evidence-based practice. *Exceptional Children, 72*(3), 299–316.

Marzano, R.J., & Kendall, J.S. (2007). *The new taxonomy of educational objectives* (2nd ed.). Thousand Oaks, CA: Corwin Press.

Massachusetts Department of Education. (n.d.). *MCAS alternate assessment.* Retrieved January 11, 2006, from http://www.doe.mass.edu/mcas/alt/resources.html

Michigan Department of Education. (n.d.). *Standard setting summary reports.* Retrieved May 6, 2008, from http://www.michigan.gov/mde/0,1607,7-140-22709_28463-202414--,00.html

Mims, P., Browder, D., Baker, J., Lee, A., & Spooner, F., (2009). Increasing participation and comprehension of students with significant cognitive disabilities and visual impairments during shared stories. *Education and Training in Developmental Disabilities, 44,* 409–420.

National Research Council. (1996). *National science education standards.* Washington, DC: National Academies Press.

National Research Council. (2000). *Inquiry and the national science education standards: A guide for teaching and learning.* Washington, DC: National Academies Press.

No Child Left Behind Act of 2001, PL 107-110, 115 Stat. 1425, 20 U.S.C. §§ 6301 *et seq.*

O'Dell, S. (1987). *Island of the blue dolphins.* New York: Dell Yearling.

Salend, S. (2008). Determining appropriate testing accommodations. *TEACHING Exceptional Children, 40*(4), 14–22.

Smith, R.M. (1999). Academic engagement of students with significant cognitive disabilities and educators' perceptions of competence. *Professional Educator, 22,* 17–31.

Snell, M.E. & Brown, F. (2006). Designing and implementing instructional programs. In M. Snell & F. Brown (Eds.), *Instruction of students with severe disabilities* (6th ed., p. 111–169). Upper Saddle River, NJ: Merrill/Prentice-Hall.

South Dakota Department of Education. (n.d.) *Extended content.* Retrieved March 18, 2006, from http://doe.sd.gov/contentstandards/extendedstandards/index.asp

Spooner, F., Baker, J.N., Harris, A.A., Ahlgrim-Delzell, A., & Browder, D.M. (2007). Effects of training in Universal Design for Learning on lesson plan development. *Remedial and Special Education, 28,* 108–116.

Texas Department of Education. (n.d.). *Texas assessment of knowledge and skills (TAKS-Alt) resources.* Retrieved April 4, 2009, from http://www.tea.state.tx.us/index3.aspx?id=3638&menu_id=793#standards

Tileston, D.W. (2004). *What every teacher should know about special learners*. Thousand Oaks, CA: Corwin Press.

Trela, K., Browder, D., Jimenez, B., & Courtade, G. (2007). *Math story* (Reading, Writing, Math, and Science Grant H324M030003). Charlotte: University of North Carolina at Charlotte.

Trela, K., Browder, D., Pugalee, D., Spooner, F., & Knight, V. (2008). *A conceptual model for mathematics for students with significant cognitive disabilities* [Brochure]. Retrieved February 22, 2010, from http://education.uncc.edu/access/PDFlinks/Conceptual%20Model%20Brochures/Math%20conceptual%20model%20brochure%202009.doc

U.S. Department of Education. (2005). *Alternate achievement standards for students with the most significant cognitive disabilities*. Washington, DC: Author. Retrieved July 11, 2008, from http://www.ed.gov/policy/elsec/guid/altguidance.doc

Wakeman, S., Mraz, M., Rickelman, B., Browder, D., Mims, P., & Knight, V. (2008). *A conceptual model for mathematics for students with significant cognitive disabilitie* [Brochure]. Retrieved February 22, 2010, from http://education.uncc.edu/access/PDFlinks/Conceptual%20Model%20Brochures/ELA%20conceptual%20model%20brochure%202009.doc

Westling, D.L., & Fox, L. (2004). *Teaching students with severe disabilities* (3rd ed.). Upper Saddle River, NJ: Merrill.

Wyss, J.D. (1990). *Swiss Family Robinson*. New York: Baronet books.

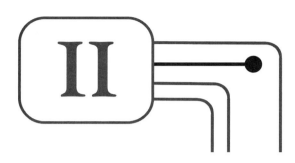

Teaching and Assessing Students with Significant Cognitive Disabilities

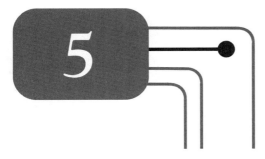

Ensuring Access

A Four-Step Process for Accessing the General Curriculum

Michael Burdge, Jean Clayton, Anne Denham, and Karin K. Hess

The social inclusion movement of the 1990s initiated sweeping changes in the educational landscape for students with significant cognitive disabilities. As students were included more frequently in academic classes, many teachers began to observe something unexpected. Although students with significant cognitive disabilities were included primarily to learn specific objectives from their own individualized education programs (IEPs; e.g., communication, socialization, motor skills), they were learning bits and pieces of the academic curriculum—things that they weren't expected to learn and certainly things that no one was clearly targeting for instruction. Teachers began to ask themselves, "Am I expecting too little? What would happen if I actually tried to teach that?"

As happens so often, practice preceded research, and teachers (these authors included) began to try many different strategies focused on teaching students with disabilities the grade-specific general curriculum content and to analyze which strategies were working and which were not. What we discovered was that it wasn't any one strategy that worked or didn't work—not surprisingly, differences in the students and differences in the general education environment precluded any conclusions about that—but a common process started to emerge. In observing and listening to teachers and then thinking about what made these classrooms and programs successful in terms of student learning of grade-specific, general curriculum, the sections and sequence of the Four-Step Process (Clayton, Burdge, Denham, Kleinert, & Kearns, 2006) emerged.

Within this process, all teachers (both general and special education) involved with the student began by *identifying the standard(s) the instructional unit addresses* (Step 1). Typically, it was the general educator who had the most information about this step, but the questions of the special educator about the meaning of the standard often deepened the understanding of both teachers about that standard. Thinking about what teachers wanted students to know and be able to do as the result of a particular curricular unit was the next step—*defining the outcome(s) of instruction from the instructional unit* (Step 2). The general education teacher had in mind the student outcomes (i.e., specific demonstrations of student performance toward the standard), and the special education teacher, with general education input, prioritized some of those outcomes for the student with significant cognitive disabilities. The next step of the process was *identifying the instructional activities to be used within the unit* (Step 3). In most cases, the general educator already had developed lesson plans for a unit of study, so this step consisted of the two teachers discussing each instructional activity in terms of delivery, format, products, and expectations. The special educator identified barriers to learning and developed accommodations and supports to allow for meaningful participation focused on academic learning for the student with disabilities. The special education teacher completed the process by *targeting specific IEP objectives and foundational skills that can be addressed during the unit* (Step 4). The special educator used this step to find appropriate opportunities to work on other student goals (most of which did not directly connect to the general curriculum, such as self-care, communication, social/behavior) that were important for the particular student without taking that student away from the academic activities of the general education classroom. The Four-Step Process really resulted from what successful teaching teams were already doing when they thought about instruction for all students. The general education curriculum is the curriculum for all students, regardless of the presence of disability or not.

The Four-Step Process has been developed to make student-by-student accommodations based on individual learning needs within general education instructional units of study. Because the unique needs of students with significant cognitive disabilities are the focus of this process, it would be inappropriate to use the Four-Step Process to plan for a *group* of learners with disabilities. Thus, the process could not be used to develop group outcomes, group participation expectations, or group supports. Certainly, more than one student with disabilities could be considered during instructional planning, but each student should have his or her individualized outcomes, participation expectations, and unique supports.

The Four-Step Process can be used for several purposes. Consider first how it can be used *as a framework for shifting the curricular emphasis from a strictly traditional special education, functional curriculum (i.e., domain oriented) and/or social inclusion to a more academic, grade-specific content curriculum*. Both the No Child Left Behind (NCLB) Act of 2001 (PL 107-110) and the Individuals with Disabilities Education Improvement Act (IDEA) of 2004 (PL 108-446) address the need for access for all students to the general curriculum. NCLB states that students with disabilities must be assessed on the same academic content standards as students without disabilities (including the provision of alternate assessment based on alternate achievement standards [AA-AAS] for students with significant cognitive disabilities who cannot take the general assessment even with accommodations and modifications). The requirements for those alternate academic achievement standards are that they "1) are aligned with the state's academic content standards; 2) *promote access to the general curriculum*" (italics added); and "3) reflect professional judgment of the highest achievement standards possible" (NCLB, 2001, § 1111 [D] [ii]). IDEA reiterates the assessment/general curriculum requirements of NCLB and adds that IEPs must include measureable annual goals that "meet the child's needs that result from the child's disability to enable the child *to be involved in and make progress in the general education curriculum*" (italics added; § 614[d][1][A][i][I][aa]).

The Four-Step Process can also be used *as a systematic means of increasing meaningful access to the general curriculum for students with disabilities*. In addition to the difficulties many special education teachers have in embracing the curricular shift as posited by NCLB and IDEA, they also labor with how to actually provide meaningful access to the general curriculum and focus learning on the grade-specific content. In one survey (Agran, Alper, & Wehmeyer, 2002), teachers of students with significant cognitive disabilities expressed that they not only felt that academic content was *not* important for this group of students but also that their instructional focus, even when these learners were participating in general education, was not on accessing the general curriculum. In addition, the same study found few schools had policies or procedures in place that promoted access.

Finally, the Four-Step Process can be used *as a structured plan for addressing IEP goals within the context of instruction on the grade-level academic content*. The Four-Step Process is designed to help educators find opportunities to work on IEP goals and benchmarks that either may not explicitly relate to the grade-specific academic content (e.g., communication, gross and fine motor skills, self-care, behavioral/social skills) or that *do* relate to academic content but not at the chronological grade level in which the student is enrolled (e.g., foundational skills within and across content areas and functional academics; Giangreco, Cloninger, & Iverson, 1998; Grisham-Brown & Kearns, 2001). Foundational skills are those skills that form the base or foundation of future, more complex learning in a content area. For example, visual discrimination and decoding are foundational skills for reading, and counting and basic computation are foundational skills for math. In our work, we have found that special education teachers often report that they perceive teaching foundational and life skills to be incompatible with access to the general curriculum and instruction on grade-level content. Yet students clearly need to learn life and foundational skills (see also Chapter 10), so it is critical that they be addressed, optimally through naturally occurring routines at times of the day when the skills are actually needed.

Effective use of the Four-Step Process is dependent on several underlying assumptions about the practices, processes, and skills of teachers, educational teams, and programs. The first assumption, that *collaboration between general and special educators is present and ongoing*, is critical for the effective utilization of the Four-Step Process. Within each step, the unique skills and experiences of both general and special educators are essential. In the initial stages of learning to use the Four-Step Process, the roles of the general and special education teachers are clearly delineated according to their respective expertise sets. Generally, once collaboration has become typical practice and teachers have internalized the Four-Step Process, overlapping of the roles significantly increases. As both general and special education teachers continue to learn, however, collaboration remains necessary for ongoing instructional improvement. Moreover, continuing collaboration is highly dependent on administrative and other sources of support. Schools may implement many effective collaborative models by creatively examining their own school culture to develop a process that works expressly for them (Conzemius & O'Neill, 2001).

A second assumption, that *educators have a working knowledge of their state and grade-level content standards*, is especially significant considering the emphasis of NCLB on proficiency on grade-specific, academic content standards. Understanding what students should know and be able to do (the function of standards) is the starting point of instructional planning (Wiggins & McTighe, 2005). The collaborative discussions of the standards ensure that the most essential elements or understandings of the skills and concepts are actively and explicitly planned within instruction. At a minimum, this planning requires the identification of pertinent student outcomes, as well as the classroom activities designed to facilitate student achievement of those outcomes. To this end, it is important not only that general and special education teachers have ongoing discussions regarding the standards but also that special education teachers be included in all standards-oriented, professional development activities. In our own work with thousands of special education teachers across a variety of states, we have found that teachers of students with significant cognitive disabilities often are not included in standards-based professional development, perhaps because of the mistaken belief that such professional development is not a priority given the needs of the students they serve.

A third assumption, that *educators are knowledgeable about and skilled in instructional unit design geared toward student achievement on those standards, including research-based instructional practices in general and special education,* addresses the implementation of a standards-based curriculum. A strong curriculum based on explicit standards can only be realized if teachers have the time and skills to practically enact it in classrooms (Brandt, 1993). In order to make standards-based instruction accessible and meaningful for the diversity of students within any classroom, general education teachers should be experts in designing unit lesson plans that incorporate the principles of Universal Design for Learning (UDL; Rose & Meyer, 2002; Rose, Meyer, & Hitchcock, 2005), differentiated instruction (Tomlinson, 2001), and other research-based instructional practices that positively affect student performance (Marzano, Pickering, & Pollock, 2001). Special educators must have skills in how to use and customize those general education teaching strategies and activities based on individual student needs (Denham, 2004; J.S. Zabala, personal communication, 2002), including providing appropriate supports.

When UDL principles are used in conjunction with unit design, the needs of all learners are addressed. This strategy reduces the need to make accommodations for the variance of learners in a typical classroom setting, thus avoiding the inefficiencies and challenges of retrofitting planned activities. UDL is a framework that when applied reduces the inadvertent development of barriers when curricula are designed to meet the needs of a broad "middle group" of learners. This focus on that middle group excludes learners with different abilities and learning styles, and thus limits learning opportunities for many students. UDL is guided by three main principles targeting *all* learners: 1) multiple means of *representation,* 2) multiple means of *action* and *expression,* and 3) multiple means of *engagement.* When educators follow UDL principles, these principles "serve as a basis for building in the options and the flexibility that are necessary to maximize learning opportunities for all students" (Center for Applied Special Technology [CAST], 2008). This is not to say that individual supports are no longer necessary. Zabala (2006) discussed how UDL focuses on introducing flexibility and options to reduce barriers within curricula, whereas assistive technology looks at specific barriers that individual students may face in different environments. Although students with significant cognitive disabilities *will* require additional supports, including the use of assistive technology, and/or systematic prompting procedures and direct instruction (Snell & Brown, 2005) to supplement the general curriculum strategies, the use of UDL *can* reduce the need for special modifications and highly individualized teaching strategies.

Although many general education strategies clearly meet the NCLB requirement of "scientifically based research and effective practices," there are questions as to whether special education strategies designed to address the needs of students with significant disabilities have been sufficiently researched *in the context of a standards-based curriculum* (Browder, Wakeman, Spooner, Ahlgrim-Delzell, & Algozzine, 2006; Council for Exceptional Children, 2006; Snell, 2007). Although there is clear documentation for a range of evidence-based strategies for teaching students with significant cognitive disabilities, there is not yet a strong research base to guide the *application* of these practices to a standards-based curriculum.

A fourth assumption, that *educators are knowledgeable about and skilled in effective and appropriate assessment (including formative and large-scale assessments)*, addresses how teachers know if and to what degree students are learning. Inherent within effective instruction is the use of formative assessment "to improve real-time teaching and learning" (Chappuis & Chappuis, 2008). Effective instruction involves more than end-of-unit summative assessments; rather, it makes use of multiple opportunities during instruction to make sure students are really "getting it" (Wiggins & McTighe, 2005). The Four-Step Process gives educators the opportunity to actively plan for and to assess the effectiveness of instruction and to make decisions about what to do next to facilitate increased learning. The Four-Step Process also is a means to improve instruction with a goal of improving student achievement on the grade-specific standards.

It is important to note that the Four-Step Process is not an assessment in itself. Use of the process, however, can yield information, including data and student products that are types of evidence required within a number of states' alternate assessments as part of their large-scale assessments (Quenemoen, 2008). Observations during instruction can yield useful data for completing checklists/rating scales and provide examples of student work to support those formats. Student work completed within the context of the Four-Step Process can also contribute to the contents of a "body of work" or portfolio assessment format. Moreover, some state AA-AAS systems are evolving into a hybrid format, combining checklists/rating scales with portfolios. Each of these large-scale assessment formats provide opportunities for the use of student work and progress data derived from the Four-Step Process, thereby making a direct connection between assessment and daily instruction.

A fifth assumption, that *educational teams and programs embrace inclusion as a school-wide philosophy*, is a critical one, supported by the last 30 years of research (IDEA, § 601, [B][c][5][A]). It is important to provide access to both the *formal* curriculum (i.e., content area knowledge and performance expectations) and the *informal* curriculum (i.e., everything else in the school milieu, from taking part in a pep rally and participating in a small-group project to following the line in the cafeteria and taking a break in the student lounge; Wehmeyer, Sands, Knowlton, & Kozleski, 2002).

Although there is a long history of purposefully including students with significant cognitive disabilities in the informal curriculum, it has only been within the past 10 years that educators have made the formal academic curriculum an area of focus. Sands, Kozleski, and French (2000) noted that the formal curriculum includes several major components—a plan for courses and classes within a school, the subject matter taught within those courses and classes, the materials used in teaching the subject matter, and planned activities for delivering the subject matter. Informal curriculum opportunities aside, without inclusion in general education classes, students with disabilities typically receive a less rigorous academic program, including less coverage and depth of subject matter and instructional activities in the absence of typically developing peers (Katz & Mirenda, 2002).

With the focus at the time of this writing on increased learning in the general curriculum (specifically higher achievement of all students), it is important to remember the findings of studies that have examined the effect of inclusion on achievement for students with and without disabilities (e.g., Cole, Waldron, & Majd, 2004; Fishbaugh & Gum,

1994; Hollowood, Salisbury, Rainforth, & Palumbaro, 1995; Hunt, Staub, Alwell, & Goetz, 1994; Jenkins et al., 1992; Sharpe, York, & Knight, 1994). Collectively, these studies have found enhanced academic achievement for both populations of students. Given the positive effect of inclusion on student performance in both the formal and informal curriculum and the right of all students to be full participants in their school communities, it is essential to consider the Four-Step Process in the context of inclusive education. To do otherwise makes it much more difficult to fulfill the other assumptions of the model.

THE FOUR-STEP PROCESS: INSTRUCTIONAL EXAMPLES

To clarify how practitioners might use this process, this section provides an extended example of a student with significant cognitive disabilities taken from a middle school language arts class. The roles of the general and special educators are explained throughout the process.

Step 1: Identify the Standard(s)
the Instructional Unit Addresses

The first step in planning an instructional unit is to identify the appropriate content standard and the related grade-level expectations that are the focus of instruction. Understanding how K–12 content standards, specific grade-level expectations, curriculum (units of study), and instruction (lessons) are linked helps all members of the instructional team make intentional connections between the broader content standard(s) and the lessons within each unit of study. Although planning most instructional activities begins with identifying one specific content standard, it is possible to address multiple standards or even multiple subject areas within a series of lessons designed for a particular topic of study. For example, a life science unit that requires students to collect and record data about the growth of plants and then share their findings in an oral report could address a mathematics standard (data representation) and a language arts standard (oral communication), in addition to the specified science inquiry grade-level expectation (conducting an investigation by collecting data to answer a question).

Most state content standards are written to encompass broad concepts and skills for K–12 learning. These standards can provide a framework for a progression of specific grade-level expectations and ensure greater continuity within the curriculum to be developed across the grades. It is important to not only know what content the broader standard embodies but also what specific *related* skills and concepts are described in the grade-level expectations before developing units of study.

The case study presented throughout the remainder of this chapter follows Mrs. Carter, a middle school language arts teacher, and Mr. Blackstone, a special education teacher, as they plan how to provide access to an instructional unit in the general education classroom for Julianne, a student with significant cognitive disabilities.

————● *Mrs. Carter is planning to provide genre studies in language arts throughout the school year. Seventh-grade genre studies could, for example, include exploring historical fiction, mythology, short stories, poetry, mysteries, and drama. Different schools and different teams will make different decisions about how to teach and assess these expectations during the school year. Mrs. Carter has decided that this particular unit will focus only on reading, analyzing, and writing mysteries.*

First Mrs. Carter needs to identify the content standard(s). *She, along with the instructional team, has developed this unit of study to address the following two state content standards in reading and writing:*

- *Reading Standard 2: Students read a wide range of literature from many periods in many genres to build an understanding of the many dimensions (e.g., philosophical, ethical, aesthetic) of human experience.*

- *Writing Standard 5: Students employ a wide range of strategies as they write and use different writing process elements appropriately to communicate with different audiences for a variety of purposes.*

Next she selects the appropriate grade-level expectations for the unit of study. *The content standards are still too broad to have meaning for unit development and daily lesson planning; therefore, Mrs. Carter has selected a small number of appropriate grade-level expectations for her seventh-grade class in this particular genre study unit. Specifically, in this unit students will*

- *Identify, explain, analyze, and apply literary elements and techniques that are characteristic of specific literary genres (e.g., historical fiction, mythology, short stories, poetry, mysteries, drama)*

- *Employ a wide range of strategies (e.g., writing process, story map, timeline, outline, text structure frame) to develop literary texts for a variety of purposes and audiences*

In this first step, the instructional team has established a clear link from the broader content standard(s) to a few prioritized grade-level expectation(s) and then to a specific unit of study. Maintaining clear links between the broader standards and the specific unit of study allows for focused instruction without eliminating important content along the way. In this case, the breadth of genre options was narrowed to focus on the mystery genre; however, the unit will go into greater depth with this genre than it would if multiple genres had been included. In Mrs. Carter's class, there will be other units during seventh-grade year that address other genres and other reading and writing grade-level expectations.

Once the broad content standard and the specific grade-level expectations have been identified, it is next important to determine what each grade-level expectation is all about, that is, what are the underlying concepts and skills that the standard and expectations define? Determining these underlying concepts and skills is essential for all students and is particularly helpful in planning for meaningful access to the curriculum for students with severe disabilities. Kleinert and Thurlow (2001) have called this the "critical function" of the standard, which has also been defined as its "essence" (Wiener, 2005) or the "unifying thread that underlies the learning across grades" (Hess, 2008). Wiggins and McTighe used the term "enduring understanding" and stated that this "represents a big idea having enduring value beyond the classroom" (1998, pp. 10–11). Measuring progress is only possible when these binding threads are clearly evident in the planned learning progression (Duschl, Schweingruber, & Shouse, 2007; Hess, 2008; Wiggins & McTighe, 1998).

————● *So what is the essence or enduring understanding(s) for the grade-level expectations selected for the unit of study on mysteries that Mrs. Carter is planning? It is good to think about why this concept or skill is important to learn and how knowing this will allow for building deeper and broader understanding over time. Mrs. Carter has decided that the following enduring understandings for reading and writing articulate something common to all genres that will be studied this year and beyond, as well as the specific skills and concepts that students will focus on in the unit on mysteries:*

- *Reading: Understanding the literary elements (e.g., setting, plot, characterization) and literary devices (e.g., description, imagery, foreshadowing, dialogue) for specific genres helps the reader make meaning of the text.*

- *Writing: Understanding that there are strategies to use in developing literary texts helps the writer use one or more of these strategies for the writer's purpose and audience.*

For Julianne and her classmates, who will be learning about the genre of mysteries, the enduring understandings will focus instructional activities on the ways that mysteries employ literary elements and techniques for specific purposes, such as building suspense and sustaining intrigue as the plot unfolds. Well-articulated, enduring understandings can be used to frame essential questions for planning and organizing learning activities in the unit of study. Essential questions are generally described as open-ended questions that lead to inquiry about a topic and are engaging for students. Often teachers begin with a few essential questions and invite students to add their own for inquiry. Figure 5.1 shows how the reading and writing enduring understandings that Mrs. Carter developed might be turned into essential questions for the unit of study on mysteries.

The elements and techniques of the mystery genre may seem difficult at first to understand as important for all students to learn; however, if one thinks about the importance of storytelling, understanding cause and effect, and problem solving in American culture, it is easy to see that these underlying ideas *are* important for all students,

Enduring understandings	Essential questions for the unit of study
Reading *Understanding the literary elements and devices used in mysteries helps the reader make meaning of the text.*	What makes a "good" mystery? How is a mystery like solving a problem? How are mysteries different from and similar to other genres? Are the setting, plot, and characters in mysteries different from those found in other texts? How can we find out? What techniques do authors use when writing mysteries to build suspense, to create interest, or to develop intriguing images of characters or settings?
Writing *Understanding the strategies used in mystery writing helps the writer to develop more engaging story lines.*	As writers of our own mysteries, what techniques can we use when writing mysteries? Can we find some good models or examples from which to learn? In planning our own stories, what do we want to accomplish and who is our audience?

Figure 5.1. Sample enduring understandings with related essential questions for unit planning. (From Hess, K. [2009]. *Applying big ideas [enduring understandings] to unit planning and assessment development.* Retrieved from http://www.nciea.org; adapted by permission.)

especially as an avenue for enjoyment and leisure. Storytelling, understanding cause and effect, and problem solving will be taught in many different ways across K–12 content areas. Having students work within the general curriculum, both within and across school years, on a variety of standards affords a wide range of opportunities to learn and to generalize the key concepts and skills that truly have enduring value. Figure 5.2 illustrates the relationship among the broad academic standard, the specific grade-level content standard, and the essence of the standard, as it applies to all students.

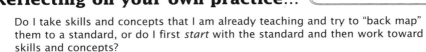

BOX 5.1

Reflecting on your own practice...

- Do I take skills and concepts that I am already teaching and try to "back map" them to a standard, or do I first *start* with the standard and then work toward skills and concepts?
- Do I teach discrete skills and facts, or do I connect them to the enduring understandings and the big ideas?

Step 2: Define the Outcome(s) of Instruction from the Instructional Unit

As a part of assisting students toward the achievement of a standard or standards through the instruction of a specific unit of study, teachers need to think about what they want all students to be able to do to demonstrate their understanding of the content (e.g., "How can my students show me what they have learned?"). The teacher should begin by enumerating end-of-unit outcomes that let him or her know just what it is that students should have learned as a result of the instruction. These outcomes are specific, provide smaller steps toward achieving the standard(s), and require observable student performances.

———● *Mrs. Carter identified the following outcomes for all students:*

1. *Using texts discussed in class, students will be able to compare and explain the literary elements and techniques of the specific genre of mysteries.*

2. *Students will be able to select a text and analyze the literary elements of mysteries by using text-specific details.*

3. *Using a wide range of strategies (e.g., writing process, story map, timeline, outline, text structure frame), students will be able to write a mystery text (of acceptable length), applying a variety of literary elements and techniques common to mystery writing.*

In planning for a student with significant cognitive disabilities, it is also important to clearly have in mind the expected outcomes that will allow the student to demonstrate what he or she knows. Based on what educators know about students with significant cognitive disabilities, they are not expected to achieve the same quantity and depth of understanding that students without disabilities will demonstrate. (But hopefully someday this will be proven wrong!) So, beginning with the outcomes identified for all students (remember that the outcomes for all students have been purposefully selected to demonstrate achievement of the content standards being addressed in the unit of study), an

Four-Step Process to Accessing Grade-Level Content Standards and Curriculum

Unit of Study: _Who-Dun-It?_

1. IDENTIFY THE STANDARD(S) THE INSTRUCTIONAL UNIT ADDRESSES.

What is the state standard?	What is the grade-level standard? (e.g., benchmark, performance indicator)	What is the standard all about? (Critical function or big idea)
Reading Standard 2: Students read a wide range of literature from many periods in many genres to build an understanding of the many dimensions (e.g., philosophical, ethical, aesthetic) of human experience.	_Students will identify, explain, analyze, and apply literary elements and techniques that are characteristic of specific literary genres (e.g., historical fiction, mythology, short stories, poetry, mysteries, drama)._	_Understanding the literary elements (e.g., setting, plot, characterization) and literary devices (e.g., description, imagery, foreshadowing, dialogue) for specific genres helps the reader make meaning of the text._
Writing Standard 5: Students employ a wide range of strategies as they write and use different writing process elements appropriately to communicate with different audiences for a variety of purposes.	_Students will employ a wide range of strategies (e.g., writing process, story map, timeline, outline, text structure frame) to develop literary texts for a variety of purposes and audiences._	_Understanding that there are strategies to use in developing literary texts helps the writer use one or more of these strategies for the writer's purpose and audience._

Figure 5.2.   Four-step process to accessing grade-level content standards and curriculum: Step 1.

educational team might, at this point, consider prioritizing the outcomes for an individual student with significant cognitive disabilities. There are several ways an educational team might go about doing this. For example, the team might

- Reduce the breadth of an outcome

- Reduce the complexity of an outcome

- Specify the information in an outcome

- Reduce the number of outcomes

If the team chose to reduce the breadth of an outcome, the team would look at the quantity of knowledge students would be required to demonstrate and choose a smaller amount that would be challenging yet realistic for the student to achieve by the end of the unit.

———● *Mrs. Carter and Mr. Blackstone decide to reduce the breadth of the first outcome. Julianne is thus expected to do a portion of that first outcome. Specifically, she will compare the literary elements of mysteries. The team has limited how Julianne needs to demonstrate knowledge of mysteries.*

If the team chose to reduce the complexity of an outcome, the team would look at the "cognitive demand" of the outcome and modify it to a less demanding level (but still a challenging and realistic level). See Chapter 10 for additional discussion of this topic.

———● *For the second outcome, the team might reduce the cognitive demand level from complex reasoning (e.g., "explain, generalize, analyze, or connect ideas, using supporting evidence from the text") to recall of information (e.g., "locate or recall facts or details explicitly presented in text"; Hess, 2004). So in this scenario, Julianne would only need to identify details from the text that related to the literary elements.*

If the team chose to specify the information in an outcome, the team would be explicit in identifying the exact information the student would need to know.

———● *Mrs. Carter and Mr. Blackstone revisit the first outcome and decide that it might be better if Julianne were expected to compare two literary elements of two specific mini-mysteries. The team selected the two mini-mysteries they felt were the most interesting to Julianne. In this example, the team actually used two strategies for prioritizing outcomes: reducing breadth (compare vs. compare/contrast) and specifying information (specifying which two literary elements and two mysteries to focus on).*

If the team chose to reduce the number of outcomes, the team would simply drop one or more outcomes it felt was less essential for the student.

———● *Another option Mrs. Carter and Mr. Blackstone might choose is to consider the outcomes for all students and focus on only one or two of the outcomes. For example, the team could choose just the first and second outcomes as the instructional focus for Julianne.*

It is important to note that prioritizing the outcomes of an instructional unit for a student with disabilities is not meant in any way to limit that student's instruction or exclude the student from any instructional activities. Students with disabilities should be given access to all of the instruction and the opportunity to learn the outcomes as identified for all students, but the expectations for their performance would be focused on a set of individually prioritized outcomes. So, even though the team decided to prioritize the writing outcome for Julianne in the examples provided, the team will still include her in all of the instruction geared toward all outcomes, and the team will provide the necessary supports to make the instruction as accessible and meaningful as possible.

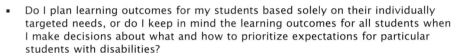

BOX 5.2

Reflecting on your own practice...

- Do I plan learning outcomes for my students based solely on their individually targeted needs, or do I keep in mind the learning outcomes for all students when I make decisions about what and how to prioritize expectations for particular students with disabilities?

As teachers develop the learning outcomes for specific units of study, they begin to think about how they will monitor student achievement toward those performances and, in turn, use that information to guide their instruction during the unit. They begin to think about formative assessment. Formative assessment differs dramatically from summative assessment in the frequency of collection and the use of the information (Chappuis & Chappuis, 2008).

Formative assessment is accomplished during the course of classroom instruction so that assessment could actually happen daily and as a result of any classroom activity that includes a student performance. Summative assessment occurs at the end of the instruction. Whereas summative assessment provides information on how well and to what level students have learned the content, formative assessment lets teachers know how well they are teaching and lets students know how well they are learning *while the classroom instruction is still occurring* (Garrison & Ehringhaus, 2007; Stiggins, 2005). Scherer (2008) stated that summative assessment answers the question, "Do you understand—yes or no?" and formative assessment answers the question, "What do you understand?" Well-planned and well-executed formative assessment activities can have dramatic effects on student achievement: "When implemented well, formative assessment can effectively double the speed of student learning" (Wiliam, 2008, p. 37).

Teachers conduct formative assessment by engaging students in a variety of activities (Brookhart, Moss, & Long, 2008; Garrison & Ehringhaus, 2007; Tuttle, 2008), and, not surprisingly, these activities parallel effective practices in special education. It seems that "good teaching is good teaching" regardless of the learner or the content. Formative assessment practices include strategies such as student goal setting, progress monitoring, and self-assessment (Brookhart et al., 2008; Garrison & Ehringhaus, 2007; Tuttle, 2008; Wehmeyer et al., 2002).

In order to involve students in their own goal setting, it is essential that they understand just what it is they need to learn. Teachers need to clearly communicate the expected learning outcomes so that students can establish their own learning goals related to those outcomes, determine how they will get there, and verify when they have "made it."

Mrs. Carter provides the general goal for all students (i.e., that they be able to iden-
tify, compare, and explain literary elements of specific genres of literature) but encour-
ages them to personalize the general goal to reflect their own interest(s) in the content.
Mr. Blackstone puts several more specific goals on Julianne's communication board
(e.g., "I want to know more about how authors put clues in mysteries"; "I want to
know why some mysteries tell you the ending and some don't"; "I want to know more
about how to look for evidence in mysteries") and lets her select a more personalized
goal from this list to monitor in addition to those goals targeted by her teachers. After
Julianne chooses her own learning goal, Mr. Blackstone will help her determine how to
best keep track of her progress.

Progress monitoring is most often accomplished by first conducting classroom observations of students' performances and the teacher's use of questioning strategies that give
some immediate insights into students' thinking and understanding. Second, the teacher
provides immediate corrective feedback regarding performance by explaining to students
exactly what they did that was either correct or incorrect and how peers can also effectively give one another corrective feedback. In addition, although it is important that
teachers monitor students' performance as a part of formative assessment, students can
and should monitor their own progress as well (Agran, 1997; Hughes et al., 2002). Having
students monitor their progress engages them and keeps them focused on that progress.

As part of her formative assessment strategies, which include in-class questions and
answers, review of students' work, and ongoing discussions with her students about their
progress and providing feedback, Mrs. Carter has her students monitor their own
progress on the learning goals specific to each unit of study in a variety of ways, includ-
ing both online and on a written chart. She periodically reviews their self-monitoring
and in-class work so that she knows where they are in acquiring the content knowledge
and skills she has identified and then adjusts her instruction as necessary. Mr. Blackstone
and Mrs. Carter confer with Julianne about her learning goals, and together they select
an online bar graphing program for Julianne because they think it will be easier for her
to see and understand her progress toward the learning outcomes they selected for her.
A teacher or a peer helps Julianne use her switch to provide input to the bar graph maker,
enabling her to chart her progress.

Having students assess their own learning is the natural continuation of goal setting
and progress monitoring and is a critical part of the formative assessment process.
Students who can self-assess (either independently or under the guidance of a teacher or
peer) are active participants in the learning process. Once goals are clear and performance
is objectively measured, students can be effective assessors of the quality of their learning.

Mrs. Carter uses rubrics to let students know what is clearly expected of them in
terms of learning specific content. Mr. Blackstone and Mrs. Carter adapt the classroom
rubrics for Julianne to better reflect the learning outcomes that have been uniquely
prioritized for her. Throughout the unit lessons, Julianne reviews her learning with
Mrs. Carter, Mr. Blackstone, or a peer, and they assist Julianne in deciding how she is
progressing. They sometimes model for Julianne what behavior she needs to perform in
order to progress to the next level. Mrs. Carter and Mr. Blackstone periodically review

the students' self-monitoring and in-class work so that they can assess individual stu-
dents in their acquisition of the learning outcomes and then adjust their instruction as
necessary.

It is important to reiterate that these and other formative assessment activities are assessments for student learning and occur throughout the teaching and learning process. They provide opportunities for teachers to modify instruction to ensure success at the end of a unit (summative assessment). Figure 5.3 summarizes the prioritized outcomes for Julianne in this unit.

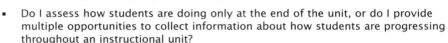

BOX 5.3

Reflecting on your own practice...

- Do I assess how students are doing only at the end of the unit, or do I provide multiple opportunities to collect information about how students are progressing throughout an instructional unit?
- Do I use the assessment information only for student grading, or do I use that information to make informed instructional decisions, such as
  1. Adjusting instructions or materials
  2. Adding more time or moving to the next activity
  3. Adding more practice
  4. Reviewing and changing the supports provided
- Do I involve students in setting goals, monitoring progress, and self-assessing?

In addition, teachers must look at the way the student is able to *interact* with the materials and demonstrate knowledge (the "how" of learning). Even when supports and scaffolds are built in from the start for all learners, there may still be specific barriers due to the complexity of a student's needs. The instructional activity needs to be closely analyzed to see if there are further barriers, such as amount of instruction provided at one time, the complexity of the steps required to complete the activity, time limitations, and so forth. It also is essential to consider whether the student has a means to communicate during instructional activities so that he or she can ask questions and demonstration of learning can occur. A close examination of possible barriers and action to reduce or remove those barriers are essential. This examination could be done as a part of Step 3, which is discussed in the following section.

Step 3: Identify the Instructional Activities to Be Used within the Unit

The purpose of this step is to take a closer look at the instructional planning process and to determine ways for a student with significant cognitive disabilities to fully participate in the instruction planned by the general education teacher. These instructional activities are the means by which the students will move toward the identified learning outcomes established in Step 2. Although it is tempting to segregate the student with disabilities and provide different instruction, it is important to start with and maintain the instructional activities planned by the general educator for all students for several reasons:

1. The general educator has the training and expertise in the requirements of the content standards.

2. DEFINE THE OUTCOME(S) OF INSTRUCTION FROM THE INSTRUCTIONAL UNIT.		
- What are the desired outcomes for all students in general education? - What evidence will document the students' understanding? - What is the best formative assessment format to gather that evidence?	Which outcomes will be prioritized for instruction and monitored for the target student with significant cognitive disabilities?	- What evidence will document the target student's understanding? - What is the best formative assessment format to gather that evidence?
1. Using texts discussed in class, students will be able to compare and explain the literary elements and techniques of the specific genre of mysteries. 2. Students will be able to select a text and analyze the literary elements of mysteries by using text-specific details. 3. Using a wide range of strategies (e.g., writing process, story map, timeline, outline, text structure frame), students will be able to write a mystery text (of acceptable length), applying a variety of literary elements and techniques common to mystery writing. *Formative assessment:* • Classroom observations • Student progress monitoring of personalized goals • Completed assessment rubric • Completed story maps	1. Julianne will compare two of the literary elements of two mini-mysteries. 2. Julianne will identify details from the text that relate to the literary elements.	• Julianne's bar graph showing progress on comparison of literary elements throughout the unit and across units • Julianne's completed assessment rubric • Julianne's completed story map

Figure 5.3. Four-step process to accessing grade-level content standards and curriculum: Step 2.

123

2. Common instructional activities facilitate inclusion, providing the opportunity to learn alongside same-age peers.

3. These common activities build communication and social skills.

4. These activities reduce the need for separate curricular materials.

The first task in Step 3 is to examine the intent of each instructional activity and each formative assessment measure to determine how to ensure access for the identified student. This involves identifying what all students are to learn from each of the instructional activities and what all students will be doing within the planned activities that result in the learning. The second task is to plan for student access by identifying any instructional, physical, or material barriers to learning that may exist within those activities so that they may be addressed in collaboration with the general education teacher and supports added as needed. The Four-Step Process form located in the appendix at the end of the book is a helpful tool to record the information used during these tasks. The following sections will describe the tasks involved in Step 3 more fully.

Focus of Student Learning

It is crucial to begin with the general education instructional plan to ensure the plan addresses the intended learning outcomes in Step 2 and the grade-level content standard(s) in Step 1. When planning instructional activities, it is important to focus on the term *instructional,* not just on the term *activity.* Wiggins and McTighe (2005) caution against any activity-oriented instruction that might be "hands-on without being minds-on" (p. 16); instructional activities must result in student *learning* rather than simply participating. In addition, student learning must connect back to the outcomes and the grade-level content standard(s) identified for the unit.

——• *Mrs. Carter is creating her unit lesson plans to address the reading standards of literary elements and techniques specific to genre and similarities and differences across genres, and to address the writing standard of developing literary texts for a variety of purposes. As she looks for lesson plan ideas, she decides that playing a "who-dun-it" type of game would highly engage students. However, as she begins to plan for formative assessments, she realizes that while engaging, the game would not result in learning the standards. Mrs. Carter then finds an activity in which the students would read short mysteries and attempt to solve the mystery. After solving the mystery, the students would complete a story map that would lead them to the standard of identifying and analyzing literary elements and technique, as well as comparing similarities and differences across genres. This activity is both engaging and instructional.*

Collaboration between the general education and special education teacher within Step 3 is essential. The general educator has specific content knowledge that keeps the focus on identified learning outcomes and student expectations high. The special educator, with expertise in how an individual student learns and what supports may be used to facilitate learning, might suggest different ways of presenting information at the beginning of each activity to address different learning styles and might suggest different ways the students might demonstrate learning. Depending on the level of the collaborative relationship, some teachers may develop activities together, whereas other teachers may limit their discussion to clarify activities and think about modifications. Regardless of the amount of collaboration, the key is to have the general education lesson plan serve as the foundation of instruction. There are cautions for both educators, given their specialized training areas. The content teacher should carefully follow UDL principles when planning instruction in order to provide the flexibility to address the needs of the widest variety of learners while maintaining the instructional focus. The special educator should ask for clarification of content when reducing content complexity for a student with significant needs to offset the risk of altering a focus or activity to such an extent that it no longer relates to the instructional outcome. It is the role of the content specialist to make further suggestions to ensure the integrity and rigor of the academic content.

———● *When Mrs. Carter and Mr. Blackstone meet to discuss the unit lesson plans, they talk about how to assist Julianne to best access the same instruction and learning as all students. While looking at the first unit activity, a brainstorming session on mysteries, the following dialogue occurs:*

Mr. Blackstone:	*What do you want students to learn from this activity?*
Mrs. Carter:	*I want them to think about the mysteries that they are familiar with and then to recognize that there are similar elements and techniques for mysteries as a genre, such as rising action, foreshadowing, imagery, and so forth.*
Mr. Blackstone:	*So, if I have Julianne activate a switch that has the prerecorded message THAT IS A MYSTERY BOOK, will that work?*
Mrs. Carter:	*That doesn't really address the elements and techniques that the content standards address. Is there a way that Julianne can at least work with some of the elements or techniques?*
Mr. Blackstone:	*Oh, maybe I can put four of the literary elements or techniques on her communication board so that she can use those terms during the brainstorming activity. I may need to pair the terms with a graphic that will help her use them correctly.*
Mrs. Carter:	*That keeps in line with the standards we are addressing.*

Mrs. Carter's and Mr. Blackstone's collaboration serves several purposes:

• Mr. Blackstone can better understand the intent of the standards, instructional activities, and the ways in which the material will be presented.

• Mrs. Carter can increase her understanding of how Julianne learns, how she communicates, and what interests her.

• Mrs. Carter and Mr. Blackstone can look at options to present the information, provide various means for the students to demonstrate learning, and find ways in which to engage the students in the learning process—all of which reflect the principles of UDL.

• Mrs. Carter and Mr. Blackstone can plan for appropriate supports so that Julianne can gain understanding of the concepts while participating in the instructional activities.

BOX 5.4

Reflecting on your own practice...

- Do I allow the student to participate in each activity without an expectation of academic learning (e.g., tracing the answers, coloring in a map, hand-over-hand prompting), or do I focus on what the student will learn?

- Do I expect the student to learn but through a completely separate activity from general education classmates with that learning not connected to the outcomes for all students (e.g., the general education students are working on geometric patterns to complete a paper quilt while the student with disabilities creates patterns using pattern blocks), or do I focus on what the student will learn within the same activity as the general education students (e.g., create the paper quilt with thicker, more durable paper)?

A Framework of Supports to Facilitate Student Learning

After carefully examining each instructional activity to determine if any additional changes will need to be made or additional supports added for the student with significant cognitive disabilities, each activity then needs to be carefully analyzed to isolate the factors that are interfering with the student moving as independently as possible toward the learning outcomes. One way to systematically approach this analysis is to use the primary principles of UDL to guide the analysis. We have adapted the primary approach and key questions advocated by CAST (2008) in formulating our points for consideration and our examples below. Specifically, with UDL, teachers should examine the following items.

1. How instructional content and materials are presented to the student (the "what" of learning). Does the student have a way to

- Perceive the information? Think about how information is presented or displayed. Does the sensory modality match the student's learning needs (vision, hearing, touch)? Is text presented in a form the student can use (e.g., digital text with a text reader, symbol-based text, summarized text)?

- Understand the language, symbols, charts, and graphics used? Think about how language and nonlinguistic information are used. Can the student understand the words and phrases used, such as content-specific terms, or does the material need to be accompanied by a summary or simplified language? Does text need to be supported by graphics, symbols, or concrete objects? Are key points illustrated, specific information highlighted, and relationships made clear?

- Comprehend the information? Think about the student's background and life experience. Activate prior knowledge, highlight critical features and big ideas, and provide correct and incorrect examples of the key concepts.

2. How the student is able to interact with the materials and demonstrate knowledge (the "how" of learning). Does the student have a way to

- Interact with the learning environment? Think about manipulating and navigating materials. For example, can the student turn a page (perhaps with the assistance of a page fluffer), use a keyboard (perhaps with a joy stick, or use an adapted keyboard and/or custom overlay), or make a selection (by pointing or eye gaze)?

- Communicate, problem-solve, and share knowledge? Think about receptive and expressive communication. Can the student communicate information (e.g., using augmentative and alternative communication) and demonstrate learning (e.g., provide an answer, draw a picture, make a selection, complete a graphic organizer, or use a model)?

- Set goals and monitor performance/progress? Think about how the student can assist with planning and managing information and resources. Can the student use guides and checklists, embedded prompts, or models of performance?

3. *What interests and engages the student in the learning process* (the "why" of learning). Does the student have a way to

- Make choices in content, materials, or challenge? Think about the student's personal preferences, interests, and values. How can the student be more involved (reduce distractions, sensory stimulation)?

- Sustain effort and persistence? Can the student maintain a goal? Think about varying levels of support and fostering collaboration and communication (e.g., flexible grouping, age-appropriate peer support, positive behavior supports).

- Self-regulate behavior? Think about appropriate behavior. How will the student manage frustration, maintain self-control, and self-reflect (e.g., schedules for overview of daily or weekly activities, mini-schedules for more detailed expectation within a class, prompts, self-reflection, occupational therapy, constructive feedback)?

Using these principles as guides, teachers can identify barriers within the classroom environment that hinder student access to the full instructional content. For Julianne, consider, in this order, *presentation, student interaction,* and *student engagement* with the instructional content and the materials for the planned unit. It is important to first analyze the *presentation* of instruction and materials (the "what" of learning). Barriers are often unintended consequences of sometimes rigid instructional methods and materials. The expectations of the unit instruction often require reading text, writing, and responding verbally, which often create barriers for students with significant cognitive disabilities. The tendency is to focus on the student's disability as the barrier to learning, whereas the barrier is actually in the activity itself. When the true barrier (e.g., printed text, level of text, amount of text) is identified, the teacher can look for ways to remove the barrier. This could include, but is not limited to, summarizing the text, pairing it with picture symbols, and providing a text reader. Consider how Julianne's teachers deal with her presentation barriers.

———● *While collaborating with Mr. Blackstone, Mrs. Carter explains her plans for having the students read mystery books. She notes that she will have the librarian pull some books that are of high interest and provide a wide variety of reading levels. This will reduce some barriers by having various reading levels. However, Julianne will need more than a reduced reading level book. Mrs. Carter plans to get digital versions of some of the books so that some students, including Julianne, can access the books using a text reader. One barrier still remains for Julianne, however, and that is the large amount of text. Mr. Blackstone plans to summarize the book Julianne chooses so that she can develop a clearer understanding of the content. This helps Julianne access the information presented—the "what" of learning.*

> **BOX 5.5**
> # Reflecting on your own practice...
> - Do I sometimes make assumptions regarding the student's capability to learn content (e.g., the work is too difficult, so the student needs a separate curriculum), or do I minimize barriers by looking at the "what" of learning and adding supports, accommodations, and/or modifications as needed?

Second, it is important to look at the way the student is able to *interact* with the materials and demonstrate knowledge (the "how" of learning).

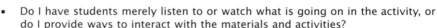

> *Mr. Blackstone is planning on providing digital options of some of the book choices. Julianne will then be able to access the text by listening; however, without the provision of assistive technology, she is unable to interact with the book independently. With the help of the assistive technology specialist, Mr. Blackstone can provide Julianne access to operate the text reader software by using a switch and scanning program. This allows Julianne to independently move to the next section, reread a section, or take a break as needed. She is then able to interact with the book rather than just listen.*
>
> *Mrs. Carter also plans on having students work in pairs to complete a story map. Julianne can work with a partner who completes the story map by asking Julianne multiple-choice questions and allowing Julianne to use eye gaze to answer. If Mr. Blackstone places possible answers on her communication board, then Julianne will also be able to independently answer questions. If she uses an adaptive keyboard with a customized overlay attached to the computer, she and her partner can both answer questions and fill in the story map. This allows Julianne the means to demonstrate her learning—the "how" of learning.*

> **BOX 5.6**
> # Reflecting on your own practice...
> - Do I have students merely listen to or watch what is going on in the activity, or do I provide ways to interact with the materials and activities?
> - Do I assume what my students know, or do I look at ways to allow students to demonstrate what they do know independently?
> - Do I provide supports that merely allow students to complete the activity, or do I provide supports that also assist students in learning the content?

Finally, in consideration of supports, it is important to analyze the activity to ensure that the student is interested and the teacher maintains the student's *engagement* (the "why" of learning). This last focus of analysis is concentrated on what will encourage students to sustain effort and regulate their own behavior within the activity. Although some classroom activities appear to be interesting to most students, a student with significant cognitive disability may appear disinterested and may even exhibit inappropriate behaviors. Offering choice, relevance, and authenticity (CAST, 2008) can facilitate interest. Having choices regarding with whom to work, in what order to complete an activity, or what materials to use, for example, may increase engagement. Helping the student make a connection to the instruction is also important. Consider how engagement is purposefully considered for Julianne.

————● *Mrs. Carter and Mr. Blackstone discuss ways to engage all students in the activities around mysteries. The activities of sharing mysteries that the students have read and trying to solve mini-mysteries should be engaging for the students. Mr. Blackstone suggests that they put the elements of a mystery on representative objects into a box and allow Julianne and classmates to pull out and use the box during class discussions and review time. This will further engage Julianne and support her—the "why" of learning.*

BOX 5.7

Reflecting on your own practice...

- Do I interpret student lack of engagement and disruptive behaviors as an indication that the activity is not appropriate for the student and remove the student from the class or the activity, or do I investigate other ways to engage the student, such as use of a schedule, positioning, reinforcement, and/or making a connection to prior knowledge?

Creating supports for individuals with significant cognitive disabilities is challenging. If barriers are not recognized, then learning is not accessible. The principles of UDL target areas that help educators systematically recognize, analyze, and reduce or remove barriers. The following questions are one way to follow up on the issue of accessibility for students with disabilities:

1. Within the context of what all students are learning (unit outcomes related to grade-level content standards), do the materials and mode of instruction facilitate the student's comprehension?

2. Within the context of what all students are doing, do the materials and activities allow independent student interaction, communication, and demonstration of learning?

3. Within the context of what all students are doing, do the materials and activities stimulate interest and promote engagement long enough for the student to learn?

Figure 5.4 summarizes the instructional activities for the unit as they are planned for all students, as well as the potential participation barriers for Julianne, and the supports to address those barriers.

Because formative assessment is closely linked to instruction, a quick review of the instructional plan completed in Step 3 reveals several opportunities for formative assessment. Although this assessment is critical, formative assessment may not be necessary for *every* activity.

————● *Mrs. Carter and Mr. Blackstone think about embedding formative assessment into the unit within several specific activities:*

- *Instructional activity #1: What prior knowledge do students already have about literary elements and techniques? About the genre of mysteries? Can I move ahead*

3. IDENTIFY THE INSTRUCTIONAL ACTIVITIES TO BE USED WITHIN THE UNIT.

What are the instructional activities planned for all students?	What barriers are keeping the student from accessing instruction, participating in activities, demonstrating learning, and so forth?	• What supports will reduce identified barriers? • How will the supports assist the student in accessing instruction, participating in activities, and demonstrating learning?

1. In small groups, students will brainstorm literary elements of mysteries, list them on chart paper, and identify illustrative details of each from specific texts.
 	
   a. Formative assessment: What prior knowledge do students already have about literary elements and techniques? About the genre of mysteries? Can I move ahead after this lesson or is some pre- or re-teaching needed before we go on? Perhaps if we save the brainstormed list at the beginning of the unit, we can come back to it to self-assess how much more we now know about mysteries. I think a KWL (what we know, what we want to learn, what we learned) format might be useful.
	1. Required auditory response
	2. Requirement of reading list from board and writing
	3. Written format of the cards; short response time allowed of just a few seconds
		1. Communication board with four common literary elements or devices: Julianne will use her communication board to participate in the brainstorming session.
		
		   a. Mr. Blackstone decides the same formative assessment will work for Julianne with the supports provided during instruction (e.g., picture symbol vocabulary).
		
		2. Objects and related picture symbols: While students are creating their picture cards, practice matching the picture symbol to the object with Julianne using system of least prompts, and place the pictures and objects together on her desk or on her communication board.

2. Students write each element on a separate index card.
 	
3. As a large group activity the teacher will read a short mystery story and have students hold up cards when they hear the element/device on the card depicted in the story. For example, when reading details about a character, students could be holding up a character card or an imagery card.
  a. Formative assessment: Holding up individual cards will tell me what each student knows. Is targeted instruction and extra practice needed for some students? Which students seem to be ready to go on independently?
		3. Objects paired with picture symbols representing literary elements/devices of mysteries: Julianne and a peer could have the objects in front of them and use those instead of index cards. The teacher would occasionally have the students hold their selected card so no one could see it and everyone show it at once. This would allow Julianne time to respond.
		  a. Mr. Blackstone assesses Julianne using her communication board so that she can demonstrate her understanding accurately considering the fast pace of the activity.

4. Review vocabulary that may be unknown to the student (e.g., alibi, deduce, red herring, sleuth) and create a student handout for students to refer to during the activity and unit.	4. Auditory and written presentation 5. Length of time required to attend to the activity 6. Requirements of reading and writing	4. Picture symbols representing each vocabulary word: Julianne will be pretaught using time delay and provided extra practice with the vocabulary during spare moments and for homework. Reduce the vocabulary as much as possible and still allow for comprehension.

(continued)

Figure 5.4. Four-step process to accessing grade-level content standards and curriculum: Step 3.

Figure 5.4. *(continued)*

3.	IDENTIFY THE INSTRUCTIONAL ACTIVITIES TO BE USED WITHIN THE UNIT.		
	5. Read a short mystery that can be read in one class period. Before reading, build anticipation by making connections to mysteries in which the students are interested. 6. Provide students with a set of questions related to the mystery. Stop periodically throughout the story and ask students to write the answers to the questions.		5. Julianne can be presented objects and picture symbols created for previous activities as the teacher reads the short mystery. 6. Julianne will be asked questions orally and will be provided choices for answering. Simplify the questions as needed.

	7. Provide a wide selection of short mysteries at various reading levels for students to choose and read independently.
	
	   a. Formative assessment: Are students able to self-select a book at the appropriate reading level for them? Which students need some redirection/assistance when choosing a book? What additional guidance can I give them?
		7. Printed text and amount of text	7. Digital version of text, adapted switch, text reader, summary of book: Julianne will listen to the book and a summary of the text by activating a text reader on the computer using an adapted switch.
			
			   a. Mr. Blackstone thinks the same formative assessment can be used for Julianne with assistance in choosing a means of accessing the text that is appropriate for her.

8. Working in pairs, have students complete a story map illustrating key elements of a mystery (characters, including suspect, investigator, witnesses; setting; plot, and clues; and the narrative structure, including introduction of characters, problem, working on solving the problem, and problem solved).
 	
   a. Formative assessment: Should I model completing the story map after I read a mystery aloud to the class? Perhaps a think-aloud with students would tell me if they understand how to complete the map before I ask them to do this independently (the extra practice might help many students).
 	
9. Reinforce and continue working on mystery literary elements by reviewing a mystery graphic organizer, which includes a prompt to decide on key elements and the story map to prompt the structure (see activity #8).
	8. Written format of the story map; required writing to complete the story map
	
	9. Written format of the mystery graphic organizer and story map
	
	10. Required writing to complete the story map
		8. Story map with added picture symbols, answers recorded on her communication board, and an adapted keyboard with a customized overlay to access the computer: Julianne and a partner could work together to complete the story map on the computer. Julianne would use the adapted keyboard while her partner uses the standard keyboard.
		
		   a. Mr. Blackstone realizes that Julianne can participate in the think-aloud by using her communication board to answer yes/no questions.
		
		9. Same as #8.
		
		10. Same as #8 with many options to describe characters, setting, clues, and plot.

(continued)

Figure 5.4. *(continued)*

3. IDENTIFY THE INSTRUCTIONAL ACTIVITIES TO BE USED WITHIN THE UNIT.		
10. Have each student complete the mystery graphic organizer or an outline in preparation for writing his or her own mystery.		
11. Ask students to complete the planning section of the rubric and to use that information to improve on their mystery graphic organizer and story map.	11. Written format of the rubric	11. Modified rubric using picture symbols and simplified, but still addressing literary elements: Peer can read to Julianne each section of the rubric while showing her the completed mystery graphic organizer and story map. Give her options of where she thinks her work would be rated on the rubric.
12. Have each student write a mystery or create a digital version of the mystery using the mystery graphic organizer and story map or outline each created.	12. Access to the computer	12. Adapted keyboard with overlay: Julianne can use each overlay with picture symbol choices, paired with objects as needed, to make choices on writing her mystery. She will need a different overlay for each element.
13. When finished, ask students to complete the second part of the rubric and make any revisions as needed based on the rubric.	13. Written format of the rubric	13. Same as #11.
14. Have students volunteer to share their mystery with the class.	14. Verbal requirement	14. Digital presentation and adapted keyboard or switch: Julianne can create her mystery on the computer using a slide show or a program that combines images into a movie clip. She can use the adapted keyboard or a switch to change slides or start the movie.

after this lesson or is some pre- or re-teaching needed before we go on? Perhaps if we save the brainstormed list at the beginning of the unit, we can come back to it to self-assess how much more we now know about mysteries. I think a KWL (what we know, what we want to learn, what we learned) format might be useful. Mr. Blackstone decides the same formative assessment will work for Julianne with the supports provided during instruction (e.g., picture symbol vocabulary). Both Mrs. Carter and Mr. Blackstone use this formative assessment information to decide which students may need some preteaching directed toward the genre of mysteries in general. If any students, including Julianne, need this, they find time within the class to provide that instruction rather than removing any student from essential learning activities for "specialized instruction."

- *Instructional activity #3: Holding up individual cards will tell me what each student knows. Is targeted instruction and extra practice needed for some students? Which students seem to be ready to go on independently? Mr. Blackstone assesses Julianne using her communication board so that she can demonstrate her understanding accurately considering the fast pace of the activity.*

- *Instructional activity #7: Are students able to self-select a book at the appropriate reading level for them? Which students need some redirection/assistance when choosing a book? What additional guidance can I give them? Mr. Blackstone thinks the same formative assessment can be used for Julianne with assistance in choosing a means of accessing the text that is appropriate for her.*

- *Instructional activity #8: Should I model completing the story map after I read a mystery aloud to the class? Perhaps a think-aloud with students would tell me if they understand how to complete the map before I ask them to do this independently (the extra practice might help many students). Mr. Blackstone realizes that Julianne can participate in the think-aloud by using her communication board to answer yes/no questions.*

Step 4: Target IEP Objectives and Foundational Skills that Can Be Addressed During the Unit

Especially for students with the most significant cognitive disabilities, the focus of special education programs has been primarily on the goals and objectives identified in the student's IEP, as required by IDEA 2004. This has sometimes resulted in the misunderstanding that the IEP goals and objectives are the student's curriculum. However, IDEA also requires that the IEP address how the student can be involved in and progress in the general curriculum. This has often left teachers feeling pressed for time and resources as they attempt to teach what is perceived as two curriculums—the IEP and the general education content (see Chapter 10 for further discussion). Assuming the IEP goals and objectives have truly been developed to assist the student in achieving his or her educational needs, instruction on the goals of the IEP and the standards-based goals of the general education curriculum are not incompatible. As the focus of instruction changes for students with significant cognitive disabilities, teachers need guidance on how to merge and/or embed these instructional goals within common activities. Step 4 provides a process to embed instruction of objectives and skills into instructional unit activities, creating an efficient way to address both requirements of IDEA. In addition, Step 4 provides a means to embed foundational skills, those skills that are typically taught at a lower grade level yet are still important for the student to learn.

IEP goals and objectives must be based on the unique needs of the individual student. Discussions on developing the objectives should also include consideration of what will help the student participate and progress in the general curriculum and be educated and participate with students without disabilities (IDEA 2004). When IEP objectives are developed with these considerations in mind, it should be easy to address most objectives within general curriculum activities. IEP objectives that are not directly connected to the general curriculum can also be embedded into the instructional unit activities and/or classroom routines if thought is given to how the student can practice each of those life skills across classroom and school settings, in the context of interactions with peers within both the formal and the informal curriculum.

————● *Julianne's IEP team, after identifying her unique needs, wrote the following IEP objectives:*

1. *Identify content-related picture symbols.*

2. *Compose simple content-related phrases and sentences using an adapted keyboard.*

3. *Answer comprehension and basic inference questions using an augmentative and alternative communication system.*

4. *Demonstrate one-to-one correspondence.*

5. *Identify concepts of more/less.*

6. *Increase time she holds her head up.*

7. *Initiate social interactions with peers and respond to their questions throughout the day.*

8. *Assist with transfers in and out of her wheelchair.*

The first task in embedding the objectives and skills is to review each instructional activity and determine which IEP objectives and foundational skills can be addressed during that activity. The matrix included in Figure 5.5 is a helpful tool to analyze each activity. In each cell of the left-hand column (Unit Instructional Activities), each of the instructional activities identified in Step 3 should be listed. Using a shorthand format such as key words or unit day and activity numbers would be sufficient. Then the goals/objectives identified on the student's IEP and other foundational skills should be listed across the first row of the matrix (IEP Objectives and Foundational Skills). Once this is completed, the instructional team should examine each academic content activity and determine when instruction on the objectives and skills can be embedded.

————● *The first activity Julianne will complete in the instructional unit is a brainstorming session on mysteries. The students will work in small groups of four and list on chart paper mysteries they have read and what literary elements each of those mysteries had. If possible, they will also list specific details in each mystery that illustrate that particular technique. Mr. Blackstone and Mrs. Carter have decided to put four literary elements on Julianne's communication board, supplemented with graphics, so that she*

4. TARGET SPECIFIC IEP OBJECTIVES AND FOUNDATIONAL SKILLS THAT CAN BE ADDRESSED DURING THE UNIT. List the instructional activity numbers or key words from Step 3 down the left column. List key words from IEP objectives and/or foundational skills across the top column. Indicate which IEP objectives and foundational skills can be addressed within each instructional activity.

IEP Objectives and Foundational Skills (Write key words) ➊ / Unit Instructional Activities (Write the number of the activity or key words) ➋	Identify content-related picture symbols	Compose simple content-related phrases and sentences using an adapted keyboard	Answer comprehension and basic inference questions using argumentative communication system	Demonstrate one-to-one correspondence	Identify more/less	Increase time head held up	Initiate social interactions with peers and respond to their questions throughout the day	Assist with transfers in and out of her wheelchair
#1: Students will work in small groups to brainstorm literary elements of mysteries, listing on chart paper the elements and corresponding, illustrative examples from mysteries they have read.	×	× using communication board				× while attending to the class activity	×	× preparation for this activity

(continued)

Figure 5.5. Four-step process to accessing grade-level content standards and curriculum: Step 4. (Key: IEP, individualized education program.)

Figure 5.5. *(continued)*

4. **TARGET SPECIFIC IEP OBJECTIVES AND FOUNDATIONAL SKILLS THAT CAN BE ADDRESSED DURING THE UNIT.** List the instructional activity numbers or key words from Step 3 down the left column. List key words from IEP objectives and/or foundational skills across the top column. Indicate which IEP objectives and foundational skills can be addressed within each instructional activity.

#2 and #3: As a large group activity the teacher will read a short mystery story and have students hold up cards when they hear the element/device on the card depicted in the story. For example, when reading details about a character, students could be holding up a character card or an imagery card.	X		X		X	X	
#4: Review vocabulary that may be unknown to the student (e.g., alibi, deduce, red herring, sleuth) and create a student handout for students to refer to during the activity and unit.	X		X		X	X	X

#5: Read a short mystery that can be read in one class period. Before reading, build anticipation by making connections to mysteries in which students are interested.	X		X			X	X
#6: Provide students with a set of questions related to the mystery. Stop periodically throughout the story and ask students to write the answers to the questions.	X	X	X			X	X
#7: Provide a wide selection of short mysteries at various reading levels for students to choose and read independently.	X		X	X Activating switch to read the next section using a text reader		X	X Transfer out of chair and into prone stander to use the computer text reader

(continued)

Figure 5.5. (continued)

4. TARGET SPECIFIC IEP OBJECTIVES AND FOUNDATIONAL SKILLS THAT CAN BE ADDRESSED DURING THE UNIT. List the instructional activity numbers or key words from Step 3 down the left column. List key words from IEP objectives and/or foundational skills across the top column. Indicate which IEP objectives and foundational skills can be addressed within each instructional activity.

#8: Working in pairs, have students complete a story map illustrating key elements of a mystery (characters including suspect, investigator, witnesses; setting; plot; and clues; and the narrative structure, including introduction of characters, problem, working on solving the problem, and problem solved).	X	X			X		X	
#9: Reinforce and continue working on mystery literary elements by reviewing a mystery graphic organizer, which includes a prompt to decide on key elements and the story map to prompt the structure (see activity #8).	X	X			X		X	X Transfer back into wheelchair

#10: Have each student complete the mystery graphic organizer or an outline in preparation for writing his or her own mystery.	X	X	X		X	X	
#11: Ask students to complete the planning section of the rubric and to use that information to improve on their mystery graphic organizer and story map.	X	X	X		X	X	
#12: Have each student write a mystery or create a digital version of the mystery using the mystery graphic organizer and story map or outline each created.	X	X	X	X	X	X	X Transfer to prone stander to use the computer

(continued)

141

Figure 5.5. *(continued)*

4. TARGET SPECIFIC IEP OBJECTIVES AND FOUNDATIONAL SKILLS THAT CAN BE ADDRESSED DURING THE UNIT. List the instructional activity numbers or key words from Step 3 down the left column. List key words from IEP objectives and/or foundational skills across the top column. Indicate which IEP objectives and foundational skills can be addressed within each instructional activity.

							transfer into wheelchair
#13: When finished, ask students to complete the second part of the rubric and make any revisions as needed based on the rubric.	X		X			X	X
#14: Students volunteer to share their mystery with the class.						X	X

can take part in the discussion. In looking at Julianne's IEP goals, Mr. Blackstone sees that he can easily provide Julianne instruction on identifying content-related picture symbols, answering comprehension and basic inference questions using her augmentative and alternative communication system, increasing the time she holds her head up, and initiating social interactions with peers and responding to their questions throughout the day. And, with a little more planning, Mr. Blackstone thinks that he can also find opportunities for Julianne to compose simple content-related phrases and sentences using an adapted keyboard.

When the activity takes place, Mrs. Carter allows the small groups to convene wherever they feel most comfortable. When Julianne's group decides to sit at a small table in the back of the room, Mr. Blackstone takes that opportunity to also instruct Julianne in her IEP objective of assisting with transfers in and out of her wheelchair.

Mr. Blackstone has figured it out. By carefully analyzing the general curriculum activities and routines, IEP goals and objectives that have been designed to 1) "meet the child's needs that result from the child's disability to enable the child to be involved in and make progress in the general education curriculum," and 2) "meet each of the child's other educational needs that result from the child's disability" (IDEA 2004, § 614[d][1][A][i][I][aa]) can be logically and meaningfully taught within the context of the general curriculum. Julianne can learn concepts across different contexts and environments. For these targeted concepts, she will not necessarily need to work on generalization as a separate programming component because instruction on specific IEP goals will be provided throughout the school day in the activities in which Julianne actually needs to use them. Figure 5.5 summarizes the embedded IEP objectives for the unit.

BOX 5.8

Reflecting on your own practice...

- Do I only focus IEP goals on functional needs, or do my student's IEP goals reflect progress in the general curriculum and/or other educational goals?
- Do I provide instruction on IEP goals in isolation, or do I provide instruction in the context of academic and other classroom routines?

CONCLUSION

The Four-Step Process is a tool for teachers to use when increasing access to the general curriculum for students with significant cognitive disabilities. This process will help teachers in making the shift to a more academically focused curriculum (the general curriculum) for this population of learners. Although the authors of this chapter believe that it is the *process itself* that is the important thing, and not the form or the tool, we must also stress the initial importance of filling out the form in the appendix at the end of the book completely for the first few times that the process is actually used. It may seem a little cumbersome and you may be tempted to skip a step or two, but using the form in its entirety will help to establish the process within your own thinking. It becomes, if you will, a learning or meta-cognitive strategy for teachers in adapting the general curriculum for students with significant cognitive disabilities. Once the process has become a routine way of thinking about instruction, the form has served its purpose.

We also want to stress the importance of involving students with significant cognitive disabilities in all activities and aspects of instruction. Just because some activities seem difficult for students to engage in and for teachers to support their participation (e.g., notetaking, research, hypothesizing), this does not mean these activities are not important. These and other research-based strategies (Marzano et al., 2001) implemented in general education classrooms are important for all students. Because of what we think we know about teaching and learning for students with significant cognitive disabilities, it is tempting to remove students from such critical instructional activities. We suggest that when you find yourself asking, "Should my student be doing this?" you instead may want to ask yourself, "What can we do to support my student in doing this?"

Something that special educators often report is that the pace of the general curriculum is too fast for students with significant cognitive disabilities to keep up. No students, with or without disabilities, are expected to achieve total mastery of standards the first time around. Standards represent concepts that students sometimes spend their entire school careers learning, hence, the idea of "spiraling standards," which receive repeated instruction over time and grades. Students without disabilities are rarely expected to show full mastery of a standard over the course of one unit of instruction. Instead they are expected to continue to learn at deeper and deeper levels of complexity as standards are repeatedly addressed through the general curriculum progression. The special education concept of "mastery" (i.e., 100% correct independent performance over 3 consecutive days) is appropriate for IEP goals and objectives and can be achieved by embedding instruction on those goals throughout a student's school day. However, that sense of mastery, focused on specific, measurable skills, is used differently than the notion of mastery as it applies to academic content standards of ever increasing complexity across grades. Mastery as we have always applied that term to instructional objectives for students with significant cognitive disabilities is, of course, very important—but it is also important that we understand the sense of that term as it is used by general educators in the context of spiraling academic content standards across the full curriculum and by the student's ability to apply or transfer concepts and skills learned in different or new contexts, reflect on one's own learning, and be able to self-correct.

So at the end of this chapter, you might ask, "Why is there a chapter on instruction in a book about alternate assessment?" The connection between instruction and assessment has long been established. Even though the connection between improved instruction and increased student achievement may seem intuitive, research is also confirming the correlation (Sanborn, 2002). If teachers have not taught "it" and taught it in the most effective ways possible using research-based strategies, we cannot say students can't learn it. We are sure that given opportunity, support, and effective instruction, students will continue to surprise us.

Finally, the Four-Step Process can be integrally connected to alternate assessment itself. For teachers and students whose state's alternate assessment is a portfolio assessment, the Four-Step Process provides direct data on performance directly linked to grade-level standards, a requirement of NCLB. For those teachers and students in states that use checklists with student performance data (e.g., graphs of student learning, student work samples), again the Four-Step Process provides a very efficient means for collecting data directly related to grade-level academic performance. And, for those teachers and students in states that require on-demand, performance event tests, the Four-Step Process—

with its continuous emphasis on removing presentation, interaction, and engagement barriers to students' learning, and its insistence on developing means for students to achieve independence and mastery—provides the ongoing classroom practice and instruction that students need to achieve success.

REFERENCES

Agran, M. (1997). *Student-directed learning: Teaching self-determination skills.* Belmont, CA: Wadsworth.

Agran, M., Alper, S., & Wehmeyer, M. (2002). Access to the general curriculum for students with significant disabilities: What it means to teachers. *Education and Training in Mental Retardation and Developmental Disabilities, 37,* 123–133.

Brandt, R. (1993). The changing curriculum: Overview: The curriculum connection. *Educational Leadership, 50,* 3.

Brookhart, S., Moss, C., & Long, B. (2008). Formative assessment that empowers. *Educational Leadership, 66*(3), 52–57.

Browder, D.M., Wakeman, S., Spooner, F., Ahlgrim-Delzell, L., & Algozzine, B. (2006). Research on reading for students with significant cognitive disabilities. *Exceptional Children, 72,* 392–410.

Center for Applied Special Technology. (2008). *Universal design for learning guidelines* (Version 1.0). Wakefield, MA: Author.

Chappuis, S., & Chappuis, J. (2008). The best value in formative assessment. *Educational Leadership, 65*(4), 14–18.

Clayton, J., Burdge, M., Denham, A., Kleinert, H., & Kearns, J. (2006). A four-step process for accessing the general curriculum for students with significant cognitive disabilities. *TEACHING Exceptional Children, 38*(5), 20–27.

Cole, C., Waldron, N., & Majd, M. (2004). Academic progress of students across inclusive and traditional settings. *Mental Retardation, 42,* 136–144.

Conzemius, A., & O'Neill, J. (2001). *Building shared responsibility for student learning.* Alexandria, VA: Association for Supervision and Curriculum Development.

Council for Exceptional Children. (2006). *Evidence-based practice—Wanted, needed, and hard to get.* Retrieved January 18, 2009, from http://www.cec.sped.org/AM/Template.cfm?Section=Home&TEMPLATE=/CM/ContentDisplay.cfm&CONTENTID=6515

Denham, A. (2004). *Pathways to learning for students with cognitive challenges: Reading, writing and presenting.* Retrieved May 15, 2009, from http://www.ihdi.uky.edu/IEI/Files/Pathways%20to%20learning%20document.pdf

Duschl, R., Schweingruber, H., & Shouse, A. (Eds.). (2007). *Taking science to school: Learning and teaching science in grades K-8.* Washington, DC: National Academies of Science.

Fishbaugh, M.S., & Gum, P. (1994). *Inclusive education in Billings, MT: A prototype for rural schools* (ERIC Document Reproduction Service No. ED369636). East Lansing, MI: National Center for Research on Teacher Learning.

Garrison, C., & Ehringhaus, M. (2007). *Formative and summative assessments in the classroom.* Retrieved January 30, 2009, from http://www.nmsa.org/Publications/WebExclusive/Assessment/tabid/1120/Default.aspx

Giangreco, M.F., Cloninger, C.J., & Iverson, V.S. (1998). *Choosing outcomes and accommodations for children (COACH): A guide to educational planning for students with disabilities* (2nd ed.). Baltimore: Paul H. Brookes Publishing Co.

Grisham-Brown, J., & Kearns, J.F. (2001). Creating standards-based individualized education programs. In H.L. Kleinert & J.F. Kearns, *Alternate assessment: Measuring outcomes and supports for students with disabilities* (pp. 17–28). Baltimore: Paul H. Brookes Publishing Co.

Hess, K. (2004). *Applying Webb's Depth-of-Knowledge (DOK) levels in reading.* Retrieved May 1, 2010, from http://www.nciea.org/publications/DOKreading_KH08.pdf

Hess, K. (2008). *Developing and using learning progressions as a schema for measuring progress.* Retrieved May 1, 2010, from http://www.nciea.org/publications/CCSSOZ_KH08.pdf

Hess, K. (2009). *Applying big ideas (enduring understandings) to unit planning and assessment development.* Retrieved from http://www.nciea.org

Hollowood, T.M., Salisbury, C.L., Rainforth, B., & Palumbaro, M.M. (1995). Use of instructional time in classrooms serving students with and without severe disabilities. *Exceptional Children, 61,* 242–252.

Hughes, C., Copeland, S.R., Agran, M., Wehmeyer, M.L., Rodi, M.S., & Presley, J.A. (2002). Using self-monitoring to improve performance in general education high school classes. *Education and Training in Mental Retardation and Developmental Disabilities, 37,* 262–272.

Hunt, P., Staub, D., Alwell, M., & Goetz, L. (1994). Achievement of all students within the context of cooperative learning groups. *The Journal of The Association for Persons with Severe Handicaps, 19,* 290–301.

Individuals with Disabilities Education Improvement Act (IDEA) of 2004, PL 108-446, 20 U.S.C. §§ 1400 *et seq.*

Jenkins, J., Jewell, M., Leicester, N., O'Connor, R.E., Jenkins, L., & Troutner, N.M. (1992). Accommodations for individual differences without classroom ability groups: An experiment in school restructuring. *Exceptional Children, 60,* 344–359.

Katz, J., & Mirenda, P. (2002). Including students with developmental disabilities in general education classrooms: Educational benefits. *International Journal of Special Education, 17,* 14–24.

Kleinert, H.L., & Thurlow, M.L. (2001). An introduction to alternate assessment. In H.L. Kleinert & J.F. Kearns, *Alternate assessment: Measuring outcomes and supports for students with disabilities* (pp. 1–15). Baltimore: Paul H. Brookes Publishing Co.

Marzano, R.J., Pickering, D.J., & Pollock, J.E. (2001). *Classroom instruction that works: Research-based strategies for increasing student achievement.* Alexandria, VA: Association for Supervision and Curriculum Development.

No Child Left Behind Act of 2001, PL 107-110, 115 Stat. 1425, 20 U.S.C. §§ 6301 *et seq.*

Quenemoen, R. (2008). *A brief history of alternate assessments based on alternate achievement standards* (Synthesis Report 68). Minneapolis: University of Minnesota, National Center on Educational Outcomes. Retrieved February 3, 2009, from http://www.cehd.umn.edu/NCEO/OnlinePubs/Synthesis68/index.htm

Rose, D.H., & Meyer, A. (2002). *Teaching every student in the digital age: Universal design for learning.* Alexandria, VA: Association for Supervision and Curriculum Development.

Rose, D.H., Meyer, A., & Hitchcock, C. (2005). *The universally designed classroom: Accessible curriculum and digital technologies.* Cambridge, MA: Harvard Education Press.

Sanborn, J. (2002). Targeted training. *School Administrator, 59,* 16–19.

Sands, D.J., Kozleski, E., & French, N. (2000). *Inclusive education in the 21st century.* Belmont, CA: Wadsworth.

Scherer, M. (2008). An answer for the long term. *Educational Leadership, 65*(4), 7.

Sharpe, M.N., York, J.L., & Knight, J. (1994). Effects of inclusion on the academic performance of classmates without disabilities. *Remedial and Special Education, 15,* 281–287.

Snell, M.E. (2007). Effective instructional practices. *TASH Connections, 33,* 8–11.

Snell, M.E., & Brown, F. (2005). *Instruction of students with severe disabilities.* Upper Saddle River, NJ: Prentice Hall.

Stiggins, R.J. (2005). *Student-Involved Assessment FOR Learning.* New Jersey: Pearson/Prentice Hall.

Tomlinson, C.A. (2001). *How to differentiate instruction in mixed-ability classrooms.* Alexandria, VA: Association for Supervision and Curriculum Development.

Tuttle, H.G. (2008). *Formative assessment: Student responses and observation of learning.* Retrieved January 30, 2009, from http://www.authenticeducation.org/bigideas/article.lasso?artId=59

Wehmeyer, M.L., Sands, D.J., Knowlton, E., & Kozleski, E.B. (2002). *Teaching students with mental retardation: Providing access to the general curriculum.* Baltimore: Paul H. Brookes Publishing Co.

Wiener, D. (2005). *One state's story: Access and alignment to the GRADE-LEVEL content for students with significant cognitive disabilities*. Retrieved January 3, 2010, from http://www.cehd.umn.edu/NCEO/OnlinePubs/Synthesis57.html

Wiggins, G., & McTighe, J. (1998). *Understanding by design*. Alexandria, VA: Association for Supervision and Curriculum Development.

Wiggins, G., & McTighe, J. (2005). *Understanding by design*. Alexandria, VA: Association for Supervision and Curriculum Development.

Wiliam, D. (2007). Informative Assessment. *Educational Leadership*, 65(4), 36–42.

Zabala, J., & Stahl, S. (2006). *AT and UDL: Complementary supports for student achievement*. Presentation at annual conference of Technology, Reading and Learning Diversity, San Francisco.

Reading Instruction and Assessment Linked to Grade-Level Standards

Lynn Ahlgrim-Delzell, Robert J. Rickelman, and Jean Clayton

The No Child Left Behind (NCLB) Act of 2001 (PL 107-110), the Individuals with Disabilities Education Act Amendments (IDEA) of 1997 (PL 105-17), and the Individuals with Disabilities Education Improvement Act of 2004 (PL 108-446) have mandated access to general education academic content and participation in state/district assessments for all students, including those with significant cognitive disabilities. Prior to this legislation, special education curricula centered on individual student needs with the long-term goal of becoming as self-sufficient as possible by teaching functional skills (Browder et al., 2003). Reading, however, was not one of these priority functional skills. The historic lack of teaching reading has been described elsewhere (e.g., Browder et al., 2009; Katims, 2000; Kliewer & Biklen, 2001; Kliewer, Biklen, & Kasa-Hendrickson, 2006). Despite the historical lack of emphasis on reading for students with significant cognitive disabilities, this chapter makes the case for why reading is so important for these students.

WHY IS READING IMPORTANT?

It should be easy to make a case that reading is probably the most important subject taught and learned in schools. Why? There are really two reasons. First, being able to read allows people a chance to lead productive lives. For instance, most people who work are required to read as part of their job. Whether it is using reading to identify labels, sort products in a warehouse, or learn new surgery procedures, reading is a major vehicle for sharing and learning new information. Second, reading can enhance the quality of life for every individual. Some people like to read books for pleasure. Some people like to take part in social networking, which involves reading and writing information to share with others. Some people like to use the computer to search for information that is helpful or just fun. Reading is all around us.

In schools, reading is a major vehicle for learning in all subject areas. In contrast, instruction in other subject areas, such as math, generally occurs only in that specific class. But reading shows up in every subject area. For example, students have to read math (both words and numbers) in order to learn mathematics principles and work out sample problems for homework. Students typically have to read in order to take tests, and a common complaint among teachers is that students may know the subject concepts but may not be able to show that knowledge because they lack the ability to read the test or to write an acceptable response to the test item. Many high school teachers feel that the lack of reading ability is one of the most frustrating challenges to them.

So, one could argue that the ability to read is probably the most important skill that one can learn in school. Reading well can make the difference between passing a class or failing, between being hired or not being hired for a job. Reading well can make a difference in day-to-day life, from shopping in the grocery store, to reading the mail, to surfing the Internet and checking e-mail, to making decisions about what to watch on television at night.

The major problem that many teachers and students face regarding reading instruction is that students cannot read at the level they need to read in order to be able to work within the grade-level classroom. What does a teacher do when a kindergarten student comes into school and does not know basic information such as his or her name or colors? What does a teacher do when a 12th-grade student cannot read 1st-grade text? These questions have perplexed teachers and students for many years.

In this chapter, we try to answer some of these important questions. We discuss the major strands of reading and how the goals of teaching and learning reading shift across grade levels. We talk about how reading may affect, for better or worse, students with both mild and severe intellectual disabilities, in addition to how research-based strategies can ensure that students have access to quality teaching and learning that pushes the limits of expectations. And, we define and discuss the differences between summative and formative assessments and how both types of assessment must be used to help students learn. Throughout the chapter, we highlight three students—Colbie, Maurita, and Juan—as we explore each of these topics. All three of these students participate in their state's alternate assessment based on alternate achievement standards (AA-AAS).

Before we continue with the chapter, however, we want to share a story as an example of what we consider "pushing the limits." A local teacher had a student in class who was nonverbal and was assumed to have both physical and intellectual disabilities. The only way the student could respond in class was through the use of a switch. Prior teachers typically would use only two switches to allow the student to make choices (e.g., "Do you want fries or tater tots for lunch?"). One day, the teacher realized that she did not really know if the student was just making random or truly deliberate choices because there was no expected right or wrong response. The other students in the class were listening to stories and giving responses related to simple comprehension questions. The teacher decided to allow this student to make a similar response. After reading a story to the class, the teacher asked the student a literal comprehension question and provided her with one switch for the correct answer and another for the incorrect answer. The teacher was somewhat surprised when the student chose the correct answer, so the teacher continued to ask similar questions, and even got into higher levels of comprehension. The student gave the correct response every time. The student was in fourth grade when this happened, and until then, no one had known for sure that she had understood anything at that level in her life. It took this teacher's "out-of-the-box" thinking to push the limits, to not make assumptions that had not been tested, and this simple decision changed the quality of life for one fourth-grade student forever.

MAJOR STRANDS OF READING

Most reading experts would agree that there are two major phases of the reading process (Herber, 1970): the learning-to-read phase and the reading-to-learn phase. The first phase, learning to read, occurs roughly from kindergarten through third grade. This phase is characterized by students learning the basic building blocks of reading, which will serve them throughout a lifetime. These building blocks include phonics, phonemic awareness, and fluency, as well as the development of vocabulary and comprehension skills. It also includes building a basic interest in and enjoyment of reading; this interest and enjoyment is fostered by reading a broad range of materials, from children's books to basic informational books about the world. The building blocks of reading were discussed in the National Reading Panel (NRP) *Teaching Children to Read* report (2000), and it is important to put the results of that study in some perspective.

The NRP report team conducted a meta-analysis of research studies that documented the skills important in teaching reading. One of the goals was to see what research had to say about how students learn to read. The report was organized around five areas: phonics, phonemic awareness, fluency, vocabulary, and comprehension—the very building blocks in the learning to read phase noted previously. However, some people mistakenly assume that the NRP report concluded that *only* these five areas had a research base of evidence, and so only these five areas should be taught in the schools. Tim Shanahan (2003), one of the NRP members, attempted to address this myth by putting the panel's work in perspective. One drawback of meta-analyses, however, is that the researchers decide beforehand what characteristics they want to examine. Some critics of the report have suggested, for example, that the panel did not study some very important elements such as reading for enjoyment and writing. One should never assume, however, that if a skill is not included in a report that the skill must not be important. Shanahan noted that the panel had to limit the areas it examined to allow the study to be finished in a reasonable time. He suggested that, if the panel included all of the areas that the members thought were important in the study, it would still be conducting the research. Also, in a meta-analysis, some research is excluded from the study if the characteristics of that research do not match the predetermined criteria. This does not mean that the excluded studies are not scientific or valuable. It only means that these studies may not have included all the criteria the panel wanted to address. Furthermore, to assume any studies not included in the report must not have been of sufficient quality is also not correct. Surely some studies were excluded for this reason, but others were excluded for wholly other reasons. So, as we talk about *what* skills need to be addressed in schools, certainly the five identified by the panel are important. But, that does not mean that other skills are not equally important.

Colbie, a third-grade student, is within the typical grade range for the learning-to-read phase. She is working on phonemic awareness by recognizing words that begin with given sounds and saying the beginning sound of words. Although she is not able to read words at this time, she can recognize objects, pictures, and picture symbols. Her teachers are using a combination of these to teach her listening comprehension and vocabulary in addition to working on phonemic awareness. She uses the same reading material content as her third-grade peers. The third-grade class is reading different books from the tall tales genre to address skills such as sequencing, vocabulary, and fluency. Colbie listens to the story as the class reads the book, and her special education teacher or a classmate shows Colbie a picture representing each major event as it is read and places it on a sequencing chart. Colbie also has picture symbol cards for some key vocabulary words used throughout the story. After finishing the story, each student in the class completes a sequencing graphic organizer. Colbie uses the picture symbols to complete her graphic organizer, as illustrated in Figure 6.1. The teacher supplements the general education research-based strategies used with all students with systematic instruction to teach phonemic awareness by using the words from Colbie's sequencing chart and vocabulary cards.

The second phase of the reading process—reading to learn—overlaps the learning-to-read phase and generally becomes important around second grade; however, first-grade students certainly take part in reading-to-learn activities. This phase assumes that students have acquired the basic building blocks of the learning-to-read phase, at least to a general level of competence, because learning to read takes a lifetime of practice to develop. This second phase becomes much more critical as students make the transition from elementary to middle school, and then again when they progress to the high school level. Most middle and high school teachers assume that students have learned to read. In other words, they assume that students have knowledge about phonics and phonemic awareness, that they have some level of fluency in reading material on grade level, and that they have developed basic skills in vocabulary and comprehension, although these skills continue to grow throughout middle and high school. So, the shift is then on reading to learn—on reading books and materials that allow a student to learn information that is important for meeting grade-level standards. For example, a first-grade student may practice phonemic awareness—the ability to separate words into sounds. It is unlikely, however, that a 10th-grade student would practice this skill because the assumption is that 10th-grade students learned to do that in the primary grades. On the other hand, it is reasonable to ask a high school student to read a biology text on cells and be able to understand some levels of basic information from that text. The teacher would not expect a first-grade student to have the background or the experience to be able to understand this information, however.

The shift from learning to read in the earlier elementary school years to reading to learn in middle and high school is reflected in a conceptual model of teaching reading for students with significant cognitive disabilities (Browder et al., 2009). This conceptual model of reading differs from what typically occurs in the general education progression in three main ways. First, is the opportunity to *interact* with literature present for students even though they may not be able to read the literature? There will be some students who will not learn to read despite teachers' best efforts, but students can learn to interact with books and receive information from books that are read to them. Access to books and the information they contain should still be related to students' grade/age level. A student in

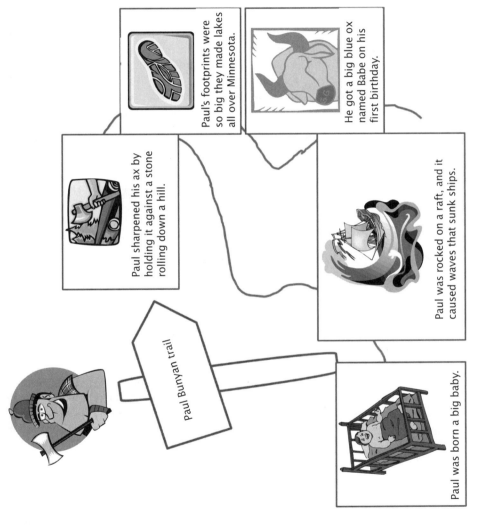

Figure 6.1. Colbie's sequencing graphic organizer.

Paul's footprints were so big they made lakes all over Minnesota.

He got a big blue ox named Babe on his first birthday.

Paul sharpened his ax by holding it against a stone rolling down a hill.

Paul was rocked on a raft, and it caused waves that sunk ships.

Paul Bunyan trail

Paul was born a big baby.

high school, for example, should be given access to the same books as those peers are reading in the general education classrooms. That means teachers will have to reduce the text
in books to a level that the student can understand by either reading or by listening to the
books as they are read. Other supports such as pictures need to be added because most
books at the middle and high school level contain few, if any, pictures to support the story
being told. This will be discussed more later in the chapter.

The second major difference in the conceptual model of teaching reading to students
with significant cognitive disabilities is the need for a *functional application* of reading.
Because some students will have limited reading vocabularies, there is still a need to teach
words that can be useful in life. Moreover, some students will need to learn to read words
and understand them in the everyday context in which they will be used. Some examples
may include reading and locating grocery items in a store, reading ingredients from product labels, or reading menu items at a restaurant.

One final difference in this conceptual model is that some students who are making
some progress in phonics skills may need to continue such learning even though they
reach an age in which this skill is not typically taught. Although students in elementary
school typically receive specific phonemic awareness and phonics skills instruction in the
learning-to-read phase, this instruction may need to be embedded within reading a book
in the reading-to-learn phase if a student is making steady yet slow progress in these skills
when entering middle school. For example, identification of letter sounds can be emphasized during the reading of a science lesson.

*Maurita is in seventh grade. She has not yet developed a consistent or conventional
method of communicating. Maurita's mother reports that Maurita will tense and turn
her head to her left side when she hears her sister and brother and that she sometimes
increases her breathing when she wants something. Her teachers are testing and observing her responses as they use voice recorded switches, objects, tactile symbols, and sign
language during work on communication and academic skills. Because Maurita is in
the seventh grade and most students are in the reading-to-learn phase, she is provided
the same type of instruction. Her teachers provide objects, pictures, and tactile symbols
representing key concepts and terms to help Maurita understand content information.
For a unit on the Middle Ages, she is provided with tactile symbols such as a circle covered in purple velvet to represent nobility and a circle covered in burlap to represent
peasants. As concepts and vocabulary are taught, Maurita is presented with these and
other symbols. These symbols can then be used when reading a related play in English
class. In addition to the research-based instructional activities used by the general education teacher (e.g., identifying similarities and differences, summarizing, learning
groups, advance organizers), Maurita's teacher will use systematic prompting and
fading to teach and assess Maurita on vocabulary.*

*Maurita's reading instruction is heavily supported and supplemented (not
supplanted) with additional reading/communication instruction. In conjunction with
Maurita's mother and speech-language pathologist (SLP), her teacher works on
learning-to-read skills in the area of phonemic awareness. They do this through reading
phrases that include rhyming words and emphasis on beginning consonant sounds.
Early phonemic awareness activities are often taught and practiced through nursery
rhymes and word/sound games. To maintain age appropriateness and to combine the
purpose of learning vocabulary and phonemic awareness, the activities designed for*

Maurita are constructed using content typically taught in her seventh-grade classes. For example, during the unit on the Middle Ages, content vocabulary words that have the same beginning sound (e.g., castle, count, constable, court) are used for phonemic awareness instruction. For this instruction, Maurita is provided with a variety of experiences throughout her day, including a switch-activated computer activity emphasizing the alliteration, a beginning sound picture/tactile symbol sorting activity, and short stories that include several vocabulary words that begin with the same beginning consonant (e.g., "The count went into the castle and into the court to meet with the constable"). On occasion Maurita may be assessed to see if she is recognizing beginning sounds by observing for a reaction when a nonrhyming word is inserted into the alliteration sequence.

IMPORTANCE OF LEARNING DIFFERENT GENRES

Reading material is traditionally divided into two categories—informational text and narrative (or story) text. Informational text, quite simply, presents information related to what is being learned. Most textbooks are informational. They discuss history, for example, or present mathematical concepts. Narrative texts are different. They tell a story (e.g., traditional fairy tales). As students progress into the upper grades, they may be expected to read books of narrative text—novels, for instance, or plays or poems. Because informational and narrative texts are organized differently, they both require some attention as students learn to read them. Narrative texts, for example, have a story line or plot. Informational texts do not have plots but might be organized by cause and effect (e.g., a major cause of the Civil War was slavery). Students must become proficient in reading multiple kinds of texts. Thinking back to the introduction to this chapter, we talked about how learning to read could greatly affect an individual's quality of life. Reading for work often involves informational texts (e.g., how to use a piece of equipment, work policies and announcements). Newspapers or magazines might include both kinds of text so that a reader can learn about what happened at the school board meeting, as well as reading the Dilbert comic or reading a story about how a local teen overcame poverty to graduate from college. People read both kinds of text for enjoyment, which is one of the important goals for reading.

Why foster reading skills, however, if students hate to read at the end? Enjoying reading, across multiple genres, is critical. Some students might enjoy being in a local theater production for relaxation, so reading dialogue becomes an important (and enjoyable for some) skill. Some people like to write poems or music. Some like to write blogs or biographies. If we buy into the assumption that learning to read and write has the potential to enhance quality of life, practicing reading across different genres (and not just for basic survival) is important.

───● *Maurita is working on informational and narrative texts in her social studies and language arts classes. Some may question the importance of this for her, asking why not just teach her how to read informational text such as her daily schedule, a lunch menu, and functional signs? As mentioned previously in this chapter, both NCLB and IDEA require access for all students to the general curriculum and assessment on state standards. Because most state standards address both narrative and informational text, providing access means teaching both genres. As we have also noted, reading can enhance quality of life. Is there anything that makes Maurita so different that reading can't enhance her life when she is provided the necessary supports? In addition, reading and being read to increase communication skills, vocabulary development, and knowledge. Each time Maurita hears a word or piece of information, that act forms another connection in her brain, and as the connections strengthen, so do her skills and knowledge.*

Maurita works on reading comprehension in narrative texts in a variety of ways. She is presented with concrete objects, tactile symbols, pictures, and picture symbols that represent characters, setting, events, and plot for each text. For example, when reading **Crispin: The Cross of Lead** *(Avi, 2002), Maurita is provided the following tactile symbols: a circle covered with burlap for Crispin, the peasant boy; a circle covered with purple velvet for Aycliffe, the noble; a circle with beads attached for Bear, the juggler; and picture symbols for the terms* **threatened, escape, friends, surprise,** *and* **free man**. *These symbols are always used when Maurita listens to the class reading the book or has a simpler paraphrased version read to her to reinforce the events of the story and during direct instruction on the vocabulary. At the end of the unit, Maurita creates a plot chart using the symbols (Figure 6.2); she is provided peer and/or teacher assistance needed to do so. This assistance includes giving her two choices at a time, observing for possible intentional choice making (e.g., eye gaze, body movement, facial expressions, vocalizations), and then pasting the selected answer on the plot chart. By actively participating in this instructional unit, Maurita has had the opportunity to hear grade/age appropriate vocabulary, connect key vocabulary to semiconcrete symbols, interact appropriately with her peers, and hear an interesting age-appropriate book. She is given every opportunity to build her reading/listening comprehension skills.*

RESEARCH ON TEACHING READING TO STUDENTS WITH SIGNIFICANT COGNITIVE DISABILITIES

Research on teaching reading to students with significant cognitive disabilities is rather limited. Browder, Wakeman, Spooner, Ahlgrim-Delzell, and Algozzine (2006) found that most reading content taught to this population was only related to learning sight words. Students learned to "read" either by saying an individual word or pointing to the word read by the teacher without either context (e.g., having the word in a sentence) or comprehension (e.g., having the student demonstrate that he or she understood the meaning of the word). Think about the description of reading presented in this chapter. Is simple recall of printed flashcards really reading? Memorizing individual words without context or comprehension would not be considered reading. It is certainly one skill necessary in learning to read fluently, but it is not in itself really reading. Sight word instruction is one component of the necessary skills listed by the NRP (2000); that component is called vocabulary. Some studies have shown that students with significant cognitive disabilities can learn other NRP skills that are necessary to learn to read, such as phonemic awareness (e.g., Browder et al., 2006; Conners, Rosenquist, Sligh, Atwell, & Kiser, 2006), comprehension (e.g., Fiscus, Schuster, Morse, & Collins, 2002; Mechling & Gast, 2003; Rehfeldt, Latimore, & Stromer, 2003), and phonics (e.g., Basil & Reyes, 2003; Bradford, Shippen, Alberto, Houchins, & Flores, 2006; Hoogeveen & Smeets, 1988).

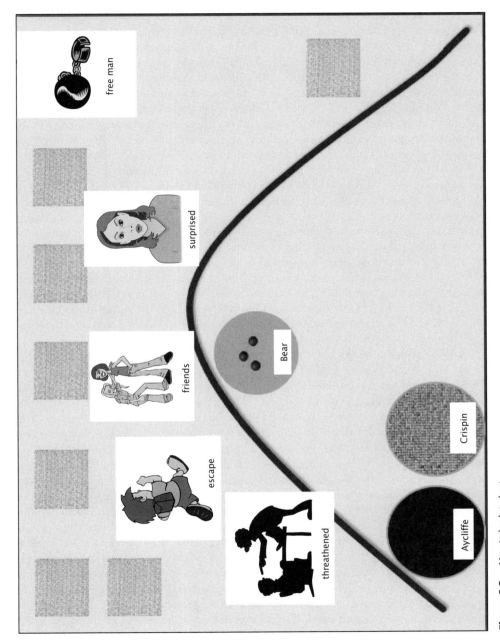

Figure 6.2. Maurita's plot chart.

Educators have a long way to go in understanding how students with disabilities best learn to read. However, the discussion of how to best teach reading still occurs among reading teachers of students without disabilities. Although many theories posit how to teach reading, at present the research in teaching reading to students with intellectual disabilities appears to fall within two main categories: a systematic instructional approach or a constructivist approach. The research cited in the previous paragraph focused on teaching students with significant cognitive disabilities to read using systematic instructional strategies commonly found in special education classrooms; these procedures include time delay, differential reinforcement, error correction, and stimulus and response prompting strategies. Specific information about these strategies can be found in Snell and Brown (2005), Browder (2001), and Downing (2005). One study (Browder, Ahlgrim-Delzell, Courtade, Gibbs, & Flowers, 2008) taught phonemic awareness and phonics skills by combining systematic prompting procedures and direct instruction. Direct instruction provides teachers with a set of scripted instructions and activities, as in *The Early Literacy Skills Builder* curriculum (Browder, Gibbs, Ahlgrim-Delzell, Courtade, & Lee, 2007). An important note about this research is the type of research design used in these studies. The type of design used determines what type of conclusions teachers can make about student performance. For example, Browder and colleagues' (2006) meta-analysis of reading research only included studies with high-quality research designs in order to allow the authors to make statements regarding cause and effect in teaching reading to students with significant cognitive disabilities. It does appear that using systematic instruction or prompting procedures (cause) is an evidence-based practice to teach reading to students with significant cognitive disabilities that increases a student's literacy skills (effect). The caution, of course, in this meta-analysis, as Browder et al. (2006) themselves point out, is that the basic focus of the studies they analyzed was on vocabulary development, which as we discussed previously, is just one element of true reading.

Within another research tradition, Erickson and her colleagues (e.g., Erickson, Hatton, Roy, Fox, & Renne, 2007; Erickson & Koppenhaver, 1998; Skoto, Koppenhaver, & Erickson, 2004) have advocated for a constructivist approach in teaching students with significant cognitive disabilities such literacy skills as interacting with books, comprehension, and writing. In a constructivist approach, students learn through interacting with literacy materials in a print-rich environment carefully constructed by the teacher to promote student-directed learning. For example, a reading center will include a variety of books selected on the basis of student interest and a variety of ways for students to interact with the books independently by teacher-made adaptations and/or technology devices. Students are provided opportunities to explore these literacy materials. This qualitative research richly describes students learning a variety of literacy skills. Although this type of research describes students' learning and gives us a deeper understanding of how literacy develops, it does not measure student performance, and therefore is not considered an evidence-based practice. Though this approach lacks measurable data on student performance, this does not mean that we should ignore this practice, especially if it is used in conjunction with approaches that are evidence-based. It does seem to be a logical consequence that students will learn literacy skills when interacting in a print-rich, literate environment. Providing that literacy environment to students with significant cognitive disabilities, while providing them with systematic instruction on the component skills of reading, maximizes opportunities to learn to read.

Let's look at our three students, Colbie, Maurita, and Juan, to see what reading instruction might look like for each of them.

——● Colbie: Third-Grade Unit on Paul Bunyan

Reading standard: *Students will paraphrase, summarize, and sequence major events or steps in a passage.*

Lesson objectives: *1) Students will sequence major events in the life of Paul Bunyan. 2) Students will summarize his life to create a book jacket.*

Instruction for the class, including Colbie: *1) After discussing the genre of tall tales, students will read a book about Paul Bunyan. Colbie will listen as the class reads the story while also looking at a version made with key words paired with picture symbols. 2) Students will draw a picture representing each major event in Paul Bunyan's life. Colbie will draw her picture using a provided model. 3) Students will scan each picture into a computer presentation with narration. Colbie will follow step-by-step picture directions to scan her pictures. She will practice with the teacher and at home so that she can say a simple phrase or sentence about each picture.*

Accommodations/supports for Colbie: *Picture symbols, simplified and shortened story paired with picture symbols for review, step-by-step picture directions for scanning, picture vocabulary cards*

Additional instruction for Colbie: *1) Colbie will practice reading simple lines from the adapted story for homework to work on decoding and fluency. 2) Colbie will listen to the simplified story read several times so that she can become more familiar with it. 3) The teacher will use time delay (a systematic instructional procedure described more fully in Chapter 10) to teach key vocabulary words prior to the class reading the story. 4) Colbie will practice what to say for each picture before she narrates it on the computer. 5) The SLP will work with Colbie on her narration to help with her articulation of specific sounds and words.*

Formative assessment for Colbie: *1) The sequencing activity will be graded.*

——● Maurita: Seventh-Grade Unit on *Crispin: The Cross of Lead*

Reading standard: *Students will identify or explain the use of literary elements (e.g., characterization, setting, plot, theme, point of view) in a passage.*

Lesson objectives: *1) Students will explain the character traits of the main characters and identify literary elements in the book that helped them determine the traits. 2) Students will map the plot structure using a plot graphic organizer including the characters, setting, rising action, climax, and conclusion.*

Instruction for the class, including Maurita: *1) The teacher will ask the students to share what they know about life in the Middle Ages and she will explain the social system, the plague, and the role of the church. The students will define vocabulary for the unit. 2) Students will read each chapter and discuss characters and events. A peer will present the vocabulary and event cards to Maurita as they are discussed or read in the book. Each student will keep a character log in which they describe the characters as they are introduced, add more information as they read about the characters, and note traits that change for each character. In addition, the students will provide details from the book that support these traits, citing page numbers. 3) At the end of the unit, students will create a plot graphic organizer. Maurita will use* *adapted vocabulary and event cards to complete a character chart, concentrating on primary characteristics for three main characters.*

Accommodations/supports for Maurita: *Tactile and picture symbols for vocabulary and character log and adapted switch with voice recording for character log.*

Additional instruction for Maurita: *1) The instructional team, peers, and Maurita's mother will take additional time to teach her the vocabulary and event cards made with the tactile and picture symbols. They will use a least-to-most prompting technique for this instruction (in which the student is first given a specified time to perform the step independently, then given a verbal prompt if necessary, followed by a model prompt, and finally physical guidance to perform the step if needed). 2) The instructional team will read vocabulary words from the book that begin with the same beginning consonant and vocabulary words that rhyme to help Maurita build her phonemic awareness. 3) The instructional team and her mother will work on building early literacy skills and communication by working on listening skills. They will read a summary of each chapter and a very simplified and shortened summary of the book to Maurita on several occasions. They will insert a repeating phrase such as, "Crispin lost everything and was declared a wolf's head" at the end of each small section and work with Maurita to activate the switch with the words WOLF'S HEAD recorded on it so that she can finish the sentence. They will attempt to shape her communication skills by first reading the sentence several times in the story; then reading it without the final words, looking for any type of response from Maurita; then shaping that response into a conventional response by prompting her to activate the switch that states the words. For example, the teacher reads the sentence without saying the final words, Maurita lifts her head a little, and the teacher helps her touch the switch and then praises her for finishing the sentence. 4) The instructional team and Maurita's mother will repeat development of the character chart after each chapter or two.*

Formative assessment for Maurita: *Data will be kept on the type of response Maurita provides for each request/question, the prompts needed, and accuracy of response (Figure 6.3).* (A blank form is included in the appendix at the end of the book.)

——● Juan: High School Language Arts Unit on Research

Reading standard: *Students will make inferences and answer questions by synthesizing concepts and ideas from multiple reading selections.*

Lesson objectives: *1) Students will use the table of contents, indices, subheadings, bold print, glossaries, graphic organizers, charts, and graphs of resources to gather pertinent information. 2) Students will provide information on the selected topic using a minimum of three sources.*

Instruction for the class, including Juan: *1) Students will sign up for one of the topics provided by the teacher (minorities in America, eco-friendly vacations, technology careers, famous authors, and severe weather events). 2) Working in topic area groups, the students will generate a list of questions they would like answered by conducting the research. Juan will be prompted to ask a question too. If he is unable to do so, he will be given two to three questions from which to choose. Each student will select the questions on which he or she would like to focus during the*

Plot Chart

Student name: Maurita

Plot Chart

Session	Accuracy/Prompt/Type of response								Independent responses	Independent and accurate responses
1	+/P/ turn head	+/G/ turn head	+/P/ turn head	+/P/ turn head	+/P/ turn head	+/P/ turn head	+/P/ turn head	+/P/ turn head	0	0
2	+/V/ look	+/G/ turn head	+/P/ turn head	+/P/ turn head	+/P/ turn head	+/G/ look	-/I/ turn head	+/P/ turn head	2	0
3	+/G/ look	+/G/ look	-/I/ turn head	-/I/ look	-/I/ turn head	+/P/ turn head	+/P/ turn head	+/P/ turn head	2	0
4	+/P/ turn head	+/P/ turn head	+/P/ turn head	+/P/ turn head	+/P/ turn head	+/G/ turn head	+/V/ look	-/I/ look	2	0
5	-/I/ look	-/I/ look	+/P/ turn head	+/P/ turn head	+/V/ look	+/V/ look	+/G/ turn head	+/P/ turn head	2	0
6*	+/V/ look	+/G/ turn head	-/I/ look	-/I/ look	+/P/ turn head	-/I/ look	-/I/ look	-/I/ look	5	0
7	+/P/ turn head	+/P/ turn head	-/I/ turn head	-/I/ turn head	-/I/ turn head	+/P/ turn head	+/P/ turn head	+/P/ turn head	3	0
8	+/I/ turn head	+/P/ turn head	-/I/ look	-/I/ look	+/I/ turn head	-/I/ look	-/I/ look	+/P/ turn head	6	2
9	-/I/ turn head	-/I/ turn head	-/I/ look	-/I/ turn head	+/P/ turn head	+/P/ turn head	+/I/ look	+/P/ turn head	5	1
10	-/I/ look	-/I/ look	-/I/ look	-/I/ look	+/G/ look	+/G/ look	+/I/ look	-/I/ look	6	2
Notes	*No minimal change in performance through Session 5, so added sound to the activity beginning with Session 6.									

Figure 6.3. Chart of Maurita's independent and accurate responses to choices for completing her plot chart. (Key: +, correct response; I, independent; –, incorrect response; I, independent; V, verbal prompt; G, gestural prompt; P, physical prompt.)

161

research. A teacher or peer will read the questions to Juan again and allow him to choose two to three questions to research. 3) Using the resources provided by the teacher, from the Internet, and the library (school and public), each student will research his or her topic. The teacher has included in each set of resources some easy to read reference books and simple web sites. Although Juan's reading ability is not sufficiently developed to independently read these resources, these adjusted-level materials do make it easier for him to comprehend what is read, which will in turn help build his listening comprehension skills. The special education teacher provides additional short pieces of information, including words that are within Juan's reading level, so that Juan can increase his decoding, vocabulary, and reading comprehension skills. 4) Each student will record on a paper or digital index card the source, title, summary (25 words or less), facts, and a picture representing the summary (student generated). Juan will copy the source, title, and at least one fact for each card and will dictate his summary. He will draw his own picture. 5) Each student will compile the research and present to the class. Juan will create his presentation on the computer so that he can practice and redo as necessary. He will then show the presentation to the class.

Accommodations/supports for Juan: Easy to read reference materials, simple web sites, short pieces of information within his reading level, and a word bank to use when writing and creating his presentation on the computer.

Additional instruction for Juan: 1) The teacher will prep Juan on the topical choices and possible questions he may want to ask. 2) The teacher and Juan's sister will preteach and practice vocabulary for the research (e.g., source, title, facts). 3) Juan will practice reading the short pieces of information to increase his reading skills. The teacher will use error correction and prompting to teach him to read these short pieces, as well as his vocabulary words. 4) Juan will use a summary pyramid to create his summary (Figure 6.4).

Formative assessment for Juan: Data will be kept on accuracy of answering comprehension questions over both pieces that he reads and those read to him. Accuracy data for identifying his vocabulary words and matching them to the correct meaning will be kept as well.

ASSESSING READING

A difficulty related to assessing student reading is that the skills that students develop in the learning-to-read phase are generally fairly easy to assess compared with assessing students' proficiency in the reading-to-learn phase. For example, if a teacher wants to test a second-grade student to see if she knows the sound the letter *l* makes, it is a fairly straightforward process. The teacher can show the student the letter written on a page and ask for the sound. To test fluency, the teacher can ask the student to read a passage and measure how quickly and accurately the student read, providing simple data to compare across time and different passages. Within comprehension, it is fairly simple to test literal understanding because the answers are in the text, and a student can actually point to the correct response. As students move from the learning-to-read phase into the reading-to-learn phase, however, especially at the higher grade levels, it becomes much more difficult to assess the higher level skills for which these students are responsible. For example, if a teacher asks a student a high-level comprehension question related to synthesizing

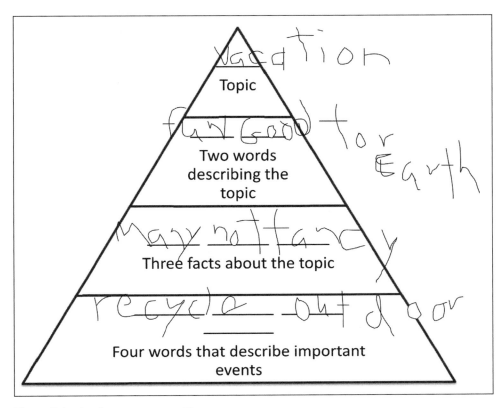

Figure 6.4. Juan's summary pyramid.

information, which is often done in the upper grades, it is much more difficult to break that task down into concrete elements. The teacher can make inferences about the student response but cannot know for sure if these inferences are correct. So, measuring learning-to-read skills is generally a much more straightforward process than measuring reading-to-learn skills. Pellegrino, Chudowsky, and Glaser (2001) have provided an outstanding overview of how we can (and should) determine what students know.

Colburn (2009) has provided a simple assessment primer that helps differentiate between the two main types of assessments: summative and formative. *Summative assessments* are the more traditional tests that are given to see what students have learned (e.g., end-of-grade tests). *Formative assessments* are meant to measure what students know to help inform instructional decisions. Teachers use the results of formative assessments to help them revise a plan or to make decisions about continuing or ending a lesson. Although the actual assessments themselves might look similar, it is the *intention* of how the results will be used that differentiates the two assessments types.

In an ideal learning setting, teachers set the objectives for what students are to learn. As the teacher provides instruction for the students, formative assessments are given during the instruction to help the teacher make decisions about student learning. Do students understand so far? Are there any general misunderstandings that need to be corrected so that we can keep going? For formative assessments, students making errors can actually be quite helpful because the teacher can look at the types of errors that students are making and try to analyze patterns across students that might lead to changing a lesson plan or modifying instruction to go over the errors and talk to students about change. For summative assessments, instruction is in the past, and the major goal is to see what was learned. Teaching is generally not modified, at least for the current students, and errors are considered incorrect responses rather than opportunities for learning.

In the real world of teaching and learning, both types of assessment are important. Formative assessments can be given to make sure that basic assumptions about students' background knowledge and general understandings are on track. Tests likely will not be graded because the point is not to assign a score or a grade but to see where things stand. These tests are diagnostic in nature and help guide future decisions, and they generally are not shared with others outside the classroom. Formative assessments might include ungraded practice tests, quizzes, homework assignments, or observing the student perform a task.

———● *For Juan's teacher to know if Juan is moving toward or mastering the desired outcomes, the teacher must first decide what evidence would clearly demonstrate that learning. His teacher decides that he needs to keep data on Juan's accurate and independent responses as evidence of his ability to decode. Evidence of Juan's ability to summarize his research is based on the accuracy of his summary pyramid. After reviewing the first couple of summary pyramids, the teacher notes that Juan is not completing them correctly, so his teacher decides that adding picture symbol cues to each part of the pyramid may help (Figure 6.5). He also decides to provide some additional instruction/practice on completing the pyramids. In addition, Juan will use a checklist (Figure 6.6) to self-monitor and evaluate his progress for completing the research assignment.*

Summative assessments, however, are almost always graded, with the results shared with others outside the classroom and often outside the school and school system. Although, in a broad sense, these tests might help shape future instruction for the next set of students, they generally provide a basic snapshot of specific student performance at a specific point in time. Summative assessments are often paper and pencil tests, are often machine scored (or at least scored by someone other than the teacher), and are often reported in broad categories that are not helpful to guide specific instruction. Alternate assessments are a form of summative assessments for students with significant cognitive disabilities.

———● *Colbie's state alternate assessment is a body of evidence, so her sequencing graphic organizer, which she completed independently and is scored, can then be submitted to partially address the required grade-level standard. Maurita's alternate assessment is a checklist. Her teacher observes her response on choosing character traits from a choice of three (two of which are reasonable distracters) and records the independence and accuracy level of the skill. She does this throughout the year for all the assessed skills. Juan's alternate assessment is a performance task. In the spring during a testing window he is given a task related to some of the grade-level standards, all of which he should have received instruction on. The teacher records his accuracy of performing the given tasks. All three students' teachers can use the assessment scores to look for areas to improve instruction for the following year.*

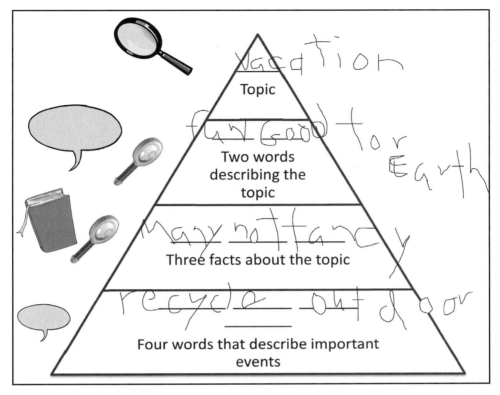

Figure 6.5. Juan's adapted summary pyramid.

Wininger (2005) came up with a hybrid of the two types of assessment, which he calls the "formative summative assessment." In this type of assessment, the teacher uses summative-type tests to teach students about testing itself. For example, when Wininger

To do	Finish			Correct mistakes
Choose topic	x			
Write two to three questions	x			
Create research card	l	2	3	
▪ Title	x	x	x	
▪ One fact	x	x	x	x
▪ Told summary	x	x	x	
▪ Drew picture	x	x	x	
Summary pyramid	x			x
Create presentation	x			x
Present research	x			

Figure 6.6. Juan's self-checklist.

gave college students a test in his educational psychology class, he went over the results of the test with the students, discussing the test items and giving feedback to students that would be helpful in terms of both students learning the content and students becoming better test takers. This process resulted in higher comprehension test scores compared with a control group of students who did not talk about the exam after it was graded. This type of hybrid assessment and subsequent feedback might also be helpful to teachers and students who are learning to take high-stakes tests.

———● *Because Juan takes a performance-type task at the end of the year, it might be helpful for him to complete similar standard-driven tasks throughout the year to gauge his progress and help him feel more comfortable with the process. The tasks, however, should cover a variety of standards and content so that he is not simply memorizing correct answers.*

SUMMATIVE AND FORMATIVE READING ASSESSMENT FOR STUDENTS WITH SIGNIFICANT COGNITIVE DISABILITIES

Alternate assessment is a form of summative assessment that summarizes student progress for students with significant cognitive disabilities who are unable to gain access to statewide assessments based on grade-level standards. Alternate assessments based on alternate, modified or grade-level achievement standards are defined by each state in compliance with NCLB and IDEA 2004 and take several different formats such as a portfolio of student work, checklist of skills learned, or a performance of a specific activity (Quenemoen, 2008). It is important to know state-specific requirements and the format of the alternate assessment.

Formative assessments in the form of homework and class assignments are common in general education classrooms but uncommon in special education classrooms for students with significant cognitive disabilities. When carefully planned and given with feedback, homework can raise student performance (Cooper & Nye, 1994; Marzano, Pickering, & Pollock, 2001; Wahlberg, 1984). Although there is no research to date on homework for students with significant cognitive disabilities, there is no reason to support a lack of homework for them. This is one form of formative assessment missing in special education classrooms.

———● *Maurita's extra practice at home and with the special education teacher on decoding, fluency, comprehension, and vocabulary could be used as formative assessments. If after reviewing the data, Maurita's teacher finds that Maurita is not responding to the tactile symbols, the teacher can meet with the speech-language, occupational, and physical therapists for additional ideas, such as using other sensory input to help increase Maurita's response.*

Collecting data for individualized education program (IEP) goals is a common practice in special education classrooms and can be used for formative assessment. Teachers can make use of the data collected on IEP goals to make educational decisions. Using frequent student data to assess student progress and to evaluate instruction can improve student outcomes and teacher decision making (e.g., Belfiore & Browder, 1992; Deno, 2003;

Good, Simmons, & Kameenui, 2001). A system of collecting and graphing data and using those data to modify instruction is described by Browder (2001), Snell and Brown (2006), and Hojnoski, Gischlar, and Missall (2009). Data can take a variety of forms, such as the number of correct responses (e.g., number of letter sounds correctly identified), steps in a task analysis (e.g., reading a recipe and cooking) completed independently, or a time-based rate (e.g., time to read a list of words). Teachers should record data at least once or twice a week and plot those data on a graph to detect changes in performance. Dates of instruction should be written along the bottom of the graph with the frequency/time scale from low to high written along the left side of the graph. Student progress can be seen by connecting the plots of student responses along a line. This line is then compared with an "aim" line drawn from the date when instruction began to the date the skill is expected to be mastered. This could be the date listed on the IEP or the date of the alternate assessment. By comparing the line of progress to the aim line, the teacher can tell if the student is making adequate progress to master the skill within the designated time frame. If the student's line of progress falls below the aim line, modification to the type of instruction is needed. This system does not require the use of a computer; graphing can be done on a piece of graph paper. An example is illustrated in Figure 6.7.

——●   *Colbie is learning the beginning letter sounds in words. The teacher is collecting data on how many times Colbie can select a picture that begins with the /s/ sound. The teacher presents Colbie with 10 sets of pictures—in each set, one picture starts with /s/ and there are three distracters—and records the number of times Colbie selects the correct picture. As in Figure 6.7, the thin line represents the aim line. The thicker line represents Colbie's progress. Colbie's line of progress is below the aim line, indicating slow progress.*

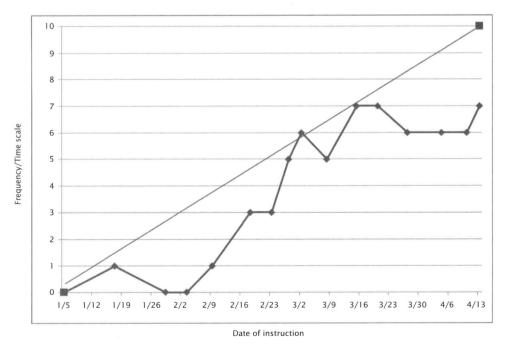

Figure 6.7.   Example of comparing a line of progress and aim line as formative assessment. (*Key:* thin line, aim line; thick line, Colbie's progress.)

Table 6.1. Application of Bloom's taxonomy to a reading assessment

Level of depth of knowledge	Description of the level	Application	Description of the assessment
Attention	Touch, look, vocalize, respond, attend	Student directed eyes toward word and reached out to touch it.	Teacher holds out individual word cards and asks student to look at and/or touch each one.
Memorize/recall	List, describe facts, identify, state, define, label, recognize, record, match, recall, relate	Student touched correct word when given four word options.	Teacher presents four word cards and asks student to find specific words.
Performance	Perform, demonstrate, follow, count, locate, read	Student selected correct word to complete a sentence provided by teacher.	Teacher presents a complete sentence (e.g., "Colbie likes to read"), then presents the same sentence with one word missing (e.g., "Colbie likes to ___") and four options to complete the sentence. Options can begin with one obvious correct word and other illogical options, then move to four similar options.
Comprehension	Explain, conclude, group/categorize, restate, review, translate, describe concepts, paraphrase, infer, summarize, illustrate	Student selected correct word to complete a sentence related to class experience.	Teacher presents an incomplete sentence related to an event in class and four word options to complete the sentence in which there is one clear correct answer. Options can begin with one activity-related item and other illogical options, then move to four similar activity-related options.
Application	Compute, organize, collect, apply, classify, construct, solve, use, order, develop, generate, interact with text, implement	Student used the cards to write sentences for the school newsletter.	Teacher presents pictures to assist the student in selecting words in an order to make a simple yet complete sentence.
Analysis/ synthesis/ evaluation	Pattern, analyze, compare, contrast, compose, predict, extend, plan, judge, evaluate, interpret, cause/ effect, investigate, examine, distinguish, differentiate, generate	Student sorted words based on categories.	Teacher gives student a stack of word cards and asks student to sort them by like/dislike, big/small, food/nonfood, and so forth.

From Flowers, C., Wakeman, S., Browder, D., & Karvonen, M. (2007). *Links for academic learning: An alternate achievement standards*. Charlotte: University of North Carolina at Charlotte; adapted by permission.

For more detailed information on creating these graphs and using them as a formative assessment, refer to Browder (2001) and Snell and Brown (2006).

One difficult area for teachers when creating assignments and summative and formative assessments for students with disabilities is the depth of knowledge required by the task. Different types of assignments and question formats require different types of thinking by the student. Bloom's Taxonomy (Bloom, 1956) is often used in general education to evaluate the depth of knowledge necessary to complete a task or answer a test question. Bloom offers a hierarchy of the level of difficulty associated with the depth of knowledge needed in order to complete a task or answer a question. A series of studies of states' alternate assessments found that most assessment items fall at the bottom end of Bloom's scale (Flowers, Browder, & Ahlgrim-Delzell, 2006; Flowers, Browder, Wakeman, & Karvonen, 2006a, 2006b, 2006c). Some creativity is needed to construct items for formative assessments that fall at the upper end of the depth of knowledge scale. These researchers have modified Bloom's description of the six levels of depth of knowledge in order to be more applicable to students with significant cognitive disabilities. An application of these descriptors on assessing reading is shown in Table 6.1. For a further discussion of depth of knowledge scales, see Chapter 10. Additional information of Bloom's Taxonomy can be found on *Big Dog & Little Dog's Performance Juxtaposition* web site (Clark, 2009).

CONCLUSION

In American society, reading is an important skill for everyone. And for many, reading is a pleasurable activity. Research has guided educators' teaching of reading in the general education curriculum. The NRP (2000) report identified five core components to successfully learning to read from a meta-analysis of the research, but other skills such as writing may also influence an individual's ability to learn to read. Research in teaching students with significant cognitive disabilities is woefully lacking. Research has found that these students can learn literacy skills, but researchers do not know nearly as much about how these students learn to read. Teachers need to be creative in designing age- and grade-appropriate reading activities. This chapter provided some ideas for how this can be accomplished. Formative and summative assessments can help teachers monitor reading success and let them know when they need to modify instruction to promote greater success. Creative teachers and researchers need to continue to work together and share what they have learned to provide all students with the opportunity to learn to read.

REFERENCES

Avi. (2002). *Crispin: The cross of lead.* New York: Hyperion Books for Children.

Basil, C., & Reyes, S. (2003). Acquisition of literacy skills by children with severe disability. *Child Language Teaching & Therapy, 19*(1), 27–48.

Belfiore, P., & Browder, D. (1992). The effects of self-monitoring on teachers' data based decisions and on the progress of adults with severe mental retardation. *Education and Training in Mental Retardation, 27,* 60–67.

Bloom, B.S. (1956). *Taxonomy of educational objectives, handbook I: The cognitive domain.* New York: David McKay.

Bradford, S., Shippen, M.E., Alberto, P., Houchins, D.E., & Flores, M. (2006). Using systematic instruction to teach decoding skills to middle school students with moderate intellectual disabilities. *Education and Training in Developmental Disabilities, 41,* 333–343.

Browder, D. (2001). *Curriculum and assessment for students with moderate and severe disabilities.* New York: Guilford Press.

Browder, D.M., Ahlgrim-Delzell, L., Courtade, G., Gibbs, S.L., & Flowers, C. (2008). Evaluation of the effectiveness of an early literacy program for students with significant developmental disabilities using group randomized trial research. *Exceptional Children, 75*(1), 33–52.

Browder, D.M., Gibbs, S.L., Ahlgrim-Delzell, L., Courtade, G., & Lee, A. (2007). *Early Literacy Skills Builder.* Verona, WI: Attainment Company.

Browder, D.M., Gibbs, S.L., Ahlgrim-Delzell, L., Courtade, G., Mraz, A., & Flowers, C. (2009). Literacy for students with significant cognitive disabilities: What should we teach and what should we hope to achieve? *Remedial and Special Education, 30*(5), 269–282.

Browder, D., Spooner, F., Ahlgrim-Delzell, L., Flowers, C., Algozzine, B., & Karvonen, M. (2003). A content analysis of the curricular philosophies reflected in states' alternate assessment performance indicators. *Research and Practice for Persons with Severe Disabilities, 28*(4), 165–181.

Browder, D.M., Wakeman, S.Y., Spooner, F., Ahlgrim-Delzell, L., & Algozzine, R. (2006). Research on reading instruction for individuals with significant cognitive disabilities. *Exceptional Children, 72,* 392–408.

Clark, D. (2009). *Bloom's taxonomy of learning domains.* Retrieved March 3, 2010, from http://www.sos.net/~donclark/hrd/bloom.html

Colburn, A. (2009). The prepared practitioner: An assessment primer. *The Science Teacher, 76*(4), 10.

Conners, F.A., Rosenquist, C.J., Sligh, A.C., Atwell, J.A., & Kiser, T. (2006). Phonological reading skills acquisition by children with mental retardation. *Research in Developmental Disabilities, 27,* 121–137.

Cooper, H., & Nye, B. (1994). Homework for students with learning disabilities: The implications of research for policy and practice. *Journal of Learning Disabilities, 27,* 465–536.

Deno, S.L. (2003). Developments in curriculum-based measurement. *Journal of Special Education, 37,* 184–192.

Downing, J.E. (2005). *Teaching communication skills to students with severe disabilities* (2nd ed.). Baltimore: Paul H. Brookes Publishing Co.

Erickson, K.A., Hatton, D., Roy, V., Fox, D., & Renne, D. (2007). Literacy in early intervention for children with visual impairments: Insights from individual cases. *Journal of Visual Impairment & Blindness, 102*(2), 80–95.

Erickson, K.A., & Koppenhaver, D.A. (1998). Using "Write Talk-nology" with Patrik. *TEACHING Exceptional Children, 31*(2), 58–64.

Fiscus, R.S., Schuster, J.W., Morse, T.E., & Collins, B.C. (2002). Teaching elementary students with cognitive disabilities food preparation skills while embedding instructive feedback in the prompt and consequence event. *Education and Training in Mental Retardation and Developmental Disabilities, 37,* 55–69.

Flowers, C., Browder, D.M., & Ahlgrim-Delzell, L. (2006). An analysis of three states' alignment between language arts and math standards and alternate assessment. *Exceptional Children, 72,* 201–216.

Flowers, C., Browder, D., Wakeman, S., & Karvonen, M. (2006a). *Alternate assessment alignment pilot study: Report to State A Department of Education.* Retrieved July 7, 2007, from http://education.uncc.edu/access/webdocs/Modified%20state%20report%20051506.pdf

Flowers, C., Browder, D., Wakeman, S., & Karvonen, M. (2006b). *Alternate assessment alignment study: Report to State B Department of Education.* Retrieved July 7, 2007, from http://education.uncc.edu/access/PDFlinks/Modified%20State%20B%20report%20012307.pdf

Flowers, C., Browder, D., Wakeman, S., & Karvonen, M. (2006c). *Portfolio alternate assessment alignment study: Report to State A Department of Education.* Retrieved July 7, 2007, http://education.uncc.edu/access/PDFlinks/Modified%20State%20C%20Alignment%20Report.pdf

Flowers, C., Wakeman, S., Browder, D. & Karvonen, M. (2007). *Links for academic learning: An alignment protocol for alternate assessments based on alternate achievement standards.* Charlotte: University of North Carolina at Charlotte. Retrieved May 4, 2010, from http://education.uncc.edu/access/PDFlinks/AlignmentManualVersion8%203%20FINAL%20110707.pdf

Good, R.H., Simmons, D.C., & Kameenui, E.J. (2001). The importance of decision-making utility of a continuum of fluency-based indicators of foundational reading skills for third-grade high-stakes outcomes. *Scientific Studies of Reading, 5,* 257–288.

Herber, H.L. (1970). *Teaching reading in the content areas.* Englewood Cliffs, NJ: Prentice-Hall.

Hojnoski, R.L., Gischlar, K.L., & Missall, K.N. (2009). Improving child outcomes with data-based decision making: Collecting data. *Young Exceptional Children, 132*(3), 32–44.

Hoogeveen, F.R., & Smeets, P.M. (1988). Establishing phoneme blending in trainable mentally retarded children. *Remedial and Special Education, 9,* 45–53.

Individuals with Disabilities Education Act Amendments (IDEA) of 1997, PL 105-17, 20 U.S.C. §§ 1400 *et seq.*

Individuals with Disabilities Education Improvement Act (IDEA) of 2004, PL 108-446, 20 U.S.C. §§ 1400 *et seq.*

Katims, D.S. (2000). Literacy instruction for people with mental retardation. Historical highlights and contemporary analysis. *Education and Training in Mental Retardation and Developmental Disabilities, 35,* 3–15.

Kliewer, C., & Biklen, D. (2001). "School's not really a place for reading": A research synthesis of the literate lives of students with severe disabilities. *Journal of The Association for Persons with Severe Handicaps, 26,* 1–12.

Kliewer, C., Biklen, D., & Kasa-Hendrickson, C. (2006). Who may be literate? Disability and resistance to the cultural denial of competence. *American Educational Research Journal, 43,* 163–192.

Marzano, R.J., Pickering, D.J., & Pollock, J.E. (2001). *Classroom instruction that works: Research-based strategies for increasing student achievement.* Alexandria, VA: Association for Supervision and Curriculum Development.

Mechling, L.C., & Gast, D.L. (2003). Multi-media instruction to teach grocery word associations and store location: A study of generalization. *Education and Training in Developmental Disabilities, 38,* 62–76.

National Reading Panel. (2000). *Report of the National Reading Panel: Teaching children to read: An evidence-based assessment of the scientific research literature on reading and its implications for reading instruction.* Washington, DC: National Institute for Literacy.

No Child Left Behind Act of 2001, PL 107-110, 115 Stat. 1425, 20 U.S.C. §§ 6301 *et seq.*

Pellegrino, J.W., Chudowsky, N.J., & Glaser, R. (Eds.). (2001). *Knowing what students know: The science and design of educational assessment.* Washington, DC: National Academy of Sciences.

Quenemoen, R. (2008). *A brief history of alternate assessments based on alternate achievement standards* (Synthesis Report 68). Minneapolis: University of Minnesota, National Center on Educational Outcomes. Retrieved May 4, 2010, from http://www.cehd.umn.edu/NCEO/OnlinePubs/Synthesis68/Synthesis68.pdf

Rehfeldt, R.A., Latimore, D., & Stromer, R. (2003). Observational learning and the formation of classes of reading skills by individuals with autism and other developmental disabilities. *Research in Developmental Disabilities, 24,* 333–358.

Shanahan, T. (2003). Research-based reading instruction: Myths about the National Reading Panel report. *The Reading Teacher, 56,* 646–655.

Skoto, B.G., Koppenhaver, D.A., & Erickson, K.A. (2004). Parent reading behaviors and communication outcomes in girls with Rhett Syndrome. *Exceptional Children, 70*(2), 145–166.

Snell, M., & Brown, F. (Eds.). (2005). *Instruction of students with severe disabilities* (6th ed.). Upper Saddle River, NJ: Merrill/Prentice Hall.

Wahlberg, H.J. (1984). Improving the productivity of America's schools. *Educational Leadership, 41,* 19–27.

Wininger, S.R. (2005). Using your tests to teach: Formative summative assessment. *Teaching of Psychology, 32,* 164–166.

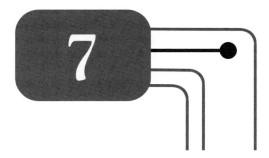

Math Instruction and Assessment Linked to Grade-Level Standards

Lou-Ann Land, David K. Pugalee, Anne Denham, and Harold L. Kleinert

Mathematics is a critical part of students' academic preparation and is a vital tool to students' life experiences both within and outside career and academic settings. Few would argue against the fact that mathematics preparation is tied to students' access to future academic studies and eventually to the level of their earning power. The National Council of Teachers of Mathematics (NCTM; 2000) has emphasized that the world is a mathematical one in which everyday activities, such as making purchases and decisions about services and products, rely on mathematical understanding. NCTM has further stressed that the level of mathematical thinking and problem solving necessary in work situations has increased dramatically. The importance of mathematics is perhaps best realized in the NCTM statement that "mathematical competence opens doors to productive futures" (2000, p. 3).

The National Mathematics Advisory Panel (NMAP; 2008), commissioned by the President to advise on improvements to mathematics education, reported that students should understand key mathematical concepts, develop automaticity with use of basic facts, develop flexible and automatic execution for standard algorithms, and employ these skills in problem solving. The NCTM (2000), in the curriculum document *Principles and Standards for School Mathematics,* has presented key mathematics goals for pre-K through 12th-grade students. The document describes 10 standards that represent a comprehensive and connected organization of key mathematical understandings and competencies of what students should know and be able to do. There are five content standards and five process standards. The content standards include 1) number and operations, 2) algebra, 3) geometry, 4) measurement, and 5) data analysis and probability. The process standards, which underscore ways of acquiring and using mathematics content knowledge, include 1) problem solving, 2) reasoning and proof, 3) communication, 4) connections, and 5) representation. For the five content standards, broad goals are presented for all pre-K through 12th-grade students, with specific expectations explicated for the various grade bands: pre-K–Grade 2, Grades 3–5, Grades 6–8, and Grades 9–12.

One noteworthy development is the importance of algebra as a focus of mathematics content. The NMAP (2008) recommended that schools ensure that all students have access to an algebra course. Such an authentic algebra course would provide a critical foundation including symbols and expressions, linear equations, quadratic equations, functions, and probability. According to the NMAP, mathematics curricula must simultaneously develop conceptual understanding, computational fluency, and problem-solving skills so that students are prepared for algebra. The centrality of algebra in the mathematics curriculum has many implications for providing special education students access to the general curriculum.

THE IMPORTANCE OF FORMATIVE
ASSESSMENT IN MATHEMATICS TEACHING AND LEARNING

Assessment is an integral part of any balanced and effective mathematics program. Formative assessment is particularly imperative if teachers are to understand students' thinking and make informed decisions about their instruction. The NCTM includes assessment as one of the underlying principles of mathematics standards, stating, "assessment should support the learning of important mathematics and furnish useful information to both teachers and students" (2000, p. 22). Although assessments include formalized measures of student performance, such as tests and inventories, assessment practices should also be an integral component of effective classroom practice, whereby teachers have information to guide their instructional decisions. The bottom line is that assessment should enhance learning. The NMAP (2008) reviewed studies related to assessment in mathematics and concluded that the use of formative assessments benefits students at all ability levels. This report also concluded that when teachers are provided with specific suggestions on *how* to use assessment data to differentiate instruction, the pooled effect on student performance is significant.

The NCTM (2000) has identified several ways in which good assessments can enhance student learning. First, tasks used in assessments convey to students ideas about the types of mathematical knowledge and performance that are valued. Techniques such as observations, interviews and conversations, and interactive journaling provide students opportunities to learn as they process ideas and answer the teacher's questions. Second, feedback from assessments help students set goals as they consider their own strengths and weaknesses. Third, scoring guides and rubrics may help teachers describe students' levels of proficiency in completing complex mathematical tasks. Assessment is inherently tied to teachers' good instructional decisions as they make judgments on when to review skills or concepts, how to revisit concepts that pose difficulty for students, and how to adapt and differentiate tasks for students who are struggling or those who need to be challenged. Consistent and quality formative assessment is tied to students' progress in achieving proficiency. The NMAP (2008) has suggested that formative assessments should lead to increased precision in how teachers use instructional time and assist teachers in identifying specific instructional needs of students. Furthermore, the NMAP advocated that teachers' regular use of formative assessment will improve students' learning if teachers have guidance on how to use such assessment to design and individualize instruction. These perspectives make certain the role of formative assessment in effective mathematics classrooms.

MATHEMATICS FOR ALL STUDENTS

The No Child Left Behind (NCLB) Act of 2001 (PL 107-110), the Individuals with Disabilities Education Act Amendments (IDEA) of 1997 (PL 105-17), and the Individuals with Disabilities Education Improvement Act (IDEA) of 2004 (PL 108-446) require schools to assure that all students make adequate annual progress toward achieving proficiency in mathematics. This requirement creates an extraordinary challenge for states as they work to provide effective instruction for students with disabilities. Students with disabilities often demonstrate ongoing and profound difficulties with multiple aspects of mathematics, such as number sense and number operations (Mazzocco, 2007), computation and problem solving (Miller, Butler, & Lee, 1998), language factors related to working with word problems, and the level of abstract thinking required to understand and apply mathematical concepts (Maccini & Gagnon, 2005).

As noted previously, the NCTM (2000) has recognized the power of mathematics for all students, as evidenced in the *Principles and Standards for School Mathematics*. In this document, the NCTM set forth several core statements that support mathematics teaching and learning. First, the equity principle provides a challenge to meet the mathematical needs of all students. "Equity does not mean that every student should receive identical instruction; instead it demands that reasonable and appropriate accommodations be made as needed to promote access and attainment for all students" (2000, p. 12). It is imperative that in embracing the spirit of this principle that the emphasis is on *all students* regardless of students' prior experiences, educational background, or type or level of disability. Though not the primary focus of this chapter, Barrera et al. (2006) have maintained that English language learners with disabilities are specifically targeted as part of NCLB and that there is an urgent need for research-based information to improve the standards-based instructional practices for English language learners with disabilities in grade-level content. Therefore, the equity principle highlights the central status that access plays in providing opportunities for all students to realize their mathematical potential.

What does it mean, however, to provide access to mathematics for students with disabilities, and how is that alignment accomplished? Too often, the emphasis in mathematics for students with disabilities has been on skill acquisition, typically within the context of number skills and operations or measurement (Browder, Ahlgrim-Delzell, Pugalee, & Jimenez, 2006; Browder, Spooner, Ahlgrim-Delzell, Wakeman, & Harris, 2008). The curriculum taught to students with significant cognitive disabilities has been limited. For example, one of the NCTM expectations defined for all students in upper elementary school (Grades 3–5) is to "propose and justify conclusions and predictions that are based on data and design studies to further investigate the conclusions or predictions" (2000, p. 178). Too often for students with cognitive disabilities, the intended outcome has been to create a graph. Although displaying data is an important expectation included in the standards, the cognitive complexity of completing a graph is typically lower than the thinking involved in making conclusions or predictions based on a graph; however, students with disabilities are often only engaged in completing a graph–a lower cognitive task. This focus does not provide access to this mathematical expectation. In order for the task to align to the intent of this expectation, students must be engaged in using the data from graphs to "propose and justify conclusions." This example illustrates the complexity involved in aligning the general mathematics curriculum in creating expectations for students with cognitive disabilities; it also shows that students may often be engaged in highly related tasks that do not necessarily meet the essence of the grade-level expectations.

Browder et al. (2006) specified seven steps in planning the link between general education standards and learning outcomes for special populations:

1. Identify the academic domains for planning.

2. Identify the state standards for the students' grade level.

3. Plan with general educators to focus on typical materials, activities, and contexts.

4. Plan alternate achievement targets; consider the students' symbolic level.

5. Review content and performance centrality.

6. Enhance the skills by applying long-standing values (values for teaching this population are reflected in the priorities chosen).

7. Identify pivotal skills for the individualized education program (IEP) and balance with other priorities.

These steps provide a coherent process by which teachers can make instructional decisions for students with disabilities. We detail these steps in an example describing a middle school algebra unit later in this chapter.

IMPLEMENTING QUALITY LESSONS

Fuchs et al. (2008) have identified seven instructional principles that promote mathematical learning for students with disabilities. First, *instructional explicitness* refers to instruction in which the teacher provides explicit and didactic teaching by sharing information focused on the goals of instruction. Fuchs and colleagues reported that a meta-analysis of 58 math studies showed that although most students advanced within programs with constructivist and inductive styles (in which students are expected to structure their own learning, discover relationships, and create their own knowledge), students with mathematics difficulties often did not profit in meaningful ways from such instruction. Students with disabilities in mathematics need very direct, clear models of how to solve problems. Second, *instructional design to minimize the learning challenge* anticipates and eliminates misunderstandings with precise details and the use of intentionally sequenced and integrated instruction focused on addressing gaps in achievement. The use of learning tools such as manipulatives and visuals enhance mathematics instruction while reducing confusion and the inability to maintain content. Third, a *strong conceptual basis* situates the procedures being taught in order to provide a solid conceptual foundation. Fourth, *drill and practice* are critical to maintaining skills through daily lessons, review, and computerized supports. Fifth, *cumulative review* reinforces practice and ongoing review, thus building a continued reliance on foundational skills being taught. Sixth, instruction must include *motivators to help students regulate their attention and behavior and work hard* integrating systematic self-regulation and motivation supports, including tangible reinforcers as necessary.

The seventh principle, considered the most essential, is *ongoing progress monitoring* to establish whether an educational intervention is effective for a particular student.

These principles have the potential to provide students with disabilities with the tools to engage in the learning process more effectively. Lee et al. (2006) have recommended the use of a variety of learning strategies during mathematics instruction, such as shadowing, verbatim notes, graphic or advance organizers, semantic maps, mnemonics, chunking, questioning, and visualizing strategies, which have been shown to be effective for students with intellectual and/or developmental disabilities. Though many associate these strategies with literacy instruction, these strategies have also shown promise as instructional supports for mathematics. The authors posit that such practices provide curriculum adaptation and augmentation strategies that can be used effectively across multiple content areas. These practices have thus shown broad promise in providing access to the general curriculum.

In a related study focusing on students with mild disabilities, Bottge, Reuda, LaRoque, Serlin, and Kwon (2007) contended that in order for special education teachers to provide instruction consistent with reform perspectives, teachers must be provided with extensive training on the way instructional materials are structured. What cannot be ignored in special education settings is the need to structure lessons in ways that are supported by the research. This is crucial given that special education students lack the conceptual foundation and sophisticated recall strategies necessary in developing problem-solving behaviors on their own. These problem-solving behaviors should be explicitly and intentionally developed while emphasizing the maintenance of basic skills.

Students with cognitive disabilities can experience relevant and substantive mathematics instruction and make progress related to grade-level content. Deliberate planning is required for this to occur. There must be clear and explicit links to grade-level mathematics goals and objectives. Lessons need to be delivered using a variety of instructional strategies that will assist students in making conceptual mathematics connections. Such strategies often employ a sequential approach, moving from concrete to representational to abstract (The Access Center, 2006; Louie, Brodesky, Brett, Yang, & Tan, 2008). Using concrete materials provides students from all backgrounds access to more abstract mathematical ideas, concepts, and processes. Such tools aid students in developing problem-solving skills and extending their understanding of important mathematical ideas.

The use of multiple supports and varied teaching strategies provides the types of accommodations necessary to address students at their level of access to particular concepts and ideas. Tools to support learning, such as manipulatives, along with research-based instructional practices, hold the potential to transform the way that mathematics is conceptualized for all students and to provide meaningful and appropriate levels of access to the general content area curriculum. When such alignment is made and coupled with solid instructional approaches, all students can make meaningful and noticeable progress toward being mathematically proficient.

Of course, many practitioners would agree that students with more mild disabilities (e.g., specific learning disabilities, mild intellectual disabilities) can make "meaningful and noticeable" progress in mathematics proficiency linked to grade-level content standards (that is linked to the five broad mathematical areas of number and operations, algebra, geometry, measurement, and data analysis and probability). And most educators would also agree that students with significant cognitive disabilities can make observable progress on mathematics related to two of these five basic mathematic content standards: number and operations and measurement. However, many educators would question whether the other three broad mathematics standards (algebra, geometry, and data analysis and probability) are appropriate subjects of study for students with significant cognitive disabilities, especially when those students are expected to master content in these areas that are linked to grade-level expectations.

This chapter is meant to accomplish two objectives: 1) to provide very specific examples of how students with significant cognitive disabilities can participate in complex mathematics instruction (including in such areas as algebra) linked to grade-level content standards, and 2) to provide teachers with strategies for formative and summative assessments of learning that will yield valuable data for student participation in alternate assessment based on alternate achievement standards (AA-AAS).

Rather than provide a number of examples in this chapter, we have chosen to illustrate curricular access, instruction, and assessment through a single extended example detailing a middle school algebra unit on linear equations. Within this example, we have also included one student with severe multiple disabilities (Joseph) because we find that teachers experience the greatest challenge in making this content meaningful to their students with the most significant disabilities.

————● Middle School Mathematics: An Instructional Unit

Maria, Isaiah, and Joseph are in the same eighth-grade inclusive mathematics class in which general and special educators collaborate to make sure all students progress within the general curriculum. As part of their middle school mathematics curriculum, the teachers need to address the following NCTM (2000) algebra goals for all students:

- Understand patterns, relations, and functions
- Represent and analyze mathematical situations and structures using algebraic symbols
- Use mathematical models to represent and understand quantitative relationships

The general education teacher plans to address these standards through a unit on linear equations. She has determined that there are two essential questions that will structure students' learning in this unit:

1. How can change be best represented mathematically?
2. How can patterns, relations, and functions be used as tools to best describe and help explain real-life situations?

The general and special education teachers collaborate to ensure that all students can gain access to the curriculum through representation (of materials), expression, and engagement (Center for Applied Special Technology, 2005). During planning meetings, the teachers work to identify supports needed for all students to gain access to the instruction and materials, as well as to show what they have learned. (See Chapter 4 for a further discussion of the terms *representation, expression,* and *engagement* as they apply to the concept of Universal Design for Learning.)

The general educator begins by giving the lesson to the special educator so that they can both review the expectations and outcomes for all students and then make any necessary modifications and adaptations for specific students. The following sections outline the process these teachers take to prioritize and/or modify grade-level outcomes without compromising the intent of the standards.

The Students

The teachers begin by looking at the strengths and needs for Maria, Isaiah, and Joseph. Maria has Down syndrome. She loves to interact with others and do what everyone else is doing. Maria's speech is extremely difficult to understand. She makes the connection between picture symbols and their representation of words and concepts, and she uses these symbols for communicating and reading, but she still prefers speech over picture symbols (because no one else uses them). She is able to write her name independently (if not required to remain on the line) and can copy printed text, but not very legibly. She can type given words and use an electronic picture writer to write sentences. Maria can identify basic high-frequency words and comprehend passages with the use of picture symbols and a text reader. She counts items to at least 20 consistently, recognizes numbers to 100, and can order numbers. She can identify coins and coin amounts; combine quarters for $0.50, $0.75, and $1.00; and use the next dollar strategy when making purchases. She is skillful at using a calculator. Maria also takes care of personal needs independently.

Isaiah has autism. He is nonverbal and uses a small set of picture vocabulary cards. He relies on a daily schedule to help him order his day and to anticipate changes in his routine. Isaiah recognizes numbers, and he can compare and order two- and three-digit numbers with supports in place. He can use a calculator for basic addition and subtraction but becomes distracted and agitated with more complex formulas. Isaiah will listen to stories for short periods of time and is able to communicate about the stories when presented picture symbols as he reads and listens. He is easily frustrated by other students and adults, and he uses Social Stories (explicit scripts for how to behave in social interactions; see Crozier & Sileo, 2005; Gray, 2000) for routine activities with some success.

Joseph has severe, multiple disabilities. He uses a wheelchair with trunk and neck support to maintain a straight posture, but he primarily leans to his left side unless fully engaged. He falls asleep often and cries when tired of his chair. Joseph can purposely hit a preprogrammed switch on command or to listen to music and stories on tape. He also demonstrates cause and effect by hitting a switch to activate various controls on the computer. Joseph has just been introduced to tactile cues and objects and to a voice output device that can be programmed to use up to eight different cells. Joseph has been working on discriminating up to four different cells, but he does not yet consistently use this device to initiate communication. He has been labeled as legally blind and wears glasses. He can see people and objects but with questionable perception.

Modifying the Outcomes

The teachers were worried about how to provide Maria, Isaiah, and Joseph access to complex mathematical concepts, such as the use of patterns and models in linear equations, as well as how to help them be a part of the classroom discussions and small-group activities. The teachers were also concerned about how Maria, Isaiah, and Joseph would engage in these grade-level mathematical processes. Yet the teachers also knew that the ability to figure out problems, create connections, and make representations would serve them well throughout their lives. The teachers decided that the complexity and/or difficulty of the outcomes needed to be modified and specified for each student. For instance, whereas Maria and

Isaiah could work on a variety of patterns (repeating patterns, expanding patterns), Joseph would work on recognizing a pattern from a nonpattern. Maria and Isaiah could work with all the models introduced in the lesson (patterns, tables, graphs, and functions), whereas Joseph would work primarily with patterns and tables. All of the students in the class would explain patterns at various degrees of complexity. The teachers first identified the most important concepts or ideas (i.e., enduring understandings) that all students should master by the end of the unit, and they then worked to ensure that each student was working toward those overarching concepts. The teachers also knew that Maria, Isaiah, and Joseph would need scaffolding and supports in order to work through each activity and be as successful and independent as possible.

The Middle School (Eighth-Grade) Lesson

Within this unit, the relationship between two variables (x, y) will be explored through patterns for all students. A six-step process will be used to teach students about linear equations (Alternate Assessment Collaborative, 2004):

1. Produce a pattern (copy, extend, and make predictions about the pattern).

2. Make and use a table (based on the pattern, make predictions).

3. Make and use a graph (based on pattern and/or table, make predictions).

4. Determine the mathematical rule.

5. Explain the rule.

6. Extend the pattern (generalize the rule).

This process was used repeatedly throughout the unit.

Throughout the next sections, we present the detailed lesson plan for all students, including the formative and summative assessments that would be embedded throughout this unit. Of course, the key for students with significant cognitive disabilities is how this general unit plan is adapted to address their unique learning needs. Teachers will want to think of how formative and summative assessments might play a role in documenting the achievement of students with significant cognitive disabilities toward these standards. Throughout this example, we provide illustrations of both modifying the instructional content and developing formative and summative assessments to provide those data for participation in state alternate assessments.

When reviewing lessons, teachers need to look at not only the content that is being taught but also the skills required for the students to participate fully in that instruction. As this unit was developed, the teachers knew they would be repeating the six-step process for teaching linear equations with each new problem introduced. The teachers also discovered that certain skills/tasks were repeated throughout the lessons, such as reading word problems, communicating ideas with peers, communicating with numbers, counting, writing, working with others, and creating models. These repeated skills were reviewed for each student to make sure the students had the necessary supports and information to participate in the lessons and to demonstrate what they knew. Identifying this repetition of tasks/skills is one way to create some consistency in the way students participate and not "reinvent the wheel" with every task. Many of these additional skills are included in the NCTM (2000) process standards noted previously in this chapter.

The teachers then created a menu of supports (Clayton, Burdge, Denham, Kleinert, & Kearns, 2006) based on the skills and tasks repeatedly presented throughout the lessons. Table 7.1 provides some suggestions to guide teachers in developing the menu of supports. This is a useful tool to record the ways in which a student will participate across a variety of tasks. The tool can be given to all those who work with the student—teachers, paraprofessionals, and even the student. Once this is completed, the teachers can concentrate on the content.

General Education Lesson: The "Big" Question   Students are given the following introductory problem as a means of framing their study of recurring linear patterns and linear equations:

> How much will it cost in materials to build a split rail fence down one side of my garden? How many total boards will I need for a fence of a given length? What will the total cost of the fence be if each board costs $4.00? What is a split rail fence? How is it made? And how can we solve this problem? We need to determine how patterns, relations, and functions can be used as tools to best describe and help explain this fence-building dilemma.

Prior to the first general activity, it will be important to reinforce or build background knowledge for Maria, Isaiah, and Joseph. The teachers brainstorm several ways in which the concept of patterns could be made accessible to Maria, Isaiah, and Joseph—these examples, taken from the students' own experiences, are provided in Table 7.2.

Breaking the Math Unit into Daily Instruction and Assessment Activities
This section describes the activities that comprise this instructional unit based on

Table 7.1. Hints in developing a menu of supports

Listen during lecture	What will the student do to demonstrate listening during lecture time?
	Hint: Provide graphics that represent elements of the lecture and have the student select the representative graphic as the teacher discusses each point. This can also be done digitally.
Read word problems	How will the student gain access to written information?
	Hint: The graphics provided to demonstrate listening may also be used in reading. Pair the graphics with the written word. If digital text is provided, a text reader may be used to read the notes. Take a digital picture. Graphics, tactile cues, or objects can all represent complete ideas.
Create models	How will the student reproduce and create patterns?
	Hint: Students may use manipulatives or computer programs using virtual manipulatives; a template may be needed to organize the manipulatives.
	How will the student create tables?
	Hint: Students may use tables labeled with picture symbols or object tables to represent the variables.
Communicate ideas	What will the student do to ask or respond to a question in class?
	Hint: Graphics may serve as possible answers to questions the teacher poses to the class. The student may select from two answers or use graphics where there is no wrong answer at the start to encourage participation and recognition.

Source: Clayton, Burdge, Denham, Kleinert, and Kearns (2006).

Table 7.2. Understanding the concept of patterns

Student	Instruction	Student performance
Maria	Point out a specific pattern found in everyday life (e.g., lines on the road) and the elements of that pattern (e.g., one white line, one space; one white line, one space) as student explores the patterns. Look at nonpatterns and point out how to determine nonpatterns. Repeat with other patterns and nonpatterns as needed (e.g., salary, the daily weather report).	Highlights elements of a given pattern Creates patterns using manipulatives or virtual patterns using interactive web sites or software Uses a checklist of elements for patterns and nonpatterns to help classify examples
Isaiah	Present student with the terms *pattern* and *nonpattern* as student explores examples of each. Terms may be in the form of written words, graphic symbols, or tactile representations. Model how to explore the elements within patterns by drawing or manipulating the elements of a pattern as the student also explores the patterns.	Explores a variety of simple patterns using a graphic representation of patterns and nonpatterns to help discriminate Sorts pattern examples into pattern and nonpatterns based on the graphic representations or objects located in the classroom After sorting patterns and nonpatterns, identifies why certain items were determined to be patterns (identifies the elements)
Joseph	Present student with tactile representations of the terms *pattern* and *nonpattern* as student explores the examples. Model how to explore the elements within patterns by guiding the student to feel the elements of a pattern.	Activates a communicator to listen to a description of a specific textured pattern while exploring the corresponding textured pattern; repeats for a nonpattern Feels the repetition of the elements in a pattern guided by a partner and identifies the correct repeated element versus a nonelement Disassembles a pattern created with manipulatives Creates a pattern using a simple jig Uses single switch input to add elements to build a pattern

the six-step process for teaching linear equations and describes how Maria, Isaiah, and Joseph participate throughout the unit. Each step could be considered a separate lesson within the unit.

Step 1: Produce a Pattern   The unit begins with students studying and producing their own patterns. Their role is to predict how the patterns operate as they are extended, specifically what are the repeating elements that make up the pattern, and is there a relationship between the elements?

The students will use straws, toothpicks, or other appropriate manipulatives to create an expanded square pattern. The pattern will describe expanded squares and focus on the relationship between the number of squares and the number of sides.

□	□□	□□□	□□□□
1 square	2 squares	3 squares	4 squares
4 straws	7 straws	10 straws	13 straws

As part of the instruction, the teacher models how to produce the square pattern. Following the teacher model, the students recreate the pattern through drawing or creating a physical model of the pattern using appropriate manipulatives.

Student Performance   Students will work in small groups and discuss the pattern; their discussion should include how the pattern is made, how it is continued, and the elements of the pattern. Students then reproduce the square pattern and explore how to extend the pattern (e.g., by using manipulatives, drawings, electronically).

Formative Assessment   The teachers will observe students as they engage in the problem (see NCTM, n.d.). The teachers take notes as they consider the following questions:

- How are students involved in the lesson activity?
- Can the students gain access to the materials?
- Are the students provided a way to communicate the concepts?
- How are the students interacting with the materials?
- Are they engaged?
- How successful are they?

The teachers work on creating the right balance between allowing students the opportunity to grapple with the concepts and offering the support and structure that the students need to complete the activity.

Building a Foundation for Linear Equations   In terms of the second major objective for the unit (i.e., using modeling and algebraic symbols to explain the structure of patterns), a variety of supports are used for each student to help scaffold the necessary skills and concepts. Throughout this activity, the teachers observe the students as a part of the formative assessment process. Although the math teacher focuses mostly on how the students understand the content in terms of the mathematical relationships inherent in the patterns, both teachers observe how the students are engaged throughout the activity. The teachers continue to ask if students

- Can gain access to and interact with the materials
- Are always provided a way to communicate the concepts
- Are interacting with the materials to represent the relationships
- Are successful in noting the patterns and solving the problems

In order to help each student engage with the materials and content, the teachers review the students' strengths and needs. Maria must reproduce and extend the pattern by drawing or using straws or other manipulatives; she then has to describe to a partner or within a small group how she knew what to do. Supports such as picture representations and/or software such as Writing with Symbols are available to her in describing the process. Her communication system also includes the relevant vocabulary needed to discuss patterns. In addition, Maria uses an interactive pattern generator (e.g., from http://www.shodor.org/interactivate/activities/Pattern Generator) to recreate and extend a pattern and then checks it with a partner. These accommodations enable her to meet the objectives set forth for the class, as well as

to work on other embedded skills such as turn taking in small groups and communication strategies (e.g., reading word problems, communicating about patterns).

Isaiah works on using modeling and algebraic symbols to explain patterns;
he uses manipulatives and describes to a partner how the pattern was created.
First, Isaiah uses step-by-step directions provided in symbol-based text to reproduce the pattern by using straws or other manipulatives. He is then given self-
correcting virtual manipulatives to recreate a pattern because errorless learning
has proven effective and has increased his opportunities for success. The teachers
also develop picture vocabulary cards that he uses as part of his communication
when reading about patterns as well as when writing or discussing patterns.
Supports such as sentence starters or choices are available to him as an option for
describing the patterns.

For Joseph, the task is scaffolded so that he has greater support at the onset
of the task, in this case to identify a pattern by copying and extending the pattern
independently. First, he is given the tactile cue for the square pattern

and asked to remove the correct number of manipulatives from a container needed
to recreate the first square of the pattern (4 sticks) and give them to a partner. He
is then given the tactile cue for continuing the square pattern

and asked to remove the correct number of manipulatives needed to continue the
pattern (3 sticks). Next his partner starts the pattern, but Joseph is responsible for
completing the third side of each section in the pattern. Once he has learned to
create the pattern with the help of a partner, he is given a cut-out of the pattern,
such as a stencil or template, to independently reproduce the pattern one section
at a time. As Joseph's skills in reproducing and extending the pattern increase, the
scaffolds are reduced. Joseph, however, always uses the tactile cues to gain access
to and communicate the information. Joseph also uses a voice output device
(Figure 7.1) that contains a number of cells of prerecorded information that he can
put together to describe how he created the pattern (e.g., cell 2: "This is a pattern
made with squares"; cell 3: "First I needed 4 sticks to make the square"; cell 5:
"Then I needed 3 sticks to complete the next square"). Joseph's voice output device
also includes several cells of prerecorded distracters that are relevant to other
parts of the algebra lesson (e.g., cell 1: "This is a nonpattern"; cell 6: "This is a triangle pattern"; cell 7: "This fence pattern has eight boards").

Reinforcing Step 1: Produce a New Pattern   The math teacher introduces a new pattern using right triangles.

She demonstrates the creation of a new pattern through at least four terms
or sequences and tells students that this new pattern will describe expanded right

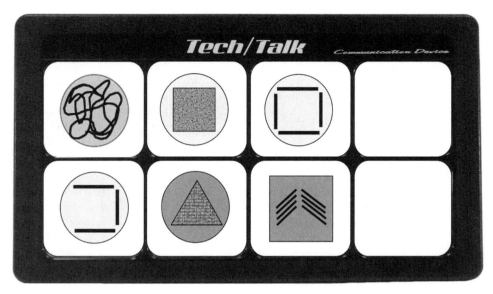

Figure 7.1. Sample voice output device for Joseph. (From Tech/Talk, Tech Series, Advanced Multimedia Devices, Inc.; adapted by permission.)

triangles. The students have to focus on the relationship between the number of triangles and the number of sides. As the teacher demonstrates the new pattern, the students copy the pattern through the four terms or sequenced repetitions and continue the pattern through at least two more terms (or sequences). Students then make a prediction for how many sides 9 triangles have.

Given the triangle pattern, students use manipulatives or drawings to reproduce the pattern and continue the pattern. Students describe the pattern (e.g., as the triangles increase by one, the sides increase by two; the first triangle required three sides, each additional triangle requires the addition of two sides). Taking into account the performance of each of the students in the previous lesson, the teachers review their menu of supports and decide to use the same supports for this portion of the lesson in which the students have to make patterns with triangles instead of squares, and again in later lessons for the fence pattern (the unit's "Big Question"). This lesson will be extended to include the use of tables and graphs to demonstrate how to record a pattern using numbers and symbols.

Maria is expected to fully participate in the lessons, using her knowledge of number sense, counting, and computation (using a calculator) to determine the patterns, create tables and graphs, and determine and describe the rule. If Maria has difficulty with the handwriting aspect of creating tables and graphs, she may use the computer to record her information. Isaiah is also expected to fully participate in the lessons with supports in place to determine the patterns and create tables and graphs. He is expected to describe the rule based on the pattern and models. Joseph is expected to participate in all the lessons to determine the pattern, create tables, and describe the rule based on the rate of change.

Special Adaptations for Joseph   Although we describe the adaptations provided for Maria, Isaiah, and Joseph to participate throughout this unit, we believe it is important to give a more in-depth description of how Joseph, our student with severe, multiple disabilities, is able to participate, especially as the lesson moves into more difficult mathematical concepts. We provide this more in-depth view of Joseph's work because teachers most frequently struggle with the adaptation of grade-level content for students with severe, multiple disabilities, especially as that content moves into progressively more abstract topics such as linear equations.

For Step 1, Joseph uses the following equipment: a computer with a monitor placed at his eye level and away from glare; an alternate keyboard with a custom overlay placed at an angle of at least 45 degrees to reduce the pressure required to control it; and single switch, instructional software that allows creation of individualized materials with voice output. The teachers make sure that Joseph is in a stable position to facilitate head control, maximize his visual field so that he is aware of both the monitor and keyboard, extend his range of motion to control a switch and alternate keyboard, and promote efficient gross and fine motor skills to distinguish textures of the keyboard surface. Note the importance of a transdisciplinary approach here—just as speech-language pathologists are essential in assisting students with significant cognitive disabilities in developing the language skills to understand and express academic content (see Chapter 3), motor specialists (physical and occupational therapists) are essential in enabling students to establish sufficient voluntary control to fully participate in learning that content.

Step 2: Make and Use a Table   In this part of the lesson, the math teacher 1) reviews the triangle pattern from the previous activity, 2) introduces the term *variables,* 3) has the students transfer their data from their patterns to a formal table, and 4) introduces the term *rate of change* (that is, how one variable changes as the other variable is changed). First, the teacher demonstrates that there are two variables: number of triangles (x) and number of sides (y). The teacher guides the students to analyze the triangle patterns and questions the students on what elements of the pattern they are analyzing. The teacher then demonstrates how to record the pattern in a T-chart by writing the numeric information in a column format. She always remembers to use the term *variables* when discussing the triangles and sides. The T-chart looks like this:

1 triangle	3 sides
2 triangles	5 sides
3 triangles	7 sides

The teacher demonstrates how to transfer the information to a table. She introduces the table format (e.g., passes out a template for the table, creates the table on an overhead projector, draws the table on chart paper, reproduces it with manipulatives) and then labels the table using the two variables (putting x in the first column to represent the number of triangles and y in the second column to represent the number of needed sides). The teacher finally models how to transfer the students' data about their pattern into the table. She explains how every time x (the independent variable) changes, so does y (the dependent variable). The teacher notes that when x has a specific number or value, so does y; they vary together. Throughout the lesson, she always remembers to reinforce the relationship between the x and y variables, expressed as the *ordered pair (x, y),* and restates that these pairs represent the number of triangles and number of sides that the students discovered in their pattern. As necessary, the teacher uses visual representation of that pattern to emphasize this point.

x		y	l
1		3	lll
2		5	lllll
3		7	lllllll
4			
5			
6			
10			

Figure 7.2. Template for relating number of triangles to the number of sides.

Students are next required to copy the information that the teacher has started within the table format and to continue to calculate or represent the pattern in the table, based on their observed predictions. Figure 7.2 presents the table template that the teacher provides the students, with the addition of picture representations.

The students are required to make predictions about the number of sides contained in 5, 6, and 10 triangles. The students record their predictions directly onto the table. As needed, students may use manipulatives to continue the pattern, count up from the numbers in the table, and so forth.

Special Adaptations for Joseph   Joseph has been working on copying and continuing the triangle pattern and needs to represent this in a table. Due to his significant needs, a range of assistive technology is used to maximize his performance and remove irrelevant factors, such as motor control, from interfering with his demonstration of learning. Using instructional software that includes the option to customize both input and output allows the teacher to design activities and overlays customized to meet Joseph's needs. Classroom Suite 4 (IntelliTools, 2003) is one software program that allows such custom design, and the IntelliKeys alternate keyboard (IntelliTools) with a custom Overlay Maker (IntelliTools) allows the control of cell size, surface texture, sensitivity, voice output, and switch input, which may be used together to provide an accessible learning environment for Joseph.

Joseph needs a way to show that he understands how to copy the pattern and represent it in a table. In the triangle activity, Joseph has learned that in order to add a triangle, he needs two sides. His teacher wants him to be able to enter this information in a table. Using Overlay Maker, the teacher has designed an overlay (Figure 7.3) that will act as an input for the computer, replacing the functions of

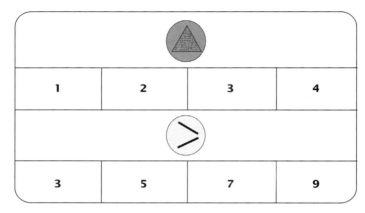

Figure 7.3. Joseph's alternate keyboard for triangle pattern.

the keyboard. The overlay has four rows. The top row acts as one large cell representing one triangle. The teacher can use manipulatives to create a tactile representation of the triangle. The third row is also one large cell that represents the two sides needed to complete another triangle. Texture is also added to this cell so that Joseph can distinguish the one triangle from the two sides. When each of these is activated or pressed, the cell inputs information into the computer. The monitor displays a table into which the information is entered, and audio output allows Joseph to hear his data entry. When the one triangle is pressed, a visual of the one triangle is displayed in the table, and Joseph hears "plus one."

The second row is divided into four smaller cells with a representation of the numbers 1, 2, 3, and 4. Each time Joseph adds a triangle to the screen, he then presses the number representing how many triangles are displayed and he hears that number. When the third row is pressed, a visual of the number of triangles is displayed in the lower half of the table and Joseph hears "plus two." The fourth row is divided into four smaller cells with a representation of the numbers 3, 5, 7, and 9. Each time Joseph presses the number of sides added to make a new triangle, he then presses the number representing the total number of sides used so far.

The rows on the keyboard are divided using texture to separate each cell with a raised line. This can be created with textured or thin pliable waxed yarn that can adhere and be removed from a surface, for example. This helps Joseph feel each cell as he enters the data and then move to the next entry. The keyboard has 10 cells, as noted in Figure 7.3. The onscreen display uses high-contrast colors so that Joseph is able to see the table as well as hear the information. If Joseph makes a mistake, it is recorded within the table, and he can also hear it. This allows the input to be erased, and Joseph can correct his mistake. The alternate keyboard also allows switch input. The switch can be programmed with different functions. For this activity, the switch is programmed to print Joseph's document. If Joseph works with a partner, his partner can make sure data are being entered correctly and within the correct row by using the regular mouse.

To enter the data, Joseph presses the cell to enter a triangle into the top row of the table. The first triangle is preprogrammed into the top row of the table on the computer screen, and each time Joseph presses the cell to continue the triangle pattern, he hears "plus one." Joseph then slides his hand down, over the raised

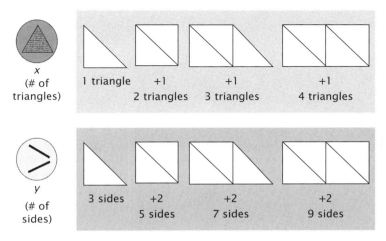

Figure 7.4.   Printout of Joseph's table.

line to the next row and the first cell (moving left to right) and presses the corresponding number to indicate how many triangles he currently has—he presses "2," a "2" is entered in the table, and he hears "2 triangles." Next Joseph moves to the third row. On pressing the cell, he enters 2 sides into the table and hears "plus two." Joseph slides his hand to the last row and moves over the raised line to the second cell and enters the data—he hears "5 sides." Moving his hand back up to the top to enter further data, Joseph repeats the process, adding a triangle (plus 1), indicating the number of triangles, adding two sides (plus 2), and then indicating the total number of sides. See Figure 7.4 for an example of the print out of Joseph's work.

    Step 3: Make and Use a Graph   The general education math teacher has introduced students to graphing in a previous unit. As a part of that instruction, students were introduced to a "coordinate plane," a plane in which the x-axis is horizontal and the y-axis is vertical, and the two intersect at the point (0,0; see Figure 7.5).

    Although coordinate planes are made up of four equal quadrants (sections), divided by the intersection of the x and y-axis, three of those four quadrants involve the use of negative numbers (which are not part of this specific unit). The teacher might even ask the students in which part of the coordinate plane they will find positive numbers for both x and y. Students will only be using that part of the coordinate plane—quadrant I—for this unit. Using the ordered pairs that students developed from their triangle patterns, (1, 3), (2, 5), (3, 7) (see Figure 7.2), the teacher reviews how to plot these ordered pairs on the coordinate grid. In pairs, students practice plotting various ordered pairs on their graph. Maria, Isaiah, and Joseph are each assigned a student partner as well. Figure 7.6 shows their work.

    Step 4: Determine the Mathematical Rule (Equation)   At this point, many teachers believe the content has become too difficult and is no longer appropriate or relevant for students with significant intellectual disabilities. As Jimenez,

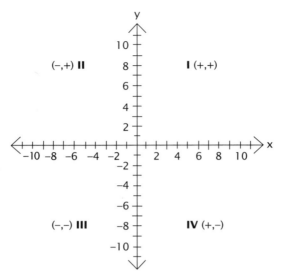

Figure 7.5. The quadrants or sections of a coordinate plane.

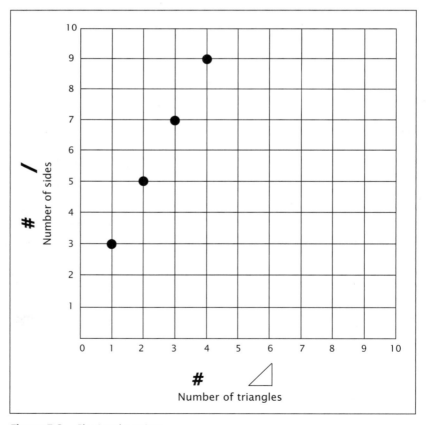

Figure 7.6. Plotting the points.

Browder, and Courtade (2008) have shown, however, students with significant intellectual disabilities can learn this important part of math.

The mathematical rule that the class will learn is based on information from the pattern, table, and/or graph. The rule will be an equation. A teacher-led discussion sharing observations of the relationship among the pattern, table, and graph is an important part of students learning to create that rule or equation themselves.

First the teacher introduces the concept of *rate of change* using the students' work on the triangle pattern, the table, and the graph they have completed (Figure 7.6). The teacher shows students how they can determine *how much change* occurs in the *y* variable with each change in the *x* variable. For example in the triangle pattern, the teacher demonstrates for the students that as the number of triangles increases by one, the number of sides increases by two. Working in pairs, the students will use the tables they completed in Step 2 to indicate the change in the *x* and *y* variables, as in the table in Figure 7.7.

Then, with the aid of the students' own graphs (Figure 7.6), the teacher shows the students how to determine the rate of change. The teacher notes that another way to say "rate of change" is "rise over run," in which "rise" represents the amount *y* increases each time (and the amount the student must count up the *y*-axis when plotting points) and "run" represents the amount *x* increases (and the amount the student must count across the *x*-axis when plotting points). Then starting with the first point or ordered pair on the students' graph (1,3), the teacher asks the students how many units they must count up and over to get to the next point on the graph (2,5). With their individual partners, students perform the visual calculations presented in Figure 7.8, showing the change (or rise and run) to get to each of the next points.

The next part of the step is to put the rule into a *mathematical formula.* The teacher explains that the rule is written as an algebraic equation and that the elements of that equation describe the value of the *y* variable (in this case, the number of needed sides for the triangles). To determine how many sides the students will need for *x* number of triangles, the teacher explains that the students have to write a formula that describes how much *y* goes up (the rise) each time *x* is increased (the run).

	x (Number of triangles)	*y* (Number of sides)	Point out/model how the number of triangles increases by 1 each time and the number of sides increases by 2 each time.
Change in *x*	0	–	Change in *y*
+1	1	3	+2
	2	5	
+1	3	7	+2
	4	–	
	5	–	

Figure 7.7. Determining the rate of change.

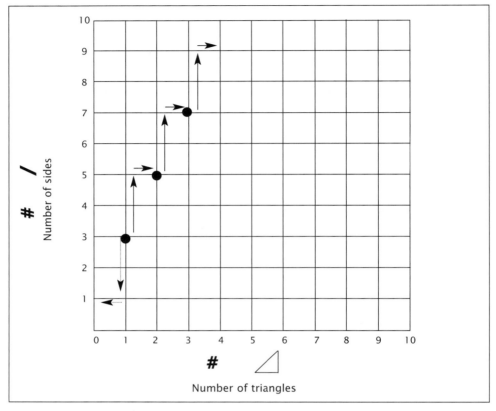

Figure 7.8. Calculating rise over run.

This formula is $y = \left(\dfrac{change\ in\ y}{change\ in\ x}\right)x + 1 = \dfrac{2}{1}x + 1$ or more simply, $y = 2x + 1$

Thus the students now have their equation that explains the rule they have been trying to discover. By practicing other patterns and problems that the teacher introduces, students will learn that there is a basic formula to describe any such pattern that rises at a constant rate. These formulas are called *linear equations*. By practicing across several patterns and problems, students will learn that the formula for linear equations is

$$y = \left(\dfrac{change\ in\ y}{change\ in\ x}\right)x + (y\text{-intercept}).$$

Or, to state it in words, where x is the independent variable and y is the dependent variable, the y-intercept is the value of y when x = 0. The formative assessment for this activity actually becomes the next step in the unit.

Special Adaptations for Joseph   In Step 4, Joseph needs to show he understands rate of change. Using the same customized overlay on the alternate keyboard (Figure 7.3), Joseph can accomplish this objective too. With the input placement kept consistent, Joseph's performance improves. This consistent placement also limits his errors and reduces fatigue. Joseph's teacher asks him to provide the rate of change, and Joseph responds by pressing the cells for triangles and number of sides in the correct order. The screen displays each triangle as it is added, as well as two sides for each additional triangle. Each time he hears "plus one" followed by "plus two." Joseph continues this pattern several times, completes the questions about rate of change, and displays it mathematically (Figure 7.9). In later parts of the lesson, as the students are taught to generalize what they have learned about the fundamental elements of linear equations and to apply those elements to different word problems, Joseph's teachers make sure that his overlay for his adaptive keyboard contains the key vocabulary for each problem he is presented (see Figure 7.10 for an example of that core vocabulary). Each time Joseph is assigned a word problem to solve, he generates the pattern expressed in numbers and determines the rate of change. Although Joseph may not have mastered all of the mathematical elements incorporated in the concept of linear equations, he has learned key principles directly linked to grade-level academic content (e.g., predicting patterns, using those predictions to determine rate of change). Moreover, predicting patterns and determining rate of change are not just academic notions unrelated to the real world; as Joseph and his peer partner learn in the final parts of this lesson, these concepts have direct applications to the problems individuals encounter in their everyday lives.

Step 5: Explain the Rule The students explain the relationship among the variables by creating a presentation. This can be done as a small group activity.

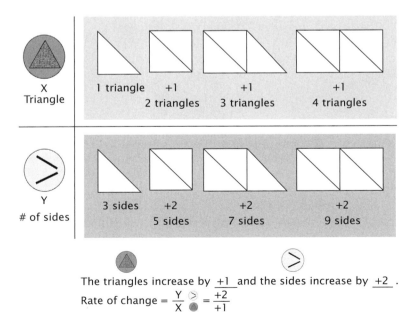

The triangles increase by +1 and the sides increase by +2 .

Rate of change $= \dfrac{Y \enspace \ominus}{X \enspace \blacktriangle} = \dfrac{+2}{+1}$

Figure 7.9. Joseph's printout of rate of change for triangles.

Information presented may include copies of the pattern, table, graph, and/or rule, along with observations such as

- Every time the number of triangles increases by one, the sides increase by two.

- On the graph, the *y*-intercept is 1 or the point on the *y*-axis is 1 when *x* is 0.

- The points on the graph have a linear relationship; a linear relationship means that the points lie along a line or look like a line.

- $y = 2x + 1$ – this is the rule for what we are seeing.

Students should use appropriate content vocabulary as they explain the rule. The use of mathematical vocabulary and symbols to share ideas, clarify meaning, and demonstrate what is learned is an important aspect of the NCTM process standard of communication. Figure 7.10 presents examples of appropriate vocabulary paired with picture representations.

Examples of how Maria, Isaiah, and Joseph each use their mode of communication to participate in the formative assessment for this important step can be found in the NCTM process standards discussed later in this chapter.

Step 6: Extend the Pattern (Generalize the Rule)

The students check predictions from the table and/or graph by using the equation or building the pattern with manipulatives. For example, students investigate how many sides there are in 12 triangles. To prove this, students can solve the equation for $x = 12$ ($y = 2[12] + 1$) or graph the line when *x* has a value of 12. In both cases, students find that the value or amount of $y = 25$ when $x = 12$.

#

number

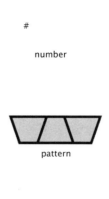

pattern

(x,y)

variable

linear

rate of change

Figure 7.10. Math vocabulary paired with picture representations.

The Culminating Activity of the Unit: Getting Back to the Big Question

It is now time for the students to use what they have learned about patterns and linear equations and to apply their new knowledge to the unit problem (the Big Question). Remember, the teachers discovered that certain skills/tasks were repeated throughout the lessons and they had created a menu of skills and supports. As they moved to the next word problem, the teachers created graphic and tactile representations needed for the problem, as well as overlays for Joseph.

Building the Fence Pattern and Creating a Table

The teachers first reintroduce the original problem to the students:

How much will it cost in materials to build a split rail fence down one side of my garden? How many total boards will I need for a fence of a given length? What will the total cost of the fence be if each board costs $4.00?

The teacher first demonstrates how the fence is built, and asks students to describe the pattern of the fence.

The students then recreate the first two or three sections of the fence based on a model. Again, working in pairs, students construct their fence sections, noting how many boards are required for each section. Students can either use picture diagrams to count the sections or actually build their sections using manipulatives, such as Popsicle sticks. As students build two to three sections, they transfer their information to a table indicating how the *y* variable (the number of boards needed) changes with changes in the *x* variable (the number of fence sections). The teacher reminds the students to be sure to label the table appropriately (i.e., putting *x* in the first column to represent sections and *y* in second column to represent boards), and instructs them to observe how every time *x* (the independent variable) changes, so does *y* (the dependent variable). The table may be modified for Maria and Isaiah using picture representations of the variables, as well as graphic representations for each element entered in the table. See Figure 7.11 for an example of an adapted table for this activity.

As students complete the table, they determine the ordered pairs or *x,y* points—(1,8), (2,16), (3,24)—that will determine their graph. Students then plot the points on their graph. The assessment product for this activity for Maria and Isaiah will be a completed graph with the *x*- and *y*-axes labeled (as it is for the other students). For Joseph it will be a print out of the table, completed using the computer program and alternate keyboard. Figure 7.12 presents his table completed via his alternate keyboard. Notice how Joseph completes his predictions for the fence pattern in much the same way as he completed his table for the triangle pattern (Figures 7.3 and 7.4).

Determining the Rate of Change

Next, the students need to determine the rate of change and make predictions about the number of boards needed for various numbers of sections. Students first describe the rate of change indicated by their tables above—that is, that the number of boards needed (*y*) increases by eight each time that the number of fence sections (*x*) increases by one. The teacher asks students to complete the table for additional sections of the fence and asks, "If we add another section of fence, what will we write in column *x*, and how many boards will we add to column *y*? For 6 sections? For 10 sections?" Students next determine the mathematical rule or equation for their problem. The teacher leads a discussion of the relationships among the pattern, table, and graph to help students develop the rule. It is now time for students to complete the final steps to solve the problem.

Summative Assessment for the Unit

Students create a presentation to identify the rule, explain the relationship among the variables in the pattern, and extend the pattern. This represents their summative assessment for the unit, and for students in the alternate assessment for that state, may be included as evidence of their achievement of the math standard related to linear equations.

x ∧∧∧	y ▱
1 ∧	8 ●●●●●●●●
2 ∧∧	16 ●●●●●●●● ●●●●●●●●
3 ∧∧∧	24 ●●●●●●●● ●●●●●●●● ●●●●●●●●
4 ∧∧∧∧	
5 ∧∧∧∧∧	
6	
10	

Figure 7.11. Calculating the fence pattern—adapted table for Maria and Isaiah. (*Key*: x, number of fence sections; y, number of boards.)

Information presented may include copies of the pattern, table, graph, and/or rule, along with observations such as the following:

- Every time the section increases by one, the boards increase by eight.
- It takes eight boards for each section of fence built.
- On the graph, the y-intercept is 0, or the point on the y-axis is 0 when x is 0.
- The points on the graph have a linear relationship or lie along a straight line.

As part of this activity, students use this information to write the rule as an equation: $y = 8x$. Joseph's print out of his work with his adapted keyboard is included in Figure 7.13. His equation is expressed with picture symbols at the bottom of his printout and is derived directly from the fence pattern the students have described.

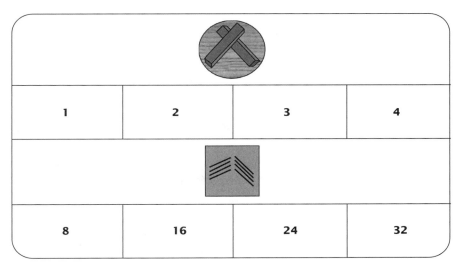

Figure 7.12. Joseph's sample alternate keyboard for the fence pattern.

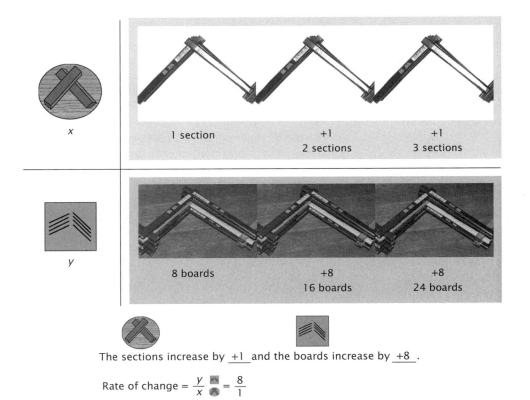

The sections increase by _+1_ and the boards increase by _+8_ .

Rate of change = $\dfrac{y}{x}$ = $\dfrac{8}{1}$

Figure 7.13. Joseph's printout of rate of change for fences problem.

If it is determined that it will require seven sections to construct a fence down the side of the garden, then the students use their rule to determine how many boards they will need: $x = 7$, therefore $y = 8(7)$ or 56 boards. The final step is for students to determine the cost of the fence if each board costs \$4.00 (56 boards $\times$ \$4.00/board = \$224.00). Students calculate this cost as part of this presentation.

In order to further stimulate their thinking about the problem and to connect it to a real-world situation, the teacher also asks the students to write a brief paragraph about how they might earn the money to construct the fence.

National Council of Teachers of Mathematics Process Standards

Remember that the teachers analyzed the lessons for repeated skills and tasks that students needed to gain access to and participate in a variety of lessons, such as reading word problems, communicating ideas with peers, and communicating with numbers. Many of these additional skills are included in the NCTM (2000) process standards noted earlier in this chapter, but we feel that it is important to describe some of these processes here.

Communication   It is important that students' communication systems provide for the opportunity to share ideas and communicate mathematically. The key ideas and vocabulary that were repeated throughout the lesson had to be included in all students' modes of communication. Mathematics has the added challenge of including numbers within that communication. The teachers discussed the relevant vocabulary needed to communicate about patterns in algebra, as well as the best way to represent those concepts using each student's mode of communication. As noted in Figure 7.10, the teachers made sure that Maria, Isaiah, and Joseph had symbols and/or objects that represented all of the important concepts and vocabulary about the content.

Furthermore, Joseph had a tactile representation of a pattern and nonpattern to use in learning to distinguish patterns from nonpatterns and communicating that understanding. Maria's speech-language pathologist came to the class for 30 minutes per week to ensure that the math vocabulary was included in her picture symbols, as well as to support her conversational skills with her peers. Because of the cooperative group and partner supports in place for these lessons, it was natural to combine content vocabulary and conversational skills. Maria and Isaiah were provided with the picture representations of specified vocabulary paired with words. All three students used the graphic and tactile representations of the vocabulary to not only participate in class and small group instruction but also to read and write about mathematics.

As the students were taught to generalize what they had learned about the fundamental elements of linear equations and to apply those elements to new word problems, Joseph's teachers made sure that his overlay for his adaptive keyboard contained the key vocabulary for each problem he was presented. Although Joseph may not have mastered all of the mathematical elements incorporated in the concept of linear equations, he learned key principles directly linked to grade-level academic content.

Connections   Thinking mathematically involves looking for connections, and making connections builds mathematical understanding. Without connections, students must learn and remember too many isolated concepts and skills. With connections, they can build new understandings on previous knowledge. The teachers wanted to help the students find connections that would enable them to not only extend their mathematical thinking but also help them navigate in their daily lives and across content areas. For instance, in a language arts lesson on writing cover letters and resumes, the students discussed how buildings were numbered in their neighborhoods. They found that even numbered buildings were on one side of the road and odd numbered buildings were on the opposite side. The students represented the building numbers that would be on the right side of the road using a table. This concept of patterns and linear equations was a connection that the students could use to build new understandings on previous knowledge across subjects.

Representation   Representation is central to the study of mathematics. Students can develop and deepen their understanding of mathematical concepts and relationships as they create, compare, and use various representations. Representations—such as physical objects, drawings, charts, graphs, and symbols —also help students communicate their thinking. To give the students more strategies for problem solving, the teachers modeled and encouraged students to use representations throughout the algebra unit, as well as throughout their day and across academic subjects. An example of how representation can be used throughout the day was discovered when Isaiah began to indicate that he did not want to have an assigned person walk with him from math to science class (assistance he had always needed in the past). His teacher decided to work with Isaiah to create representations of the route to his next class, after Isaiah had learned to use graphs, to find the shortest route between two points. Isaiah practiced using the models for the route between math class (point A) and science class (point B) and matching the representations to the actual physical route. Through this process, he learned how to walk through the hall himself after being released from math class 3 minutes early (which enabled him to follow the route without the distractions of a hallway full of students). See Chapter 10 for further examples of how functional or life skills, essential to student independence, can be related to the academic content of the general curriculum.

CONCLUSION

The study of mathematics is truly meant for all students—students can gain access to even complex grade-level content when they have appropriate support and representations and when that content is connected to experiences in their own lives. The extended example we provided in this chapter was meant to illustrate how formative and summative assessments, including performance data, student work samples, and graphs of student performance (perhaps constructed by the students themselves as part of their learning of the math standards), can be used in the context of the documentation required for AA-AAS. For example, as part of the students' summative evaluation, they were assigned to small groups to present how the group used the concept of linear equations to solve a problem

Student name:_____	**Date:**_____	
1) Student communicated the correct information.		
a) Student gave facts.	Yes	No
b) Student organized facts logically.	Yes	No
c) Student used facts to state conclusion.	Yes	No
2) Student remained on topic.	Yes	No
3) Student referred to the following to support his or her presentation:		
a) Pattern	Yes	No
b) Table	Yes	No
c) Graph	Yes	No
d) Rule	Yes	No
4) Student used the following content vocabulary:		
a) Variable	Yes	No
b) Rate of change	Yes	No
c) Line/linear	Yes	No

Figure 7.14. Summative evaluation for a student's presentation.

of interest to the students in that group. Each student, including Maria, Isaiah, and Joseph, had a specific role in his or her group. Their roles reflected both an opportunity to demonstrate their knowledge of the math content of the unit and an opportunity to embed essential communication and social skill objectives from their respective IEPs within their presentations.

In Figure 7.14, we present an evaluation form for how teachers might record each student's performance in their small-group presentation. For students such as Maria, Isaiah, and Joseph, this evaluation form could be adapted to their mode of communication so that they could review their work. It could also be included as part of the alternate assessment in many states, with notations of the supports used, any modifications of the content, and the independence or prompt level of student responses directly recorded on the form. This documentation would be appropriate for students whose respective states' alternate assessments used either a portfolio or checklist format.

We understand the immense challenge teachers face in creating access to grade-level math content standards for students with significant cognitive disabilities. We also understand that this challenge becomes even more difficult when teachers are trying to make connections among complex, higher-level mathematical concepts (e.g., linear equations) for students who have not previously had training in each of the major strands of mathematics (number and operations, algebra, geometry, measurement, and data analysis and probability). We really do not know what students are capable of learning unless we provide carefully planned access to each of the major strands of mathematics and engage the students with that content through connections personally relevant to their own lives. As teachers engage students in more complex content, teachers may be surprised by both what the students learn and the problems that they can solve in both classroom and large-scale assessments.

REFERENCES

The Access Center. (2006). *Strategies for accessing algebraic concepts K–8*. Retrieved October 19, 2009, from http://www.k8accesscenter.org/training_resources/AlgebraicConceptsK-8.asp

Advanced Multimedia Devices, Inc. (2009). *8 message communicators*. Retrieved December 30, 2009, from http://www.amdi.net/communicators

Alternate Assessment Collaborative. (2004). *Instructionally embedded assessment: High school mathematics*. Denver: Colorado Department of Education. Retrieved February 3, 2009, from http://www.measuredprogress.org/resources/inclusive/research/grants/co/download/ EAG_Math_IEA.pdf

Barrera, M., Liu, K., Thurlow, M., Shyyan, V., Yan, M., & Chamberlain, S. (2006). *Math strategy instruction for students with disabilities who are learning English* (ELLs with Disabilities Report 16). Minneapolis: University of Minnesota, National Center on Educational Outcomes.

Bottge, B.A., Reuda, E., LaRoque, P.T., Serlin, R.C., & Kwon, J. (2007). Integrating reform-oriented math instruction in special education settings. *Learning Disabilities Research & Practice, 22*(2), 96–109.

Browder, D.M., Ahlgrim-Delzell, L., Pugalee, D.K., & Jimenez, B.A. (2006). Enhancing numeracy. In D.M. Browder & F. Spooner (Eds.), *Teaching language arts, math, and science to students with significant cognitive disabilities* (pp. 171–196). Baltimore: Paul H. Brookes Publishing Co.

Browder, D.M., Spooner, F., Ahlgrim-Delzell, L., Wakeman, S.Y., & Harris, A. (2008). A meta-analysis on teaching mathematics to students with significant cognitive disabilities. *Exceptional Children, 74*, 407–432.

Center for Applied Special Technology. (2005). *UDL guidelines*. Retrieved July 14, 2009, from http://www.cast.org/publications/UDLguidelines/version1.html#intro

Clayton, J., Burdge, M., Denham, A., Kleinert, H., & Kearns, J. (2006). A four-step process for accessing the general curriculum for students with significant cognitive disabilities. *TEACHING Exceptional Children, 38*(5), 20–27.

Crozier, S., & Sileo, N. (2005). Encouraging positive behavior with social stories: An intervention for children with autism spectrum disorders. *TEACHING Exceptional Children, 36*(6), 26–31.

Fuchs, L.S., Fuchs, D., Powell, S.R., Seethaler, P.M., Cirino, P.T., & Fletcher, J.M. (2008). Intensive intervention for students with mathematics disabilities: Seven principles of effective practice. *Learning Disability Quarterly, 31*(2), 79–92.

Gray, C.A. (2000). *The new Social Story book: Illustrated edition*. Austin: TX: Future Horizons.

Individuals with Disabilities Education Act Amendments (IDEA) of 1997, PL 105-17, 20 U.S.C. §§ 1400 *et seq.*

Individuals with Disabilities Education Improvement Act (IDEA) of 2004, PL 108-446, 20 U.S.C. §§ 1400 *et seq.*

IntelliTools, Inc. (2003). *Classroom suite* [Computer software]. Petaluma, CA: Author.

Jimenez, B., Browder, D., & Courtade, G. (2008). Teaching an algebraic equation to high school students with moderate developmental disabilities. *Education and Training in Developmental Disabilities, 43*(2), 266–274.

Lee, S., Amos, B.A., Gragoudas, S., Lee, Y., Shogren, K.A., Theoharis, R., et al. (2006). Curriculum augmentation and adaptation strategies to promote access to the general curriculum for students with intellectual and developmental disabilities. *Education and Training in Developmental Disabilities, 41*(3), 199–212.

Louie, J., Brodesky, A., Brett, J., Yang, L.M., & Tan, Y. (2008). *Math education practices for students with disabilities and other struggling learners: Case studies of six schools in two Northeast and Islands Region states* (Issues and Answers Report, REL 2008–No. 053). Washington, DC: U.S. Department of Education, Institute of Education Sciences, National Center for Education Evaluation and Regional Assistance, Regional Educational Laboratory Northeast and Islands.

Maccini, P., & Gagnon, J.C. (2005). Mathematics and technology based interventions. In D. Edyburn, K. Higgins, & R. Boone (Eds.), *Handbook of special education research and practice* (pp. 599–622). Whitefish Bay, WI: Knowledge by Design.

Mazzocco, M.M.M. (2007). Defining and differentiating mathematical learning disabilities and difficulties. In D.B. Berch & M.M.M. Mazzocco (Eds.), *Why is math so hard for some children? The nature and origins of mathematical learning difficulties and disabilities* (pp. 29–47). Baltimore: Paul H. Brookes Publishing Co.

Miller, S.P., Butler, F.M., & Lee, K. (1998). Validated practices for teaching mathematics to students with learning disabilities: A review of literature. *Focus on Exceptional Children, 31*(1), 1–24.

National Council of Teachers of Mathematics. (2000). *Principles and standards for school mathematics.* Reston, VA: Author.

National Council of Teachers of Mathematics. (n.d.). *Alternate forms of assessment.* Retrieved February 5, 2009, from http://www.nctm.org/resources/content.aspx?id=17290

National Mathematics Advisory Panel. (2008). *Foundations for success: The final report of the National Mathematics Advisory Panel.* Washington, DC: U.S. Department of Education.

No Child Left Behind Act of 2001, PL 107-110, 115 Stat. 1425, 20 U.S.C. §§ 6301 *et seq.*

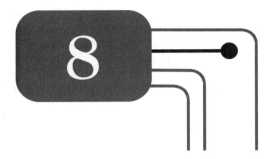

Science Instruction and Assessment Linked to Grade-Level Standards

Ginevra Courtade, Deborah A. Taub, and Michael Burdge

In 1996, the National Research Council (NRC) published the *National Science Education Standards* (NSES), which focused on "science standards for all students…regardless of age, gender, cultural or ethnic background, disabilities, aspirations, or interest and motivation in science" (p. 2). Goals for school science outlined in these standards are meant to develop a "scientifically literate society" by educating students who know and understand about the natural world, use scientific processes and principles to make decisions, engage in public discussion about scientific and technological matters, and increase economic productivity by using their knowledge and skills in their careers.

Four principles underlie the NSES:

1. Science is for all students.

2. Learning science is an active process: Students engage in and create their own learning experiences.

3. School science reflects the intellectual and cultural traditions that characterize the practice of contemporary science: Students understand how science contributes to culture.

4. Improving science education is part of systematic education reform: The standards are one component of overall science education reform.

Although these science standards target all students, there were few discussions of applications for students with significant cognitive disabilities until the No Child Left Behind (NCLB) Act of 2001 (PL 107-110) required the assessment of all students in science by

2007. As with other content areas, these students' participation in large-scale testing could take the form of alternate assessments. However, even with the stipulation of an alternate assessment for accountability purposes, the questions of how to teach and assess science in an everyday classroom setting still remained. A comprehensive literature review (Courtade, Spooner, & Browder, 2007) of science instruction for students with significant cognitive disabilities uncovered a limited number of studies to help answer these questions. Of the 11 studies that were discovered, 8 dealt with concepts that related to only one content area of the NSES (Content Standard F: Science in Personal and Social Perspectives). Nearly all of these studies were designed to address daily living skills but had content that overlapped with science. Although the literature review revealed a limited number of ideas for teaching science content, it was clear that formative assessments were used in all cases to make responsive changes to instruction.

None of the studies analyzed by Courtade et al. (2007) addressed a fundamental aspect of science: the process of inquiry. The NRC asserted that "inquiry is a set of interrelated processes by which scientists and students pose questions about the natural world and investigate phenomena; in doing so, students acquire knowledge and develop a rich understanding of concepts, principles, models, and theories" (1996, p. 214). Within the NSES, inquiry is described as a critical component of a science program. Inquiry-based instruction requires more than hands-on activities. Students also learn to follow a problem-solving process that is applicable to the real world. For students with significant cognitive disabilities, learning more about the world around them (content of science) could enhance quality of life. What may be even more useful for this population, like all science learners, is to acquire a process for gaining and evaluating new information through inquiry. Inquiry-based learning is a process that can be used across the life span and in any content or life skill area.

In addition, one study investigating what employers were looking for in their employees indicated that

> For high school graduates, the five most frequently reported applied skills considered "very important" for successful entry level job performance are: *Professionalism/Work Ethic* (80.3 percent), *Teamwork/Collaboration* (74.7 percent), *Oral Communications* (70.3 percent), *Ethics/Social Responsibility* (63.4 percent), and *Critical Thinking/Problem Solving* (57.5 percent). (The Conference Board, Corporate Voices for Working Families, the Partnership for 21st Century Skills, & the Society for Human Resource Management, 2006, p. 20).

Teamwork, work ethic, communication, and critical thinking/problem solving are all a part of the national expectations for students learning science. In order to prepare students for a job, these skills must be taught, and this can be done in the context of science. Furthermore, teachers must understand how to assess these skills as they are teaching science in their classrooms.

FOUNDATIONS OF SCIENCE ASSESSMENT

In a publication titled *Classroom Assessment and the National Science Education Standards* (2001) the NRC provides teachers with "A Framework for Formative Assessment," which includes the following questions:

1. Where are you trying to go? (identify and communicate the learning and performance goals)

2. Where are you now? (assess or help the student to self-assess current levels of understanding)

3. How can you get there? (help the student with strategies and skills to reach the goal) (p.14)

Teachers considering these questions will not only be able to make important instructional changes to meet the needs of the students but also will foster self-determination skills by providing students the opportunity to self-assess and work toward the goal.

To facilitate knowledge across all areas of science and make instruction relevant for all students, teachers must be aware of the science content standards and the main concepts that relate to each standard. Table 8.1 lists the eight categories of content standards (NRC, 1996) and their main concepts, as well as examples of what might be taught related to each standard.

Table 8.1.   Eight categories of content standards

Category	Concept	Teaching examples
Unifying concepts and processes in science	*General:* Students learn overall concepts and processes to help them understand the natural world, such as systems, order, and organization; evidence, models, and explanation; change, constancy, and measurement; evolution and equilibrium; and form and function. *Grade-specific:* Occurs throughout all grades	Understanding the concept of a model
Science as inquiry	*General:* Students learn skills, such as observation, inference, and experimentation. They also learn the abilities necessary to perform scientific inquiry and understand scientific inquiry. *Grade-specific:* Occurs throughout all grade	Supporting statements with facts found through research; designing investigations that incorporate the skills, attitudes, and values of scientific inquiry; designing, conducting, evaluating, and revising experiments
Physical science	*General:* Students learn science facts, concepts, principles, theories, and models that are important for all students to know, understand, and use related to physical science *Grade-specific:* K–4: Properties of objects and materials; position and motion of objects; light, heat, electricity, and magnetism 5–8: Properties and changes of properties in matter; transfer of energy 9–12: Structure of atoms; structure and properties of matter; chemical reactions; motions and forces; conservation of energy and increase in disorder; interactions of energy and matter	Relating changes in states of matter to temperature; examining the various sources of energy; explaining the relationship between electricity and magnetism

(continued)

Table 8.1. *(continued)*

Category	Concept	Teaching examples
Life science	*General:* Students learn science facts, concepts, principles, theories, and models that are important for all students to know, understand, and use related to life science. *Grade-specific:* K–4: Characteristics of organisms; life cycles of organisms; organisms and environments 5–8: Diversity and adaptations of organisms; populations and ecosystems; regulation and behavior; reproduction and heredity; structure and function in living systems 9–12: Behavior of organisms; matter, energy, and organization in living systems; interdependence of organisms; biological evolution; molecular basis of heredity; the cell	Identifying structures of living things; constructing models of plant and animal cells and comparing similarities and differences; applying knowledge of cells to variations in cells, tissues, and organs of different organisms
Earth and space science	*General:* Students learn science facts, concepts, principles, theories, and models that are important for all students to know, understand, and use related to earth and space science. *Grade-specific:* K–4: Properties of earth materials; objects in the sky; changes in earth and sky 5–8: Structure of the earth system; earth's history; earth in the solar system 9–12: Energy in the earth system; geochemical cycles; origin and evolution of the earth system; origin and evolution of the universe	Describing the alignment of the earth, moon, and sun and how this alignment affects the earth; comparing the earth's tilt and rotation to seasonal changes; analyzing the evolution of the ocean floor
Science and technology	*General:* Students establish connections between the natural and designed worlds, which provide them with opportunities to develop decision-making abilities. *Grade-specific:* K–4: Abilities to distinguish between natural objects and objects made by humans; abilities of technological design; understanding about science and technology 5–8; 9–12: Abilities of technological design; understanding about science and technology	Describing how modern tools affect daily lives; illustrating the advantages of simple machines; collaborating to present research on current environmental and technological issues to predict possible solutions

Category	Concept	Teaching examples
Science in personal and social perspectives	*General:* Students are provided a means to understand and act on personal and social issues. *Grade-specific:* K–4: Personal health; characteristics and changes in populations; types of resources; changes in environments; science and technology in local challenges 5–8: Personal health; populations, resources, and environments; natural hazards; risks and benefits; science and technology in society 9–12: Personal and community health; population growth; natural resources; environmental quality; natural and human-induced hazards; science and technology in local, national, and global challenges	Developing responsibility for the environment; critically analyzing mass media reports of scientific events; evaluating environmental factors that affect populations and communities; constructing and defending potential solutions for current science-technology-societal issues
History and nature of science	*General:* Students learn to use history in school science programs to clarify different aspects of scientific inquiry, the human aspects of science, and the role that science has played in the development of various cultures. *Grade-specific:* K–4: Science as a human endeavor 5–8: Science as a human endeavor; nature of science; history of science 9–12: Science as a human endeavor; nature of scientific knowledge; historical perspectives	Exploring science careers in individual states; relating societal, cultural, and economic issues to key science innovations; formulating explanations based on historical observations and experimental evidence

Source: National Research Council (1996).

SCIENCE IN THE LIVES OF STUDENTS WITH DISABILITIES

Learning about science is theoretically important for everyone, yet how does it make a difference for students with disabilities? The following examples illustrate how science instruction made a difference in the lives of three students.

——● *When Essie was in fourth grade, a good portion of the curriculum was spent on learning about her home state of Kentucky. While in class, Essie did not demonstrate a high degree of interest in the geological points of interest, but something must have "clicked." On a family trip to visit relatives, she pointed to and verbally identified the "knobs" (cone-shaped hills caused by erosion) as they passed them on the highway. It wasn't long before her favorite video (a popular preschool cartoon) was replaced by a new favorite—a documentary produced by the statewide public television network on the geology of Kentucky.*

As part of a middle school science class, Jordan was required to enter the science fair. From a list of possible projects, she chose making models of various chemical compounds. Her brother, a high school senior, helped her make the models out of marshmallows and toothpicks. Now, when Jordan's brother comes home from college, one of the activities they love to do together is select a compound from an old science text, research it on the Internet, and make a model.

Ben's science instruction had mostly consisted of planting a bean in a paper cup until he was in an inclusive high school science class, in which part of the course was devoted to botany. He seemed totally disinterested until the class began soil sampling and testing and experimenting with growing plants under various conditions. On a trip with his mother to a local greenhouse, Ben caused quite a stir when he wandered off and was found in the "Employees Only" section where different soils were kept. Using his augmentative and alternative communication (AAC) device in his daily living class, Ben chose to write and send his resume to that same greenhouse where, after high school graduation, he began working on a supported work placement.

These examples show how science can have an impact on students with significant disabilities, but what does science instruction actually look like for this population of students? The following sections illustrate how two teams of teachers (one elementary and one high school) think about, plan for, and deliver science content for a highly diverse classroom of learners.

———● An Elementary School Example

Mr. Martino is a new special education teacher. He is excited to begin his career in a fully inclusive elementary school. He looks forward to collaborating with general education teachers to provide modifications and adaptations in content areas to meet the needs of his students. Mr. Martino is especially impressed with what he has heard about Mrs. Knowles and her inquiry-based science instruction. Three of the students on Mr. Martino's caseload are in Mrs. Knowles fourth-grade class this year. The two teachers have a common weekly planning time, and Mr. Martino's schedule is flexible enough to allow him to be in certain classes (he collaborates with more than one general education teacher at the school) at critical times. When he is not in a specific class, the students on his caseload are supported in a variety of ways according to their needs and the demands of the instruction. At times, a paraprofessional may be present, or a peer or the general education teacher may provide support. Mr. Martino makes sure that the supports are in place and being delivered appropriately, and the general education teachers are responsible for delivering the content instruction.

In their first collaborative planning meeting, Mr. Martino and Mrs. Knowles discuss the first science unit for this year. Mrs. Knowles arrives at the meeting with a unit plan called *Rocks Really Rock!* (see LEARN NC, n.d.). She gives Mr. Martino the following information on the standards and goals with which the unit aligns so that he fully comprehends what the unit is about (i.e., classifying rocks using mineral identification tests):

- The unit aligns with NSES Content Standard D, Earth and Space Science: Properties of Earth Materials (Grades K–4).

- Earth materials are solid rocks and soils, water, and the gases of the atmosphere. The varied materials have different physical and chemical properties, which make them useful in different ways, for example, as building materials, as sources of fuel, or for growing the plants we use as food.

- The unit also aligns with Goal 2 of the fourth-grade state standard: The learner will conduct investigations and use appropriate technology to build an understanding of the composition and uses of rocks and minerals.

- Objective 2.02: Recognize that minerals have a definite chemical composition and structure, resulting in specific physical properties including: hardness, streak color, luster, magnetism.

Mr. Martino looks over the standards, goal, and objectives, and feels comfortable with the concepts. However, he is not sure about the inquiry process Mrs. Knowles uses to teach her lessons. Mrs. Knowles uses Box 8.1 and the variations of classroom inquiry (e.g., a student posing his or her own question, selecting among several questions, clarifying a question posed by the teacher, or simply engaging in the question initially assigned by the teacher; NRC, 2000) to explain the process to Mr. Martino.

BOX 8.1

Content standard for science as inquiry: Fundamental abilities necessary to do scientific inquiry (Grades K–4)

- Ask a question about objects, organisms, and events in the environment
- Plan and conduct a simple investigation
- Employ simple equipment and tools to gather data and extend the senses
- Use data to construct a reasonable explanation
- Communicate investigations and explanations

Source: National Research Council (2000).

After looking over the skills necessary to "do scientific inquiry," Mr. Martino immediately begins to think about how his students who have individualized education programs (IEPs) communicate and how difficult abstract concepts may be for them to understand and communicate during the lesson. The variations in the essential features of inquiry, however, give him a guide with which to work. Using this continuum of student self-direction and structured teacher guidance, Mr. Martino believes that he can help his students understand the process of inquiry, as well as the concept of composition and uses of rocks and minerals, without losing the "big idea" of the unit.

Mrs. Knowles is a veteran teacher. She has worked with many students over the years and believes that all students can learn from her inquiry-based science instruction. However, she knows that collaborative preplanning is a must. She can explain precisely what the outline, outcomes, and assessments for the unit and lessons look like from the general education curriculum, and, in turn, will rely on Mr. Martino to explain the modifications and adaptations needed for the students with IEPs.

Lesson outline: Students will collect rocks to be used in the unit; students will test rocks for physical properties; students will record conclusions of assessments.

Learning outcomes: Students will use scientific inquiry to analyze and classify rocks by their physical properties; students will engage in hands-on activities to analyze and classify various rocks (e.g., they will collect several different rocks and test each one for hardness, streak [i.e., does the rock leave a mark when scratched on concrete], and the presence of carbonate).

Assessment: Students will determine which of their rocks is hard (it scratches glass) and which is soft (it can be scratched by a fingernail, a penny, or a paper clip) and classify them by the results; students will classify their rocks according to whether or not the rocks leave a streak; students will classify their rocks according to the presence or absence of carbonate using their recorded results on the matrix.

Cross-curriculum/embedded skills: Same/different, math (numbers), English and language arts/communication (use oral and written language to present ideas), inquiry and logical argument (prediction, conduct an experiment, observation), cooperative learning/social behavior.

The Students

The three students who will need modifications and adaptations to meaningfully gain access to the curriculum and instruction are Neil, Katy, and Tim. Mr. Martino and Mrs. Knowles discuss the strengths and needs of each student as they plan for the rocks unit.

Neil has a moderate disability and is independent in his daily living, social, and communication skills. He primarily uses a walker but can ambulate with crutches for short distances around the classroom. Positive behavior supports help him complete academic tasks. He can read at approximately the first-grade level but has difficulty with comprehension. He can remember concrete information when read to, but he still struggles with abstract thoughts. He uses basic phonics to sound out simple words and can write most of those words independently. He copies text easily and neatly. Neil has basic competencies on the computer but uses it primarily for games. He can complete most computation problems using a calculator and has a sense of quantity with any amount he can relate to money (e.g., he knows that 255 is more than 200 because he knows that $2.55 is more than $2.00). He works well with peers but is sensitive to the differences in his learning needs when he feels set apart from other students. Neil's IEP objectives include 1) improving reading fluency and comprehension, 2) dictating or writing a complete paragraph using descriptors (adjectives and adverbs), 3) completing a three-step computation problem, and 4) independently transitioning from sitting to standing with crutches.

Katy has a severe disability. She uses an electric wheelchair that she can propel safely and accurately for distances less than 25 feet in typical school environments (e.g., classroom, hallway, cafeteria, gymnasium). Given verbal cues, she uses an AAC device with up to five messages. She can identify common objects by direct selection and is beginning to use black and white picture symbols. She needs prompting beyond naturally occurring cues to attend to an activity or task for longer than 3 minutes (e.g., Katy needs a verbal reminder from her teacher approximately every 3 minutes to keep her "eyes on me"). Katy frequently needs to rest following seizures, which occur approximately six times per day. Katy's IEP objectives include 1) identifying content-related picture symbols, 2) self-propelling her wheelchair safely and accurately for moderate distances (up to 150 feet), 3) following verbal and/or pictorial directions involving up to three steps, 4) matching shapes (geometric, symbolic, letters, numbers), 5) using 1-to-1 correspondence, 6) independently initiating communication using her AAC system, and 7) remaining on task for 5 minutes with natural cues.

Tim also has a severe disability. He uses a walker to get around and a double-switch (i.e., two pressure switches presented simultaneously that allow the user to choose from two different responses) communication device for expressive communication (but he needs verbal reminders and physical assistance to use it). Picture symbols and objects are used with Tim to supplement verbal information. Because of limited communication skills, he sometimes uses inappropriate behaviors (e.g., scratching, screaming) to express frustration. He can repeat single words verbally. He is supposed to wear hearing aids but generally will not leave them in without frequent reminders and supervision. Tim's IEP objectives include 1) using an AAC device to answer verbal questions related to content and/or social situations, 2) ambulating more efficiently (increase distance and speed), 3) following three-step classroom routines, 4) decreasing the number of inappropriate behavior responses (scratching and screaming), 5) using 1-to-1 correspondence, 6) identifying objects/pictures/symbols by direct selection related to content and social contexts, and 7) wearing hearing aids for increasing lengths of time.

Modifying the Lessons

After Mr. Martino and Mrs. Knowles discuss the students, they decide to delve into the five individual lessons that make up the unit. They develop a matrix that breaks down each lesson into smaller components (listed under the column General Education Lesson) and then design modifications for Neil, Katy, and Tim. Figure 8.1 presents this matrix. (A blank form is located in the appendix at the end of the book.) The teachers also draft a list of materials and adaptations that they will need to have ready for each student. A separate plan is also developed to positively support behavioral needs and maintain engagement in the lessons. With this type of thorough planning, the teachers ensure that these three students will have in place the supports they need to receive the information in ways they can understand, show what they have learned, and stay actively involved and interested in the activities. (See Chapter 5 for a further description of this process.)

Although this unit is clearly designed for instructional purposes, it is precisely under each of the "Assessment" portions in Figure 8.1 (especially in Days 4 and 5) that work samples so essential to many states' alternate assessments can be compiled for Neil, Katy, and Tim. Furthermore, any unit similar to this offers ongoing assessments that can be used to make decisions about daily student progress, as well as the instruction itself. The results of formative assessments offer the teacher the chance to monitor student progress and design instruction as necessary. The results of a summative assessment not only offer work samples that could be used in state alternate assessments but also help the teachers and parents gauge the student comprehension of the concepts taught in the unit overall. Sample assessment forms from this unit are shown in Figures 8.2 and 8.3.

Matrix Lesson Plan

General education lesson	Modifications for *Neil*	Modifications for *Katy*	Modifications for *Tim*
Day 1 Students will examine different rocks in the classroom.	Neil will touch rocks one at a time and verbally describe characteristics of the rocks.	Katy will touch the rocks one at a time and match characteristics of the rocks to pictures preprogrammed on her augmentative and alternative communication (AAC) device (e.g., color, texture).	With a peer partner, Tim will touch the rocks one at a time and select a characteristic of the rocks (given two picture choices preprogrammed on his AAC device, e.g., hard/soft). Tim's peer partner will verbally state the word Tim has chosen, and Tim will verbally repeat the word his peer partner verbalizes.
The teacher will introduce vocabulary words/definitions related to rock properties (hard, soft, streak, carbonate).	Neil will copy the vocabulary word and definitions from a worksheet and will match the written definitions to the vocabulary words.	Katy will match pictures of the rocks labeled with the vocabulary words to the actual rocks.	With a peer partner, Tim will match rocks with similar characteristics (given two picture choices preprogrammed on his AAC device, e.g., hard/soft). Tim's peer partner will verbally state the word Tim has chosen, and Tim will verbally repeat the word his peer partner verbalizes.

Figure 8.1. Matrix lesson plan illustrating modifications for Neil, Katy, and Tim.

(continued)

	Neil	Katy	Tim
The teacher will demonstrate rock properties (hardness: scratches glass; softness: can be scratched by a fingernail or paper clip; streak: rock leaves mark on concrete; absence or presence of carbonate—fizz from vinegar).	Neil will verbally participate in a class choral response of the rock property.	Katy will participate with her AAC device in a class choral response of the rock property (given the choices hard, soft, streak, and carbonate).	With a peer partner, Tim will verbally participate and use his AAC device in a class choral response of the rock property (given two choices).
The teacher will model classification of the rocks using the "Rock Discovery Chart" with five rocks.	Neil will observe the teacher as she models the rock classification.	Katy will observe the teacher as she models the rock classification and will be given one reminder (teacher pointing to a picture symbol for "eyes on teacher") if Katy is inattentive.	With a peer partner, Tim will observe the teacher as she models the rock classification and will be given reminders from a peer (peer pointing to a picture symbol for "eyes on teacher") if Tim is inattentive.
Assessment: The students will practice classification of five more rocks (teacher performs tests and whole group classifies).	Neil will answer questions about where rocks belong on a chart and give answers based on the characteristics (e.g., "the rock is soft because it could be scratched with a paper clip").	Given two picture choices, Katy will indicate to the teacher/peer partner by pointing to which area on the chart a rock belongs.	Given two choices of rocks with symbols for the properties shown underneath them, Tim will match the rock to be classified with the correct choice or property.
Day 2 Students will review vocabulary.	Neil will copy the vocabulary word and definitions from a worksheet and will match the written definitions to the vocabulary words.	Katy will work with a peer partner who will use a constant time delay (CTD)* procedure to teach her to identify picture symbols with written words that represent the rock properties.	Tim will work with a peer partner who will use a CTD procedure to teach him to identify rocks with written words attached to them that represent the rock properties.

*Constant time delay is an errorless learning procedure in which a request is given to a student (e.g., point to the word *hard*), a simultaneous prompt is used (e.g., instructor points to the word as she makes the request), and the student is given corrective feedback (e.g., "Yes, you pointed to the word *rock*"). This immediate prompt is called 0-second delay. After a set number of trials at 0-second delay, the request is given again, without the simultaneous prompt, and a delay period (e.g., 4 seconds) is given to wait for the student to respond. If the student responds within the delay period, corrective feedback is given. If the student does not respond within the delay period, the correct answer is given (Collins, 2006).

Figure 8.1. *(continued)*

Matrix Lesson Plan

General education lesson	Modifications for Neil	Modifications for Katy	Modifications for Tim
Students will collect five rocks to be used in the lesson.	With a peer partner, Neil will choose five rocks outside (the partner will pick up the rocks Neil asks for and put them in a bag for Neil, who uses crutches).	Katy will use her electric wheelchair to get outside. A peer partner will gather a tray full of rocks (15–20) and bring them to Katy. Katy will choose five rocks with help from the partner to count them.	Tim will use his walker to get outside. A peer partner will gather a tray full of rocks (10) and bring them to Tim. Tim will select five rocks with help from the partner to count them.
Assessment: The students will label rocks 1–5.	Neil will write the numbers 1–5 on flash cards and stick the rocks on the flash cards with putty.	Katy will attach the rocks to flashcards labeled 1–5 and touch the numbers 1–5 on her AAC device as her peer partner touches and reads the numbers on the flashcards.	Tim will attach the rocks to flashcards labeled 1–5 and repeat the numbers as his peer partner verbalizes them.
Day 3 Students will review vocabulary.	Neil will copy the vocabulary word and definitions from a worksheet and will match the written definitions to the vocabulary words.	Katy will work with a peer partner who will use a CTD procedure to teach her to identify picture symbols with written words that represent the rock properties.	Tim will work with a peer partner who will use a CTD procedure to teach him to identify rocks with written words attached to them that represent the rock properties.

	Neil	Katy	Tim
Students will examine rocks and make predictions about the properties each rock has (e.g., hard, soft, streak, carbonate). **Assessment:** The students will record predictions on the "Rock Properties Prediction Form."	With a peer partner, Neil will read the choices on the prediction form. Neil will independently make a choice about what properties he thinks his rocks have and circle his choices. Neil will independently circle his choices.	A peer partner will read the choices on the prediction form to Katy and point to the picture symbols; Katy will use her AAC device to verbalize the choices. Katy's partner will circle the choices that Katy selects.	A peer partner will read the choices on the prediction form to Tim and point to the photos; Tim will repeat the choices (vocabulary words) after the peer partner has read them. Tim's peer partner will help him place his rocks on his choices.
Day 4 Students will test rocks for hardness (scratch rocks on glass) and record results. Students will test rocks for softness (scratch rocks with paper clip or finger nail) and record results. Students will test rocks for streak (scratch rocks on cement and look for color) and record results. Students will test rocks for carbonate (drop vinegar on rocks and watch for fizz) and record results. **Assessment:** The students will record results on the "Rock Discovery Chart."	Neil will follow written directions to perform each test to determine his rocks' properties. He will be asked to raise his hand for teacher assistance if needed. Neil will record his results on the chart by writing yes or no in the appropriate box after each property test is conducted.	Katy will follow picture directions to perform each test to determine her rocks' properties. She will work in a small group of peers for support if she is not sure of the picture directions. Katy will record her results on the chart by placing a symbol for yes or no in the appropriate box after each property test is conducted.	Tim will work in a small group of peers who will read him picture directions and support him as he tests his rocks' properties. Tim will record his results on the chart by placing his rock in the appropriate box after each property test is conducted (with peer support). Note: after each set of tests is done, a photograph is taken so that Tim will have a record of where he put the rocks. He can also move them for the next set of tests.

(continued)

Figure 8.1. *(continued)*

Matrix Lesson Plan

General education lesson	Modifications for *Neil*	Modifications for *Katy*	Modifications for *Tim*
Day 5 Students will compare their predictions to results of rock properties tests to decide if their predictions were correct.	Neil will compare his prediction chart to his discovery chart to determine if his predictions were correct.	Katy will compare her prediction chart to her rock properties chart to determine if her predictions were correct. Her peers will read her prediction chart and discovery chart and ask her if her answers were the same or different. Katy will use her AAC device to answer yes or no.	With paraprofessional support, Tim will compare his prediction chart to his discovery chart to determine if his predictions were correct. The teacher assistant will read his prediction chart and discovery chart and work on the concepts of same and different with him.
Assessment: The students will answer questions related to the properties of their rocks. For example: Which of your rocks is hard? How do you know (e.g., scratched glass)?	Neil will verbally answer questions about the predictions and comparisons he made. Neil will write a paragraph about his discoveries given a word bank and his discovery chart. He will read his paragraph to the class.	Katy will use picture symbols to fill in sentences based on her discoveries (e.g., rock number 1 was hard). Katy will use her AAC device to read her sentences to the class.	Tim will use photos to fill in sentences based on his discoveries (e.g., rock number 2 was soft). A peer will assist Tim as he reads his sentences to the class (the peer will read the beginning of the sentence and Tim will read the word he filled in).

Rock Properties Prediction Form

Student name: _____

I think that:				
Rock 1	is hard	is soft	will leave a streak	has carbonate
Rock 2	is hard	is soft	will leave a streak	has carbonate
Rock 3	is hard	is soft	will leave a streak	has carbonate
Rock 4	is hard	is soft	will leave a streak	has carbonate
Rock 5	is hard	is soft	will leave a streak	has carbonate

Figure 8.2. Rock properties prediction form (form can also be created with picture symbols).

Rock Discovery Chart

Student name: _____

	Rock 1	Rock 2	Rock 3	Rock 4	Rock 5
Hard					
Soft					
Streak					
Carbonate					

Figure 8.3. Rock discovery chart (students can write in answers, pick symbols for answers, or place rock in appropriate square).

———● A High School Example

Ms. Fay is a high school biology teacher and is getting ready to teach a unit titled Genetics and Disease to answer the question: Why are some people born with diseases even though their parents do not have them? The unit plan she has used in the past should work, but she needs to collaborate with Mrs. Hamon, the special education teacher, to make sure that the students with disabilities in the class get what they need from the instruction. The teachers do this through their regularly scheduled monthly meeting. Ms. Fay teaches several other science content classes and has students on Mrs. Hamon's caseload in all of those classes, so the teachers use this monthly planning period to talk about all of their shared students. Ms. Fay knows that Mrs. Hamon will provide support as needed throughout each lesson even if she is not in the class directly. They may plan supports that students can use independently or that can be implemented with some naturally occurring peer help or from Ms. Fay, a paraprofessional, or Mrs. Hamon, who will be in the class occasionally (she also supports students in arts and humanities classes as well as science) to monitor the progress of the students. When Mrs. Hamon is in the class, the teachers use this time together to supplement their monthly meeting with some informal discussions about how to best support the learning of all students.

Table 8.2. Genetics and Disease Unit lesson benchmarks and learning outcomes

Benchmarks for Science Literacy (Project 2061, AAAS, 1993)	6E:The Human Organism: Physical Health: Grades 9-12: Faulty genes can cause body parts or systems to work poorly. Some genetic diseases appear only when an individual has inherited a certain faulty gene from both parents.
	1B:The Nature of Science: Scientific Inquiry: Grades 9-12: Investigations are conducted for different reasons, including the need to explore new phenomena, to check on previous results, to test how well a theory predicts, and to compare different theories.
Learning outcomes	Students will understand the differences among three of the major causes of genetic diseases and be able to identify and explain the likelihood of each of these genotypes being inherited by offspring.
	Students will use the scientific process to design experiments to answer questions about genetic inheritability.
Essential question to lead instruction	Why are some people born with diseases even though their parents do not have them?

Source: American Association for the Advancement of Science (1993).

More often than not these discussions center on students who do not have IEPs. They have found that their collaboration helps both teachers support all students.

Ms. Fay begins by reviewing the general education lesson benchmarks and learning outcomes with Mrs. Hamon (see Table 8.2) so that they can both review the expectations and outcomes for all students and then make any necessary modifications and adaptations.

The three students with disabilities in Ms. Fay's class and on Mrs. Hamon's caseload—Elaine, Susanna, and Charlie—will all participate in the state's alternate assessment based on alternate achievement standards (AA-AAS). Ms. Fay is worried that the information will be too difficult for these students and wonders what she will be expected to do differently for them. When Ms. Fay and Mrs. Hamon meet to discuss the unit, Ms. Fay expresses her concerns, but Mrs. Hamon notes that she needs to know more about the unit before they make any decisions. They start by discussing the standard (see Chapter 5 for a more detailed explanation of this process). Mrs. Hamon has a pretty good idea of what the standard means, but to make that concept accessible to her students with disabilities, she needs to know a lot more about it. After Mrs. Hamon gets a "crash course" in genetic diseases, she feels she understands the concepts but is still unsure of how to make instruction work for her students. The teachers both agree that even if they could "exempt" some students from the general curriculum content (and they can not), this is good information for everyone to know, and the process of problem solving in genetics can be generalized across many areas and topics.

The Students

Mrs. Hamon and Ms. Fay began by looking at the strengths and needs for Elaine, Susanna, and Charlie. Elaine has a moderate disability. She is verbal but hard to understand due to articulation difficulties. She is able to write her name independently (if not required to remain on the line) and can copy printed text. She can identify approximately 50 high-frequency sight words and short sentences when picture cues are provided. She rote counts to 39 consistently and to 100 with some mistakes. She can count by 5s if provided with number cues. She manages her self-care skills independently but needs verbal reminders.

Susanna has severe disabilities. She can move her head to the left approximately $\frac{1}{4}$ of an inch and will contract her arms if excited (either positively or negatively). Susanna has impaired vision; this is corrected by glasses, but she still requires enlarged text and symbols. If her trunk is totally supported, she can sit for about 45 minutes. She has difficulty holding her head in a neutral position, so she must sit tilted slightly back with items/text presented slightly above eye level. Susanna blinks quickly for "yes" and holds her eyes shut briefly for "no." She can use a pillow switch activated by a slight head turn to the left to operate a computer and a rotary scanner with up to four object messages. She uses a ventilator, has a seizure disorder, and frequently misses school due to illnesses. Susanna seems to have good receptive language skills, and with her rotary scanner, yes/no response, or eye gaze, she can answer verbal questions in conversations or in academic discussions.

Charlie has a profound intellectual disability. He is nonverbal with his only observed consistent response being a startle upon hearing a loud noise. He vocalizes, cries, and occasionally laughs but does not appear to do so in response to external stimuli. He can see light and objects with questionable perception, and he is nonambulatory and requires someone to push his wheelchair. Charlie has movement of his upper extremities and is working on using them appropriately in learning and social environments. He uses objects and big button switches to supplement and expand his communication repertoire, but he often ends up banging on his wheelchair tray and knocking things off. Charlie communicates inconsistently through crying and changes in muscle tone. He is provided with parts of objects to represent upcoming activities (e.g., the strap of a seat belt to represent his bus ride). Charlie requires positioning devices such as supported seating and a side-lyer.

Modifying the Lessons

Mrs. Hamon was particularly worried about how to give Elaine, Susanna, and Charlie access to complex scientific concepts, such as genes and inheritance, as well as how to help the students be a part of the classroom discussions and small-group activities. Ms. Fay was concerned about how her students would engage in the scientific process. She knew the ability to figure out problems would serve her students well throughout their lives. Yet she was not sure how they would do with such difficult content, and she wondered how best to scaffold the scientific process so that each of the students could meaningfully engage in it. The teachers decided that for each of the students, there needed to be some modifying of the complexity and/or difficulty of the outcomes. For instance, although Elaine and Susanna could work on all three of the major causes of genetic disease, they might want to prioritize two for them to focus on and really develop a strong understanding of those causes. The teachers decided that for Charlie they would really focus on one cause of genetic disease: either autosomal dominant or X linked. (See Chapter 5 for a more detailed explanation of prioritizing student outcomes.)

In terms of the second major outcome for the unit—developing an experiment—modifications would be made so that the students had some scaffolding to answer specific questions that were integral to the lesson. Elaine's overarching goal would be to work on sequencing the events of the experiment and then helping her team follow that sequence to complete the experiment. Susanna would help design the experiment by choosing from a set of genotypic and phenotypic fruit fly characteristics, in order to direct the experiment, and then by choosing the correct icon on the computer to match the step being completed. Charlie's overarching goal would be to observe and recognize what was happening during the experiment by following the process with a visual model illustrating each step. He would help design the experiment by choosing from objects representing possible fruit fly characteristics (e.g., yellow wings/short body versus plain wings/long body). He would then take notes on the experiment by creating an object representation of the results.

In addition to these unit outcomes, individual lesson outcomes would have to be reviewed and modified when appropriate. The teachers worked hard to ensure that each student was working toward the enduring understanding of the lesson, first by identifying the most important overarching concepts or ideas that they wanted all students to leave the unit having mastered. For instance, during the lecture on sexual reproduction, Charlie's objective was to be able to identify which genes came from the female and which ones came from the male. And, for the activity in which students would be completing Punnett squares for each major type of heredity, Charlie would have already completed Punnett squares and focused on identifying the most likely, least likely, or same probability for each outcome. For instance, given a Punnett square outlining parents who each have one recessive gene, Charlie would use his communication device to choose from three options (more, less, or same) to answer questions about whether one genotype or another would be more likely to occur. The teachers also knew that all three students would need scaffolding and supports in order to work through each activity and be as successful and independent as possible.

Mrs. Hamon and Ms. Fay reviewed the lesson to look for common activities throughout (see Table 8.3). For instance, there were multiple places where students were expected to communicate with peers and teacher, make predictions and demonstrate cause/effect, and take notes. These larger categories of expectations needed to be reviewed for each student to make sure the student had the necessary supports and information to participate and demonstrate what he or she knew.

Table 8.3. The lesson

Days	General education lesson
1–2	Teacher will give the students the essential question: "Why are some people born with diseases even though their parents do not have them?" As a class, students will brainstorm different types of diseases that people may be born having. Students will work in small groups to complete a graphic organizer to help them develop possible hypotheses for why this might happen. **Formative Assessment:** Review the graphic organizers and hypotheses for organization and logic as well as any background knowledge included.

Days	General education lesson
3–4	Teacher will review different causes of illness/disease (e.g., genetic, bacterial, viral).
	As a class, students and teacher will sort the diseases they brainstormed earlier into genetic versus nongenetic causes.
	In small groups, students will choose one genetic disease from the list and if it is different than their initial hypothesis, they may work with their groups to revise their hypotheses.
	Formative Assessment: Review revised hypothesis to determine how much new information is included and the logic of the argument.
5	Teacher will review basic genetics in sexually reproducing organisms by asking students to remember what they know about how genes are passed from parents to offspring. (Focus: Half the genes come from each parent.) Teacher will use a physical model to show this transference.
	Students may revise their hypotheses based on this review.
	Formative Assessment: Class discussion of sexually reproducing organisms; review revised hypotheses.
6–7	Teacher will introduce various case studies on specific genetic diseases (including autosomal recessive, autosomal dominant, and X linked).
	Students will complete Punnett squares for each category of disease to examine the likelihood of two parents having a child with a dominant or recessive disease.
	Formative Assessment: Review Punnett squares.
8–10	Working in small groups, students will research the disease they chose earlier to determine which type of disease it is and outline its common symptoms, treatments, and outcomes for the patients.
	Students will examine their earlier hypothesis and compare it with what they have learned during their research.
	Formative Assessment: Review hypotheses.
11–12	As a class, students will debate the benefits and drawbacks of genetic counseling based on their findings with the Punnett squares and their research on their specific disease.
	Formative Assessment: Review the logic of the argument, the depth of information from their research (using specific traits from their research to prove or refute a point), and the use of Punnett squares to support the argument.
13–15	In small groups, students will design an experiment to test their best hypothesis. Virtual fruit flies using computer programs can be used for the experiment (e.g., where they are given three sets of fruit flies):
	1. One of the parents has a physical (not genetic) difference (e.g., broken wing).
	2. One of the parents has a genetic disease (e.g., Huntington chorea).
	3. Both of the parents seem fine.
	Students will examine the offspring of these parents to see what (if any) ailments are passed down through genetics.
	Formative Assessment: The small groups will compare their findings to their hypotheses and present a lab report (written or oral) on their results.
16	**Summative Assessment:**
	Students will be given individual assessments that include family histories and information about genotype and phenotype of 10 different patients. Students will then develop Punnett squares to determine if the disease is autosomal recessive, autosomal dominant, X linked, or not genetic. They must write an explanation for their answers, as well as show the completed Punnett squares.

Communicating   Mrs. Hamon was not concerned about how the students would participate in the brainstorming session. She saw it as a great opportunity for the students to work on building their communication systems, as well as meet some of the social goals in their IEPs. She talked with Ms. Fay about what the key vocabulary or ideas were and which ones would be repeated throughout the unit. From there, the teachers prioritized which vocabulary words the students would have added to their communication systems. Mrs. Hamon then considered pictures and objects that would best exemplify the concepts (see Figure 8.4). For instance, they chose three diseases from which the students could choose to contribute to the class discussion and small group sessions.

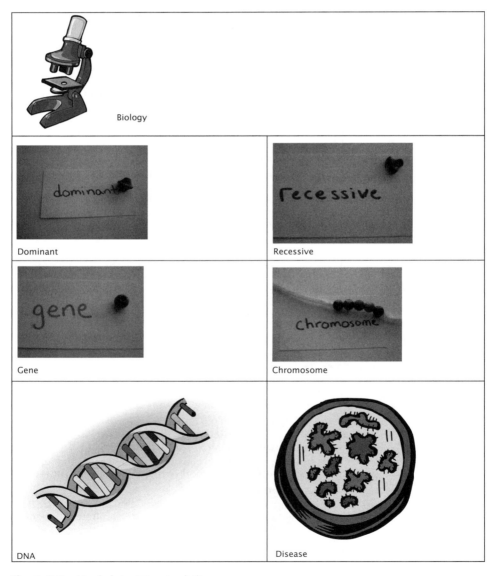

Figure 8.4.   Vocabulary picture symbols.

Phenotype	Genotype
Inherit	Parents
Hypothesis	X linked
Fruit fly	Yellow wings

(continued)

They also developed several sentence starters/objects that would illustrate possible hypotheses for why some people are born with diseases even though their parents are healthy. Communication is a skill that both teachers knew was an important part of every lesson. Understanding and using science vocabulary are important skills for all students. Mrs. Hamon thus made sure that Susanna and Charlie had symbols and objects that represented all of the important concepts and vocabulary about the content (Figure 8.5), and not just those that related to achieving their specific outcomes. For instance, Charlie had a tactile representation of a broken DNA sequence to indicate a genetic disease; this helped him frame the activities of the

Figure 8.4. *(continued)*

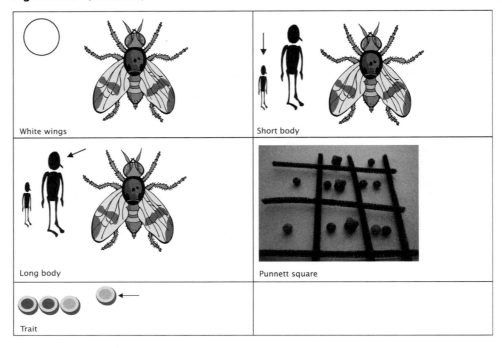

unit into a context that he understood, as did having a 3-dimensional grid, which he used for the Punnett square activities. Elaine's speech and language therapist came in to the class for ½ an hour per week to help her with articulation of the science vocabulary, as well as conversational skills in small-group activities.

Predictions and Cause and Effect　　Elaine, Susanna, and Charlie made their predictions using graphic organizers, which were then used throughout the lesson, as the class learned more about the topic and continued to revise their hypotheses. The continually revised hypotheses that the students eventually used to develop an experiment became an ongoing form of formative assessment not only of the content being learned but also of the scientific process itself. Mrs. Hamon particularly liked this idea, as the revision of the hypotheses allowed for a wide range of scaffolding (e.g., graphic organizers, cloze sentences, yes/no questions), and her students had multiple opportunities to practice cause/effect and problem solving around the same general concepts. Mrs. Hamon also used the same prediction scaffolds for other prediction opportunities that occurred throughout the remainder of the school day, such as "If I do not have all of my social studies materials with me in class, what should I do? What will happen next?" and "If I do not have enough money to buy the snacks the Student Council is selling, what could I do?"

Notetaking　　One of the areas that presented a challenge for Ms. Fay was how the students would take notes during lectures. She wanted the students to be able

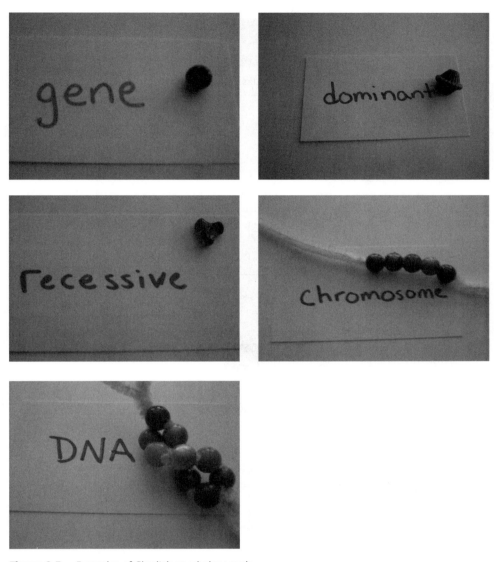

Figure 8.5. Examples of Charlie's vocabulary cards.

to just copy a peer's notes at a later time, but Mrs. Hamon felt that the skill of listening for particular information would be a skill the students would need throughout their lives. In the end, Elaine took notes by highlighting information as the teacher covered it and by completing cloze sentences (choosing the word the teacher was defining and matching it to the definition), again by using picture symbols and words. Susanna took notes with the help of her scanner. She was given a graphic organizer naming the diseases that were going to be discussed during the lecture. Her scanner was then set up with the two icons so that she could make decisions about whether a particular disease was genetic or not genetic (see Figure 8.6). Charlie took notes by hitting his big button switch to activate a recorder. With

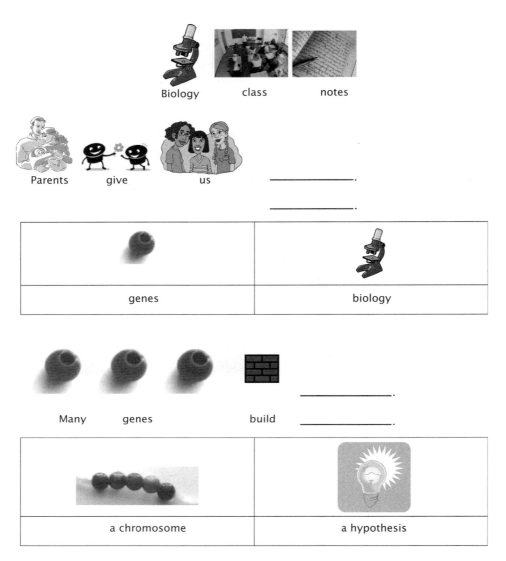

Figure 8.6. Examples of class notes.

assistance, he could start and stop the recorder throughout the lecture. He then listened to the notes before the activity in which students sorted diseases into genetic and nongenetic, and his peer wrote down important information from his recordings about the names of genetic versus nongenetic diseases. Each of these strategies allowed the students to be as independent as possible while still having to actively listen to the information the teacher was presenting. The students could then use this information within their small group to sort diseases into categories (e.g., genetic versus nongenetic for one lecture). Each small group would then use its graphic organizers to revise its hypotheses if necessary. All of these note-

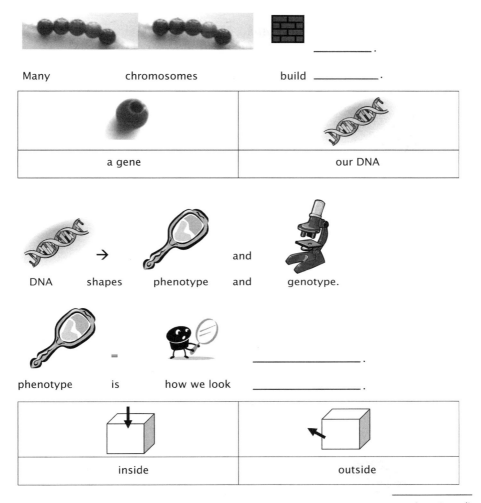

Many   chromosomes   build _____.

a gene	our DNA

DNA   shapes   phenotype   and   and   genotype.

phenotype   is   how we look _____.

inside	outside

(continued)

taking strategies were used within the context of Elaine's, Susanna's, and Charlie's other content classes too, so they really were learning the generalized concept of notetaking versus using a skill for only one specific instance.

Teaching Modifications   Ms. Fay found that for this lesson she had to supplement her usual lecture style with the addition of manipulatives to represent sexual reproduction inheritance of genes from both parents. In this way, the students all had the added opportunity of using their own models to copy what Ms. Fay was demonstrating at the front of the class. Charlie was presented with object and tactile representations in conjunction with the lecture to aid his understanding and build his vocabulary, whereas Susanna had a choice of using either the objects or pictures of these objects for her own notes.

Figure 8.6. *(continued)*

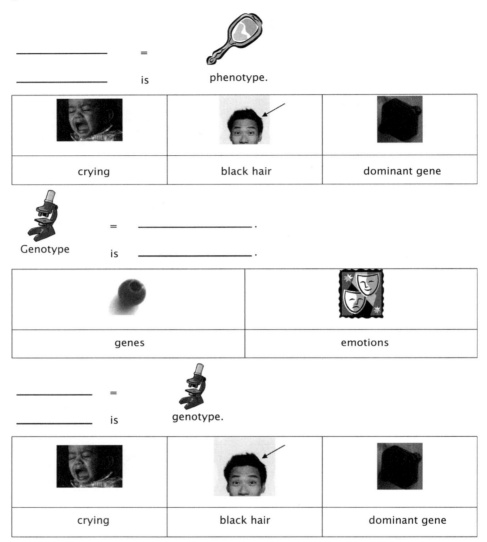

Conducting Research   Both Ms. Fay and Mrs. Hamon struggled with how to make this activity meaningful for Charlie. They felt comfortable that with the content vocabulary and identified supports already in place, Elaine and Susanna could learn more about the science concepts by participating in this critical instructional activity. But the two teachers just were not sure about Charlie. In their initial planning, they hit upon connecting his big button switch to the computer and printer so that he could learn to turn the computer on and print materials. But after watching the first day of class research, they realized that although he was actively participating, just performing the computer functions was not teaching him either the

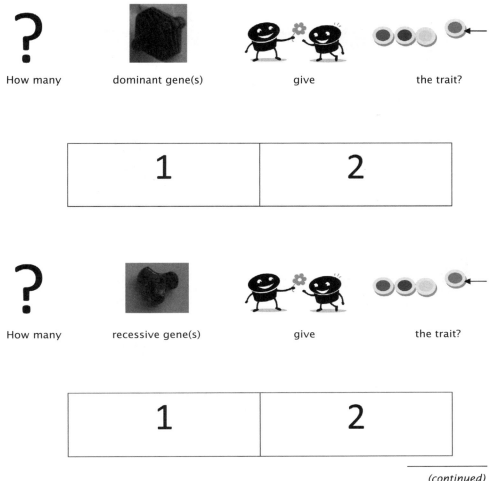

(continued)

science concepts or how to conduct research. On the second research day, Mrs. Hamon did some preteaching on differentiating science content web sites from nonscience web sites, using a tactile-based T-chart to sort different web sites. Charlie was given two shallow boxes, one lined with felt for the content web sites and the other lined with sandpaper for the nonscience web sites. Charlie then worked in a small cooperative group that chose several web sites from an online search engine to review. The web sites were identified by the group as content based or not content based. The general education students went on to critically evaluate the information within the content-based sites, but for Charlie, the priority was on recognizing whether or not a web site was content based. Therefore, a graphic from the site or the web address (depending on the site), was paired with either Charlie's tactile clue for "science" class or the tactile symbol for "not" + "science." Charlie then sorted the web sites into the boxes. Although sorting was an activity with which Charlie was familiar and one he had been working on for several

Figure 8.6. *(continued)*

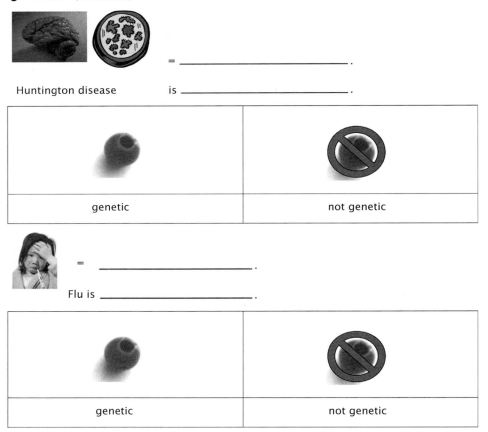

= _____ .

Huntington disease   is _____ .

genetic	not genetic

= _____ .

Flu is _____ .

genetic	not genetic

years, using this concept in the context of research was new. After the second and third days of conducting research, Mrs. Hamon still was not sure how well this activity was helping Charlie learn the content or how to conduct research (it did provide opportunities for him to maintain his sorting skills and work on crossing midline, both of which are important skills for Charlie). Still, she decided to support the process of student-directed research in this and all his other classes until her data confirmed if he was learning that process or not and if she needed to provide additional support. She was not willing to say research was something that Charlie could never learn to do.

Assessment Modifications

There were multiple formative assessments throughout this lesson, as well as the larger summative assessment at the end of some of the larger projects (e.g., the debate and the experiment). After reviewing how each lesson would be modified, Mrs. Hamon and Ms. Fay turned to how the assessments would be adapted to

=   _____ .

Sickle cell anemia is _____ .

genetic	not genetic

=   _____ .

Chicken pox is _____ .

genetic	not genetic

ensure that Elaine, Susanna, and Charlie were being assessed on their individual outcomes while also maintaining fidelity with the general education expectations. In addition, Mrs. Hamon used this planning to embed each student's cross-curricular goals, such as "identifying more and less" or "asking peers a question." She was able to assess these student-specific IEP goals within the instruction and assessment designed for the lesson.

One of the most important formative assessments within the unit was for students to complete various Punnett squares. Mrs. Hamon saw many cross-curricular opportunities for these squares, and she was able to embed the concept of Punnett squares into other academic areas, such as figuring out fractions and percentages in mathematics, as well as some more basic concepts such as same/different and more/less. Whereas Elaine worked on three different types of Punnett squares (autosomal dominant, autosomal recessive, and X linked), Charlie and

Susanna worked on one and two types of Punnett square models, respectively. Each student needed different accommodations in order to successfully complete the Punnett squares. For instance, Elaine used two colored/textured manipulatives to represent the genes passed from the mother and father, mirrored from the class notes she took during Ms. Fay's lecture on sexual reproduction, with red signifying recessive and black signifying dominant. Elaine then placed the pieces in a graphic organizer to show what genes the offspring could inherit. Another option presented to Elaine was colors that matched specific traits (e.g., sickle cell anemia, normal blood cells) so that she had additional practice making direct connections to specific diseases being targeted by the class. Susanna and Charlie had their Punnett squares already set up (Susanna's on her scanner and Charlie's with a 3-dimensional Punnett square grid) so that they used a combination of yes/no questions and the manipulatives from taking notes in Ms. Fay's lecture to complete their Punnett squares. See Figures 8.7 and 8.8 to see Susanna's and Charlie's Punnett squares, respectively.

There was another important use of the Punnett squares and related questions completed on Day 16 as a summative assessment of the unit, which could also be used as evidence for the state AA-AAS. Based on decisions made by their respective IEP teams, Elaine, Susanna, and Charlie participated in the state large-scale assessment through the AA-AAS. This assessment format in their state is a body of evidence (e.g., portfolio), which includes samples of student work. Mrs. Hamon made sure that she kept the originals of the students' Punnett squares and their answers to the questions on the classroom assessment so that she could include those as a part of their alternate assessments. Elaine's evidence was a paper worksheet with her completed Punnett square with her answers to the questions scribed, Susanna's evidence was a photo of the completed Punnett square on her scanner and her scribed yes/no response to the questions, and Charlie's evidence was a photo of his completed 3-dimensional Punnett square and his scribed answers. As part of the required evidence for the state alternate assessment, Mrs. Hamon was sure to include a brief note on each piece of evidence explaining how the student answered the questions, which answers/performances were independent and correct, and any prompting that was given during the assessment.

Huntington disease

Parents	H	h
h	Hh	hh
h	Hh	hh

Teaching process: Susanna first needs to identify the dominant gene (capital letter/big bead) by touching, or scrolling through answers with her switch and the computer.

How many squares would show the dominant trait? (0, 1, 2, 3, 4)

How many squares would not show the dominant trait? (0, 1, 2, 3, 4)

What are the chances that a child will have Huntington disease?

Figure 8.7. Susanna's Punnett square.

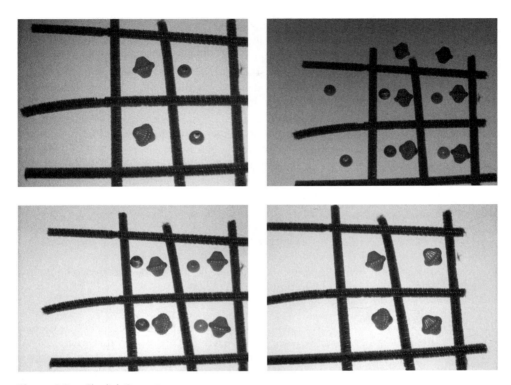

Figure 8.8. Charlie's Punnett square.

CONCLUSION

Although assessment of students to show their progress in the general curriculum is now a federal mandate, it is important that assessments are used as ongoing progress monitoring tools and not simply as a one-shot answer to the law. Throughout the two examples presented in this chapter are classroom activities that are based on general and special education research (e.g., identifying similarities and differences, notetaking, nonlinguistic representation, cooperative learning, time delay, generating and testing hypotheses; Collins, 2006; Marzano, Pickering, & Pollock, 2001; Wolery et al., 1992). It is important that all students, with or without identified disabilities, be actively engaged in instruction that has been proven to be effective in increasing student achievement. As teachers strive to use the most effective instructional practices with their students, it is important that they note what is and is not working with their students (as evidenced by ongoing student instructional and assessment data) and change instruction accordingly. For example, on Day 1 of the elementary school rocks lesson, a quick review of Neil's classification of rocks may have shown that Neil (and maybe other students as well) experienced difficulty with the classification and thus needed more explicit instruction. That instruction could be easily delivered by the teacher or a peer later on in the day, or prior to the next lesson, so that Neil would not fall behind.

Ongoing formative assessments also provide insight into a student's understanding of skills and concepts that may be supplemental to the content area but not directly assessed in the content area. For instance, in the high school example, the concepts of more/less or fractions are instrumental in understanding Punnett squares, even though these are not strictly science concepts. Through observation, classroom work, and more formal daily or weekly assessments, it is possible to pinpoint exactly where a student is struggling and thus provide the support necessary to help that student succeed.

Summative assessments can be used to determine if the students understand the concepts taught in the unit of study. In both the elementary and high school examples, the students were expected to go beyond just identification of facts and be able to explain why a concept holds true or a phenomenon occurs. As mentioned in the high school example, summative assessments that require a work sample or artifact can provide excellent data to demonstrate student progress or mastery in an alternate assessment. The examples of assessments that can be used in science vary according to content but can all be used as progress monitoring tools and documentation of student learning for students with disabilities.

REFERENCES

American Association for the Advancement of Science. (1993). *Benchmarks for science literacy: Project 2061*. New York: Oxford University Press.

Collins, B. (2006). *Moderate and severe disabilities: A foundational approach*. Upper Saddle River, NJ: Prentice Hall.

The Conference Board, Corporate Voices for Working Families, the Partnership for 21st Century Skills, & the Society for Human Resource Management. (2006). *Are they really ready to work? Employers' perspectives on the basic knowledge and applied skills of new entrants to the 21st century U.S. workforce*. Retrieved March 30, 2009, from http://www.21stcenturyskills.org/documents/FINAL_REPORT_PDF09-29-06.pdf

Courtade, G., Spooner, F., & Browder, D. (2007). A review of studies with students with significant cognitive disabilities that link to science standards. *Research and Practice for Persons with Severe Disabilities, 32*, 43–49.

LEARN NC. (n.d.). *Rocks really rock! A lesson on the classification of rocks*. Retrieved January 22, 2010, from http://www.learnnc.org/lp/pages/3891

Marzano, R.J., Pickering, D.J., & Pollock, J.E. (2001). *Classroom instruction that works: Research-based strategies for increasing student achievement*. Alexandria, VA: Association for Supervision and Curriculum Development.

National Research Council. (1996). *National science education standards*. Washington, DC: National Academies Press.

National Research Council. (2000). *Inquiry and the national science education standards: A guide for teaching and learning*. Washington, DC: National Academies Press.

National Research Council. (2001). *Classroom assessment and the national science education standards*. Washington, DC: National Academies Press.

No Child Left Behind Act of 2001, PL 107–110, 115 Stat. 1425, 20 U.S.C. §§ 6301 *et seq.*

Wolery, M., Holcombe, A., Cybriwsky, C., Doyle, P.M., Schuster, J.W., Ault, M.J., et al. (1992). Constant time delay with discrete responses: A review of effectiveness and demographic, procedural, and methodological parameters. *Research and Intervention in Developmental Disabilities, 13*, 239–266.

9

Social Studies and the Arts Instruction and Assessment Linked to Grade-Level Standards

Karen M. Guettler, Jacqueline M. Norman,
James M. Zeller, and Mariel L. Zeller

Social studies and the arts are not always assessed in large-scale assessments. However, these subjects are always an important part of the curriculum. To deliver effective instruction in these disciplines, formative assessment is a helpful tool. When social studies and the arts are assessed in summative large-scale assessments (as they are in at least some states' regular and alternate assessments), formative assessments help guide learning and develop materials in preparation. We discuss in this chapter why it is important to teach and assess social studies and the arts.

People are citizens of a global community, and within that community all have a place in a specific society and culture. Social studies enable people to understand how societies and cultures in the global community relate to each other, how communities and nations work together and establish international relations, and their role within their society. Social studies analyze the function of societies, defining components that structure their communities and nations: political, economic, and cultural structures; geographic features and constraints; and historical origins. In an era of information sharing and mass communication, it is important for all students to understand the forces driving the actions of global communities and how their own nation is part of the world system. To understand these concepts, it is essential that students have a historical perspective, as well as an understanding of political and economic structures.

Historical perspective is essential in understanding the unique society and culture within which students live. Each student has a right and a responsibility to be an active and contributing member in his or her society. It is imperative that all students learn the origin of their political and social structures so they understand the events that have led to their modern world and can predict the results of their own actions within their communities. Understanding the history of their nation will allow students to make sense of the institutions within their communities, including how and why those institutions exist and the purposes these institutions serve.

Political institutions and economic systems that shape our societies provide guidelines for both individual and group actions. Students taught in social studies and actively participating in a social studies curriculum grow to understand these guidelines and, most important, learn to apply them to their own decision-making processes. Although students with significant cognitive disabilities have traditionally not had the opportunities to participate in social studies to the full extent of their abilities, this lack of curricular access can be remedied with thoughtful instruction. All students, including those with significant cognitive disabilities, are expected to live within, and abide by, the conventions, laws, and institutions of their respective societies. It is vital that all students are educated in social sciences so they can meet these expectations.

The arts infuse the political and economic aspects of a society with the character and culture of its people. Many of the decisions people make are influenced or driven by their cultures, therefore, it would be impossible to understand those decisions without some knowledge of how culture shapes their lives. Studying the arts of differing cultures opens a window into the characteristics of societies and the individuals within them. The arts are simultaneously an expression of a people and a person, and as students study the cultures of others, they also gain insight into their own. Gaining knowledge of the arts provides students with the skills and abilities to interpret the world around them and to express their interpretations of that world. Through the arts, people can express the most intimate human knowledge and feelings, and bring individuals together in a common experience. Whether the arts are created to entertain or to inform, for ceremony or for recreation, to narrate history or a story, to evoke a desired response or just to amuse, they are a bonding force. In order for students to have a common basis for relationship with members of their society and culture, they must have an understanding of the arts.

Just as reading, mathematics, and science are important in the lives of all students, so is instruction in these *other* areas of the general education curriculum. The areas of social studies and the arts may not be assessed by a particular state or district (or even as part of large-scale accountability assessments), but it is important to note that many of the skills and concepts practiced in reading, mathematics, and science are reinforced and extended within the instruction taking place in these classes. If a state *does* assess social studies and/or the arts as a part of its regular large-scale educational assessment, then it must provide an opportunity for students with significant cognitive disabilities to participate in that assessment as well, typically through an alternate assessment in those content areas.

A RATIONALE FOR SOCIAL STUDIES INSTRUCTION FOR ALL STUDENTS

It would be very fair to say that social studies instruction is essential in the education of all students. It is, after all, at the heart of the United States' most basic beliefs. The founding fathers felt that the nation's very survival depended upon the education of its citizens to ensure that the populace was knowledgeable and civically responsible. The goal of social studies is therefore to prepare students to make connections between knowledge and action in order to promote social competence. This is a goal that is important not only for students who have typically participated in the general education curriculum but also for all students, including students with significant cognitive disabilities (Spooner & Browder, 2006).

Social studies instruction offers many avenues for evaluating student understanding of key concepts and provides ample opportunities for students to take their new knowledge and put it into action in everyday life (National Council for the Social Studies [NCSS], 2009b). Many teachers have found formative assessment valuable in planning for further instruction of social studies, to promote a deeper understanding of the concepts and knowledge (Erickson, 2001). In social studies, teachers use such methods as discussions, questioning, displays, and small group projects to assess students' level of understanding.

Social studies typically cover content from civics and government, history, geography, and economics. According to NCSS (2009b), 10 themes recur throughout these content strands: 1) culture; 2) time, continuity, and change; 3) people, places, and environments; 4) individual development and identity; 5) individuals, groups, and institutions; 6) power, authority, and governance; 7) production, distribution, and consumption; 8) science, technology, and society; 9) global connections; and 10) civic ideals and practices.

The ultimate goal of social studies is to promote the growth and development of an informed and thoughtful citizen. Social studies are thus an important part of the curriculum for all students in making connections between knowledge and action and promoting enduring understanding. As educators who work with students who have significant cognitive disabilities, it is essential to enable students to make these same connections in instruction between knowledge and action. Many educators refer to this as making the knowledge useful, practical, or functional. Making connections to "real-world activities," and incorporating these activities in lesson plans whenever possible, assists in the generalization of the knowledge and skills. These types of activities promote deeper learning and understanding.

Social studies instruction is typically broken down into disciplines: civics and government, history, geography, and economics.

Civics and Government: In civics and government instruction, students gain such knowledge and skills as recognizing the need for and acquiring the ability to evaluate rules and laws, understanding the rights and responsibilities of citizenship, and understanding how different countries have different governments (NCSS, 2009b). In elementary school, civics instruction may focus on how students relate to one another with an emphasis on how rules help to resolve issues and disputes. In middle school, it is important to emphasize how personal responsibility leads to ensuring the common good (e.g., the rights of the individual must always be balanced with the rights of society). High school students should focus on how our country's values have shaped our culture, society, and government (NCSS, 2009b).

History: In history instruction, students gain knowledge and skills related to historical thinking such as evaluation, analysis, and interpretation of historical evidence in an effort to understand current issues (NCSS, 2009b). In elementary school, students should learn to differentiate past, present, and future and may start with their own families and family histories. In middle school, students should learn how to construct timelines and how events may be grouped into eras; they may also learn about historical context and how it relates to values and beliefs. By high school, students should be using their knowledge of history to make inferences about possible consequences of potential actions (NCSS, 2009b).

Geography: In geography instruction, students gain knowledge and skills related to the interdependency of living things and the physical environment, including the impact of human and natural processes on the environment, how to use geographic tools to understand people and their culture, and how resources are related to territorial conflicts (NCSS, 2009b). In elementary school, students should learn about the world in which they live and how they have an impact on their own environment. In middle school, students should begin to use geographic tools, such as thematic maps, to understand how human and physical characteristics affect the ecosystem of the region. In high school, students should use geographic knowledge and skills to analyze problems and develop possible solutions (NCSS, 2009b).

Economics: In economics instruction, students gain such knowledge and skills as the role of consumers and producers, costs and benefits of individual decisions and public policies, and the government's role in the market economy (NCSS, 2009b). Economics instruction should be personally relevant for students (in ways that directly connect to their everyday experiences). In elementary school, students should learn that a shortage of resources means having to decide how limited resources will be used. By the end of middle school, students should understand the trade-offs, costs, and benefits of economic decisions. In high school, students should understand how the economy affects many public policy decisions (NCSS, 2009b).

Although expectations have increased for students with intellectual disabilities over the years (Browder, Wakeman, Flowers, Rickelman, & Pugalee, 2007), the attainment of academic expectations in social studies appears to be mostly related to functional skills in the area of civics and geography, such as rights and responsibilities or map-reading skills (Collins, Branson, Hall, & Rankin 2001; Polloway, Patton, Payne, & Payne, 1989). Academic expectations truly reflective of the content of social studies have not been a priority. The lack of exposure to the *academic* content of social studies has left students with significant cognitive disabilities at a disadvantage in making sense of their community and their country. Social studies content cultivates skills and understandings essential for all students and citizens. For students with significant cognitive disabilities, social studies can be made personally relevant and can be embedded into the context of their lives.

A RATIONALE FOR ARTS INSTRUCTION FOR ALL STUDENTS

Arts education promotes deeper learning and understanding of skills and concepts in much the same way social studies reinforce knowledge and skills learned. The integration of the arts into the instruction of mathematics, science, reading, writing, and social studies results in a deeper understanding of each of these academic areas; the study of art becomes an "organizer" for students, leading them to make deeper connections and develop creative thought (Consortium of National Arts Education Associations, 1994). Formative assessments have been used to assess student competence in the arts for many years and often take the form of performance (e.g., dance, plays), student creation of their own art, and responding to questions about the meaning of whatever art the students are currently studying. Such assessment strategies also lend themselves to documenting the learning of students with significant cognitive disabilities.

Arts education consists of four disciplines: music, drama, dance, and visual arts. Each of these disciplines has standards and achievement expectations by the end of Grade 4, the end of Grade 8, and upon graduation (Consortium of National Arts Education Associations, 1994). The arts promote an understanding of the world in which people live and how they "experience" that world. The arts also provide for ways to communicate thoughts and ideas as well as enhance the lives and education of all students. As with social studies, the arts lend themselves to making "functional" connections to life and everyday activities. In addition, the arts provide many opportunities for students with significant cognitive disabilities to make connections within and across each discipline of the arts (e.g., dance, drama), as well as across other content areas. The arts also provide a means of self-expression, as well as a valued present and/or future leisure activity or avocation. Below the major areas of the arts and the broad grade-level expectations for each area are briefly discussed:

Music: In music instruction, students gain such knowledge and skills as the creation, performance, appreciation, and analysis of music (Consortium of National Arts Education Associations, 1994). In elementary school, students should experience music through singing, playing, and creating music. In middle school, students should make connections between music and other disciplines, such as math through the use of rhythm or patterns. By high school, students should gain an understanding of the cultural and historical value of music (Consortium of National Arts Education Associations, 1994).

Drama: In drama instruction, students gain knowledge and skills that allow them to relate to the world in which they live and to understand other cultures (Consortium of National Arts Education Associations, 1994). In elementary school, students should be encouraged to use role-playing as a way to communicate ideas. In middle school, students should learn to communicate a "world view," understand how a world view defines one's perceptions, and evaluate the effectiveness of a world view in relating to the world. By high school, students should be able to analyze the works of others and identify key elements (Consortium of National Arts Education Associations, 1994).

Dance: In dance instruction, students gain knowledge and skills related to movement and expression, including communication of thoughts and ideas through movements, cultural expression, and historical relevance (Consortium of National Arts Education Associations, 1994). In elementary school, students should learn to move their bodies in relation to music. In middle school, students should learn how to reflect upon what is communicated through dance. By high school, students should be able to gain cultural and historical perspective through experiencing a variety of dance forms (Consortium of National Arts Education Associations, 1994).

Visual Arts: In visual arts instruction, students gain knowledge and skills in the exploration and creation of various art forms such as sculpture, illustration, and painting (Consortium of National Arts Education Associations, 1994). In elementary school, students should learn the basic elements of design. They should be encouraged to create their own works and identify the basic elements (i.e., line, shape, form, value, texture, color, space) in other works. In middle school, students should be able to develop works reflecting the basic elements and themes, and evaluate their individual work. By high school, students should identify and develop their own style, identify different styles and movements, express ideas through their work, and understand that art reflects politics and culture, as well as a historical perspective (Consortium of National Arts Education Associations, 1994).

As with social studies, we found very little research regarding academic expectations for students with significant cognitive disabilities related to the arts. When students with significant cognitive disabilities did receive instruction in the arts, it was often dependent upon the special educator's knowledge and comfort level in the discipline (Polloway, Patton, Payne, & Payne, 1989). Often the emphasis was mainly on participation in the activity and social interaction (Hunt, Alwell, Farron-Davis, & Goetz, 1996). Frequently, the outcome of the activity was not academic in nature, but rather focused on the development of fine or gross motor skills, hand–eye coordination, or social skills. If students with significant cognitive disabilities received instruction from a general education teacher, that student was often included for social purposes (Stainback & Stainback, 1990) and rarely was expected to have academic outcomes as a result of that participation. Although students may have been exposed to the same instruction as general education students, the final products or performances were often not assessed based on the same expectations as those of their general education peers, but on the student's learning of other behaviors (social, motor, communication) and/or his or her simple participation in the activity. Of course, these more basic life skills are important—but they are not art. The arts offer a multidimensional method of interpreting and conveying information related to all content areas and are an essential tool for *all* students; the arts are a window to our world, and that world includes students with significant cognitive disabilities!

PUTTING IT INTO PRACTICE:
SOCIAL STUDIES AND THE ARTS FOR ALL STUDENTS

In the first part of this chapter, we made the case for the inclusion of students with significant cognitive disabilities in the academic content (not just their physical presence) in social studies and the arts. In this section, we provide strategies for making access to grade-level academic content in these subjects truly meaningful for students with significant cognitive disabilities. In describing these lesson plans, and their accompanying adaptations and modifications, we also provide strategies for formative and summative (end of unit) assessments for students. We realize that not all teachers work in districts or states that require large-scale assessments in these subjects, yet we also believe that anything worth learning is also worth documenting how well students have learned it.

Each of the lessons we describe in the following sections include the identification of the national standard(s), grade-level expectations, and the "enduring understanding" or the "Big Idea" (see Chapter 5 for a thorough discussion of "enduring understandings") for each standard taught during the instructional activity. Social studies and the arts are connected in culminating projects for each grade level. Within each content area, the lessons begin with elementary school examples and are followed by middle school and high school samples. The social studies themes addressed in each lesson are part of the 10 themes from NCSS. The national standards are also used for the arts content. Finally, the culminating projects that we present can be very appropriate for documenting student performance on alternate assessments in social studies and the arts, when states do require alternate assessments in these subject areas.

———● Social Studies Lessons

The following sections present sample social studies lessons for students with significant cognitive disabilities at the elementary, middle, and high school levels.

Elementary School Example: Holidays Around the World

Although the theme of culture and cultural diversity is included in the social studies curriculum of several states, the national standards for this theme are included in sociology, anthropology, geography, and history instruction. Studying culture enables students to appreciate the similarities and differences among cultural groups and better understand their role in society. Because culture is an outgrowth of human lifestyles, it is dynamic and changing. At the same time, culture is a way of sharing ideas, beliefs, values, and traditions that are passed on through generations. Sharing culture can be accomplished in a variety of ways, including storytelling, music, dance, and art. We begin with a Grade 5 lesson taken from social studies "Standard I-Culture" (NCSS, 2009a), specifically Standard I-c, which states that "the learner can describe ways in which language, stories, folktales, music and artistic creations serve as expressions of culture and influence behavior of people living in a particular culture" (NCSS, 2009a, p. 1).

Big Idea   As noted in Chapter 5, it is important that teachers "translate" the standards into essential understandings or the main ideas teachers want all students to take away from those standards. Of course, teachers, working in collaboration with each other, can develop their own Big Idea (the process is described in detail in Chapter 5). Sometimes, state program of studies documents themselves translate the standard(s) into that essential idea for teachers. Here is the Big Idea for the above standard as taken from one state's program of studies document:

> Culture is the way of life shared by a group of people, including their ideas and traditions. Cultures reflect the values and beliefs of groups in different ways (e.g., art, music, literature, religion); however, there are universals connecting all cultures. (Kentucky Department of Education, 2006, p. 4)

Overview of the Unit   During winter months, people across the world celebrate many different holidays. After discussing a few winter holidays and the traditions that accompany those holidays, each student is given a country to study (countries may be chosen or assigned). Students will present to the class an overview of their chosen or assigned country's winter traditions. In their presentation, students will demonstrate one traditional artistic component of the holiday (e.g., song, dance). After all students have presented, they will identify similarities and differences of the holidays.

General Activity 1: Brainstorm, Explore, and Research   Brainstorming, exploring and researching are essential prefatory steps for presentation development. These instructional activities and assessment procedures are described in detail in the following paragraphs.

Instruction   The teacher reads a story (or article) about a winter holiday (e.g., Hanukkah, Kwanzaa, Christmas) and traditions associated with that holiday.

After the reading, students are asked to reflect on the holidays they celebrate during winter. Together, the class conducts a brainstorming activity listing the winter holidays with which the students are already familiar. The class also identifies traditions that are associated with the various holidays and discusses similarities and differences of these holidays. After the brainstorming activity, the teacher discusses how students can learn about other countries and their holiday celebrations, and describes the various research options available to the students. Each student then conducts research to learn more about a holiday in a given country. The student may select the origins, traditions, customs, and/or rituals of winter holidays in a country of their ancestry, or simply present from a chosen or assigned country. The student's research identifies customs, traditions, rituals, foods, and a traditional song or dance associated with the holiday.

Student Performance   Students use various research tools (e.g., Internet, encyclopedias, books, interviews) to find relevant information on the winter holidays of their assigned country. Students identify foods, traditions, customs, rituals, and a traditional song or dance associated with their holiday. They must also select a traditional song or dance to present.

Formative Assessment   The teacher observes the students to ensure they are collecting relevant information. The teacher has the students complete a research template (Figure 9.1) to ensure that they are answering the research questions. The teacher asks questions appropriate for the type of research each student is conducting.

In Table 9.1, we identify how students at three different levels of communicative development (presymbolic, emerging symbolic, and symbolic) can participate in both instruction and assessment within this "explore/research activity."

Country:	Foods	Traditions	Customs	Song/dance
Name of holiday:				Style: Rhythm:
Religious affiliation:				Meaning: Origin:
Miscellaneous information:				

Figure 9.1. Holiday research template.

Table 9.1. Access to explore/research activity based upon student's current level of communication

	Symbolic learner	Emerging symbolic learner	Presymbolic learner
Instruction	Have a shortened or paraphrased version of the story available for the student to read or read this aloud to the student.	Have a paraphrased and shortened version of the story read aloud and paired with pictures representing the main idea or theme for each paragraph or chapter.	Have a paraphrased and shortened version of the story read aloud and paired with objects representing the main idea or theme for each paragraph or chapter.
	Describe and provide examples for each of the different research tools that could be used to find this information. Provide the student with a copy of the research template (Figure 9.1) and explain how to fill the template with relevant information.	Describe and provide examples for each of the different research tools that could be used to find this information. Demonstrate how books and research can be read aloud using computer software programs. Provide the student with a copy of the research template (Figure 9.1) and explain how to use pictures or other graphics to fill out the template with relevant information.	Describe and provide tactile or object representations for each of the different research tools that could be used to find this information. Provide the student with a copy of an enlarged research template (Figure 9.1) attached to foam board and have the student work with a peer who reminds the student of the meaning of each object, reads the template and provides models or physical assistance as needed for the student to match the tactile/object representations to complete the template.
Student performance	Student conducts research with a peer, using various sources (e.g., Internet, articles, books) and records the needed information on the research template.	Student conducts research on a computer equipped with read-aloud software and paired with pictures or graphics. The student uses pictures or graphics to record the needed information on the research template.	Student follows along, touching/handling the objects or tactile representations related to the research as they are read aloud to the student. Working with a peer who reads the template categories and names each object as the student feels the object, the student selects the objects needed to complete the template with verbal cues and physical assistance, if needed, from the peer.
Formative assessment	Student accurately completes the research template to demonstrate required knowledge of the holiday.	Student accurately completes template using pictures or graphic representations to demonstrate required knowledge of the holiday.	Student accurately completes template using tactile/object representations to demonstrate required knowledge of the holiday.

(See Chapter 3 for a full description of each of these levels of communication, and a discussion of how the student's current ability to understand and express symbolic language is perhaps the single most critical factor in determining how that activity should be modified to make it personally relevant for the student.) Student work from both formative assessments (e.g., student work samples or instructional data) and summative assessments (e.g., creative or research products) can be used in many states' alternate assessments to document student achievement linked to grade-level content standards.

General Activity 2: Presentations The culminating activity, Holidays Around the World, is a student presentation. This activity is described in detail in the following paragraphs.

Instruction Students are provided with a note-taking template (Figure 9.1) to write down the country of origin, any religious affiliation, customs, traditions, rituals, foods, and song/dance for each student presentation.

Student Performance Student presentations include country of origin, religious affiliation (if any), customs, traditions, rituals, foods, and the presentation of either a traditional song or dance. Students may conduct the presentation in a variety of ways (e.g., PowerPoint, poster session, dramatization, classroom lecture, prepared foods, customs, dances). All students complete the note-taking template (Figure 9.1) for each of their classmates' presentations.

Formative Assessment The student presentations make up the assessment. Students' scores are based on a rubric specifically designed to reflect all elements of the students' research. The style of presentation does not affect the presentation score, as long as required components are present. Table 9.2 describes how students with significant cognitive disabilities at each of the three communication levels (symbolic learner, emerging symbolic learner, presymbolic learner) can participate in this assessment activity. Figure 9.2 presents a poster presentation by a student with a significant cognitive disability (a symbolic learner) for her presentation, entitled *Christmas in Norway*.

Middle School Example: Road Trip

This unit targets an eighth-grade–level lesson using the social studies standard III "People, Places and Environments" (NCSS, 2009a, p. 2) and standard VII "Production, Distribution, and Consumption" (NCSS, 2009a, p. 4). Although social studies encompass many subdisciplines (i.e., sociology, anthropology, history, geography, economics, civics), the themes associated with social studies are designed to assist students in developing the skills necessary to become productive citizens. These skills include applying knowledge of self, community, nation, and world issues to make informed decisions or choices. This lesson focuses on geography and economics and the interrelationship of the two studies.

Standards: Geography and Economics Geographic characteristics affect or determine many economic aspects of a region. Combining geography and

Table 9.2. Access to instructional activity #2 (presentations) for students at different communication levels

	Symbolic learner	Emerging symbolic learner	Presymbolic learner
Instruction	Provide student with the note-taking template and a word bank to facilitate completion of the chart.	Provide student with the note-taking template prefilled with the holiday and/or country of origin. Also, provide the student with a picture bank to facilitate the completion of the chart.	Provide student with the note-taking template prefilled with the holiday and/or country of origin. Also, provide the student with an object/tactile representation bank to facilitate the completion of the chart. The student works with a peer or teacher to complete the template.
Student performance	*Presentation:* The student develops and delivers a poster presentation to inform the class of the winter traditions of their chosen country (see Figure 9.3). The presentation also includes audio and/or visual representation of the selected song and/or dance. *Notetaking:* The student uses the word bank to complete the note-taking chart. The student demonstrates the traditional song/dance with descriptions as appropriate.	*Presentation:* The student uses pictures to represent themes and ideas on the poster; the student either selects the pictures from a choice of three, or independently selects pictures. The student also demonstrates the traditional song/dance (i.e., performs the song or dance, plays a piece of music, shows a dance video, etc.). *Notetaking:* The student uses the picture bank to complete the note-taking chart.	*Presentation:* The student develops a PowerPoint presentation to inform the class of the winter traditions of his or her chosen country. The student is given a template PowerPoint and a choice of two items to complete each slide by using an eye-gaze system as the teacher reads the slide and labels each choice as the student eye-gazes to the objects. With verbal reminding (and physical assistance as needed), the student selects the items that represent the missing information for each slide. The PowerPoint includes a video clip of the traditional song or dance with descriptions as appropriate. *Notetaking:* The student uses objects/tactile representations and works with a peer who reads the template out loud and verbally reminds the student of the meaning of the objects to complete the note-taking chart that is enlarged and affixed to foam board.
Formative assessment	The student presents his or her chosen holiday to the class and the presentation is scored using the presentation rubric.	The student presents his or her chosen holiday to the class and the presentation is scored using the presentation rubric. The student may play a prerecorded presentation as he/she points to the graphic representation being discussed on the recording.	The student uses a single button switch to advance the PowerPoint slides.

Figure 9.2. *Christmas in Norway* presentation—symbolic learner.

economics teaches students to consider geographic factors in their understanding of economic environments.

Geography   The specific geography standards for this unit are standard III-c, "use appropriate resources, data sources, and geographic tools such as atlases, data bases, grid systems, charts, graphs, and maps to generate, manipulate, and interpret information" (NCSS, 2009a, p. 2), and standard III-e, "locate and distinguish among varying landforms and geographic features, such as mountains, plateaus, islands, and oceans" (NCSS, 2009a, p. 2). The Big Idea for this unit is that geographic knowledge provides ability to analyze issues regarding human interaction with the environment, settlement and population of a geographic area, and how geographic features may affect economy, culture, and climate.

Economics   The specific economics standards for this unit are standard VII-g, "explain and demonstrate the role of money in everyday life," and VII-h, "describe the relationship of price to supply and demand" (NCSS, 2009a, p. 4). The Big Idea is that the study of economics looks at production, distribution, and consumption of goods and services and that economics helps students understand their individual economic status as it relates to the global economy.

Overview of the Unit   Students will review economic principles and use of geographical tools (e.g., reading topography, map keys). The teacher (or collaborating teachers) will conduct group discussions about possible points of interest within the continental United States. The students must plan a road trip to a specified number and type of sites or locations (e.g., specific landforms and geological features). Students are presented with limitations for the trip: 1) restricted budget; 2) restricted rate of travel—driving an old Volkswagen Rabbit and therefore unable to drive above 55 miles per hour; 3) restricted daily time allotment for travel—no more than 8 hours a day; and 4) restricted travel within the continental United States during the trip.

Grade-Level Instructional Activities for All Students: Road Trip Plan
Planning a road trip is an authentic activity which requires an understanding of geography and economics. The Road Trip Plan is described in detail in the following paragraphs.

Instruction   The teacher (or collaborating teachers) reviews the differences between *wants* and *needs,* as these concepts pertain to maintaining a budget, and leads a discussion about the implications of *supply and demand, cost/benefit,* and the role *competition* plays in the cost of goods and services. The teacher then reviews how to read a map using a map legend to identify landforms (e.g., mountains, deserts), water sources (lakes, rivers, and oceans), cities, rural areas, and roads (county roads, highways, and interstates). Students then do research to determine which sites to visit based on their budget, their preferred sites, and other relevant details. Students must complete a trip planner that contains all the daily stops and provides the miles driven each day, road time, and amount of money spent on gas, food, and lodging per day. The trip planner includes a final total of miles traveled, total number days the trip required, and total amount spent on gas, lodging, and food. The teacher assigns students to work in groups of two to three.

Student Performance   The students investigate various routes to each location and research prices of fuel, food, and lodging across the United States; in doing so, students must pay particular attention to tourist areas and areas with specific geological features. The students describe the variations in prices of fuel, food, and lodging based on location or other factors. They study a U.S. map to find geographical features (e.g., mountains, deserts, geysers, small towns, large cities) and determine the distance between chosen and assigned visit/site locations. The students must identify a mountain range, natural water source, a desert, a geological anomaly, a natural hot spring or geyser, a large city, a historically relevant site, and one place of personal interest. Students then plan a road trip that incorporates all required components and stays within budget (determined by teacher at the time of activity based on national averages). Students write up the trip to include cost of food, fuel, and lodging, the significance of the sites visited (e.g.,

Yellowstone National Park: hot springs and Old Faithful). Finally, they prepare a poster map with a legend to mark the route and identify the relevant sites or locations visited on the trip. They are expected to research locations and use the Internet and library resources in their work.

Formative Assessment   The formative assessment includes the cost analysis research, map and geographic locations research, as well as the poster of the planned trip and presentation of the trip planner to include accurate use of math to calculate economic goals. The poster presentation includes accurate use of the route and clarity of map key developed, as well as the clarity of the representation of the sites/locations visited and effectiveness of communicating or expressing the significance of the location. In Table 9.3, we again identify how students at three different levels of communicative development (symbolic, emerging symbolic, and presymbolic) can participate in both the instructional and the assessment activities. Figure 9.3 presents a tactile map and trip planner by a student at a presymbolic level of communication (i.e., a student who may not yet have a regularized or formalized means of communication). As noted in Chapter 3, it is essential to make the general curriculum accessible to all students, including students with the most significant cognitive disabilities.

High School Example: Revolutionary War Battles

Our high school example is taken from social studies standard V "Individuals, Groups, and Institutions" (NCSS, 2009a, p. 3) and standard VI "Power, Authority, and Governance" (NCSS, 2009a, p. 4) at the 10th-grade level. In order to understand the framework of the U.S. government and its division of power, one must first study the impact that foreign authority and unjust governing had on the individual colonists. The Revolutionary War resulted from individuals standing together against an institution to create an independent nation. Through the study of this unit, students learn that history is a series of cause-and-effect relationships.

Standards   The standards for this 10th-grade unit are taken from standard V-d, "identify and describe examples of tensions between and among individuals, groups, or institutions, and how belonging to more than one group can cause internal conflicts"; and V-e, "identify and describe examples of tensions between an individual's beliefs and government policies and laws" (NCSS, 2009a, p. 3). In addition, standard VI-f, "identify and describe factors that contribute to cooperation and cause disputes within and among groups and nations" (NCSS, 2009a, p. 4) is used in this lesson. The Big Idea for the unit is that history is the study of people, ideas, and events over time. By reviewing cause and effect within an historical context, students apply their knowledge to understanding recurring patterns and preparing for the future.

Overview of the Unit   Students will learn about the Declaration of Independence and will review the basic ideas and historical forces leading up to its development. Students will research the cause-and-effect relationship of these events and identify how these events led to the commencement of the Revolutionary War.

Table 9.3. Access to the road trip instructional activity for students at different levels of communication

	Symbolic learner	Emerging symbolic learner	Presymbolic learner
Instruction	Provide student with a graphic organizer labeled with required components of trip planner. Review requirements with student group. Provide student with template of required information for the presentation.	Provide student with a graphic organizer labeled (using pictures/graphic representation) with required components of trip planner. Review requirements with student group. Provide student with template poster board to include required information and a bank of information that can be used to create the presentation.	Provide student with a graphic organizer labeled (using pictures or other tactile representation) with required components of trip planner. Provide student with a computer-generated template, an adaptive switch to access the computer, adaptive software, and a bank of information that can be used to create the presentation.
Student performance	The student conducts research about the different locations he or she wants to visit including location and costs of food, fuel, and lodging for given locations. The student completes a map poster detailing the scheduled route, cities visited, and geographic features.	The student conducts research about the different locations he or she wants to visit including location and costs of food, fuel, and lodging for given locations. The student completes a map poster detailing the scheduled route, cities visited, and geographic features.	The student uses an adaptive single switch to access the computer and, with a peer, conducts research about locations and costs of food, fuel, and lodging for given locations. Peer helps student match object representations to objects paired with pictures to create chart. The student and peer partner complete a map poster detailing the scheduled route, cities visited, and geographic features. Peer reads the topics and provides verbal prompts or physical assistance as needed for student to select the tactile representation from a choice of two to complete the tactile map of the trip (see Figure 9.3).
Formative assessment	Student presents the poster map and the description of the total number of days, mileage, and cost analysis.	Student presents the poster map and the description of the total number of days, mileage, and cost analysis.	Student creates a tactile map of trip planned and description of total number of days, mileage, and cost. Student matches object to picture of object and peer places answers for student. Final presentation of tactile map and trip data via LCD projector operated by adaptive switch.

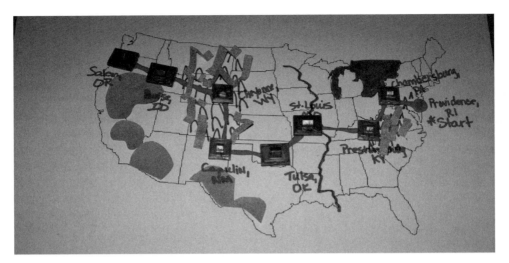

Figure 9.3. Tactile map and trip planner—presymbolic learner.

They will conduct Internet research to create a prewar cause-and-effect timeline. Then using a list provided by the teacher, each student will pick one Revolutionary War battle and become an "expert." Students will conduct Internet research on the battle and explain the relevance (i.e., political, economic) of the battle to the war, how the topography of the battlefield affected the outcome, and troop movements throughout the battle.

Revolutionary War Activity   Timelines, research, and discussion of causal factors help students understand the significance of singular events in the course of history. This activity is described in detail in the following paragraphs.

   Instruction   The teacher explains that many of the actions taken by the British led not only to the colonists' rebellion, but also to the creation of a new American government aimed at preventing abuses as set forth in the Declaration of Independence. To ensure students understand the cause-and-effect relationship, given a variety of situations, the teacher has the students indicate possible reactions or outcomes to specific situations. The teacher reviews the events leading up to the Revolutionary War by emphasizing the cause and effect of each event. She provides students with a list of relevant web sites to use, in addition to their text book, so they can further research the events leading to the Revolutionary War. Together, the class develops a comprehensive timeline of the events leading up to the war. The teacher provides information about a variety of the battles fought during the Revolutionary War. The focus of the discussion is on battles that had an impact on the outcome of the war (e.g., time of war, loss of troops, loss of supply route). The teacher explains why the battle was important (e.g., capture of munitions, supply route) and the factors (e.g., terrain, timing, access to resources) that influenced each battle.

   Student Performance   Students assist in the creation of the classroom cause-and-effect timeline of the events leading up to the war. After the completion of the timeline, each student chooses one battle on which to become the expert. Students research their chosen battle and determine the relevance of the battle and the significance of outcomes of the battle, such as retreat or strategic gain/advantage (e.g., control of transportation or supply routes, capture of munitions, turning point in the war). The project includes a topographically accurate diorama of the battlefield (see the arts "scale and perspective" lesson later in this chapter).

Formative Assessment   The formative assessment for this activity is twofold. First, each student's participation in the development of an accurate timeline is assessed, including dates, cause of the event (law or action taken by British), and effect of the event. The second part of the assessment is the student's explanation of how the battle was relevant to the outcome of the war.

Consider how this might look for students with significant cognitive disabilities at each of the three levels of communication (Table 9.4). Figure 9.4 presents an example of how a student at an emerging symbolic level of communication (i.e., communicating through pictures and beginning words/signs) might communicate the relevance of the battle.

————● The Arts Lessons

The following sections present sample lessons in the arts for students with significant cognitive disabilities at the elementary, middle, and high school levels.

Elementary School Example—Holidays Around the World

In *Learning Improved Through Arts Training,* Gardiner, Fox, Knowles, and Jeffrey (1996) found that arts education that included actual student performances resulted in higher educational achievement in other subjects for a targeted group of students in comparison with a control group that did not participate in arts education with student performance. The relationship between music and dance instruction and improved learning, particularly in the area of mathematics and spatial relationships, is a strong argument for increasing arts programs for all students. Dance and music offer students the unique opportunity to express their thoughts, knowledge, and feelings. Incorporating the fine arts into the academic instruction of other content areas not only reinforces instruction in each of these areas, but may also increase student interest in a variety of topics. In the example below, we provide an extension of our social studies unit (Holidays Around the World) presented earlier in this chapter, to include the subjects of music and dance as an integral part of that same unit.

Dance Standards   The dance standards for this unit are taken from *The National Standards for Arts Education*:

- *Dance Content Standard 3:* "Understanding dance as a way to create and communicate meaning" (ArtsEdge, 1994)
- *Dance Content Standard 5*: "Demonstrating and understanding dance in various cultures and historical periods" (ArtsEdge, 1994)
- *Dance Content Standard 7*: "Making connections between dance and other disciplines" (ArtsEdge, 1994)

Table 9.4. Access to the Revolutionary War instructional activity for students at different levels of communication

	Symbolic learner	Emerging symbolic learner	Presymbolic learner
Instruction	Provide prewritten notes and a highlighter for student to follow along with the lecture to assist in comprehension.	Provide prewritten notes to be read aloud and paired with pictures to assist in comprehension.	Provide prewritten notes to be read aloud and paired with objects to assist in comprehension.
Student performance	Student identifies and provides one event leading up to the war, including date, cause, and effect. Student selects one battle from the teacher-created list and conducts research (i.e., using a computer, text book, encyclopedia). Student works to determine the relevance and outcomes of the battle selected.	Student provides one picture of an event with date, cause and/or effect from a choice of three when asked "What happened next?" Student selects one battle from the teacher-created list and conducts research (i.e., using a computer with adaptive software, using books read aloud and paired with pictures). Student works in small group to determine the relevance and outcomes of the battle by filling in blanks of a template describing the battle. The sentences are read aloud by a peer and the student is given three picture choices to complete each sentence (see Figure 9.4).	Working with a peer who provides verbal reminding and physical assistance as needed, the student matches an object representation of an event to picture representing the cause and/or effect of that event. Student selects one battle from the teacher-created list and conducts research with a peer (i.e., using a computer with adaptive software, or books read aloud and paired with objects). Student works in a small group to determine the relevance and outcomes of the battle by filling in blanks of sentences describing the battle. The sentences are read by a peer, and the student is given two object choices that are verbally stated as the student touches the objects to complete each sentence. The peer provides verbal, gestural, or physical assistance as needed.
Formative assessment	Student explains the selected battle, including the relevance to the outcome of the war.	Student explains the selected battle, including the relevance to the outcome of the war (see Figure 9.4).	Student explains the selected battle, including the relevance to the outcome of the war.

The battle of Fort Ticonderoga. Fort Ticonderoga situated on Lake Champlain in New York was captured

by the Green Montain Boys in May 1775. The Green Mountain Boys captured the fort without firing one shot.

They captured 78 large weapons including 59 cannons. The weapons were later used to remove the

British from Boston.

Figure 9.4. Student description of events occurring at Fort Ticonderoga—emerging symbolic learner.

Music Standards   The music standards for this unit are also taken from *The National Standards for Arts Education*:

- *Content Standard 6*: "Listening to, analyzing, and describing music" (ArtsEdge, 1994)
- *Content Standard 8*: "Understanding relationships between music, the other arts, and disciplines outside the arts" (ArtsEdge, 1994)
- *Content Standard 9*: "Understanding music in relation to history and culture" (ArtsEdge, 1994)

The Big Idea for this unit (and for the subsequent arts lessons we present in this chapter) is that the study of the arts reflects the beliefs and ideals of a culture and conveys meaning, history, and feeling. Exploring the arts of different cultures gives students insight into these cultures and their history, as well as an understanding of how the arts affect our society. Students improve their understanding of their world when they are able to recognize and interpret the many art forms that express the core beliefs and views of their culture and others.

Overview of the Unit   Dance and music can be connected to all content areas. Styles, rhythm, melody, and movement of songs and dance vary greatly, being influenced by culture, region, religion and other factors. Throughout history, music and dance have been an important means of recreation, communication, and ceremony. In this lesson, students will study the historical and/or traditional relevance of song and dance and learn how to interpret and/or react to the art form(s).

Understand, Analyze, and Share the Arts Music/Dance Activity   Discussion and performance help students understand how music and dance have meaning and shape culture. This activity is described in detail in the following paragraphs.

Instruction   The teacher explains how music and dance have been used to celebrate events and communicate meaning. Discussion includes a description of the functions and purposes of dance and music throughout history. Students are provided with examples of ceremonial song/dance versus recreational song/dance. The teacher also describes the role of songs and dance in culture and tradition. Based on previously provided examples and the students' research (Holidays Around the World, Grade 5), they are asked to perform or demonstrate a traditional song and/or dance and have the class identify the purpose of the art form.

Student Performance   Students are provided with a variety of different traditional songs/dances. Students are asked to identify the purpose of each song/dance (i.e., ceremonial, artistic expression, recreational) and describe the function of each song/dance. Students are then asked to compare the song/dance to a similar song/dance related to their own culture or traditions. Each student performs or demonstrates a traditional song or dance associated with the winter holiday the student has researched for the social studies unit Holidays Around the World. The class analyzes each of the performances and determines the purpose (i.e., ceremonial, recreational, or artistic expression) of the traditional song or dance.

Formative Assessment   The formative assessment for this activity is tied to the culminating project for our social studies unit on Holidays Around the World. Students must incorporate a traditional song or dance associated with the winter holiday from their selected or assigned country. Students perform or demonstrate (i.e., using an audio or video clip) the song or dance (see Activity 2 from our social studies unit). In Table 9.5, we again identify how students at three different levels of communicative development (presymbolic, emerging symbolic, and symbolic) can participate in both the instructional and the assessment activities. In Figure 9.5 we present sample slides from a PowerPoint presentation demonstrating how a student with significant cognitive disabilities (symbolic learner) and a peer partner might complete this activity. This work sample can be used as evidence linked to grade-level content standards for alternate assessments.

Middle School Example: Road Trip

Why are the visual arts such an important part of any academic curriculum? The arts are not only a part of most memorable or auspicious occasions, but art has a way of imbuing the most commonplace experience with a special significance. For many students, art is the most engaging aspect of a lesson; a fascinating picture in a biology book, a dramatic reenactment of a historical event, a fun dance or creative pottery project in social studies. Art is enticing, drawing the observer in, capturing his or her attention. Art makes learning fun, but art is more than just fun. Art conveys meaning, and students who are instructed in the arts learn to interpret and gain perspective from art in academic content and in the world around them. The meaning that art conveys not only informs but helps the student make decisions about the world and its people.

Visual Arts Standards   The standards for the visual arts for this unit are taken from *The National Standards for Arts Education*:

Table 9.5. Access to the music/dance instructional activity for students at different levels of communication

	Symbolic learner	Emerging symbolic learner	Presymbolic learner
Instruction	The teacher explains how music and dance have been used to celebrate events and communicate meaning, as well as the role of songs and dance in culture and tradition. The discussion examines what differentiates a ceremonial song or dance from a recreational song or dance. Additionally, the class discusses artistic expression as a purpose of song and dance. Finally, the teacher discusses how song and dance can be connected to a variety of holiday customs.		As noted in the left-hand (symbolic learner) column, except the teacher provides pictorial or video representations of various types of songs and dances. The teacher provides object representations for the vocabulary that a peer reviews with the student to help the student match the correct object to its picture.
Student performance	Given knowledge of the purposes of song and dance, the student conducts research on the Internet or in research articles about songs and dances associated with the country that he or she has selected for the "Holidays Around the World" social studies lesson. The student selects either a song or a dance with which to become familiar and present to the class. The student explains the background information regarding why the song is sung or the dance is danced and how it pertains to the traditions of the holiday selected.	The student conducts research as noted in the left-hand (symbolic learner) column, except the student is provided with Internet sites and articles that have been paraphrased and paired with pictures to conduct research about the songs and dances associated with the country that he or she has selected for the "Holidays Around the World" social studies lesson. The student selects either a song or a dance with which to become familiar and present to the class. The student explains (e.g., with picture symbols) the background information regarding why the song is sung or the dance is danced and how it pertains to the traditions of the holiday selected.	The student conducts research as noted in the left-hand (symbolic learner) column, except the student uses adaptive software and a single button switch to have information from Internet sites read aloud and works with a peer who pairs the objects to the research and verbally assists (e.g., reminding the student to click the switch to advance the screen or providing physical assistance, as needed) the student in conducting his or her research about the songs and dances associated with the country he or she has selected. The peer assists the student in selecting a song or a dance to present. The student selects an object (from a choice of two) to represent why the song/dance is performed.
Formative assessment	The student either performs the song or dance for the class or prepares a presentation (e.g., recording of a song, video of a dance) of the art form to present to the class and then describes how the dance or song relates to the holiday celebration (see Figure 9.5).	The student describes how the dance or song relates to the holiday celebration using a pictorial representation.	The student presents the art form (e.g., recording of a song, video of a dance) by activating an adaptive switch to play the recording.

Figure 9.5. Sample slides from the PowerPoint presentation about two Norwegian Christmas carols—symbolic learner.

- *Visual Arts Standard 1*: "Understanding and applying media, techniques, and processes" and its associated achievement standard, "students select media, techniques, and processes; analyze what makes them effective or not effective in communicating ideas; and reflect upon the effectiveness of their choices" (ArtsEdge, 1994)

- *Visual Arts Standard 6*: "Making connections between visual arts and other disciplines" and its associated achievement standard, "students describe ways in which the principles and subject matter of other disciplines taught in the school are interrelated with the visual arts" (ArtsEdge, 1994)

Overview of the Unit   Students will investigate the cultural influence on the arts in each location they visit on their "road trip" (see social studies eighth-grade lesson). Using their research results, they will develop a "Travel with the Arts" brochure that describes local art forms and cultural influences for each location visited. In addition, they will incorporate each local art form into their visual poster map representation of the trip. The poster will include sample art work for every location visited (e.g., sand painting from the Grand Canyon, totem pole from Pacific Northwest, quilting from the Appalachian mountains).

Grade-Level Instructional Activities for All Students: Creating a Multimedia Work of Art

Students learn to understand differences in cultures by creating a visual representation of their road trip and art forms of specific geographic regions. This activity is described in detail in the following paragraphs.

Instruction   The teacher explains how art forms vary based on histories, lifestyles or customs, resources, and traditions. Along the route traveled in the Road Trip lesson, students "encounter" many cultural examples of art in different forms. The teacher describes various art forms from a variety of cultures and discusses similarities and differences based on culture and location; she leads a discussion on how differing media are used to express artistic and cultural meaning. Instruction includes a description of resources available in locations visited on the road trip (e.g., sand in the Southwest, trees in Pacific Northwest, cotton in the Southeastern states) and how resources are used to develop various media for artistic expression (e.g., sand painting, totem poles, textiles). Students learn about a variety of images and objects representing these different media and art forms. They are shown examples of multimedia art works and asked to think about how they would incorporate different art forms into a multimedia poster map.

Student Performance   Students create samples of regional art work using information from their "Travel with the Arts" brochure. Using a map of the continental United States, students place their art samples in each location on the Road Trip map.

Formative Assessment   Students describe how resources from each location are used to develop the media used in regional art forms. They explain the purpose (i.e., artistic expression, ceremonial use, narrative use, and functional use) of the art form. The formative assessment for this activity is tied to the culminating project of the Grade 8 social studies lesson. See Table 9.6 to identify how students at three different levels of communicative development (presymbolic, emerging symbolic, and symbolic) can participate in both the instructional and the assessment activities. Figure 9.6 presents a student work sample that fulfills the formative assessment requirements for a student at the presymbolic level.

Table 9.6. Access to the multimedia work of art instructional activity for students at different levels of communication

	Symbolic learner	Emerging symbolic learner	Presymbolic learner
Instruction	The teacher leads a class discussion about the types of art that might be found in a particular region. The teacher discusses the media typically used to create that particular art form, and provides vocabulary for the various art media.	Within the instruction noted in the left-hand (symbolic learner) column, the teacher also provides vocabulary for the various art media paired with picture cues.	Within the instruction noted in the left-hand (symbolic learner) column, the teacher also provides vocabulary for the various art media paired with picture or object cues. The student works with a peer who helps assign meaning to the objects by stating the media type and assisting (e.g., verbal reminders, gestures, physical assistance as needed) the student to match the media type to the object representation.
Student performance	The student selects at least four different types of artwork to research and learn about the history of the work of art and the media used to create the art piece.	To assist with student performance, the student may work with a peer or in a small group.	The student may work with a peer, in a small group, or use a single switch that reads the computer screen aloud when activated.
Formative assessment	The student selects at least four different types of artwork found from his or her "Road Trip" and recreates the work of art. The student also places the art work on the map in the correct geographic location. The teacher uses the map as the formative assessment, and evaluates the authenticity of the replication and accuracy of the artwork found within the region. If the student is physically unable to create certain works of art, he or she can answer questions to complete a work of art (e.g., color, design).	See the formative assessment for the symbolic learner in the left-hand column of this table.	Given a variety of art pieces prepared by peers representing various geographic areas, a preselected area of the map, and peer verbal reminders about what type of media is typically found in that geographic area, the student selects the correct art form from a choice of two (with assistance as needed). The peer places that representation on the map for the student in the area that they had been discussing (see Figure 9.6).

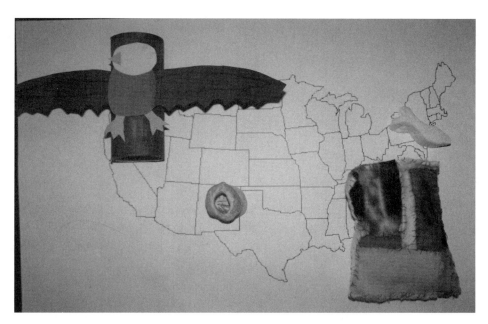

Figure 9.6.   Student artwork for Road Trip lesson—presymbolic learner.

High School Example: Revolutionary War

In this final unit, we present an example of how the visual arts can be embedded into the Revolutionary War unit for 10th-grade students. The study of history can be made to come alive by the incorporation of the arts for all students, as the example below illustrates.

Visual Arts Standards   The standards for the visual arts for this unit are taken from *The National Standards for Arts Education*:

- *Visual Arts Standard 1*: "Understanding and applying media, techniques, and processes" (Arts Edge, 1994)
- *Visual Arts Standard 6*: "Making connections between visual arts and other disciplines" (ArtsEdge, 1994)

Overview of the Unit   Students will incorporate their knowledge of various media, scale, and perspective in the construction of a diorama that accurately reflects a Revolutionary War battlefield. The diorama should be used as part of a culminating project for the Grade 10 Revolutionary War activity. The students will be expected to understand how the topography of a battlefield affected the outcome of the battle and use a variety of media to represent topographical features of their battlefield. Students will use their knowledge of scale and perspective to demonstrate realistic representation of the battle and use the diorama to describe the battle, including troop movements and outcome. Students will reflect on the significance of the battle.

Grade-Level Instructional Activity for All Students: Working with Scale and Perspective Activity   By using art to reconstruct a specific historical event, students understand the importance of scale and perspective. This activity is described in detail in the following paragraphs.

Instruction   The teacher explains that a diorama is a realistic representation of a moment and place in time and space. For a diorama to appear realistic, it must be constructed with scale and perspective in mind. A battlefield diorama must include setting and characters, as well as topographical features and other constructions (e.g., buildings, fences, monuments, harbor). The teacher explains that setting is used as a background and instructs students as to what constitutes the setting in a battlefield diorama (e.g., *time:* season, day/night; *place:* countryside, mountains, forest, city, harbor). The characters in a battlefield diorama include soldiers and other relevant individuals (e.g., civilians, government officials or personnel, livestock). The teacher also discusses how scale and perspective are used in the development of a diorama. Students learn that all objects in the diorama must maintain the appropriate relationship in size. Various techniques for maintaining scale and perspective are demonstrated and described for the students (e.g., objects in the background appear smaller; depth perception can be created by the convergence of two or three planes in the background; and objects on a tilted plane appear to be in the distance) through the use of a variety of examples.

Student Performance   Students develop a plan for their battlefield diorama. The plan must include the scale and how perspective is attained and must accurately represent the battle, the setting, and the characters. It may be constructed using a computer program or paper.

Formative Assessment   The completed plan consists of a description of the scale and background for the diorama, a list of appropriate materials (e.g., characters, setting), and an accurate representation of perspective (near and distant). Table 9.7 illustrates how instruction, performance, and formative assessment are modified or adapted for students with significant cognitive disabilities communicating at symbolic, emerging symbolic, and presymbolic levels. Figure 9.7 represents a graphic or visual organizer for an emerging symbolic learner to plan exactly what he is going to place on his diorama. The graphic organizer prompts the student to consider the scale as well as the essential questions of who, what, where, and when.

CONCLUSION

Formative assessments are used to guide instruction and to assess student progress on an ongoing basis, so that teachers can design and implement activities that target the specific needs of all students. Formative assessments may be as simple as anecdotal record keeping or as complex as the culminating projects that have been outlined in this chapter. Observing students' work in progress allows the teacher to identify areas in which the students may need more instruction or practice, or the next steps or tasks in their learning process. This results in more effective instruction, as well as more efficient use of teacher

Table 9.7. Access to the battlefield diorama instructional activities

	Symbolic learner	Emerging symbolic learner	Presymbolic learner
Instruction	The teacher conducts a lesson about setting, scale, perspective, and media and how all of these components work together to assist in the development of a work of art. The teacher leads a discussion of why smaller items sometimes look larger than bigger items (e.g., a small tree that is nearer to us may appear larger than a tall building farther away) and have students provide examples of perspective in a variety of settings.	As described in the left-hand (symbolic learner) column, the teacher also has the student match pictures to indicate understanding of perspective, that the nearer an object, the larger it appears.	As described in the left-hand (symbolic learner) column, the teacher also demonstrates perspective by showing the student two objects the same size, stating "these objects are the same size," and letting the student feel the objects. The teacher moves one object farther away until it appears smaller to the student. The teacher then says, "See, this one seems smaller, but it is because it is farther away" and brings the item back to the student saying, "See, they are still the same size."
Student performance	The student develops the plan for the diorama including the scale to be used (the student may use a calculator), the setting/background for the diorama, characters, and actions to be represented within the diorama. The student also includes any other details that he or she wants the diorama to depict.	As noted in the left-hand (symbolic learner) column, the student may need a mathematical model to determine the scale. The student can use pictures to assist with writing the plan and also include any other details that he or she wants the diorama to depict (see Figure 9.7).	As described in the left-hand (symbolic learner) column, the student develops the plan with the following modifications. Given a template of five questions to answer (scale, who, what, when, and where) and working with a peer, the student makes a diorama plan. Given two choices for each question represented by pictures and paired with objects, the peer hands an object to the student and reads the question aloud. The student then matches the object to the picture/object pair and works with the peer to glue the pictures in the appropriate places. The peer provides verbal reminding and physical assistance as needed.
Formative assessment	The student completes an evaluation of the plan for the diorama.	The student completes an evaluation of the plan for the diorama.	The student completes an evaluation of the plan for the diorama.

261

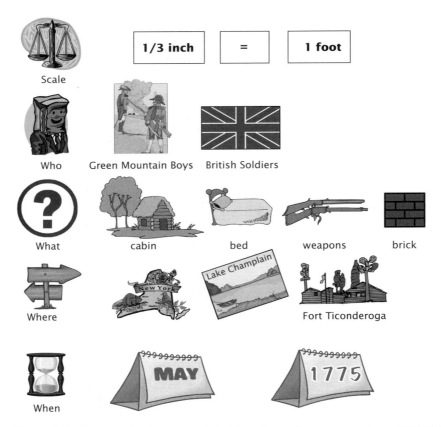

Figure 9.7. Scale plan for the capture of Fort Ticonderoga diorama—emerging symbolic learner.

and student instructional time and classroom materials and resources. For students with significant cognitive disabilities, these assessments can yield both student work samples and instructional performance data required to demonstrate student proficiency on alternate assessments linked to grade-level content standards.

Social studies and the arts are broadly encompassing fields of study in and of themselves. Most important, they also provide a means to articulate holistic viewpoints of other content and can be easily integrated with other content areas. This integration allows teachers to reinforce critical skills in such areas as reading and math, while permitting the teacher to work toward multiple academic goals simultaneously. Formative assessments may incorporate numerous content standards and academic tasks. For instance, the "Travel with the Arts" brochure (the arts component of the Road Trip unit) is designed as an arts activity, but also incorporates study of geography and culture (social studies), a writing task, and reading, reviewing, and editing (as students review their research). The activity could be easily modified to include a math component by requiring the students to develop alternative "trip packages" that combine differing costs or offer special discounts, or a science component by requiring the students to identify natural resources or elements used as media in the various art forms.

Formative assessments provide students with opportunities to practice and use new skills. A student may become not only proficient, but comfortable with his or her knowledge of the content. In a testing situation, confidence can make a difference in student performance. For example, in some states, alternate assessments for students with significant cognitive disabilities take the form of performance-event or testing situations; opportunities to practice are essential preparation for such tests. Formative assessments also provide evidence that can be used in alternate assessments that require work samples or other documentation of student work. Many formative assessments include writing samples and use mathematical computations and tools such as charts, graphs, or function tables. For example, topographical maps developed during the Road Trip activity in this chapter's activities could be used to meet state science standards. Identifying the sequence of events or identifying the main characters in an historical event (as in the Revolutionary War unit) may address required reading content standards.

Formative assessments should target content standards, as well as develop and utilize strategies that provide access to the curriculum for the student. These strategies might be provided in the form of a graphic organizer or a mnemonic (or memory) strategy, for instance, and could address standards that require comparing and contrasting, inquiry, problem solving, or the use of the scientific method. These types of supports should be taught and incorporated in instruction and formative assessment. Typically, supports that are used in instruction, and that do not lead a student to an answer, may also be used in large scale alternate assessments.

Formative assessment is an effective means of guiding and developing instruction, as well as an important source of learning for the student. Outcomes of these assessments include improved learning opportunities, evidence of student knowledge, application of skills and knowledge to authentic tasks, and generalization of these skills and knowledge to both summative assessments and real world situations. For students with significant cognitive disabilities, these outcomes can also include the needed work samples, instructional data, and/or learning opportunities necessary to prepare them for successful participation in their state's respective alternate assessment based on alternate achievement standards.

REFERENCES

ArtsEdge. (1994). *The national standards for arts education*. Retrieved October 20, 2009, from http://artsedge.kennedy-center.org/teach/standards/standards.cfm

Browder, D.M., Wakeman, S.Y., Flowers, C., Rickelman, R.J., & Pugalee, D. (2007). Creating access to the general curriculum with links to grade-level content for students with significant cognitive disabilities: An explication of the concept. *The Journal of Special Education, 41*, 2–16.

Collins, B.C., Branson, T.B., Hall, M., & Rankin, S.W. (2001). Teaching secondary students with moderate disabilities in an inclusive classroom setting. *Journal of Developmental and Physical Disabilities, 13*, 41–59.

Consortium of National Arts Education Associations. (1994). *National standards for arts education: What every young American should know and be able to do in the arts*. Reston, VA: MENC Publications.

Erickson, L. (2001). *Stirring the head, heart and soul: Redefining curriculum and instruction* (2nd ed.). Thousand Oaks, CA: Corwin Press.

Gardiner, M.F., Fox, A., Knowles, F., & Jeffrey, D. (1996). Learning improved by arts training. *Nature, 381*, 284.

Hunt, P., Alwell, M., Farron-Davis, F., & Goetz, L. (1996). Creating socially supportive environments for fully included students who experience multiple disabilities. *The Journal of The Association for Persons with Severe Handicaps, 21*, 53–71.

Kentucky Department of Education. (2006). *Combined curriculum document: Social studies, Grade 5.* Retrieved June 26, 2009, from http://www.education.ky.gov/kde/instructional+resources/ curriculum+documents+and+resources/teaching+tools/combined+curriculum+documents/

National Council for the Social Studies (2009a). *Curriculum standards for social studies.* Retrieved October 19, 2009, from http://www.macmillanmh.com/socialstudies/2009/teacher/pdf/ncss.pdf

National Council for the Social Studies (2009b). *Expectations of excellence: Curriculum standards for social studies.* Retrieved October 21, 2009, from http://www.socialstudies.org/standards

Polloway, E.A., Patton, J.R., Payne, J.S., & Payne, R.A. (1989). *Strategies for teaching learners with special needs* (4th ed.). Columbus, OH: Merrill.

Spooner, F., & Browder, D.M. (2006). Why teach the general curriculum? In D.M. Browder & F. Spooner (Eds.), *Teaching language arts, math, & science to students with significant cognitive disabilities* (pp. 1–13). Baltimore: Paul H. Brookes Publishing Co.

Stainback, W., & Stainback, S. (Eds.). (1990). *Support networks for inclusive schooling: Interdependent integrated education.* Baltimore: Paul H. Brookes Publishing Co.

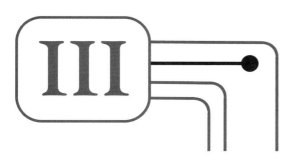

Enhancing Student Outcomes

The Role of Students and Families and Directions for Future Research

10

Embedding Life Skills, Self-Determination, Social Relationships, and Other Evidence-Based Practices

Harold L. Kleinert, Belva C. Collins,
Donna Wickham, Leah Riggs, and Karen D. Hager

For students with disabilities, access to and progress within the general curriculum are requirements of both the Individuals with Disabilities Education Act Amendments (IDEA) of 1997 (PL 105-17) and the Individuals with Disabilities Education Improvement Act (IDEA) of 2004 (PL 108-446). IDEA also requires that all students with disabilities participate in state educational assessments linked to the general curriculum, either through the state's regular assessment or through an alternate assessment. State assessments directly tied to core academic content also are required for all students under the No Child Left Behind (NCLB) Act of 2001 (PL 107-110). In its nonregulatory guidance to NCLB, the U.S. Department of Education (2005) has further explicated this relationship between the general curriculum and alternate assessments by noting that alternate assessment based on alternate achievement standards (AA-AAS) must be linked specifically to grade-level content standards. See Chapter 4 for a detailed set of criteria for grade-level content alignment for alternate assessments.

Yet students with significant cognitive disabilities have other learning needs that arise from the nature of their disability. Such needs can include direct instruction in vocational and other community settings to prepare for postschool life, explicit instruction in initiating and sustaining social interactions in order to develop friendships, and intensive programming to address adaptive and self-care needs to increase independence. Teachers have an obligation to ensure that both sets of needs are met: that students receive academic instruction—linked to grade-level content standards—in the general curriculum, as well as instruction on those other life-skills needs, as identified within each student's individualized education program (IEP). Addressing both sets of needs poses a considerable challenge for many, if not most, teachers (Flowers, Ahlgrim-Delzell, Browder, & Spooner, 2005; Towles-Reeves, Kleinert, & Muhomba, 2009). This chapter provides examples that illustrate how academic content can retain the "enduring understandings" of grade-level content standards and be personally relevant to the other (life-skills) needs of the student.

Fortunately, there are evidence-based practices that enhance student outcomes in both academic and life-skill domains. In this chapter, we illustrate how instruction and assessment linked to grade-level content standards can promote life skills, social relationships, independence, and postschool outcomes. We also will show how academic outcomes can be applied in "real-life" contexts and how the core components of self-determination (problem-solving, evaluating, and self-monitoring) can be enhanced through instructional and assessment tasks with increasing Depth of Knowledge (DOK).

CONTENT CENTRALITY

Content centrality (i.e., sufficient linkage—see Chapter 4) to grade-level content standards is required under NCLB, but what about "linkage" to functional life skills, social and communication skills, and the components of self-determination? Are these other life domains still a part of AA-AAS? When authorities in alternate assessment use the term *content centrality* (see Browder et al., 2007), it is to grade-level content standards that they are implying this essential linkage. Yet can we also talk about content centrality to the critical life skills that a student needs in order to be as independent as possible in his or her present environment and to be prepared for a satisfying and productive outcome in his or her postschool life?

Everything that a student with a significant cognitive disability learns, or needs to learn, cannot, of course, be measured by an AA-AAS. IDEA 2004 clearly states that each student's IEP must address both student performance in the general curriculum and the student's other needs that arise from his or her disability (§ 614 [d][1][A]). Thus, the overall educational program for the student will necessarily be broader than what is measured on the AA-AAS, but instruction on grade-level content standards can nevertheless embed these other elements essential to life outcomes for students with significant cognitive disabilities. In this chapter, we suggest several strategies that teachers can use to embed these other critical elements and provide examples of each within both instruction and assessment.

DEPTH OF KNOWLEDGE AND SELF-DETERMINATION—LINKING ACADEMIC SKILLS TO CRITICAL LIFE SKILLS

Depth of Knowledge (DOK) is an assessment term that refers to the level of complexity or conceptual thought required to derive an answer or to solve a problem. DOK can range from simple recall or remembering (e.g., "2 + 2 = 4," "the capital of the United States is Washington, D.C.") to basic application (e.g., "John has four apples and Mary has six apples. How many apples do they have all together?") to more complex problems involving analysis and synthesis of data or even creation of new products or solutions (e.g., creating a personal narrative, determining the number of days in which the temperature exceeded the mean through a visual analysis of a graph). For examples of how DOK has been applied and studied within the context of alternate assessments, the reader is referred to Flowers, Browder, and Ahlgrim-Delzell (2006) and to Roach, Elliott, and Webb (2005), as well as to Chapter 4 of this text. Although AA-AAS might be expected to reflect achievement standards of reduced breadth, depth, and complexity than the grade-level content upon which they are based, students with significant cognitive disabilities should still have opportunities, in both instruction and assessment, to work on questions and problems that sample the full range of DOK.

Although there are different scales used to determine DOK, all of these scales have common elements at their highest levels. Generalization of concepts to new situations, self-evaluation of one's work, and monitoring of one's own performance in the steps of solving a problem (or creating a new solution) are all examples of these higher-level skills. Of course, these are all component skills under the broad rubric of self-determination. *Self-determination* is the capacity to set one's own goals, develop a plan to achieve those goals, and evaluate one's success toward reaching those goals (Holub, Lamb, & Bang, 1998; Martin & Marshall, 1995). Although self-determination historically has not been emphasized in programs for students with significant cognitive disabilities (Agran, King-Sears, Wehmeyer, & Copeland, 2003; Falvey, 1995), there has been an increasing recognition that self-determination can be systematically taught to students with intellectual disabilities (Agran et al., 2003; Wehmeyer, Palmer, Agran, & Mithaug, 2000) and embedded in the elements of alternate assessment (Kleinert et al., 2001). Most importantly, students who evidence higher levels of self-determination have more positive postschool outcomes (Wehmeyer & Palmer, 2003; Wehmeyer & Schwartz, 1998).

Yet it would appear that, even though students with significant cognitive disabilities have ample opportunities to learn and practice the skills of self-determination in school, they often do not develop and use those skills. Carter, Owens, Trainor, Sun, and Swedeen (2009) found that high school students in one state's alternate assessment did not evidence those higher order components of self-determination in the context of their school and everyday routines. Carter et al. found that, although students with significant cognitive disabilities expressed their own interests, set goals, and made choices, students less frequently engaged in more complex skills, such as evaluating their own learning, problem solving, and self-management.

To the extent that we can embed academic instruction and alternate assessments with tasks or problems that capture these elements of self-determination (and thus require increasing DOK), we increase the likelihood that academically aligned instruction will result in essential life skill acquisition (problem solving, generalizing learned concepts to novel situations) for students with significant cognitive disabilities. In this section, we first describe DOK dimensions in greater detail; we then provide two examples (of a middle school and a high school student) of how increased DOK can be related to problem-solving and life applications.

A Closer Look at Cognitive Complexity

Several approaches exist to represent complexity of thinking (e.g., Anderson & Krathwohl, 2001; Bloom, 1956; Webb, 1997). Webb's DOK scale describes cognitive demand as recall, basic application of skill or concept, strategic thinking, and extended thinking. Webb's DOK most commonly is used as a tool for states to align their assessment and content standards. As a result, many states have assigned DOK levels to their state assessment standards. On the other hand, Bloom's Taxonomy is by far the most familiar to educators. As a means to categorize degrees of cognitive complexity, Bloom proposed six different levels of learning. In the 1990s, those six levels were revised by Anderson and Krathwohl (2001) to reflect advanced understanding of cognition and learning. The revised Bloom's Taxonomy includes six levels of learning: remembering, understanding, applying, analyzing, evaluating, and creating. Because educators and assessment experts may use different approaches, Table 10.1 shows how the two most frequently used approaches (those of Bloom and Webb) can be compared and equated.

Many resources are available for educators to show how instructional activities can be designed for all cognitive complexity levels; however, few resources in this area exist for students with significant cognitive disabilities. Because students with significant cognitive disabilities historically have not participated in grade-level academic content, it is tempting to believe that the lower level activities, such as rote memorization of discrete facts and skills, are the appropriate beginning point for these students. Moreover, academic content areas have extensive technical vocabularies that often are associated with solving mathematics problems or conducting scientific experiments, and these technical vocabularies also may present barriers for students with significant cognitive disabilities in learning academic content. Yet, without understanding the content and its practical use, it is difficult to understand the relationship between the academic concepts and requisite

Table 10.1. A comparison of Bloom's and Webb's measures of cognitive complexity

Bloom's *revised* Taxonomy	Webb's Depth of Knowledge
Remembering: Retrieving relevant knowledge from long-term memory (e.g., recognizing, recalling)	*Recall*: Recalling a fact, information, or procedure
Understanding: Determining the meaning of instructional messages, including oral, written, and graphic communication (e.g., interpreting, exemplifying, summarizing, explaining)	
Applying: Carrying out or using a procedure in a given situation (e.g., executing, implementing)	*Basic application of skill/concept*: Using information, conceptual knowledge, and/or procedures; following two or more steps
Analyzing: Breaking material into its constituent parts and detecting how the parts relate to one another and to an overall structure or purpose (e.g., differentiating, organizing, attributing)	*Strategic thinking*: Reasoning, developing a plan or sequence of steps; problems involve some complexity, with more than one possible answer
Evaluating: Making judgments based on criteria and standards (e.g., checking, critiquing)	
Creating: Putting elements together to form a novel, coherent whole or make an original product (e.g., generating, planning, producing)	*Extended thinking*: Using investigative thinking, with time to reflect and process multiple conditions of the problem.

Sources: Anderson and Krathwohl (2001); Webb (1999).

skills. As educators unfortunately learned from the field's use of a developmental model to guide learning for students with significant cognitive disabilities in the 1970s, many students—if a similar "developmental" model to learning grade-level content is adopted—will spend their entire educational career learning all of the "requisite" skills to the academic content. As a result, they will not have the opportunity to integrate those skills into their lives or understand the practical reasons for learning them.

Special educators may also be more comfortable teaching specific skills and concrete facts, because skills and facts lend themselves well to task analysis and systematic instruction. Similarly, teachers may provide instruction on relevant discrete skills associated with academic content before they teach students to apply the academic content in more integrated, complex, and authentic ways. In some cases, especially with high school academic content, teachers may not understand how to apply grade-level content in more integrated or practical ways.

Although hierarchical in nature, cognitive complexity models such as Bloom's Taxonomy never were intended to be a "ladder for students to climb" from the most simple to the most complex rungs in a stepwise fashion. Educational models that differentiate complexities of learning serve as a valuable way to explicate content and ensure that students have the opportunity to apply that content in authentic or practical contexts at each point in their learning progression. Matrices that have been useful to teachers for many years to plan opportunities for instruction on students' IEP objectives within general education classes also can be helpful in planning how to teach problem-solving skills, DOK, and component skills of self-determination within academic content areas (see Figure 10.1). Many times, these skills are not necessarily age- or grade-content-specific (i.e., they go across grades), and they are important for students across all ages. How they occur within grade-level-appropriate routines should be determined by examining what a typical peer would do within those routines.

The matrix in Figure 10.1 is similar to what special education teachers have used to embed a student's IEP objectives in activities throughout the school day, to ensure that there are ample opportunities to practice each of these IEP objectives, and as a simple data collection tool (i.e., classroom staff could use this matrix to indicate how many times the student performed each objective or skill successfully in the activities of that day). What is new to our matrix in Figure 10.1 are the specific component skills of self-determination (shaded in gray), and each element of Bloom's Taxonomy of Knowledge. Inclusion of the component skills of self-determination and the skills associated with high levels of knowledge allows the student's team to make sure that the student has the opportunity to practice these higher-order skills across school routines in both academic and nonacademic class times. For example, during morning meeting, the student could "differentiate (choosing salient features)" by responding to a question about the science project the class conducted the day before. Similar, the student could plan colors and materials to make a ceremonial Native American mask during art class by explaining why or how a color or material relates to the Native American tribe or ritual.

Table 10.2 provides examples of how Bloom's six levels can be practiced with students to promote instruction in life skills, social relationships, and improved independence and postschool outcomes, while at the same time retaining applications to grade-level academic content. Some of the activities that follow are directly linked to promoting life skills, independence, social relationships, and postschool outcomes, although others (e.g., classifying categories of literature) reinforce academic concepts that can contribute to students' enjoyment and understanding of literature and shared stories.

Individualized Education Program Planning Matrix

General class activities / IEP goals	Morning work	Morning meeting	Word study	Related arts	Reading workshop	Writing workshop	Read aloud	Math	Science/ social studies
Follow two-step directions									
Answer yes/no questions across activities									
Expand expressive vocabulary to 100 words									
Initiate and sustain social interactions									
Use calculator to solve real-life math problems									
Work effectively in small groups to complete class projects									
Improve fine motor skills (writing)									
Independently follow own daily pictorial schedule									
Healthy habits (e.g., wash hands, oral hygiene)									
Embedded self-determination skills related to Depth of Knowledge									
Pose a question/identify a problem									
Identify and analyze/compare solutions									
Choose a solution									
Predict outcome									
Execute/carry out/monitor one's own steps in solving									
Evaluate solution: Did it work/not work?									
Communicate results: What happened?									

Figure 10.1. Individualized education program (IEP) goal/activity matrix.

Table 10.2. Applying Bloom's Taxonomy of Knowledge to grade-level content for students with significant cognitive disabilities

Examples of activities at each of Bloom's levels of knowledge	General classroom activities that promote or support instruction in life skills, social relationships, improved independence, and postschool outcomes
Remembering: Students *remember* information about community resources, important for survival and life skills.	*Example*: As part of a local government unit, students take field trips to specific government and city agencies (e.g., courthouse, police station, library, bank, bus station, hospitals) to learn the services each agency provides and how to gain access to those services. Students gather information and write notes in a personal booklet.
Understanding: Students have the opportunity to interpret, explain and infer new knowledge or experiences and learn how to respond (skills important in developing social relationships and essential survival skills).	*Example*: 1) In an extension of the example above, as part of a group project, students create a "welcome to their city" book, for people new to their city, that explains each of the above agencies and its services. 2) In an elementary science class, students learn what happened to families after several such disasters as the 9/11 attacks and the Katrina and Rita hurricanes, and about agencies that helped victims. Students use resources developed by the Federal Emergency Management Agency (FEMA), especially those developed for students. In small groups the students then produce their own books using pictures, words, or objects, to retell people's stories.
Applying: Students match the characteristics of a concept to a *novel* situation to determine if the new situation is a true example of that concept. This promotes both higher order thinking and independence.	*Example*: In a primary level reading workshop, students listen to a teacher read either a biography or a work of fiction. Using a worksheet with the characteristics of biographies and fictional works listed in a matrix, the students check when they recognize a characteristic of either a biography or a work of fiction as the story is read. At the conclusion of the story, the student individually determines whether the story was a biography or work of fiction.
Analyzing: Students describe or defend whether an example represents a concept by applying the characteristics of the concept (important to developing both higher order thinking and life skills).	*Example*: Extending the example above, the student describes and defends why the story of Paul Bunyan is a work of fiction (specifically a folk tale) by stating that elements of the story are characteristic of a folktale (e.g., it was written for children and features magical characters and animals). The story of Harriet Tubman, although it also contains great elements of danger, is a true life story (a biography) of an inspirational American, because it contains historical facts in the life of a person that can be verified or "checked".
Evaluate: Students use a process to *evaluate and critique* how to value a possible activity (e.g., a leisure activity); evaluation is important for promoting life skills, social relationships, and independence.	*Example*: In consumer economics class, students compare several spring break packages to state parks in their own state, as well as trips to Florida. In small groups they evaluate the packages based on cost, time, and package features and vote on the best deal.

(continued)

Table 10.2.   *(continued)*

Examples of activities at each of Bloom's levels of knowledge	General classroom activities that promote or support instruction in life skills, social relationships, improved independence, and postschool outcomes
Creating: Students use a process to *create* a story (perhaps using picture symbols with the assistance of a story-writing template and a topic provided by the teacher). This activity promotes choice-making and self-expression, important for self-determination and leisure skills. Or (in science), students use the scientific method to *create* a novel experiment; this experiment may be directly related to improving life skills.	*Example*: During a middle school writing work-shop focused on generating and organizing ideas for story writing, students use a story organizer to plan for and write the exposition (introduction), rising action, climax, and conclusion of a fiction story. Or (in science), after learning about the scientific method, students design their own experiment to test a hypothesis around an interest area, such as which type of exercise best improves flexibility or endurance, and promotes healthy lifestyles.

Choice Making and Cognitive Complexity

Choice making is one of the nine component elements of self-determined behavior proposed by Wehmeyer and Field (2007). Choice making is commonly practiced as a part of daily instruction for students with significant cognitive disabilities by providing students with two or more choices to a question and asking the student to select the correct option. The choices may be presented orally and/or may be paired with pictures, representations of objects, or the actual objects. This common classroom activity is representative of Webb's recall level or Bloom's remembering level, and allows for a quick formative assessment that a teacher can use to check a student's grasp of academic content (e.g., subject matter terms, vocabulary). For example, a teacher can present the correct answer and a distracter and ask the student to identify the correct answer to gain a better understanding of what the student has learned.

Although it is important for all students to make choices, the real importance of choice making is that the choices must be meaningful for that person and the effect or result of making that choice must be personally relevant. This level of self-examination about choices is beyond Bloom's remembering level and requires that some instruction occur at Bloom's levels of analyzing and evaluating, so that students learn to make a judgment about the choice based on criteria or analyze a choice based on an overall structure or purpose.

Although special education teachers are familiar with offering and teaching choice making in special education activities, choice making also can be taught and practiced in all academic content areas. Below is an example of how Jenna, a student with a significant cognitive disability, learned to analyze and evaluate her city's choice of adopting solar energy as one of several possible alternative energy sources.

———● *Jenna is a 16-year-old student enrolled in an 11th-grade ecology and environmental science class. She has emerging symbolic skills in communication (e.g., communicating primarily with the use of picture symbols) and uses assistive technology in her instruction and in demonstrating what she has learned. Along with her classmates, she participated in a 2-week unit to study alternative energy options, culminating with a report of her city's choice to adopt solar energy in the construction of all new city buildings.*

The example that follows illustrates how an 11th-grade standard, "explore the causes, consequences and possible solutions to persistent, contemporary and emerging global issues relating to environmental quality" (which is, in part, about making a reasoned choice from a variety of options), can be taught within Bloom's analyzing and evaluating levels. Because Jenna does not take notes, she follows along with graphic symbols of the teacher's lecture notes. The lectures discuss the cost, availability, and carbon emissions of nine different energy sources. These notes allow her to preview and review the content at a later time by following tapes of the class lecture at her own pace. She then uses her class notes to complete a T-chart (Figure 10.2) to help her organize what she has learned about the positive and negative aspects of each energy source, based on three main criteria: cost, availability, and carbon emission.

Students also have class time to research various types of alternative energy on a computer. A panel from the community is invited to share its research and decision making for pursuing solar energy for the city. The panel describes the cost, availability, and carbon emissions of the city's current sources of energy. For the culminating classroom assignment, students evaluate their city's pursuit of solar energy in comparison to one of the other nine potential energy sources.

Jenna prepares her presentation using facts and figures she has learned and uses her T-chart to compare the two energy sources. She uses graphic symbols to state which source she thinks is superior and provides three reasons for her choice (expressed with those symbols).

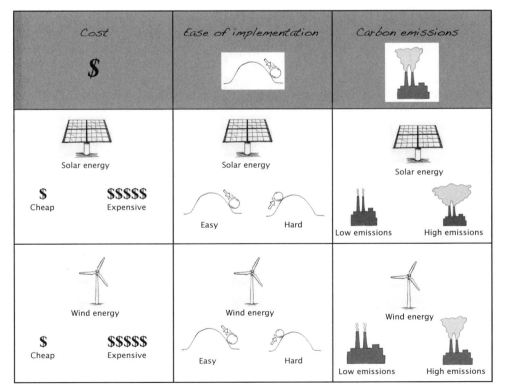

Figure 10.2.   Jenna's T-chart for her ecology project. (Original art drawn by Daniel Livingston, Human Development Institute, University of Kentucky; adapted by permission.)

As the highest level in Bloom's Taxonomy, creating promotes self-determination and higher-order thinking for students with significant cognitive disabilities. Creating is about generating, planning, and producing to make an original product. An example of this highest level within the taxonomy follows, describing a middle school student learning to research and write a position paper as part of English class.

> *Whitney and his classmates are learning first-hand the features of a position paper by first selecting a topic provided by the teacher. Students work in pairs to conduct the research and then take opposing views for the paper. Whitney decided to write about why it's important for teenagers to work during their high school years (as he himself is preparing to enter high school). Whitney and his partner designed a survey to determine how many of their classmates work and, if so, why they work. Together, Whitney and his peer partner compile the results of their survey. Together, they also search the Internet to research the history of child labor laws and the advantages and disadvantages of teenagers working. Whitney's teacher ensures that all materials that Whitney uses for this unit are made accessible for him by using picture symbols to represent the information and facts.*
>
> *As part of the ongoing unit, the teacher covers the steps to writing a position paper (eHow, n.d.). The process includes the following five steps: 1) write an introduction to include the main idea of the position paper; 2) explain your position by telling the reader why you are taking the position you have chosen and offer evidence supporting your opinion; 3) present a counter (or opposite) argument by picking a position that is against your view; 4) explain why the counterargument does not apply and restate your position and why your position is better; 5) conclude by restating your position. Using picture symbols with his teacher's assistance, Whitney first sorts the information he has learned with his partner into "contributing to" or "belonging within" one of the five steps (e.g., stating my position, telling reasons for my position, stating an opposite position). Finally, he creates his position paper using picture symbols to complete each of the five steps. Figure 10.3 provides an excerpt of his position paper. This example, with notations on the level of prompts and supports that Whitney received, could well be used to document performance on a state alternate assessment in English linked to important grade-level content.*

Although the examples described are illustrative of embedding the component skills of self-determination and the higher-order thinking skills associated with increased cognitive complexity into instructional activities for students with significant cognitive disabilities, they also are related to alternate assessments for these students. For teachers whose states use portfolio assessments, work samples taken directly from activities such as these can illustrate mastery of academic content that goes beyond just simple recall. For teachers whose states use more of a checklist format, activities such as the ones described can yield samples of student work that provide documentation of teacher ratings of work linked to grade-level content. For states that use more of a performance-event approach (i.e., students are expected to demonstrate mastery on a predetermined task), these instructional activities can equip the student with the problem-solving skills often required in these on-demand, performance-event assessment tasks.

Moreover, the approach described enables teachers and other school staff to directly embed the component skills of self-determination into both academic and nonacademic activities throughout the day. Self-determination skills are essential for all students and,

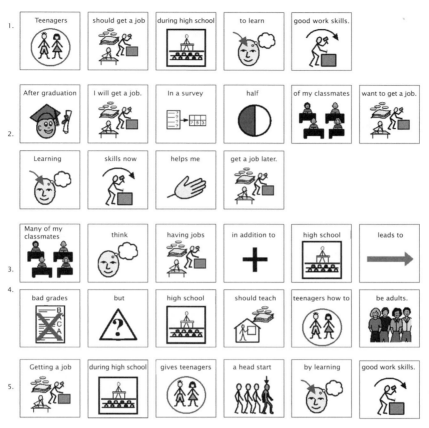

Figure 10.3. Whitney's position paper in English. (The Picture Communication Symbols© 1981–2010 by Mayer-Johnson LLC. All Rights Reserved Worldwide. Used with Permission. Boardmaker™ is a trademark of Mayer-Johnson LLC.)

as noted, are important predictors of successful postschool outcomes for students with intellectual disabilities (Wehmeyer & Palmer, 2003; Wehmeyer & Schwartz, 1998). Finally, this approach allows teachers to take into account "all that is important" in instructional programs for students with significant cognitive disabilities by including both the student's IEP objectives and the higher-order levels of knowledge and application. This "total view" of a student's instructional program is designed to promote both high expectations in the general curriculum and preparation for successful participation in present and future environments.

EMBEDDING LIFE-SKILL INSTRUCTION INTO GRADE-LEVEL ACADEMIC CONTENT

We have tried to emphasize in this chapter that academic content from the general curriculum can be meaningfully taught to students with significant cognitive disabilities in ways that have direct applicability to their daily lives. The following three examples (an elementary, middle, and high school example) illustrate how grade-level core content can be truly functional for students with significant cognitive disabilities. We also have tried to illustrate another fundamental principle within the examples: that core academic content can be taught with evidence-based, systematic instructional procedures, with careful consideration given to both maintenance and generalization of that content (Collins, 2007; Snell & Brown, 2006; Westling & Fox, 2009; Wolery, Ault, & Doyle, 1992). We also have illustrated through each of these examples another powerful teaching principle: the embedding of nontargeted information (Collins, Hendricks, Fetko, & Land, 2002) within targeted skill instruction enables students with significant cognitive disabilities to learn at even greater rates and to make additional individualized "connections" to the core academic content. Finally, although each of the following examples represents effective instruction, it is precisely in the systematic collection of daily performance data that teachers often can find the required evidence to demonstrate that their students in the AA-AAS have mastered the core content.

Collins, Karl, Riggs, Galloway, and Hager (2009) have described two approaches to designing lesson plans for teaching grade-level core content in a meaningful way. The first approach is to embed core content in functional lessons or activities, and the second approach is to insert functional applications when using direct instruction to teach core content. In each of these approaches, the teacher must follow six steps: 1) develop instructional objectives, 2) identify the instructional context, 3) select an evidence-based instructional procedure, 4) embed nontargeted information, 5) design a data collection system and graph data, and 6) plan for maintenance and generalization. The steps will be illustrated in the following three examples from elementary, middle, and secondary school. These examples also illustrate how the principles of systematic instruction (Wolery et al., 1992), the concepts of generalization and maintenance, and the participation of peer buddies in school and community environments (Hughes & Carter, 2008) can be built into student acquisition of academic targets required on alternate assessments.

Elementary Example: Science Lesson on the Effects of Human Interactions on the Environment

As suggested by Collins (2009), teaching a science lesson on protecting the environment to a student with a significant cognitive disability can go awry if care is not taken to ensure that the lesson is presented in a meaningful way. For example, a student who is shown a picture of car and asked to label whether it is beneficial or harmful to the environment may not recognize that air pollution (an unseen factor) is the detrimental variable. Instruction needs to go beyond asking students to memorize a yes/no response and must be presented in an applied manner that will influence the way a student interacts with the environment on a daily basis. Although a student with a significant cognitive disability may never have the opportunity to purchase or drive a car, some activities in which the student may engage will contribute to protecting the environment, and these are the activities that should be targeted for instruction.

Objectives   The instructional objectives for this lesson are linked to the following elementary science core content standard: "The student will classify human interaction in the environment where he or she lives as beneficial or harmful to the environment using data/evidence to support the conclusions." The core content instructional objective is as follows: "When shown a photograph of an item to be recycled and shown a replica of a labeled disposal bin, the student will indicate whether the designated disposal bin is a beneficial or harmful choice to the environment by activating the appropriate switch with 100% accuracy for 5 days." The corresponding functional objective goes across domestic, community, educational, and vocational domains as follows: "When given the opportunity to dispose of paper, glass, plastic, and food scraps and a choice of labeled disposal bins during a daily activity, the student will place items in the appropriate container with 100% accuracy for 5 days."

Instructional Context   The teacher will conduct instruction on core content in a small-group format during science class. Materials for instruction will include a variety of photographs of items to be recycled (e.g., plastic, paper, glass, food scraps) with a variety of labeled waste disposal bins, including a generic garbage can and a container clearly marked for recycling. The student will have two pressure switches to use in responding; a blue switch will have a label of *beneficial* under a smiling face, and a red switch will have a label of *harmful* under a frowning face.

Instructional Procedure   Within this instructional unit, all instructional sessions will begin with the instructor securing the student's attention (e.g., "Look," "Are you ready?") and then giving background on recycling (e.g., "Our environment is where we live. Recycling is good for our environment because we can reuse items without having to make more and because we will not need so much land filled with the things we throw away"). Instruction using the *system of least prompts,* a systematic and evidence-based instructional procedure, will follow. With this procedure, the teacher will wait 5 seconds for an independent response after asking a question (e.g., "Is this container a good or beneficial choice or is this a bad or harmful choice for throwing away a glass bottle?"). If the student fails to make a correct response within 5 seconds, the teacher will give a verbal prompt that tells the student what to do (e.g., say "Putting a glass bottle in a container labeled *glass* is a good or beneficial choice for the environment"). If the student still fails to make a correct response within 5 seconds, the teacher will give a model prompt that shows the student what to do (e.g., point to the switch that is labeled *beneficial*). If the student still fails to make a correct response within 5 seconds, the teacher will give a physical prompt that assists the student in making the correct response (e.g., use hand-over-hand physical guidance to help the student press the switch labeled *beneficial*). Whenever the student makes a correct response, regardless of whether the response was prompted, the teacher will praise the student. Each student in the group will receive a minimum of six trials (three beneficial and three harmful) per session, and daily instruction will continue until all students in the group reach the criterion set in the core content instructional objective.

Nontargeted Information   Research has shown that students with disabilities can acquire at least some of the information that is presented to them in a systematic way, even if the information has not been targeted for direct instruction (Collins, 2007; Collins et al., 2002). During core content instruction, the teacher will add information on why recycling is beneficial to the environment following each instructional trial (e.g., "Putting glass bottles in a container labeled *glass* is beneficial to the environment because the glass can be used again instead of filling up landfills," "Putting glass bottles in a garbage can instead of a container labeled *glass* is harmful to the environment because it makes the landfill too large and causes us to have to make more glass"). After the student reaches criterion on the instructional objective, the teacher will then assess whether the student has acquired the nontargeted information (e.g., ask, "Why is it beneficial to recycle glass?" when giving a choice of photographs that include a person buying a glass container; ask, "Why is it harmful to throw away glass without recycling?" when giving a choice of photographs that include garbage being dumped in a large landfill).

Data Collection   To determine when the student has acquired the skill, the teacher will collect daily instructional data. To do this, the teacher will record an *I* for a correct independent response, a *V* for a correct response following a verbal prompt, an *M* for a correct response following a model or demonstration prompt, and a *P* for a correct response following a physical prompt. It is possible that a student will learn to perform a response with a less intrusive level of prompting over time even if independence is not reached, but instruction should continue to the independent level, if possible, in order to reach criterion, and to demonstrate independent performance (or mastery) on the core content objective. We should also note that independent performance is an essential element of most states' alternate assessments; independence is an essential element in evidencing proficiency in almost all states' assessments.

Generalization and Maintenance   Generalization can be demonstrated by the ability to apply a concept with novel materials across real-life settings. In this lesson, generalization will be facilitated through instruction on recycling conducted by peer buddies without disabilities in the cafeteria after lunch and during an after-school recycling service learning project. (For more information on organizing peer buddy service learning projects, see Hughes & Carter, 2008, and Kleinert et al., 2004). Materials for generalization sessions in the cafeteria will consist of the items left on the cafeteria tray from the student's lunch and appropriately labeled disposal bins. Materials for generalization during the service learning project will consist of bags of trash from classrooms (e.g., aluminum cans, recyclable paper) and appropriately labeled disposal bins.

During generalization sessions, the peer buddy will secure the student's attention and then give the task direction (e.g., "Put the can in the correct container."). The peer will wait 5 seconds to see if the student makes the correct response before using the system of least prompts to systematically assist the student in making the correct response (e.g., verbal prompt: say, "You need to put the can in the container with the word *aluminum* on it"; model prompt: point to the disposal bin that is labeled *aluminum*; physical prompt: use hand-over-hand physical guidance to help the student put the can in the container labeled *aluminum*). Again, although the student may need less intrusive assistance over time, instruction should continue until a criterion of independence is attained. Also, the peer can insert nontargeted information in each trial, explaining why the student has made a choice that is beneficial or harmful to the environment. The teacher will monitor data collected by peer buddies. When criterion is reached, the teacher assesses generalization through a probe in which the student is asked to recycle a novel material in a novel setting (e.g., dispose of a paper napkin at a community sandwich shop).

Maintenance is facilitated by thinning reinforcement (i.e., praise) to a natural schedule or frequency. Once the student reaches criterion of 100% correct, independent responses for a single day, the instructor (e.g., teacher, peer buddy) will thin reinforcement by only praising every other correct response (i.e., Fixed Ratio or FR2 schedule; Alberto & Troutman, 2009) until criterion is reached for 5 days. To ensure that the student maintains the skill of recycling, the teacher will conduct monthly probes on the core content for the remainder of the school year and peer buddies will continue to engage in lunch and after-school recycling activities with the student. Finally, we should note that the inclusion of this core academic content into extracurricular and service learning opportunities does more than just provide additional opportunities to master that core content. It also enables students to expand their opportunities to interact with same-age peers to shared activities beyond the classroom, and to contribute to the well-being of their community by performing an important service.

Middle School Example: Math Lesson on Fractions

Fractions can be a complex concept to teach. Although teaching that two halves make a whole (e.g., a pizza) may appear to be an easy concept for students to grasp, teaching students that two halves of a set make a whole set (e.g., eggs) can be more difficult to grasp. Equivalencies and conversion are even more difficult (e.g., $2/4 = 1/2$). The following lesson is planned to teach fractions to a student with significant cognitive disabilities who is just beginning to work with fractions.

Objectives   The instructional objectives for the lesson are linked to the following middle school mathematics core content standard: "The student will provide examples of and identify fractions, decimals, and percents." The core content instructional objective is as follows: "When shown a picture of a whole item divided into parts, the students will point to $1/2$, $1/3$, and $1/4$ with 100% accuracy for 5 days." The corresponding life-skill or functional objective goes across domestic, community, educational, and vocational domains as follows: "When given the opportunity to divide real items into halves, thirds, or quarters during a real-life activity, the student will perform the task with 100% accuracy for 5 days."

Instructional Context   The teacher will conduct instruction on core content in a small-group format during math class. Materials for instruction will include a variety of photographs of whole items (e.g., food items, art materials, science materials such as seeds and liquids) and corresponding pictures of the items divided into halves, thirds, and quarters. The teacher will also have cards labeled $1/2$, $1/3$, and $1/4$.

Instructional Procedure   All instructional sessions will begin with the instructor securing the students' attention (e.g., "Are you ready?") and then setting up a problem that requires fractions (e.g., "If we have a cookie and we want to share it with one friend, we need to divide it in two parts. When a whole cookie is divided into two equal parts, each part is one half."). The teacher would then show a photograph of a cookie divided into two halves and give the task direction (e.g., "Show me one half."). Another trial may involve the materials that are used in science class: "In our science experiment we need to divide this seed into two equal parts— show me one half." Instruction using *constant time delay* (Collins, 2007), a systematic and evidence-based instructional procedure, will follow. With this procedure, the initial session will consist of a set of 0-second-delay trials in which the teacher immediately uses a model prompt to demonstrate the correct response for the student (e.g., points to a piece of a cookie or part of a seed that equals one half). The student will then have 3 seconds to perform the response modeled by the teacher. During all subsequent instructional sessions, the teacher will give the student 3 seconds to perform the correct response independently before giving a model prompt. Whenever the student makes a correct response, regardless of whether the response was prompted, the teacher will praise the student. Instruction during each session will continue until each student in the group has the opportunity to identify one half, one third, and one fourth of each depicted object or material. Daily instruction will continue until each student in the group meets the criterion of 100% accuracy for 5 days.

Nontargeted Information   During core content instruction, the teacher will add nontargeted information each time feedback is given on a student's response. This will be done by pointing to a card showing the fraction in written form (e.g., $\frac{1}{2}$) and making a statement regarding equivalency (e.g, "Good job. This is one half. Two halves make a whole"). After the student reaches criterion on the instructional objective (e.g., "show me one half, one fourth"), the teacher will then assess whether the student has acquired the nontargeted information (e.g., ask the student to point to the written form of the fraction from an array of cards showing $\frac{1}{2}$, $\frac{1}{3}$, and $\frac{1}{4}$, then ask, "How many halves does it take to make one whole?" or "How many fourths does it take to make one whole?").

Data Collection   To determine when the student has acquired the skill, the teacher will collect daily instructional data. To do this, the teacher will record whether a student makes one of the following responses on each trial: 1) correct response before the prompt (+B), 2) correct response after the prompt (+A), 3) incorrect response before the prompt (–B), 4) incorrect response after the prompt (–A), and 5) no response after the prompt (0). Criterion is reached when all responses are correct before the prompt.

Generalization and Maintenance   In this lesson, generalization will be facilitated by additional instruction during real-life activities (e.g., dividing a pizza for the class or dividing clay with peer buddies during art class). During generalization sessions, the teacher will secure the student's attention, set up the problem (e.g., "We need to divide the pizza to share with four students"), and then give the task direction (e.g., "Show me how to divide the pizza into fourths"). The teacher will wait up to 15 seconds for the student to perform the task (e.g., divide pizza into four slices) before giving a prompt of physical guidance (e.g., hand-over-hand assist the student in dividing the pizza into four slices). The teacher will provide feedback as described previously (e.g., "Good job. Four quarters make one whole").

Once the student reaches criterion of 100% correct, independent responses for a single session, the instructor (e.g., teacher) will thin reinforcement by only praising every other correct response (i.e., FR2 schedule) until criterion is reached for 5 days. To ensure that the student maintains the skill of identifying fractions, the teacher will conduct monthly probes on the core content for the remainder of the school year and will continue to conduct generalization activities at natural times with natural materials throughout the school year.

High School Example: Science Lesson on Genetics

Chapter 8 of this book described how a unit on genetics and disease can be collaboratively planned and implemented to include students with significant cognitive disabilities at the high school level and how the instructional products or performance data from that unit could be used as documentation within state AA-AAS. In this chapter, we will extend this example with a lesson plan based on the work of a secondary special education teacher (Riggs, 2009) to demonstrate how that same standard ("Faulty genes can cause body parts or systems to work poorly. Some genetic diseases appear only when an individual has inherited a certain faulty gene from both parents"; National Research Council, 2000) can be used to systematically teach students with significant cognitive disabilities to identify what they could do to improve their own current and future health. This example is based on a unit designed by a classroom teacher who made that science instruction on grade-level content personally relevant for her students by focusing on wellness tips for genetic diseases, especially if students' own family histories indicated that they might be at risk for those diseases, such as diabetes or heart disease. In this example, we have also shown how this teacher documented her students' performance on their state's alternate assessment. The complete lesson across levels of complexity (i.e., dominant trait, recessive trait, mixed dominance) has been described by Collins et al. (2009).

Objectives   The instructional objectives for the lesson are linked to the following secondary school science core content standard: "The student will draw conclusions/make predictions based on hereditary evidence/data (pedigrees, Punnett squares)." The core content instructional objective is as follows: "When shown a photograph of a father with two dominant genes for a trait and a photograph of a mother with two dominant genes for a trait, the student will select a photograph of a child with the dominant trait from a selection of three photographs with 100% accuracy for 5 days." The corresponding functional objective goes across domestic, community, and leisure domains as follows: "When presented with a health care trait that can be inherited from parents, the student will state a minimum of two precautions that can be taken by the parents' child." Note that the functional or life-skill objective does not have a set criterion, because identifying precautions will be treated as nontargeted information. After the teacher assesses whether the student has acquired the nontargeted information once the content objective has been met, the teacher may decide to use direct instruction to teach this information to criterion (e.g., 100% for 5 days).

Instructional Context   A peer buddy will conduct instruction on core content in a one-to-one format during science class. Materials for instruction will include photographs of male and female adults with dominant traits (e.g., brown eyes) and male and female children with both dominant and recessive traits (e.g., brown and blue eyes). A notation will be written on each photograph of a dominant (BB) or a recessive (bb) trait. During each session, there will be a minimum of three trials across examples of dominant traits (e.g., brown eye color, freckles, right-handedness). This instruction can occur during transition or brief "down" times within science class, which often allow time for a series of rapid but very structured learning trials; this method of focused instruction, termed *embedded instruction* (see Jameson, McDonnell, Johnson, Riesen, & Polychronis, 2007; McDonnell, Johnson, Polychronis, & Riesen, 2002), can be very effective in providing sufficient instructional trials on key concepts to students with significant cognitive disabilities in academic classes. Moreover, classroom peers can be taught to implement systematic instruction with students with significant cognitive disabilities with a high level of instructional fidelity (see Godsey, Schuster, Lingo, Collins, & Kleinert, 2008).

Instructional Procedure   The instructional strategy will be *simultaneous prompting,* an evidence-based strategy (see Rao & Mallow, 2009; Singleton, Schuster, Morse, & Collins, 1999) that requires the instructor (in this case, a peer buddy) to conduct daily probe trials to assess the student's ability to perform the targeted skill each day prior to conducting training trials, in which the student is immediately prompted to perform the skill. In this lesson, all daily probe trials consist of the peer buddy securing the student's attention (e.g., "Are you ready?"), giving the task direction (e.g., "This father has the dominant trait of brown eyes and this mother also has the dominant trait of brown eyes. Which photograph shows someone who could be their child?"), and then waiting 5 seconds for the student to respond (i.e., point to the picture of the child with the appropriate eye color). If the student responds incorrectly or fails to respond on any of the probe trials, a training session with prompted trials will follow the probe trials.

All training sessions will begin with the peer buddy first securing the student's attention and then giving some background information followed by the task direction (e.g., "When two parents both have the same dominant trait, the child will also have that trait. This father has the dominant trait of brown eyes and this mother also has the dominant trait of brown eyes. Which photograph shows someone who could be their child?"). During training trials, the peer buddy will immediately prompt the student to make the correct response (e.g., point to correct choice and say, "This is the child with the dominant trait of brown eyes like the parents"). Training sessions will continue until the student meets criterion during probe sessions.

Nontargeted Information   Several types of nontargeted information will be presented during training trials. First, functional information on precautions that can be taken if a disease is inherited (the functional objective) will be presented as instructive feedback following the student's response on each training trial, regardless of whether the student made the correct response. For example, the peer buddy might say, "Good job. Brown eyes are a dominant trait that can be inherited from parents by their child. We can see brown eyes, but there are some traits that cannot be seen. One of these is diabetes. If a child inherits diabetes from her parents, the child should have regular check-ups from her doctor" (or "eat a healthy sugar-free diet" or "get plenty of exercise").

Core content also will be embedded in each training trial as nontargeted information, and the teacher will want to assess if this has been acquired when criterion on the core content objective is met. This will include vocabulary (e.g., *trait, inherit, dominant*) and notations for the Punnett square (e.g., BB, bb) that are written at the bottom of each photograph. (See Figure 8.4 and 8.7 in Chapter 8 for examples of how to adapt and teach the use of Punnett squares to students with significant cognitive disabilities).

Data Collection   Data will be collected during probe trials only, because these are the data that count toward criterion (i.e., unprompted responses, as are required on most states' alternate assessment). A + will be recorded for each correct response within 5 seconds, a − for each incorrect response within 5 seconds, and a *0* for each failure to respond within 5 seconds. Although it is optional for the instructor to record training data (i.e., trials in which the correct response is immediately given to the student), some instructors may find that this provides useful information for modifying instruction (e.g., changing the type of prompt) if a student is not making progress through the use of the simultaneous prompting instructional procedure. All probe data (unprompted trials) should be graphed on a daily basis for visual analysis. It also should be noted that, when using instructional data for inclusion on alternate assessment tasks or entries, it is only these unassisted probe data that should be included as evidence of content mastery, because only unassisted student performance is really indicative of what the student has learned.

Generalization and Maintenance   In this lesson, generalization is facilitated by providing varying instruction on the traits that can be inherited (e.g., eye color, freckles). Once criterion is reached, the teacher can check to see if the student has mastered the concept of trait dominance by presenting a novel example (e.g., right-handedness) and waiting for a response. If the student has not mastered the concept, then additional instruction on new examples is indicated before moving to instruction on mixed dominance or recessive traits.

The same holds true for the nontargeted information. The peer buddy may provide varying instruction on inherited health conditions (e.g., diabetes, high blood pressure) during instruction and then check for mastery of the concept by presenting a novel example (e.g., cancer) and waiting for a response once criterion has been met on the targeted skill.

Once the student reaches criterion of 100% correct, independent responses during a single probe session, the instructor (peer buddy) will thin reinforcement by only praising every other correct response (i.e., FR2 schedule) until criterion is reached for 5 days. To ensure that the student maintains the concept of inherited traits, the classroom teacher will conduct monthly probes on the core content and the functional or life-skill content (i.e., things the students can do to improve their own current and future health) for the remainder of the school year. Instructional data on both the targeted academic objective (traits inherited from parents' genes) and the nontargeted information (what one can do to improve one's current and future health) can be included in the student's alternate assessment entry on this high school science content standard.

Although the high school example clearly addresses the grade-level content standard, "Faulty genes can cause body parts or systems to work poorly. Some genetic diseases appear only when an individual has inherited a certain faulty gene from both parents," and also provides measurable and observable probe data to demonstrate student mastery on that content standard (as required on alternate assessments for students with significant cognitive disabilities), it also provides instruction on a valued life skill directly related to health and wellness. It is precisely in this way that teachers can teach grade-level academic content, target very specific instructional and assessment targets for their students with significant cognitive disabilities, and ensure that the learning does have personal relevance and meaning for their students' daily and future lives.

CONCLUSION

Life-skill instruction—embedded whenever possible into general education instruction and integrated throughout the school day across school and community settings—is still an essential part in the education of students with significant cognitive disabilities. Although it is true that AA-AAS are designed to measure achievement on academic skills linked to grade-level content standards, this does not mean that teachers should neglect the value of life-skill or functional skills instruction for their students. Yet, we also recognize teachers' often overwhelming feelings of "not having time to do it all" (see Flowers et al., 2005). Examples of how teachers can embed personally relevant life-skill instruction into grade-level academic content designed to prepare students for their states' respective alternate assessments are clearly needed.

In this chapter we argued that teachers can use DOK hierarchies (which are often embedded within the scoring criteria or item construction of state alternate assessments) to ensure that students have opportunities to practice higher-order cognitive skills, including those skills most directly related to the acquisition of self-determination (e.g., problem solving, self-monitoring and self-evaluation, goal setting). Self-determination is itself an essential life outcome for students with significant cognitive disabilities, but one not exhibited often by students with significant disabilities even at the high school level (Carter et al., 2009). Teachers can also carefully consider how academic content can be systematically taught to include functional life applications (perhaps through the use of nontargeted information within instructional trials as we illustrated in the examples). The effectiveness of instructional strategies, such as time delay, simultaneous prompting, and system of least prompts, are well-documented for students with significant cognitive disabilities, and represent evidence-based strategies for teaching academic content to students with significant disabilities (e.g., Browder, Ahlgrim-Delzell, Spooner, Mims, & Baker, 2009; Browder, Wakeman, Spooner, Ahlgrim-Delzell, & Algozzine, 2006; Rao & Kane, 2009). Moreover, we argued that such instruction can occur with peer buddies, in the context of embedded instruction in general education classrooms (McDonnell et al., 2002), and across school and community settings, including service learning projects designed to help students give back to their community (Hughes & Carter, 2008). We also note that the performance data collected through these strategies can provide documentation, in the forms of student graphs and work samples, of student achievement required in alternate assessments, especially for portfolio and checklist assessment formats. Systematic practice of independent responses to core content questions and concepts can help to prepare students for the on-demand performance-event tests that are used by some states as a part of their respective alternate assessments.

These life skills—taught to students with significant cognitive disabilities alongside typical peers in the context of general education classes, other school routines, and extracurricular activities—also build opportunities for the development of friendships, for health and wellness, and for inclusion in one's community when school is over. Along with the general curriculum on grade-level content standards, these skills are the other part of the "enacted curriculum," essential to the lives of students with significant cognitive disabilities.

REFERENCES

Agran, M., King-Sears, M., Wehmeyer, M., & Copeland, S. (2003). *Student-directed learning: Teachers' guide to inclusive practices*. Baltimore: Paul H. Brookes Publishing Co.

Alberto, P.A., & Troutman, A.C. (2009). *Applied behavior analysis* (8th ed.). Saddlebrook, NJ: Prentice Hall.

Anderson, L.W., & Krathwohl, D.R. (2001). *A taxonomy for learning, teaching, and assessing: A revision of Bloom's Taxonomy of educational objectives*. New York: Addison Wesley Longman.

Bloom, B.S. (1956). *Taxonomy of educational objectives, handbook I: The cognitive domain*. New York: David McKay.

Boardmaker (Computer software). Pittsburgh: DynaVox Mayer-Johnson.

Browder, D., Ahlgrim-Delzell, L., Spooner, F., Mims, P., & Baker, J. (2009). Using time delay to teach picture and word recognition to identify evidence-based practice for students with severe developmental disabilities. *Exceptional Children, 75,* 343–364.

Browder, D., Wakeman, S., Flowers, C., Rickelman, R., Pugalee, D., & Karvonen, M. (2007). Creating access to the general curriculum with links to grade-level content for students with significant cognitive disabilities: An explication of the concept. *Journal of Special Education, 41*(1), 2–16.

Browder, D., Wakeman, S., Spooner, F., Ahlgrim-Delzell, L., & Algozzine, B. (2006). Research on reading instruction for individuals with significant cognitive disabilities. *Exceptional Children, 72,* 392–408.

Carter, E., Owens, L., Trainor, A., Sun, Y., & Swedeen, B. (2009). Self-determination skills and opportunities of adolescents with severe intellectual and developmental disabilities. *American Journal of Intellectual and Developmental Disabilities, 114,* 179–192.

Collins, B.C. (2007). *Moderate and severe disabilities*. Upper Saddle River, NJ: Pearson.

Collins, B.C. (2009). What happened to functional curriculum? In W.L. Heward, *Exceptional children: An introductory survey of special education* (9th ed., pp. 472–474). Upper Saddle River, NJ: Merrill/Prentice Hall.

Collins, B.C., Hendricks, T.B., Fetko, K., & Land, L. (2002). Student-2-student learning in inclusive classrooms. *Teaching Exceptional Children, 38*(4), 56–61.

Collins, B.C., Karl, J., Riggs, L., Galloway, C.C., & Hager, K.L. (2009). *Teaching core content with real life applications to students with moderate and severe disabilities*. Manuscript submitted for publication.

eHow. (n.d.). *How to write a position paper*. Retrieved September 1, 2009, from http://www.ehow.com/how_2106307_write-position-paper.html

Falvey, M.A. (1995). *Inclusive and heterogeneous schooling: Assessment, curriculum, and instruction*. Baltimore: Paul H. Brookes Publishing Co.

Flowers, C., Ahlgrim-Delzell, L., Browder, D., & Spooner, F. (2005). Teachers' perceptions of alternate assessments. *Research and Practice for Persons with Severe Disabilities, 30*(2), 81–92.

Flowers, C., Browder, D.M., & Ahlgrim-Delzell, L. (2006). An analysis of three states' alignment between language arts and mathematics standards and alternate assessments. *Exceptional Children, 72*, 201–215.

Godsey, J., Schuster, J., Lingo, A., Collins, B., & Kleinert, H. (2008). Peer implemented time delay procedures on the acquisition of chained tasks by students with moderate and severe disabilities. *Education and Training in Developmental Disabilities, 43*(1), 111–122.

Holub, T.M., Lamb, P., & Bang, M.Y. (1998). Empowering all students through self-determination. In C.M. Jorgensen, *Restructuring high schools for all students: Taking inclusion to the next level* (pp. 183–208). Baltimore: Paul H. Brookes Publishing Co.

Hughes, C., & Carter, E.W. (2008). *Peer buddy programs for successful secondary school inclusion.* Baltimore: Paul H. Brookes Publishing Co.

Individuals with Disabilities Education Act Amendments (IDEA) of 1997, PL 105–17, 20 U.S.C. §§ 1400 *et seq.*

Individuals with Disabilities Education Improvement Act (IDEA) of 2004, PL 108–446, 20 U.S.C. §§ 1400 *et seq.*

Jameson, J., McDonnell, J., Johnson, J., Riesen, T., & Polychronis, S. (2007). A comparison of one-to-one embedded instruction in the general education classroom and one-to-one massed practice instruction in the special education classroom. *Education and Treatment of Children, 30*, 23–44.

Kleinert, H., Denham, A., Groneck, V., Clayton, J., Burdge, M., Kearns, J., & Hall, M. (2001). Systematically teaching the components of self-determination. In H. Kleinert & J. Kearns, *Alternate assessment: Measuring outcomes and supports for students with disabilities* (pp. 93–134). Baltimore: Paul H. Brookes Publishing Co.

Kleinert, H., McGregor, V., Durbin, S., Blandford, T., Jones, K., Owens, J. et al., (2004). Service learning opportunities that include students with moderate and severe disabilities. *Teaching Exceptional Children, 37*(2), 28–35.

Martin, J., & Marshall, L. (1995). ChoiceMaker: A comprehensive self-determination transition program. *Intervention in School and Clinic, 30*(3), 147–156.

McDonnell, J., Johnson, J.W., Polychronis, S., & Riesen, T. (2002). The effects of embedded instruction on students with moderate disabilities enrolled in general education classes. *Education and Training in Mental Retardation and Developmental Disabilities, 37*, 363–377.

National Research Council. (2000). *Inquiry and the national science education standards: A guide for teaching and learning.* Washington, DC: National Academics Press.

No Child Left Behind Act of 2001, PL 107–110, 115 Stat. 1425, 20 U.S.C. §§ 6301 *et seq.*

Rao, S., & Kane, T. (2009). Teaching students with cognitive impairment chained mathematical task of decimal subtraction using simultaneous prompting. *Education and Training in Developmental Disabilities, 44*, 244–256.

Rao, S., & Mallow, T. (2009). Using simultaneous prompting procedure to promote recall of multiplication facts by middle school students with cognitive impairment. *Education and Training in Developmental Disabilities, 44*, 80–90.

Riggs, L. (2009). *The use of constant time delay with multiple exemplars and non-targeted information when teaching principles of heredity to high school students with moderate and severe disabilities in accordance with the Kentucky alternate assessment.* Unpublished master's thesis, University of Kentucky, Lexington.

Roach, A.T., Elliott, S.N., & Webb, N.L. (2005, January). Alignment of alternate assessment with state academic standards: Evidence for the content validity of the Wisconsin alternate assessment. *Journal of Special Education, 38*(4), 218–231.

Singleton, D.K., Schuster, J.W., Morse, T.E., & Collins, B.C. (1999). A comparison of antecedent prompt and test and simultaneous prompting procedures in teaching grocery words to adolescents with mental retardation. *Education and Training in Mental Retardation and Developmental Disabilities, 34*, 182–199.

Snell, M., & Brown, F. (2006). *Instruction of students with severe disabilities* (6th ed.). Upper Saddle River, NJ: Pearson/Merrill Prentice Hall.

Towles-Reeves, E., Kleinert, H., & Muhomba, M. (2009). Alternate assessment: Have we learned anything new? *Exceptional Children, 75,* 233–252.

U.S. Department of Education. (2005). *Alternate achievement standards for students with the most significant cognitive disabilities: Non-regulatory guidance.* Washington, DC: Author.

Webb, N. (1997). *Criteria for alignment of expectations and assessments in mathematics and science education* (NISE Research Monograph No. 6). Madison: University of Wisconsin–Madison, National Institute for Science Education.

Webb, N. (1999). *Alignment of science and mathematics standards and assessments in four states* (NISE Research Monograph No. 18). Madison: University of Wisconsin–Madison, National Institute for Science Education.

Wehmeyer, M.L., & Field, S.L. (2007). *Self-determination: Instructional and assessment strategies.* Thousand Oaks, CA: Corwin Press.

Wehmeyer, M., & Palmer, S. (2003). Adult outcomes for students with cognitive disabilities three years after high school: The impact of self-determination. *Education and Training in Developmental Disabilities, 38*(2), 131–144.

Wehmeyer, M., Palmer, S., Agran, M., & Mithaug, D. (2000). Promoting causal agency: The self-determined learning model of instruction. *Exceptional Children, 66*(4), 439–453.

Wehmeyer, M., & Schwartz, M. (1998). The relationship between self-determination and quality of life for adults with mental retardation. *Education and Training in Mental Retardation and Developmental Disabilities, 33*(1), 3–12.

Westling, D.L., & Fox, L. (2009). *Teaching students with severe disabilities* (4th ed.). Upper Saddle River, NJ: Pearson.

Wolery, M., Ault, M.J., & Doyle, P.M. (1992). *Teaching students with moderate to severe disabilities.* New York: Longman.

For more information on Picture Communication Symbols:

DynaVox Mayer-Johnson
2100 Wharton Street
Suite 400
Pittsburgh, PA 15203

Phone: 800-588-4548
Fax: 866-585-6260
Email: mayer-johnson.usa@mayer-johnson.com
Web site: www.mayer-johnson.com

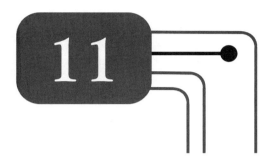

Alternate Assessments, Families, and the Individualized Education Program

Jacqui Farmer Kearns and Rachel Quenemoen

In our first book on alternate assessments, Grisham-Brown and Kearns (2001) described the relationship between the individualized education program (IEP) required by the Individuals with Disabilities Education Act Amendments (IDEA) of 1997 (PL 105-17) and the content standards required in most standards-based accountability systems. Since then, the requirements for annual assessments in reading and math in Grades 3–8 and one assessment in high school between Grades 10–12 under the No Child Left Behind (NCLB) Act of 2001 (PL 107-110) necessitated the specification of content standards for each of those grades. The grade-level content standards form the foundation for the curriculum upon which the assessments are designed. Also, as required by NCLB and described in Chapters 2 and 4 of this book, alternate assessments must be linked to the content standards identified for each of these grades. The linkage to content standards at each grade is important to facilitate the inclusion of students with significant cognitive disabilities in general education classrooms or the least restrictive environment. Inclusion in general education classrooms through access to the general curriculum is "value added" because of the increased learning opportunities for the development of age-appropriate communication, social skills, and independent living skills. However, the relationship of the IEP to the content standards and curriculum as described in Grisham-Brown and

Kearns continues to be relevant today, even though the relationship between the academic standards and curriculum is now stronger than ever for students with significant cognitive disabilities. In this chapter, we again explicate the relationship between the IEP and the content standards. We discuss the important elements of high-quality IEPs. Finally, we provide strategies for working collaboratively with families before, during, and after the IEP meeting to develop IEPs that maximize the student's access to the general curriculum.

CONTENT STANDARDS AND THE INDIVIDUALIZED EDUCATION PROGRAM

The concentric circles in Figure 11.1 illustrate the relationship between the content standards, the curriculum materials and activities used to teach the content standards, and a goal for a student's IEP. This relationship was originally described by Grisham-Brown and Kearns (2001).

The content standards define the material that should be taught across classrooms of the same grade. In the Figure 11.1 example, students are required to sequence the events in a literary passage or book and identify the problem/solution in the passage/book. It is important for IEP teams to note that the content standard may also be taught across grades, but the materials and sophistication of the activities allow students to reach a particular achievement standard. The curriculum materials and activities change across grades. A third-grade teacher uses a variety of children's literature across the school year to teach reading content standards such as identifying the main character's problem and retelling the sequence of story events.

Although we used third-grade literature in the Figure 11.1 example, middle school students addressing the same content standard may use Mildred Taylor's Newberry Award winner *Roll of Thunder, Hear My Cry* (1998) or Lois Lowry's *The Giver* (1993) to identify the character's problem and solution. Similarly, high school students may read classics such as Shakespeare's *Romeo and Juliet* (2009) or John Steinbeck's *Of Mice and Men*

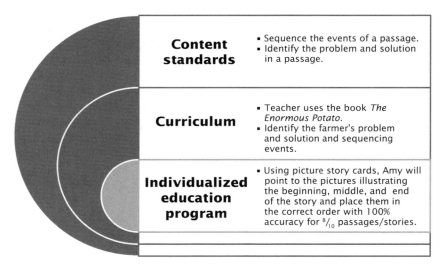

Figure 11.1. Content standards, curriculum, and individualized education program. (*Source:* Grisham-Brown & Kearns, 2001.)

(1993). To learn this content standard, students may listen to or read the original or an abbreviated version of the story in order to practice the required content standards. See Chapter 7 for more examples addressing reading content standards.

Two common concerns have emerged related to the content standards requirement in NCLB (Quenemoen, Kearns, Quenemoen, Flowers, & Kleinert, 2010) that are particularly important to discuss with families. First, the term *grade-level* is used to describe the content standards requirements for each grade. This is a concern for two reasons: first, students with significant cognitive disabilities previously were not generally placed in grades, and second, the term *grade-level* often carries the presumption of achievement on grade level. The assignment of students in grades, or grade placement, ensures that students are connected as closely as possible with peers of the same chronological age, as well as provided age-appropriate curriculum activities and materials. Moreover, there is no presumption of a specified level of achievement associated with the term *grade-level* as it applies to content standards. Indeed, content standards simply define the content that should be taught at each grade and ensure that similar content is taught across classrooms. Although some content standards may receive differential emphasis at particular grades, many content standards are even repeated from grade to grade. The complexity and themes as illustrated in the literary examples above are used to teach content standards changes across grades. For this reason, McLaughlin, Nolet, Rhim, and Henderson (1999) have suggested that IEP teams should have a deep understanding of curriculum within and across grades in order to identify appropriate measureable annual goals as well as supports and services.

CHOOSING ACADEMIC SKILL PRIORITIES

Choosing goals and objectives for the IEP can be a daunting task, particularly for students who experience significant cognitive disabilities. Giangreco, Cloninger, and Iverson (1998) recommended working with families to identify life outcomes and then selecting priority goals and objectives for the IEP that are appropriate for the student as he or she advances through the grades. In selecting academic skills for the IEP, teams should first consider academic skills related to the content standards that other students will be learning in reading, math, science, and social studies, and approximate those skills as closely as possible. Because many of those skills will be taught in the general curriculum as a matter of course, the IEP team can then select the most important of these skills for the IEP. As such, selecting those academic skills that will be necessary for the development of future competence in reading and math is critically important and should be a priority for the IEP.

Selecting Personal Management, Social, and Communication Skill Priorities

Students with significant cognitive disabilities typically need to develop skills related to communication, social behavior, and independent living/personal management in addition to academic skills. The IEPs for these students necessarily must include such skills. As discussed in Chapter 3 of this book, communication skills underpin the development of literacy skills. However, communication skills are also tightly intertwined with the development of appropriate social skills and form the foundation for academic skills (Cafiero, 1998; Goossens, Crain, & Elder, 1992; Kliewer, 2008; Miller & Eller-Miller, 2000; Mirenda, 2003; Romski & Sevcik, 1996). For example, Dana, a student with autism, used oral speech to communicate but needed a socially appropriate way to greet peers in addition to speech. Once he and his peers were coached to initiate a "high five" greeting, his inappropriate greeting behavior was replaced by this more appropriate social greeting. These skills are often of highest priority for families and as such should be included on the IEP.

Likewise, skills that promote personal independence and are commensurate with the student's chronological age should be included on the IEP. Keeping up with one's belongings, completing homework, and traveling within the school or community are examples of skills that may also be included on the IEP, as might self-feeding and toileting, for example. Indeed, the criterion of ultimate functioning (Brown, Nietupski, & Hamre-Nietupski, 1976) suggests that if someone else must perform the skill for a student if he or she cannot do it, then that skill may be considered a learning priority for the student. We would add that in many cases, an accommodation for a particular skill deficit may save valuable instructional time and that these skills should be taught within an age-appropriate context and taught to the extent other students learn similar skills. For example, shoe tying can be accommodated with hook and loop fasteners, toileting and hygiene taught within the student's daily routine, and perhaps skills like tooth brushing can be best taught at home, because although students do learn about tooth brushing at school, most students do not practice such a skill at school often enough to ensure acquisition. We recognize the health benefit of tooth brushing and recommend providing practice opportunities at naturally occurring times (e.g., after meals).

DETERMINING THE SOCIAL VALIDITY OF INDIVIDUALIZED EDUCATION PROGRAM PRIORITIES

Considering the social validity of some skills may also help in choosing priorities for the IEP. For example, identifying one's address and telephone number may be important, but the IEP team must evaluate the chronological age-appropriateness of such a skill and the teaching time requirements as compared to accommodating such a skill with an ID card. For example, primary-school students may regularly use their name and street address, their teacher's name and room number, and the number for the bus they ride to and from school.

Furthermore, if the IEP team has a question about a skill that promotes independence, the team should socially validate that skill by checking the extent to which students without disabilities at the same chronological age perform the skill and at what level of independence. A simple survey of same-age peers without disabilities or of teachers who work with children of a similar age may help the IEP team to identify or modify priorities. Figure 11.2 illustrates an example of such a survey.

ENSURING OPPORTUNITIES TO TEACH AND PRACTICE

The extent to which students will achieve the objectives on their IEPs depends on the frequency of opportunities to practice the goals and objectives. Villa and Thousand (1995) recommended that IEP teams consider the opportunities to practice independent living skills across the school day. Using a tool such as an IEP matrix will help teams identify appropriate times to teach such skills. Figure 11.3 shows an IEP matrix for a middle school student.

The student's IEP goals are represented down the left side of the matrix, and the student's routine is listed across the top. The x within each cell in the matrix denotes an opportunity to practice skills. Research shows that providing more opportunities to practice a skill within natural routines increases the likelihood of skill acquisition and

Respondent: Teacher _____	Parent _____	Student _____		
Age/grade _____				
Students at this grade*				
1. Write first and last name independently	None	Some	Most	
2. Write address	None	Some	Most	
3. State telephone number	None	Some	Most	
4. Write city, state, zip code	None	Some	Most	
5. Write telephone number	None	Some	Most	
6. Manage belongings (e.g., backpack)	None	Some	Most	
7. Identify and locate bus number	None	Some	Most	
8. Count money for lunch	None	Some	Most	
9. Pay for lunch weekly	None	Some	Most	
10. Pay for lunch daily	None	Some	Most	
11. Use a locker with combination	None	Some	Most	
12. Manage personal schedule independently	None	Some	Most	
*For use with peers, substitute the words *my friends* or *students*.				

Figure 11.2.   Social validation survey of chronologically age-appropriate personal management skills.

generalization (McDonnell, 1998). If there aren't sufficient opportunities to practice a particular skill (e.g., tooth brushing), then the IEP team may want to include skills on the IEP that are more likely to be accomplished.

Functionality

IEP teams should perform a careful ecological analysis of the validity of care skills that are labeled "functional skills" or "life skills." For example, reading signs such as *hospital* may be identified as a "functional or life skill," but the opportunities to use such words in daily life are relatively few, whereas reading the comics in the newspaper can occur daily and provide a useful leisure-time skill. Finally, we caution IEP teams to remember that for students with complex levels of educational needs, terms such as *readiness* and *prerequisite* essentially represent "never"—that is, it is highly probable the student will never learn all of the prerequisite skills required to even begin instruction on the critical skill. For example, learning to make a bed is not a prerequisite to learning to read, and although bed-making may be important, students without disabilities learn to make their bed at home or summer camp. The IEP team should carefully consider whether a skill is really "functional" for the student in terms of the opportunity to acquire and fluently use the skill(s) across a wide variety of age-appropriate environments. We argue that academic skills are critically important functional skills and are only taught at school. Therefore, as IEP teams select priorities for the IEP, three elements are critical for determining the functionality of skills: The IEP should document the extent to which the student has 1) access to the general curriculum; 2) opportunities to develop and enhance communication, social, and personal management skills; and 3) instructional opportunities that are consistent with the skill sets of students without disabilities of similar age.

Writing Goals and Objectives

Grisham-Brown and Kearns (2001) recommended the following format for writing IEP goals that integrate all of the recommended components: 1) choose a generic skill;

Class routine data sheet	Morning meeting	Language/Arts reading	Language/Arts writing	Science	Math	Social studies	Music	Art
1. Use new vocabulary	×	×	×	×	×	×	×	×
2. Increase communication exchanges with peers	×	×	×	×	×	×	×	×
3. Identify main idea and two details	×	×	×	×		×		
4. Follow three-to four step rocedure/directions		×	×	×	×		×	×
5. Ask questions	×	×	×	×	×	×	×	×

Figure 11.3. An individualized education program matrix for an elementary school student.

2) include a sample of the range of activities; and 3) specify the range of adaptations, modifications, strategies, and people responsible within the objective itself. The example that follows integrates all of the components.

1. Choose a generic skill: The student will use a communication device switch to choose among three options. When involved in the following activities and given a choice of three pictures of objects, activities, or people, Megan will choose one option by activating a communication switch paired with the actual object in five of five opportunities across three consecutive days.

2. Sample a range of activities:

    a. Choose a book

    b. Choose a friend to work on a project

    c. Choose an answer from a picture/object array during reading or science activity

    d. Choose a classroom chore

    e. Choose a snack

    f. Choose an activity

3. Include the adaptations/modifications/specialized instruction:

    a. Visual consultation

    b. Contrasting background without clutter

    c. Proper positioning

    d. Switches with messages paired with objects/pictures

    e. Vertical presentation of switches and objects

    f. Time-delay procedures

    g. Small-motor preparation

4. Implementers: teacher, occupational therapist, physical therapist, speech-language pathologist, vision specialist

This approach guarantees that goals and objectives are coordinated with specially designed instruction and that related services are integrated into each objective, ensuring a seamless approach to integrating the primary components of the IEP.

Working with Families to Develop the Individualized Education Program

Now that we have provided specifications for writing IEPs, we turn to the equally important task of working with families to develop the IEPs. The role of the family is essential in developing an IEP that addresses priority academic, social, and independent living needs. Communicating effectively with families and recognizing the important role they play throughout the process ensures successful student outcomes.

Families and caregivers are tremendous resources for every student and for every IEP team. Their insights are especially important as the team makes decisions about assessment participation and use of assessment results. In order to be sure that the family representative is able to be a full member of the team as the team makes decisions about assessments, it is important to provide the family with accessible information. The U.S. Department of Education has developed a guide for parents to explain alternate assessments, *Learning Opportunities for Your Child Through Alternate Assessments* (Quenemoen & Thurlow, 2007). This guide describes why these assessments are used, how the student can benefit from the assessment, and how results can be used in future IEP meetings. Remember that not all family members will feel comfortable going through these materials on their own. Offer support to walk them through the guide, answering questions as you work together. That time invested will pay off in their increased understanding and contributions to the important work of the IEP team.

Preparing Families Before the Individualized Education Program Meeting

The shift to an academic as well as functional focus for IEPs can be confusing for parents and guardians. In the past, IEPs for many students with significant cognitive disabilities have included very limited academic goals or objectives. Those that have been included often were on narrowly defined academic content, such as time, money, and very basic number sense. The teacher/case manager can provide all members of the IEP team with examples of what instruction linked to grade-level content (but with a different achievement expectation) looks like as an introduction to the IEP team meeting. For example, in *Learning Opportunities for Your Child Through Alternate Assessments* (Quenemoen & Thurlow, 2007), team members can see concrete representations of what students can do with grade-level content on a different achievement expectation. These examples build on best practices in teaching students with severe cognitive disabilities. Concepts like *partial participation, age appropriateness,* and *inclusion* should be very familiar to the team, including the parent/guardian. Team members can work together to clarify how linkage to grade-level academic content extends these concepts to the academic content typically developing peers are learning.

Meaningful Participation of Families During the Individualized Education Program Meeting

Parents or guardians will have unique perspectives on what strategies and supports are effective for their students. All team members should recognize and respect this important expertise on the team. Families spend far more time with the student than teachers and related service providers, but sometimes do not feel confident to share the important insights they have gained. They may also contribute to the team a unique perspective that helps them see past the sometimes arbitrary structures and organizational barriers in schools. The focus should be on what works, not on the usual routine or procedure, and parents or guardians can often recognize the difference from their view as an external observer. Conversely, sometimes it is intimidating to the team members when parents or guardians speak to what they see. Teams can be sensitized to these potential tensions within the IEP team meetings and work to facilitate full involvement and understanding of the family representatives. Finding a way to safely discuss different perspectives and concerns will make the team far more effective in decision making. It may be helpful to have one member of the team serve as a process observer, checking to be sure the family representative understands the discussion and is able to voice observations, questions, and concerns.

Families often are facing many challenges in the present, and thus they struggle to construct a vision for their child's future, either in later grades in public school or in adult life. Most families have only their personal experience to help them think about what skills and knowledge their child will need to be successful in future settings, and often, the future may seem like a frightening prospect. The steps outlined in the content standards and the IEP section of this chapter can provide necessary social validation for the families as well as for other team members, and they should be specifically included in all steps of the process. For example, the social validation survey (Figure 11.2) is useful as presented, but the concept of looking at what typical peers do and the skills they are developing can be helpful for clarifying goals and possible outcomes in the academic domains as well.

Placing the conversations about the content of IEP in the context of the larger community of peers, and focusing on what other students at that age are doing in school and community, will help all of the IEP team members avoid focusing solely on deficits and short-term gains. There are multiple tools for doing this, including Personal Futures Planning (Mount & Zwernik, 1991) and the McGill Action Planning System; now known as Making Action Plans (Vandercook, York, & Forest, 1989). Team members may need training to ensure they respect and encourage alternatives to what currently exists in the school or community. For example, even though at one time, no students with severe disabilities were included in regular classrooms, some pioneering families and teams opened that door by imagining what was possible.

Remember that families or guardians are a resource to school staff, just as educators are a resource to families. As families see the school becoming more available for rich academic experiences, the family's role in working on skills of daily living and community participation can be enhanced. Family members may be very skilled at working on cooking, shopping, and money skills in the context of family life, but may feel unskilled at teaching academics. In contrast, educators are uniquely situated to teach academics. For many students with severe disabilities, their school years are the only time in their life during which they will have academic support; most adult services focus only on daily living types of supports. A team can best understand how to use the precious time each student has in school.

Communicating Successfully with Families
After the Individualized Education Program Meeting

Once the IEP team meeting is over, the work has just begun. It is especially important for families or guardians of students who participate in alternate assessment based on alternate achievement standards (AA-AAS) to be involved in the student's progress throughout the year. Successful teaching strategies will include ongoing data collection and analyses. Many family representatives will find that periodic updates on progress using these data, along with actual samples of student work to illustrate what the student is learning in concrete terms, can spur continued interest and support at home. Educators should send materials for the family members to work on at home. Most families will welcome new and engaging activities that relate to what typical peers may be doing, such as simplified, picture-based or simple-text versions of grade-appropriate literature, along with picture or simplified versions of recipes, hobbies typical for the student's age, or other recreation and leisure activities. All families want to see how their child can have experiences similar to those typical peers may be having; such information also spurs conversations on the content itself with other families of children the same age. The family may also be interested in having its own data-charting tools to record how the student is doing on skills of daily living, community participation, and recreation and leisure in the course of family life. That can be a powerful addition to the team's understanding of progress made by the student, beyond the goals defined in the IEP. And, recording such data empowers families and guardians to recognize the important work they do to prepare their child for adult life. IEP team members can help problem-solve and provide alternative strategies to both the family and the educators throughout the year with informal connections and check-in processes that truly make the team a *team*.

CONCLUSION

Understanding the requirements of the IEP and the integration of the IEP within the context of the general curriculum are important skills for teachers. Understanding that the IEP may include both academic content and other essential life skills is critical for both teachers and families. Families also need to know that AA-AAS, although linked to grade-level content standards, do represent different achievement standards, and that alternate assessments are required by law to measure standards that are linked to grade-level content. Conversely, alternate assessments cannot measure everything on the IEP that the team has identified as important for the student to learn, especially those "life skills" that are personalized to the needs of each student.

All that said, communicating effectively with families to translate the IEP into an effective educational program represents the highest priority for students with significant cognitive disabilities. This chapter outlined some strategies for working with families to make this communication and this partnership as clear and strong as possible. It also outlined strategies for developing an IEP that is a usable, working document, linked whenever possible to the academic standards identified for all students. Combined, these strategies hold tremendous promise in supporting higher levels of achievement than previously thought possible for this population.

REFERENCES

Bishop, K., Rankin, J., & Mirenda, P. (1994). Impact of graphic symbol use on reading acquisition. *Augmentative and Alternative Communication, 10*(2), 113–125.

Brown, L., Nietupski, J., & Hamre-Nietupski, S. (1976). The criterion of ultimate functioning and public school services for severely handicapped children. In M. Thomas (Ed.), *Hey, don't forget about me!* (pp. 8–12). Reston, VA: Council for Exceptional Children.

Cafiero, J. (1998). Communication power for individuals with autism. *Focus on Autism and Other Developmental Disabilities, 16*(3), 113–121.

Giangreco, M., Cloninger, C., & Iverson, V. (1998). *Choosing outcomes and accommodations for children (COACH): A guide to educational planning for students with disabilities* (2nd ed.). Baltimore: Paul H. Brookes Publishing Co.

Goossens, C., Crain, S., & Elder, P. (1992). *Engineering the preschool classroom environment for interactive symbolic communication: 18 months to 5 years developmentally*. Birmingham, AL: Southeast Augmentative Communication Conference Publications.

Grisham-Brown, J., & Kearns, J. (2001). Creating standards-based individualized education programs. In H. Kleinert & J. Kearns, *Alternate assessment: Measuring outcomes and supports for students with disabilities* (pp. 17–28). Baltimore: Paul H. Brookes Publishing Co.

Hetzroni, O., Rubin, C., & Konkol, O. (2002). The use of assistive technology for symbol identification by children with Rett syndrome. *Journal of Intellectual & Developmental Disability, 27*(1), 57–71.

Individuals with Disabilities Education Act Amendments (IDEA) of 1997, PL 105-17, 20 U.S.C. §§ 1400 *et seq.*

Kearns, J., & Burdge, M. (2007). *Student observation tools.* Unpublished manuscript, University of Kentucky, Human Development Institute, National Alternate Assessment Center, Lexington.

Kliewer, C. (2008). Joining the literacy flow: Fostering symbol and written language learning in young children with significant developmental disabilities through the four currents of literacy. *Research and Practice for Persons with Severe Disabilities, 33*, 122–133.

Lowry, L. (1993). *The giver.* Boston: Houghton Mifflin Harcourt.

McDonnell, J. (1998). Instruction for students with severe disabilities in general education settings. *Education and Training in Mental Retardation and Developmental Disabilities, 33*(3), 199–215.

McLaughlin, M.J., Nolet, V., Rhim, L.M., & Henderson, K. (1999). Integrating standards: Including all students. *Teaching Exceptional Children, 31*(3), 66–71.

Miller, A., & Eller-Miller, K. (2000). The Miller Method: A cognitive-developmental systems approach for children with body organization, social and communication issues. In *Interdisciplinary Council on Developmental and Learning Disorders practice guidelines: Redefining the standards of care for infants, children, and families with special needs* (pp. 489–515). Bethesda, MD: ICDL Press.

Mirenda, P. (2003). Toward functional augmentative and alternative communication for students with autism: Manual signs, graphic symbols, and voice output communication aids. *Language, Speech, and Hearing Services in the Schools, 34*, 203–216.

Mount, B., & Zwernik, K. (1991). *Making futures happen: A manual for facilitators of personal futures planning.* Publication No. 421–90–036, Metropolitan Council of the Twin Cities Area, St. Paul, MN. Retrieved December 5, 2009, from http://www.eric.ed.gov/ERICDocs/data/ericdocs2sql/content_storage_01/0000019b/80/13/23/a1.pdf

No Child Left Behind Act of 2001, PL 107-110, 115 Stat. 1425, 20 U.S.C. §§ 6301 *et seq.*

Orelove, F., Sobsey, D., & Silberman, R. (Eds.). (2004). *Educating children with multiple disabilities: A collaborative approach* (4th ed.). Baltimore: Paul H. Brookes Publishing Co.

Quenemoen, R., Kearns, J., Quenemoen, M., Flowers, C., & Kleinert, H. (2010). *Common misperceptions and research based recommendations for alternate assessments on alternate achievement standards.* Minneapolis: University of Minnesota, National Center for Educational Outcomes.

Quenemoen, M., & Thurlow, M. (2007). *Learning opportunities for your child through alternate assessments.* Retrieved December 5, 2009, from http://www.cehd.umn.edu/NCEO/OnlinePubs/LearningOpportunities.pdf

Rankin, J., Harwood, K., & Mirenda, P. (1994). Influence of graphic symbol use on reading comprehension. *Augmentative and Alternative Communication, 10*, 269–281.

Romski, M.A., & Sevcik, R.A. (1996). *Breaking the speech barrier: Language development through augmented means.* Baltimore: Paul H. Brookes Publishing Co.

Shakespeare, W. (2009). *Romeo and Juliet.* New York: Harper Collins.

Steinbeck, J. (1993). *Of mice and men.* New York: Penguin Books.

Taylor, M. (1998). *Roll of thunder, hear my cry.* New York: Random House.

Vandercook, T., York, J., & Forest, M. (1989). The McGill action planning system (MAPS): A strategy for building the future. *Journal of The Association for Persons with Severe Handicaps, 14*, 205–215.

Villa, R., & Thousand, J. (1995). *Creating an inclusive school.* Alexandria, VA: Association for Supervision and Curriculum Development.

What We Have Learned from Alternate Assessment Research and What We Still Need to Know

Harold L. Kleinert and Elizabeth Towles-Reeves

The purpose of this final chapter is to summarize what the field has learned from research on alternate assessment based on alternate achievement standards (AA-AAS), the implications of these "lessons learned" for practitioners, and directions for future research. We have intentionally taken a "teacher perspective" in writing this chapter—we have focused on the relationship of alternate assessment to classroom practice, in elucidating what we presently know and what we yet need to learn. We consider 1) the critical role of key stakeholders—including teachers and families—in shaping and refining each state's AA-AAS; and 2) elements of effective access to instruction and assessment for students with significant cognitive disabilities. In the final part of this chapter, we consider the challenges and direction for future research in AA-AAS.

THE CRITICAL ROLE OF KEY STAKEHOLDERS

AA-AAS require key stakeholders be involved in supporting both the development of these assessments and their implementation, from the state policy level to the individual student level. In the following sections, we note key considerations for the strategic stakeholders in this process: state departments of education, district administrators, principals, teachers, and parents. We discuss what the field has learned of the essential role of each of these stakeholders in turn.

State Departments of Education

State departments of education must clearly communicate to constituents all the issues related to the assessment system, including the federal requirements for AA-AAS. School staff including principals, special education coordinators, and teachers, along with parents and students, should understand the expectations for students with significant cognitive disabilities. This understanding starts with leadership and communication from the state department of education. Information that must be shared includes the purpose of the AA-AAS, the use of students' scores on the AA-AAS, and how all students' scores will be reported and calculated in measures of school, district, and state accountability. State-level leadership must support the development for the state of a guiding philosophy for students with disabilities (specifically, students with the most significant cognitive disabilities) that includes beliefs about what these students know and can do as they work toward proficiency on grade-level academic content standards, as well as the development of a statewide network of training and technical assistance for district-level administrators and teachers in implementing the assessment (Thurlow et al., 2008). In essence, the state department of education sets the tone for the state regarding expectations for students with the most significant cognitive disabilities and the AA-AAS. As noted by Kohl, McLaughlin, and Nagle (2006), the complex challenges of implementing high-quality alternate assessments "create a need for open lines of communication with personnel from state and local districts, school administrators, teachers, and parents" (p. 121).

District Administrators

District administrators are also key stakeholders in the AA-AAS process. Ahlgrim-Delzell, Flowers, Browder, and Wakeman (2006) investigated school administrators' perceptions of the impact and consequences of AA-AAS. The total sample for this study consisted of principals; school, district, and state level coordinators/supervisors/specialists; and other administrators/directors. From the perspective of these administrators, Ahlgrim-Delzell et al. found that AA-AAS have increased teachers' stress level and workload, while also increasing the amount of training and workload for administrators. Interestingly, few administrators agreed with the potential benefits of students taking alternate assessments (e.g., raising teacher expectations for students, communication between schools and parents, collaboration). In addition, only half of the administrators in the study reported the AA-AAS was beneficial to student outcomes or helped teachers track student progress.

District-level administrators, including both special education and assessment coordinators, must be well versed in the requirements both from the federal and state level regarding AA-AAS. These administrators are crucial for providing support on multiple levels, as outlined by Ahlgrim-Delzell et al. (2006). For example, these coordinators can provide support regarding instructional issues related to teaching students with significant cognitive disabilities; development of the assessment, completion, and submission of the assessment; assistive technology for students; access to the general education curriculum; and collaboration between general and special education teachers. Yet in order to provide necessary supports and timely information to their teachers, district-level administrators must be trained in these areas and have access to assessment materials and resources. District-level administrators, as the results of the study of Ahlgrim-Delzell et al. have shown, also need positive examples of how inclusion in the AA-AAS can provide new opportunities for learning, and benefit both students and teachers.

Principals

Principals are inherently key stakeholders in the AA-AAS process, in that they are responsible for everything that happens within their school. In a very early study, Costello, Turner, Kearns, and Kleinert (as reported in Kleinert et al., 2001) completed teacher and principal telephone surveys in schools purposely chosen to reflect both high- and low-performing schools in 1) the general assessment for all students and 2) the alternate assessment for students with significant cognitive disabilities. Although principals in schools with high alternate assessment scores were typically more supportive of the alternate assessment than principals in lower performing schools, principals in both groups generally lacked knowledge of the alternate assessment. A more recent study by Towles-Reeves, Kleinert, and Anderman (2008) also found that principals appear to lack an indepth knowledge of the structure of alternate assessments. This was evidenced by the number of principals who reported unfamiliarity with the AA-AAS and the number of principals who indicated they did not know what type of approach (i.e., portfolio, checklist, or performance event) to AA-AAS was used by their state.

Furthermore, the Towles-Reeves et al. (2008) study suggested a need for principals to provide increased support for teachers in time and resources for collaboration. Collaboration is critically important for general and special education teachers; its significance is underscored by both an increase in inclusion for students with intellectual disabilities in the general education classroom (Data Accountability Center, 2008), as well as a clear link to the grade-level content standards for this population in large-scale assessments (U.S. Department of Education, 2005). Students must be taught the content with high expectations from both general and special education teachers. In addition, shared instructional responsibilities between general and special education teachers often enhance special education teachers' understanding of academic content standards, as the general education teacher is considered the "expert" in that academic content and can share that knowledge with the special education teacher. In turn, student mastery of the content comes from the academic expertise of the general education teacher in collaboration with the special education teacher's knowledge of how to make that content accessible to the student. Planning time for increased collaboration is essential in providing high-quality instruction on grade-level academic content standards for students with significant cognitive disabilities.

Finally, in the Towles-Reeves et al. (2008) study, principals reported that functional skills were more important for students with the most significant cognitive disabilities to learn than academic skills aligned to the grade-level curriculum. However, principals agreed that students can effectively learn functional skills when those skills are embedded in academic instruction through the grade-level curriculum. Teaching these students grade-level academic content is novel for teachers and principals (Browder, Karvonen, Davis, Fallin, & Courtade-Little, 2005; Browder, Spooner, Ahlgrim-Delzell, Flowers, Algozzine, & Karvonen, 2003; Flowers, Ahlgrim-Delzell, Browder, & Spooner, 2005). It was only with the Individuals with Disabilities Education Act Amendments (IDEA) of 1997 (PL 105-17) that individualized education program (IEP) teams were required to document the extent to which all students with disabilities participated and made progress in the general curriculum, and it was only with the No Child Left Behind (NCLB) Act of 2001 (PL 107-110) that the requirements for assessment on grade-level academic content were explicated. As a result, there is a critical need for the development of models that help teachers understand how to teach students the grade-level curriculum while also embedding functional skills into this instruction. Many teachers (and principals) do not have workable exemplars or models to help them merge the two worlds of academic and functional skill instruction, as indicated by Flowers et al. (2005). Certainly, the field of severe disabilities is moving away from a focus on teaching only functional skills to students with the most significant cognitive disabilities, yet teachers often perceive this as an either/or equation (Flowers et al., 2005). In other words, a portion of the day can be devoted to functional skill instruction and a portion of the day can be devoted to academic skills and, from the perception of many teachers, these represent wholly separate portions of the school day. As a result, there does not appear to be sufficient time in the day to do both adequately. We have tried throughout this book to give examples of a well-rounded, blended curriculum of academic and functional skills (see especially Chapter 10).

Finally, Towles-Reeves et al. (2008) found that principals strongly agreed that they were the instructional leaders for all of their students, including students with significant cognitive disabilities. Certainly, having principals provide that leadership in encouraging high expectations and teaching a blended curriculum is essential to the effective performance of their students with significant cognitive disabilities in both the alternate assessment and in the achievement of life skills.

Teachers

One of the most important stakeholder groups for supporting and implementing AA-AAS is teachers, both general and special education teachers. Kleinert, Kennedy, and Kearns (1999) found that most teachers recognized the benefits of inclusion in the state assessment system for their students, were positive about the benefits for their students, and were incorporating the elements of the alternate assessment (i.e., individualized schedules, student self-evaluation) into their daily instruction. Conversely, teachers also expressed frustration with the time required to complete the assessment and increased paperwork (teachers noted lack of experience incorporating the assessment into daily instruction), although some teachers reported that the assessment was not beneficial for students. In addition, Kampfer, Horvath, Kleinert, and Kearns (2001) found that certain instructional variables—clearly under the control of teachers—were related to student scores on the alternate assessment. These variables included 1) the extent to which the assessment was embedded into daily instruction, 2) the extent to which the student was involved in developing his or her portfolio, and 3) the teacher's perception of the benefit of the assessment for the student.

In a subsequent teacher survey, Flowers et al. (2005) examined teachers' perceptions of AA-AAS with a sample of 983 teachers from five states. Supporting findings from the Kleinert et al. (1999) study, the results suggested that teachers believed students with the most significant cognitive disabilities should be included in school accountability indices. Flowers et al. suggested that teachers need additional models of how to address state academic content standards in ways that are meaningful for students with significant cognitive disabilities, as was also noted in Towles-Reeves et al. (2008).

Parents

Parents are also important stakeholders in supporting and implementing AA-AAS. Although parents' wishes for their children's educational goals are often heard at the IEP meeting, discussion of the AA-AAS during this meeting is typically limited. However, parents can play a large role in helping their children achieve proficiency by advocating for high expectations from teachers and by advocating for embedding functional skill instruction in the general education content, inclusion in general education settings, and the use of technology or appropriate supports for making the general education curriculum accessible. In fact, Palmer, Fuller, Arora, and Nelson (2001) noted parents' concerns for student skills stagnating without access to the general education curriculum. One parent commented, "The special education program is very limiting and acts to confine people to expected limitations, closing the door to the ability or opportunity to learn because they are not expected to or thought able" (p. 475). As advocates for their children, parents are critical stakeholders in the AA-AAS process. As we discuss later in this chapter, parents need increased opportunities to learn of the role of alternate assessments for their children, so that they can be full partners in this process.

Although research does indicate that at least some stakeholders report a positive impact of the AA-AAS, research also suggests that many teachers are finding it difficult to teach and assess students on grade-level academic content standards, although required by federal legislation (IDEA 2004; NCLB 2001). It appears the lack of support, resources, and training for key stakeholders regarding AA-AAS results in a struggle for these constituents—especially teachers and families—in understanding exactly how to support and implement the AA-AAS. In the section "What We Still Need to Learn: Considerations for Additional Research," we clarify our key recommendations for addressing these issues.

LINKING TO GRADE-LEVEL CONTENT: EFFECTIVE ACCESS

The following elements are essential to effective academic instruction and assessment for students with significant cognitive disabilities: 1) consideration of both the defined and enacted curriculum, 2) the relationship of alternate assessment to research-based instructional practices, and 3) equal participation and equal weight in the state's accountability system for all students. We discuss each of these elements in turn.

The Defined and the Enacted Curriculum

The grade-level academic content standards in each state are what all students, including students with the most significant cognitive disabilities, are expected to learn as defined by NCLB. From these grade-level academic content standards is derived the defined curriculum for all students. Students with significant cognitive disabilities often have special considerations (i.e., attention to stimuli, memory, generalization, self-regulation, limited motor response repertoires, metacognition, skill synthesis, sensory impairments, and special health care needs) that affect the time it takes to learn the defined curriculum and the amount of material that can be learned within a school year (Kleinert, Browder, & Towles-Reeves, 2009). Given these special considerations, the *enacted curriculum* (that which is actually taught) for these students is often very limited.

Limiting the curriculum even more are the demands for reaching proficiency in reading, math, and science on the AA-AAS. Unfortunately, in many cases, one consequence of standardized testing is a narrowing of the curriculum as teachers "teach to the test" to ensure their students show progress toward proficiency. In the case of AA-AAS, this too can happen as the high-stakes demands on students with significant cognitive disabilities to reach proficiency leave teachers feeling forced to work on only those skills assessed by the AA-AAS rather than all skills in the defined curriculum. As a result, the enacted curriculum for these students is often only those goals or objectives set forth for assessment within the AA-AAS, along with separate functional skill instruction.

Consideration of the enacted curriculum is important, because it is the enacted curriculum that students actually experience. This consideration of an enacted curriculum grounded in state standards for all students reflects the next step in the evolution of what our field has thought is most important for students with significant cognitive disabilities to learn. At the time of passage of the Education for All Handicapped Children Act of 1975 (PL 94-142), the developmental model represented the fundamental curricular paradigm for students with significant cognitive disabilities. Experts in our field reasoned that the content of what educators teach these students should be aligned with the student's mental age derived from his or her special education assessments. But the developmental model did not result in students achieving the life skills essential for their independence (Brown, Nietupski, & Hamre-Nietupski, 1976). As a result, the field's paradigm for instruction for these students in the 1980s moved toward a functional curriculum where educators designed tasks that addressed students' needs in the areas of self-care, social functioning, and adaptive behavior (Browder et al., 2004), in both current and future environments. Subsequently, the educational movement in the 1990s for students with significant cognitive disabilities focused on inclusion in general education settings, with an emphasis upon such embedded basic skills as social, communication, and motor, supported by the infusion of new assistive technology practices. Most recently, curricula and instruction for these students has focused specifically on grade-level academic content instruction. However, functional skill instruction embedded in the general education content and opportunities for students to be included in general education settings are both critical pieces to providing a well-rounded school experience for students with significant cognitive disabilities. As also argued in Chapter 10, life skills—embedded whenever possible into general education instruction and integrated throughout the school day across school and community settings—are still an essential part of the enacted curriculum for students with significant cognitive disabilities.

Alternate Assessments and Effective Instructional Practices

The field has research illustrating the relation of alternate assessment to effective instructional practices for students with significant cognitive disabilities. Kleinert and Kearns (1999) found, in a validity study of Kentucky's alternate assessment for students with significant cognitive disabilities, that national experts in the field of severe disabilities rated the performance criteria identified in Kentucky's alternate assessment as reflecting essential components in programming and outcomes for students with significant cognitive disabilities. In another early study, Turner, Baldwin, Kleinert, and Kearns (2000) found that student scores in one state's alternate assessment were strongly correlated with implementation of effective instructional practices for those same students. Kampfer et al. (2001) found that student scores in that same state's alternate assessment were related to how effectively the teacher was able to embed assessment activities into ongoing instructional routines (the state had a portfolio assessment) and also were related to the extent to which the student was included in the development of his or her own portfolio. Student choice making and evaluation of one's own work are essential components of the concept of self-determination, which is an important predictor of successful postschool outcomes (Wehmeyer & Palmer, 2003; Wehmeyer & Schwartz, 1998).

In a year-long case study of teachers whose students performed well in their state's alternate assessment, Karvonen, Flowers, Browder, Wakeman, and Algozzine (2006) found that these teachers used extensive amounts of direct, systematic instruction;

collected ongoing progress data; and embedded student self-evaluation and self-monitoring into their instructional and assessment activities. All of these are fundamental elements of research-based classroom practices (Snell & Brown, 2006). Similarly, Browder et al. (2005) found that when teachers were provided instruction in direct instruction and data-based decision making, their students' scores on the AA-AAS improved significantly, as did overall student progress on IEP objectives.

Together, the studies would suggest that effective, evidence-based instructional strategies are related to student performance on AA-AAS. Although the studies were conducted before the requirement that each state's AA-AAS be linked to grade-level content standards, there is no reason to expect that an enhanced focus on grade-level academic skills would diminish this relationship of alternate assessment performance to effective classroom instructional practices.

Equal Participation and Equal Weight in the Accountability System

An essential aspect of AA-AAS is that, like all assessments under NCLB, the results of these assessments must "count." In other words, students' scores in the AA-AAS in reading, math, and science must carry equal weight to those of all other students, and should be publicly reported as part of the results of all other students at the school, district, and state levels. Scores for students in the AA-AAS should be disaggregated as well (reported as a separate category), as long as disaggregated results do not result in the loss of student confidentiality. Disaggregation enables the public and parents to see how student overall scores in the AA-AAS compare with those of students with and without disabilities in the regular assessment. For an excellent set of principles delineating how all students can be effectively included in state assessment and accountability systems, the reader is referred to Thurlow et al. (2008).

Statewide surveys of teachers have noted that teachers believe that students with significant cognitive disabilities should be included in their state's respective assessment and accountability systems (Flowers et al., 2005; Kleinert et al., 1999). Moreover, Flowers et al. found that when teachers perceived that their students' participation in the AA-AAS contributed to overall school accountability, those teachers were also more likely to report a positive impact. It is essential that both practitioners and parents understand how AA-AAS are reported within their state, how they are disaggregated, and most important how they are calculated to reflect a full and equal weight to that of all other students in their state's assessment and accountability system.

WHAT WE STILL NEED TO LEARN: CONSIDERATIONS FOR ADDITIONAL RESEARCH

In this final section we discuss directions for future research, including 1) more precisely defining the students, 2) articulating grade-level academic progressions for students with significant cognitive disabilities, 3) examining the relationship of alternate assessments to other measures of student learning and to postschool outcomes, 4) defining "sufficient" linkage to grade-level content standards for this population, 5) examining the extent to which alternate assessment scores are actually used in school improvement efforts; and 6) ensuring that the voices of students and families are heard in the implementation and interpretation of alternate assessments.

The Importance of Precisely Defining the Student Population

Clearly the field needs to more precisely describe the population of learners who participate in AA-AAS, as well as explicate a theory of learning for this population. Chapter 3 of this text argued that there is evidence for three subgroups of learners defined by the key dimension of communicative competence or development: presymbolic, emerging symbolic, and symbolic learners (see also Kearns, Towles-Reeves, Kleinert, Kleinert, & Thomas, in press;. Towles-Reeves, Kearns, Kleinert, & Kleinert, 2009). Teachers need evidenced-based strategies for enabling learners at each of these communicative levels to have access to and make progress within the general curriculum; alternate assessments need to be designed to allow each of these groups of students to meaningfully participate. As we have noted elsewhere,

> How to design alternate assessment systems, especially alternate assessments linked to grade-level content standards, for students at emerging and pre-symbolic levels, in a way that allows these students to demonstrate what they do know, is an immense challenge for the field. (Towles-Reeves, Kleinert, & Muhomba, 2009, p. 246)

Grade-Level Academic Progressions

Researchers also need to examine something that has not historically been part of the "nomenclature" or the "educational perspective" of the field of severe disabilities—that is, the concept of learning progressions in academic content (especially reading, math, and science) across grade levels for students with significant cognitive disabilities. The field has always focused on a wholly individualized approach; true, practitioners have been guided by curriculum paradigm shifts that have focused on a functional curriculum (but *functional* has always been defined in terms of the needs of the individual student), by academic inclusion and embedded skills (again with both of these concepts defined by the specific needs of the student), and more recently by the concept of self-determination (focused on teaching the student to set and to achieve his or her own goals). All of these curricular shifts have represented true advances in the field. Yet practitioners are now faced with a new challenge: the design of learning progressions (e.g., a common curricular framework and set of expectations) that represents what students with significant cognitive disabilities should achieve in core academic content areas.

At the date of this writing, little research has been conducted regarding the development and understanding of learning progressions for students with significant cognitive disabilities in reading, mathematics, and science. Some work is starting to emerge from Diane Browder and her colleagues (see Browder, Ahlgrim-Delzell, Courtade, Gibbs, & Flowers, 2008; Browder et al., 2009). One question raised by this discussion is, "Do these students have truly different learning progressions than students in the general assessment?" Perhaps an even more important question is whether these students have communication systems, consistent response modes, and ways to demonstrate what they know and can do. A priority for this population is ensuring all students have a way to consistently communicate so they can demonstrate what they have learned. The work regarding learning progressions brings to the surface many more questions than answers at this point. Content experts and special educators need to continue to work together to better understand how students with significant cognitive disabilities gain competence in the academic domains of reading, mathematics, and science.

Alternate Assessments and Relations
to Other Measures of Student Learning

It is also important to show that alternate assessment scores relate to something other than themselves. Providing evidence of increasing numbers of students scoring *proficient* in alternate assessments, although a positive trend (see Thompson, Johnstone, Thurlow, & Altman, 2005; Thurlow, Quenemoen, Altman, & Cuthbert, 2007), is not enough. Simply put, are higher alternate assessment scores reflective of improved student learning, or rather of increased teacher experience and familiarity with doing alternate assessments with their students? Are there other measures of academic performance for students with significant cognitive disabilities that one should expect to correlate with state alternate assessment scores? Given the amount of time, teacher and student effort, and costs associated with alternate assessments, it seems reasonable that researchers investigate the relationship of alternate assessments to other recognized measures of academic competence for students with significant cognitive disabilities. Although the field has not historically focused on the development of academic measures for these students (as opposed to, for instance, more functional measures of performance in the area of adaptive behavior), measures of academic competence are being developed specifically for this population. For example, Browder and colleagues are designing assessments for students with significant cognitive disabilities that measure competence in the five key domains of reading: phonemic awareness, decoding, fluency, vocabulary, and comprehension (see Browder, Ahlgrim-Delzell, Courtade, Gibbs, & Flowers, 2008). Future research should focus on the extent to which state alternate assessment scores relate to these measures.

At the time of this writing, two studies have considered the relationship of AA-AAS scores to other measures of student achievement. Elliott, Compton, and Roach (2007) examined the extent to which student scores on the AA-AAS correlated with other measures of academic learning, academic engagement, and functional skills. Specifically, these researchers examined the relationship of student performance on the Idaho Alternate Assessment (IAA) for students with significant cognitive disabilities with their performance on the Academic Competence Evaluation Scales (ACES; DiPerna & Elliott, 2000) and a measure of adaptive behavior, the Vineland Adaptive Behavior Scales (Sparrow, Balla, & Cicchetti, 1985). The ACES measured both academic achievement (rated in comparison to grade-level achievement in academic skill areas) and academic enabling skills (e.g., interpersonal skills, study skills). These authors found that, although AA-AAS scores did correlate positively with the ACES academic skill ratings, the strongest correlations were found between AA-AAS scores and measures of academic enabling skills (requisites to academic achievement) and adaptive (or functional) skills. Although Elliott et al. (2007) noted that adaptive and academic enabling skills are important for student success, the findings of that study, if replicated, "could cause concern because they suggest that the IAA may be a broader measure of student functioning than called for by the state's content standards" (p. 42). In other words, alternate assessments—like all large-scale assessments—are purported to measure academic achievement linked to grade-level content standards but may in fact be measuring constructs other than just academic performance.

In a second, related study, Kettler et al. (in press) examined the relationship of student AA-AAS scores in reading and math across six states to those same measures of academic skills, academic enablers, and adaptive or life skills that were used in the Elliott et al. (2007) study. Kettler et al. further considered these correlations for students eligible for their respective state AA-AAS and for students with disabilities not eligible for their state

AA-AAS; this latter group allowed the authors to examine the relationship of regular assessment and AA-AAS scores for a common set of students across these six states. For AA-AAS-eligible students, AA-AAS scores generally had moderate to strong correlations with student academic skills and even stronger correlations to adaptive behavior. For AA-AAS noneligible students (students with disabilities who did not qualify for their states' AA-AAS), there were small to moderate correlations between AA-AAS and regular assessment scores, suggesting that the AA-AAS and the regular assessments across these six states measured related, but clearly not the same, constructs.

For the AA-AAS eligible students in the Kettler et al. (in press) study, several findings were noted. First, reading and math scores were highly related: students who scored very highly in reading also scored very well in math, and vice versa. As these authors noted, one might reasonably ask if reading and math AA-AAS across these six states represented truly distinct academic constructs for these students. Second, as these authors noted, "The results of this study indicate that alternate assessments often measure a number of constructs," including adaptive behavior, academic enabling skills, and grade-level academic content. Although all of these represent important skill domains for students with significant cognitive disabilities, the question is, of course, whether AA-AAS is first and foremost a measure of academic achievement linked to grade-level content standards.

It will be essential for the field to continue to study how well alternate assessments measure what they purport to measure (academic achievement linked to grade-level content standards) and how well alternate assessments correlate with other measures of academic achievement for this population. At this point, the field simply does not have the research data to tell us how well alternate assessment scores relate to other measures of academic learning for these students. This question is essential to fully explaining to policy makers, administrators, teachers and, perhaps most important, families, what these scores really mean for their students with significant cognitive disabilities.

Alternate assessment scores should also correlate, at least to some extent, with future outcomes for students. For example, for students taking the alternate assessment in their final high school years, one would expect at least some correlation with postschool outcomes. Although the only study that did attempt to correlate alternate assessment scores with postschool outcomes did not find a correlation (Kleinert et al., 2002), that study had a small sample size and was conducted before the requirements that alternate assessments be linked to grade-level content standards. Our field will have an increased capability to investigate the relationship of alternate assessment scores to postschool outcomes, as states put into place the student postschool outcomes data sets required by IDEA 2004. This is a golden opportunity for states to integrate two federally mandated state data sets—performance of students in AA-AAS with their respective postschool outcomes— and thus determine the relationship of alternate assessment performance (especially at the high school level) to postschool outcomes for students with significant cognitive disabilities. Integrating these required data sets would truly allow states to determine the extent to which they are addressing both academic achievement standards and the life-skill needs of their students for the future, and if gains in one area (academic content achievement) are correlated with improvements in postschool outcomes.

Sufficient Linkage to Grade-Level Content Standards: What Does This Mean?

As the field learns more about what students with significant cognitive disabilities are capable of learning academically, we need to thoughtfully consider what constitutes *sufficient linkage* to grade-level content standards for students with significant cognitive disabilities. Although NCLB guidance allows for reduced depth and breadth in AA-AAS (and this is a very reasonable stance, given that these are alternate academic achievement standards for students who cannot participate in the regular assessment even with accommodations), this does not mean that any skill that remotely resembles the grade-level content standard meets this requirement for "linkage" or, for that matter, is meaningful for students. At what point does reduced scope and complexity result in the measurement of skills that trivialize the "enduring understandings" or the essential underpinnings of grade-level content standards? Indeed, Johnson and Arnold (2004, 2007) found that for one state's alternate assessment, the relationship between the actual student skills evidenced in the AA-AAS and the identified state content standards was often tenuous at best.

Researchers need to clearly document the extent to which alternate assessments are improving access to the general curriculum, even for students with the most significant cognitive disabilities. The data in this area are just preliminary. For example, Thurlow, Quenemoen, Altman, & Cuthbert (2007) found that for students with disabilities participating in their state's AA-AAS, there did appear to be strong trends of increased proficiency for the limited number of states for which these trend data are available. Within the six states with 3 or more years of successive performance data on their AA-AAS, the gains were far more substantial than were comparable gains for students with disabilities who were participating in the regular assessment, and these gains held over all grade levels (reading: 22% average gain at the elementary, 21% at the middle, and 32% at the high school level; math: 24% average gain at the elementary, 22% at the middle, and 30% at the high school level). However, as Thurlow et al. (2007) noted, the reasons for these gains in alternate assessment scores are unclear. The gains could reflect substantial improvement in student learning at each grade level or could also reflect a less rigorous approach to alternate assessment or the fact that alternate assessments have reflected "moving targets" in recent years. We simply do not have enough information to tell. That is part of the issue with alternate assessment, and begs the question of whether states see the AA-AAS as fairly easy mechanisms for at least getting some of their students with disabilities to proficiency, or whether AA-AAS truly do represent the highest professional judgment of what students with significant cognitive disabilities are able to learn.

How Are Alternate Assessment Scores Used in School Improvement Efforts?

Most teachers believe that students with significant cognitive disabilities deserve to be part of school and district accountability systems (see Flowers et al., 2005; Kleinert et al., 1999), and yet, researchers have not really documented the broader administrative or policy consequences to these students from that involvement. For example, how are alternate assessments scores used, if at all, by districts and schools in formulating district and school improvement plans? Do the results of alternate assessments really make a difference in classroom and school-level practices? Are school and district administrators, as well as general educators, more supportive of the inclusion of students with significant cognitive disabilities in grade-level curricular activities as a result of inclusive large-scale assessment? As we discuss next, our field has really very limited research to answer these pivotal questions.

In a study of principal perceptions of two states' AA-AAS described earlier in this chapter, Towles-Reeves et al. (2008) found that principals saw the greatest impacts of the AA-AAS in teachers' instruction in two areas: 1) instruction on grade-level academic content, and 2) time spent by students in the general education classroom. Similarly Towles-Reeves and Kleinert (2006) found a much higher percentage of teachers (44%) in one state's alternate assessment who perceived a positive impact of their state's alternate assessment on instruction than that of teachers (16% of respondents) who perceived a negative impact, though this study did not specifically address increased access to the general curriculum.

However, in a study of five states' alternate assessments, Flowers et al. (2005) found that teachers saw increased paperwork as a greater impact than increased access to the general curriculum of the AA-AAS: only 28% of responding teachers saw increased access to the general curriculum as an impact of their state's alternate assessment (though this study was conducted before the requirement for linkage to grade-level content standards), and only 25% believed that their state's AA-AAS had an impact upon the quality of the student's educational program. Even in the Towles-Reeves et al. (2008) study of principal perceptions, the perceived positive results of increased access to the general curriculum were mitigated by the fact that principals strongly perceived that functional or life-skills instruction is a higher priority for students in the AA-AAS than academic content linked to grade-level content standards.

Without coherent models and examples of how to merge academic and functional skill instruction within daily classroom routines, it is doubtful that alternate assessments will achieve their promise—that is, that they will be perceived as meaningful tools for school improvement efforts. Both teachers and principals will continue to struggle with what is most important for students with significant cognitive disabilities to learn, and how to balance competing curricular demands. Without effective models for "blended" instruction, both principals and teachers will continue to question whether alternate assessment scores really reflect what students most need to learn.

We return then to our original questions: how are alternate assessments scores used, if at all, by districts and schools in formulating district and school improvement plans? Do the results of alternate assessments really make a difference in the classroom and in school-level practices? In truth, the field really does not have good answers to these questions for students with disabilities in general, whether they are participating in alternate assessments or state regular assessments. For example, Altman, Lazarus, Thurlow, Quenemoen, Cuthbert, and Cormier (2008) found, in their 2007 Survey of States: Activities, Changes, and Challenges for Special Education, that with all the effort devoted to the inclusion of students with disabilities in large-scale assessments, a full 20 states do not have the ability to track individual student performance across time. Although 16 states did report that they tracked individual performance for those students who consistently performed poorly on state assessments, the fact that the majority of states (58%) did not track the performance of students with disabilities who perform poorly shows how states might be fulfilling the letter of the law, but greatly missing key benefits (e.g., improving instructional effectiveness) of including students with disabilities in the first place.

There would appear, therefore, to be two issues related to the meaningful use of alternate assessments in school improvement efforts. First, teachers and administrators must gain assurance that alternate assessments measure critical learning for students with significant cognitive disabilities. Second, state departments of education must build the capacity to track student performance over time, including students who participate in AA-AAS.

Researchers do have good examples of how teachers are using alternate assessments at the district level to improve classroom instruction and access to the general curriculum for their students. For example, Brown (2009) described a districtwide model used in which the teachers who have students in the AA-AAS meet in the beginning of the year to review their students' scores in math, reading, and science (if science had been assessed at that grade level); examine the standards in each academic area that scored the highest within their schools and district and those standards that were scored the lowest; identify trends and patterns from previous years; and consider if portfolio entries accurately represented what students were capable of doing in those academic areas or if there had been instructional weaknesses in their programs that prevented students from fully learning the material. Then, at subsequent meetings, teachers identify one standard in each content area (math, reading, science) to be addressed in the current school year, and share materials and strategies for addressing those content standards each month. Because the alternate assessment is a portfolio assessment (based on instruction and progress for the entire year), teachers develop working portfolio binders for each of their students; these working portfolios are organized by standard and academic area and are then used to provide the assessment probe data and work samples for the final portfolio. Again, teachers share their working portfolio binders, as specific examples of how they can modify the content or its presentation to enable their students to achieve mastery.

Understanding the Perspectives of Families and Students

Finally, two sets of voices are conspicuously absent in the research on alternate assessment conducted thus far: those of parents and of the students themselves. We could find only one study to date that systematically sampled parental perceptions of the impact of alternate assessments on the education of their children (Roach, 2006), and no studies that asked the students who participate in alternate assessments if these assessments have helped them to learn, have resulted in increased control or decision making over their own learning, or have enabled them to understand what they have accomplished in school. Clearly, researchers need to investigate the perspectives of families and students if we are to fully understand the consequences of alternate assessments.

Although Roach (2006) did find that parents believed that their children benefited from participation in the AA-AAS, and that the AA-AAS score in reference to their own child was accurate, they placed less confidence on the accuracy or utility of the AA-AAS as their son or daughter reached high school age and as their son or daughter's IEP reflected a higher percentage of life-skill objectives as opposed to clearly academic objectives. This is a delicate balance, but clearly parents are most concerned at this point with what will happen after high school for their son or daughter; it would also seem that parents believe that school accountability at the secondary level must take into account all that is important for their son or daughter to learn. The need to further study the perspectives of parents of students at each school level (elementary, middle, and high school) is obvious. Parental support is essential to the achievement of student outcomes, and an understanding and support for the AA-AAS process is an important part of parents' participation in their son or daughter's educational planning.

CONCLUSION

As we have noted, "Very significant gaps remain in scholars' ability to provide practitioners and policy makers with research-based strategies that will enable alternate assessment to truly achieve its promises to students, teachers, and parents" (Towles-Reeves, Kleinert, & Muhomba, 2009, p. 249). It becomes the charge of the "next generation" of alternate assessment researchers to 1) establish how all students (including students at a presymbolic level of communication) can be fairly and validly included in their respective states' AA-AAS; 2) articulate grade-level academic progressions for students with significant cognitive disabilities; 3) examine the relationship of alternate assessments to other measures of student learning and to postschool outcomes; 4) define "sufficient" linkage to grade-level content standards for this population; 5) examine the extent to which alternate assessment scores are actually used in school improvement efforts; and 6) ensure that the voices of students and families are heard in understanding the impact of AA-AAS. This next generation of alternate assessment research can only be done in full partnership with practitioners. Teachers are not just a part of the alternate assessment "system"; they play a key role in furthering the field's knowledge regarding how students with significant cognitive disabilities learn best and how we can measure what they have learned in the context of the learning standards that we have identified as essential for all students.

REFERENCES

Ahlgrim-Delzell, L., Flowers, C., Browder, D., & Wakeman, S. (2006). *School administrators' perceptions of the impact of alternate assessments.* Unpublished manuscript.

Altman, J., Lazarus, S., Thurlow, M., Quenemoen, R., Cuthbert, M., & Cormier, D. (2008). *2007 survey of states: Activities, changes and challenges for special education.* Minneapolis: University of Minnesota, National Center on Educational Outcomes.

Browder, D., Alhgrim-Delzell, L., Courtade, G., Gibbs, S., & Flowers, C. (2008). Evaluation of the effectiveness of an early literacy program for students with significant developmental disabilities. *Exceptional Children, 75,* 33–52.

Browder, D., Flowers, C., Ahlgrim-Delzell, L., Karvonen, M., Spooner, F., & Algozzine, R. (2004). The alignment of alternate assessment content with academic and functional curricula. *Journal of Special Education, 37*(4), 211–223.

Browder, D., Gibbs, S., Ahlgrim-Delzell, L., Courtade, G., Mraz, M., & Flowers, C. (2009). Literacy for students with significant cognitive disabilities—What should we teach and what should we hope to achieve? *Remedial and Special Education, 30,* 269–282.

Browder, D., Karvonen, M., Davis, S., Fallin, K., & Courtade-Little, G. (2005). The impact of teacher training on state alternate assessment scores. *Exceptional Children, 71,* 267–282.

Browder, D., Spooner, F., Ahlgrim-Delzell, L., Flowers, C., Algozzine, R., & Karvonen, M. (2003). A content analysis of the curricular philosophies reflected in states' alternate assessment performance indicators. *Research and Practice for Persons with Severe Disabilities, 28*(4), 165–181.

Brown, H. (2009, July). *Organizing your alternate assessment effort.* Paper presented at the Kentucky Alternate Assessment Advisory Board Meeting, Frankfort.

Brown, L., Nietupski, J., & Hamre-Nietupski, S. (1976). The criterion of ultimate functioning and public school services for severely handicapped children. In M. Thomas (Ed.), *Hey, don't forget about me!* (pp. 8–12) Reston, VA: Council for Exceptional Children.

Data Accountability Center. (2008, June). *Profiles of Parts B and C programs in states and outlying areas.* Rockville, MD: DAC/Westat, Data Accountability Center.

DiPerna, J.C., & Elliott, S.N. (2000). *Academic competence evaluation scales.* San Antonio, TX: Psychological Corporation.

Education for All Handicapped Children Act of 1975, PL 94-142, 20 U.S.C. §§ 1400 *et seq.*

Elliott, S., Compton, E., & Roach, A. (2007). Building validity evidence for scores on statewide alternate assessment: A contrasting groups, multi-method approach. *Educational Measurement: Issues and Practice, 26*(2), 30–43.

Flowers, C., Ahlgrim-Delzell, L., Browder, D., & Spooner, F. (2005). Teachers' perceptions of alternate assessments. *Research and Practice for Persons with Severe Disabilities, 30*(2), 81–92.

Individuals with Disabilities Education Act Amendments of 1997 (IDEA), PL 105-17, 20 U.S.C. §§ 1400 *et seq.*

Individuals with Disabilities Education Improvement Act of 2004 (IDEA), PL 108-446, 20 U.S.C. §§ 1400 *et seq.*

Johnson, E., & Arnold, N. (2004). Validating an alternate assessment. *Remedial and Special Education, 25*(5), 266–275.

Johnson, E., & Arnold, N. (2007). Examining an alternate assessment: What are we testing? *Journal of Disabilities Studies, 18*(1), 23–31.

Kampfer, S., Horvath, L., Kleinert, H., & Kearns, J. (2001). Teachers' perceptions of one state's alternate assessment portfolio program: Implications for practice and preparation. *Exceptional Children, 67*(3), 361–374.

Karvonen, M., Flowers, C., Browder, D., Wakeman, S., & Algozzine, B. (2006). Case study of the influence on alternate assessment outcomes for students with disabilities. *Education and Training in Developmental Disabilities, 41*(2), 95–110.

Kearns, J., Towles-Reeves, E., Kleinert, H., Kleinert, J., & Thomas, M. (in press). Characteristics of and implications for students participating in alternate assessments based on alternate academic achievement standards. *Journal of Special Education.*

Kettler, R., Elliott, S., Beddow, P., Compton, E., McGrath, D., Kaase, K. et al. (in press). What do alternate assessments of alternate academic achievement standards measure? A multitrait-multimethod analysis across six states. *Exceptional Children.*

Kleinert, H., Browder, D., & Towles-Reeves, E. (2009). Models of cognition for students with significant cognitive disabilities: Implications for assessment. *Review of Educational Research, 79*(1), 301–326.

Kleinert, H., Garrett, B., Towles, E., Garrett, M., Nowak-Drabik, K., Waddell, C. et al. (2002). Alternate assessment scores and life outcomes for students with significant disabilities: Are they related? *Assessment for Effective Intervention, 28*(1), 19–30.

Kleinert, H., & Kearns, J. (1999). A validation study of the performance indicators and learner outcomes of Kentucky's alternate assessment for students with significant disabilities. *Journal of the Association for Persons with Severe Handicaps, 24,* 100–110.

Kleinert, H., Kearns, J., Costello, K., Nowak-Drabik, K., Garrett, M., Horvath, L., Kampfer, S., & Turner, M. (2001). Research on the impact of alternate assessments. In H. Kleinert & J. Kearns, *Alternate assessment: Measuring outcomes and supports for students with disabilities* (pp. 213–227). Baltimore: Paul H. Brookes Publishing Co.

Kleinert, H., Kennedy, S., & Kearns, J. (1999). Impact of alternate assessments: A statewide teacher survey. *Journal of Special Education, 33*(2), 93–102.

Kohl, F., McLaughlin, M., & Nagle, K. (2006). Alternate achievement standards and assessments: A descriptive investigation of 16 states. *Exceptional Children, 73*(1), 107–123.

No Child Left Behind Act of 2001, PL 107-110, 115 Stat.1425, 20 U.S.C. §§ 6301 *et seq.*

Palmer, D., Fuller, K., Arora, T., & Nelson, M. (2001). Taking sides: Parent views on inclusion for their children with severe disabilities. *Exceptional Children, 67,* 467–484.

Roach, A. (2006). Influences on parent perceptions of an alternate assessment for students with severe cognitive disabilities. *Research & Practice for Persons with Severe Disabilities, 31*(3), 267–274.

Snell, M., & Brown, F. (2006). *Instruction of students with severe disabilities* (6th ed.). Upper Saddle River, NJ: Pearson/Merrill Prentice Hall.

Sparrow, S.S., Balla, D.A., & Cicchetti, D.V. (1985). *Vineland adaptive behavior scales: Classroom edition.* Circle Pines, MN: American Guidance Service.

Thompson, S., Johnstone, C., Thurlow, M., & Altman, J. (2005). *2005 state special education outcomes: Steps forward in a decade of change.* Minneapolis: University of Minnesota, National Center on Educational Outcomes. Retrieved December 12, 2005, from http://www.education. umn.edu/nceo/OnlinePubs/2005StateReport.htm

Thurlow, M., Quenemoen, R., Altman, J., & Cuthbert, M. (2007). *Trends in the participation and performance of students with disabilities (Technical Report 50)*. Minneapolis: University of Minnesota, National Center on Educational Outcomes.

Thurlow, M., Quenemoen, R., Lazarus, S., Moen, R., Johnstone, C., Liu, K., Christenson, L., et al. (2008). *A principled approach to accountability assessments for students with disabilities (Synthesis Report 70)*. Minneapolis: University of Minnesota, National Center on Educational Outcomes.

Towles-Reeves, E., Kearns, J., Kleinert, H., & Kleinert, J. (2009). An analysis of the learning characteristics of students taking alternate assessments based on alternate achievement standards. *Journal of Special Education, 42,* 241–254.

Towles-Reeves, E., & Kleinert, H. (2006). The impact of one state's alternate assessment upon instruction and IEP development. *Rural Special Education Quarterly, 25*(3), 31–39.

Towles-Reeves, E., Kleinert, H., & Anderman, L. (2008). Alternate assessments based on alternate achievement standards: Principals' perceptions. *Research and Practice in Severe Disabilities, 33,* 122–133.

Towles-Reeves, E., Kleinert, H., & Muhomba, M. (2009). Alternate assessment: Have we learned anything new? *Exceptional Children, 75,* 233–252.

Turner, M., Baldwin, L., Kleinert, H., & Kearns, J. (2000). An examination of the concurrent validity of Kentucky's alternate assessment system. *Journal of Special Education, 34*(2), 69–76.

U.S. Department of Education. (2005). *Alternate achievement standards for students with the most significant cognitive disabilities: Non-regulatory guidance*. Washington, DC: U.S. Department of Education, Office of Elementary and Secondary Education.

Wehmeyer, M., & Palmer, S. (2003). Adult outcomes for students with cognitive disabilities three years after high school: The impact of self-determination. *Education and Training in Developmental Disabilities, 38*(2), 131–144.

Wehmeyer, M., & Schwartz, M. (1998). The relationship between self-determination and quality of life for adults with mental retardation. *Education and Training in Mental Retardation and Developmental Disabilities, 33*(1), 3–12.

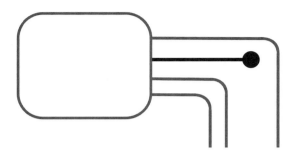

Appendix

Blank Forms

Student Communication Observation Recording Log

Student Communication Competency Inventory

Potential Barriers and Supports to Clear Communication

Decision Chart for Developing a Communication Program

Mathematics Story-Based Lesson

Four-Step Process to Accessing Grade-Level Content Standards and Curriculum

Plot Chart

Matrix Lesson Plan

Individualized Education Program Planning Matrix

Student Communication
Observation Recording Log

Date _____

Student's output and/or behaviors that may signal expressive or receptive communication (Mode/Form)	What's happening around or with the student? (Antecedent)	What could the student have meant to communicate? (Intent/Function)	Did the student receive any type of a response from others? (Consequence/Response)

Alternate Assessment for Students with Significant Cognitive Disabilities: An Educator's Guide by Harold L. Kleinert & Jacqui Farmer Kearns

Student Communication Competency Inventory

Student:　　　　　**Age:**　　　　　**School:**

Content/ Intent/Function	Mode/ Form of output	Suggested responses to the student
(List the intents the student exhibits below.)	(List the mode or form the student uses to express his or her intents listed in the previous column.)	(Record the manner in which everyone should respond to the student and indicate which **augmentative and alternative communication** should be used, if appropriate. Also list any **adaptive equipment needed** for the student to participate in ongoing activities.)

Potential Barriers and Supports to Clear Communication

Student: **Age:**   **School:**

Sensory/ Receptive systems (Describe each type)	Strengths (Facilitating abilities)	Weaknesses (Inhibitory/ Distracting)	How is communication affected?
Auditory			
Vision			
Touch/Tactile			
Cognition/ Receptive abilities			
Motor characteristics			
Muscle tone			
Abnormal movement patterns and reflexes			
Environmental opportunities to communicate			

Alternate Assessment for Students with Significant Cognitive Disabilities: An Educator's Guide
by Harold L. Kleinert & Jacqui Farmer Kearns
Copyright © 2010 by Paul H. Brookes Publishing Co., Inc. All rights reserved.

Decision Chart for
Developing a Communication Program

Student	What the student already has/does		Challenges/ Abilities	What the student needs	What actions can satisfy the communication needs of this student?
	Intents:	Modes:			

Mathematics Story-Based Lesson

Math Strand:
Skill (objective):
Manipulatives:
Graphic organizer:

What the teacher will do	Materials to present	What the student will do	Examples of student responses

Four-Step Process to Accessing Grade-Level Content Standards and Curriculum

Unit of Study:

1. IDENTIFY THE STANDARD(S) THE INSTRUCTIONAL UNIT ADDRESSES.

What is the state standard?	What is the grade-level standard? (e.g., benchmark, performance indicator)	What is the standard all about? (Critical function or big idea)

(continued)

Four-Step Process to Accessing Grade-Level Content Standards and Curriculum

2. DEFINE THE OUTCOME(S) OF INSTRUCTION FROM THE INSTRUCTIONAL UNIT.

What are the desired outcomes for all students in general education? • What evidence will document the students' understanding? • What is the best formative assessment format to gather that evidence?	Which outcomes will be prioritized for instruction and monitoring for the target student with significant cognitive disabilities?	• What evidence will document the target student's understanding? • What is the best formative assessment format to gather that evidence?

Alternate Assessment for Students with Significant Cognitive Disabilities: An Educator's Guide by Harold L. Kleinert & Jacqui Farmer Kearns
Copyright © 2010 by Paul H. Brookes Publishing Co., Inc. All rights reserved.

3. IDENTIFY THE INSTRUCTIONAL ACTIVITIES TO BE USED WITHIN THE UNIT.

What are the instructional activities planned for all students?	What barriers are keeping the student from accessing instruction, participating in activities, demonstrating learning, and so forth?	▪ What supports will reduce identified barriers? ▪ How will the supports assist the student in accessing instruction, participating in activities, and demonstrating learning?

(continued)

(continued)

Four-Step Process to Accessing Grade-Level Content Standards and Curriculum

4. TARGET SPECIFIC IEP OBJECTIVES AND FOUNDATIONAL SKILLS THAT CAN BE ADDRESSED DURING THE UNIT.
List the instructional activity numbers or key words from Step 3 down the left column. List key words from IEP objectives and/or foundational skills across the top column. Indicate which IEP objectives and foundational skills can be addressed within each instructional activity.

IEP Objectives and Foundational Skills *(Write key words)* ➦							
Unit Instructional Activities *(Write the number of the activity or key words)* ➥							

Alternate Assessment for Students with Significant Cognitive Disabilities: An Educator's Guide by Harold L. Kleinert & Jacqui Farmer Kearns

Plot Chart

Student name:

Plot Chart

Session	Accuracy/Prompt/Type of response							Independent responses	Independent and accurate responses
1									
2									
3									
4									
5									
6									
7									
8									
9									
10									
Notes									

Matrix Lesson Plan

General education lesson	Modifications for	Modifications for	Modifications for
Day 1			
Assessment:			
Day 2			
Assessment:			
Day 3			
Assessment:			

Day 4

Assessment:

Day 5

Assessment:

Individualized Education Program Planning Matrix

General class activities
IEP goals

Embedded self-determination skills related to Depth of Knowledge

Pose a question/identify a problem									
Identify and analyze/compare solutions									
Choose a solution									
Predict outcome									
Execute/carry out/monitor one's own steps in solving									
Evaluate solution: Did it work/not work?									
Communicate results: What happened?									

Index

Page numbers followed by *b*, *f*, and *t* refer to boxes, figures, and tables, respectively.